The Unfinished Business of Liberation and Transformation

Revisiting the 1958 All-African People's Conference

edited by

Dzodzi Tsikata
Edem Adotey
Mjiba Frehiwot

Daraja Press

Published by
Daraja Press
https://darajapress.com
Wakefield, Quebec, Canada
2024

ISBN: 9781998309030

This publication was made possible with the support of the
Institute of African Studies and the University of Ghana.

Library and Archives Canada Cataloguing in Publication

Title: Unfinished business of liberation and transformation : revisiting the
    1958 All-African People's Conference / edited by Dzodzi Tsikata,
    Edem Adotey, Mjiba Frehiwot,
Names: Tsikata, Dzodzi, editor. | Adotey, Edem, editor. | Frehiwot, Mjiba, editor.
    | All-African People's Conference (1958 : Accra, Ghana)
Description: Includes bibliographical references.
Identifiers: Canadiana 20240284372 | ISBN 9781998309030 (softcover)
Subjects: LCSH: All-African People's Conference (1958 : Accra, Ghana) |
    LCSH: Africa—Social conditions. | LCSH: Decolonization—Africa. |
    LCSH: Africa—Politics and government. | LCSH: Africa—Economic conditions.
Classification: LCC HN773.5 .U54 2024 | DDC 306.096—dc23

The Unfinished Business of African Liberation and Transformation is a path-breaking collection of proceedings commemorating the 1958 landmark All African People's Conference. Masterfully curated by a new generation of radical Pan-Africanist thinkers, the resulting volume is essential reading for all those interested in pursuing African decolonization and liberation in the 21st century.

Amina Mama
Professor, Gender, Sexuality & Women's Studies
University of California, Davis and fourth Kwame Nkrumah Chair in African Studies at the University of Ghana

The ideas discussed in this book are crisp, lucid and refreshingly unconventional. As the biggest threat to the unipolar world order, the Pan-African movement is more relevant than ever before. Hence, this book is a must-read for all who care about the contemporary plight of African people.

Sylvia Tamale
Decolonial feminist & Professor of Law
School of Law, Makerere University, Uganda, and Editor, Feminist Africa Journal

This collection of essays from the Institute of African Studies 2018 conference commemorating the 1958 All African Peoples Conference convened by Ghana's Prime Minister Kwame Nkrumah, present critical thinking by a wide spectrum of Pan-African workers, youth, women, students, diasporans, intellectuals, businesspeople, activists, and academics, and politicians as they explore current challenges and how to overcome them. They are well worth studying to learn some of the ways in which African people, and others, can make progress in advancing towards the full spectrum of possibilities inherent in the right to self-determination.

Adotey Bing-Pappoe
Senior Lecturer, Department of Economics and International Business, University of Greenwich, London, United Kingdom, Founding Member and co-Chairperson of Executive Council, Cooperation Africa

TABLE OF CONTENTS

Section 3

Exhortation

List of Contributors

Acknowledgements

This book, which documents the commemoration of the sixtieth anniversary of the AAPC, exists because of the remarkable partnership to organise the Conference in the first place. We want to acknowledge the Conference Partners—the Institute of African Studies at the University of Ghana, the Trades Union Congress (TUC) of Ghana, Socialist Movement of Ghana (formerly Socialist Forum of Ghana), Lincoln University, USA, and Third World Network Africa. We also acknowledge the financial support of sponsors such as Tricontinental: Institute for Social Research, The Open Society Initiative for Eastern Africa, the Institute of African Studies, Prudential Bank Ltd., Embassy of the Republic of China in Accra, Embassy of Algeria in Accra, the African Women's Development Fund, and Organisation of African Trade Union Unity (OATUU), who made it possible to invite participants from across the world and support programming and logistics.

We owe special thanks to Prof Akilagpa Sawyerr, the Conference Chair who steered the proceedings from start to finish, and to the keynote speakers, Prof Nzongola-Ntalaja, the Opening Keynote Speaker, and Prof Horace G. Campbell, the Closing Keynote Speaker for their insightful perspectives on African liberation and transformation, which are presented in this book.

We are also extremely grateful to the Conference Planning Committee—Profs Dzodzi Tsikata, Akilagpa Sawyerr, Kofi Anyidoho, Horace Campbell, Takyiwaa Manuh, Akosua Adomako Ampofo, Esi Sutherland-Addy, Audrey Gadzekpo; Dr Yao Graham, Mr Akunu Dake, and Mr Kyeretwie Opoku for their stimulating deliberation on the unfinished business of liberation and transformation and for setting the agenda of the Conference.

We acknowledge the support of members of the Conference Secretariat—Drs Mjiba Frehiwot Dzodzi Tsikata, Edem Adotey, Michael Kpessa-Whyte, Chika Mba, Peter Narh, Genevieve Nrenzah, Pius Siakwah, Obodai Torto, Mr William Asare, Mr Akunu Dake, Mrs Philomina Aku Anebo, Mr Peter Bembir, Mr Kafui Tsekpo, Mr Eric Tei-Kumadoe, Ms Harriet Boateng Akuako, Ms Aseye Tamakloe, Ms Prisca Kyei-Sayki, and Mr Kingsley Orleans Thompson.

We also appreciate the work of the Resolutions Committee—Mr Kyeretwie Opoku, Prof D. Zizwe Poe, Drs Peter Narh, Msia Kibona Clark, Obodai Torto, and Mr Kafui Tsekpo. The group of conference rapporteurs, Mr Peter Narh, Mr Kafui Tsekpo, Mr Peter Bembir, Ms Mary S. Ayim-Segbefia, Ms Ruth Mango, Ms Ifeanyi-Ajufo Nnenna, Mr Kofi Emmanuel Akpabli, Ms Juliet Oppong-Boateng, Mr Kwaku Darko Ankrah, Ms Mina Tetteh, Ms Gertrude Sarah Aidoo, Mr Aaron Nii Ayitey Komey, Mr Emmanuel Nii Addotei Baddoo, Mr Bryant Samona, Ms Grace Opare, Mr Joseph Fosu-Ankrah, Mr Joseph Aketema, Ms Janet Zeylisa Dauda, Ms Evelyn Aku Adzandeh, Mr Emmanuel Asante, Dr Edwin Asa Adjei, Mr Isaac Sekyi Nana Mensah, and Rev. Bonaventure Kweku Quaidoo, did a sterling job. The IT support for the conference was ably provided by Mr Emmanuel Ekow Arthur-Entsiwah, Mr Dennis Ayeh, and Mr Frimpong Opuni, while Mr Emmanuel K. Kuto, Ms Pamela Amoah, Mr Abel Yao Aji, and Ms Fifime Sandrine Adangnihoun provided interpretation services.

We were privileged to welcome Mr G. A. Balogun, who had participated in the 1958 Conference to the commemoration. He graciously agreed to the interview which is presented in the book. We are indebted to the Editor-in-Chief, Prof Akosua Adomako Ampofo, the Editorial Coordinator, Dr Edwina Ashie-Nikoi, and editors of the *Contemporary Journal of African Studies* for publishing a special issue of the journal in which six of the chapters of this book were first published and for permission to use these in this book. We also acknowledge the anonymous reviewers of the articles for their valuable feedback, and the publishers, Daraja Press for their pivotal role and invaluable technical support in finalising the manuscript and publishing the book.

We recognise Mr Allotey Bruce Konuah for curating the photo exhibition, Mr Bice Osei Kuffour (Obour) former president of the Musicians

Union of Ghana (MUSIGA) for partnering with IAS for the 1 *Africa Musical Concert*, and the artistes who participated in the various programmes—Prof Arthur Flowers, Atentenben, Palmwine Tappers Band, Ghana Police Band, M.anifest, Dr Knii Lantey, Blacka Tee, Ann Philogene, Mykal Belle, Kojo Kombolo, Trudy, Osagyefo, Ras Appiah Levi, Xali, Hali, Miss Millar, Dr Temitope Fagunwa, and DJ Ashmen. Special appreciation also goes to Mr Ahuma Ocansey (Daddy Bosco) for coordinating the musical concert and Dr Alhaji Sidick, station manager of *Radio Univers 105.7fm* for publicity for all the conference events.

We say a very big thank you to the staff of J. H. Kwabena Nketia Archives, IAS (Mrs Judith Opoku Boateng, Mr Nathaniel Kpogo, and Mr George Gyesaw), the Audio-Visual Lab, IAS (Mrs Fidelia Ametewee and Mrs Selina Laryea), and the IAS Museum (Mr Philip Owusu) for the sights and sounds of the conference. To the Artistic Director and members of the Ghana Dance Ensemble, IAS, we are indeed extremely grateful for the wonderful African dance performances that set the tone for the conference. Finally, we express our thanks and appreciation to the Director of the Institute of African Studies (IAS), Prof Samuel Ntewusu for his unwavering support for the book. We also thank all the Fellows, staff, and students of the Institute and the wider University of Ghana, and all the participants, especially the youth and women who travelled from all over the world to participate in the conference and made it a memorable one. There is indeed hope for the future of Pan-Africanism and for Africa!

INVOCATION

Ancestral Roll-Call*

Kofi Anyidoho[1]

On this Solemn Day of our Re-Membering
In this Troubled Year of Their Lord
In this Hopeful Hour of our Re-Gathering

Elder Statesman John Henrik Clarke
One who recently stepped out into Twilight

It is I *Kofi Anyidoho menya tatam o*

I am but a child with an infant tongue
called in haste to invoke
Our Ancestral Roll-Call of Honour

---

* Published in *The Place We Call Home and Other Poems* (2011)

1 Composed in my office in the English Department, University of Ghana, one busy morning following an urgent call from the National Commission on Culture to come to the National Theatre early afternoon prepared with a commemorative poetic prelude to the launch of the **First Emancipation Day Celebrations**, to be presided over by the then President Jerry John Rawlings, broadcast live on Ghana Television and National Radio.

Taflatse Taflatse Taflatse Seven Times
Mine is but a trembling infant Tongue
a fledgling voice that cannot presume
to know or even faintly recall
the full lineup of our illustrious Ancestors

But I still must stand before you all
and on behalf of all the Elders of this House
on behalf of all the People of this Land
and on behalf of the Head of this Household

I call on you once more
Elder Statesman John Henrik Clarke
One who recently stepped into Twilight
to hold and guide my tongue
as I invoke
Our Ancestral Roll-Call of Honour.

I must begin with those countless millions
who perished on our many fields of sorrow
agony fields long grown to harvest point.

They who died fighting the slave raiders
And they who died on the shackled march to the Coast.

They who died in dark dungeons
And those who died on the turbulent Middle Passage.

They who died on the countless auction blocks
And those who died in endless chain gangs
on the cotton fields in the sugar mills
in the gold and silver mines
and in boiling plants of urban jungles.

And of those who survived
even against unreasonable odds

I must invoke Pedro Alonzo Nino
who in 1492
sailed tempestuous seas with Christoph Colomb

And I must invoke Estavanico
Explorer and Pathfinder
who in 1527
guided Navaez to Florida and Mississippi
and in 1538
led Friar Marcos on his search
for the Seven Cities of Cibola.

I cannot count all the Ancient Pathfinders
So when I invoke only two
Please know I invoke you all.

Some say too many of our Elders and Rulers
Soiled their Name with Shame
Selling their own into the Thunderstorm.

But Taflatse Taflatse Taflatse Seven Times
On this solemn day of our Re-Membering
in this Troubled Year of Their Lord
in this Hopeful Moment of our Re-Collecting
I must recall the many other Elders
who fought and fought
and fought to the Death of the Last Warrior
fought to the Death and the Resurrection
of the Final Hope.

Above them all I must recall
Peerless Ancestral Mothers
who led their children to war
against the arrogance of Alien Lords.

Saraounia of the DesertLands
Queen Amina of HausaLand
Queen Ann Nzinga of Angola
and
Nana Yaa Asantewaa of Asanteman.

And I must invoke
the many brave warriors
who led their people in revolt
against the enslavers chains.

Unconquerable Nat Turner
and Matchless Sojourner Truth
and Harriet Tubman
of the Unstoppable Underground Freedom Train.

And I must invoke the many other warriors
who broke the enslaver's chains
and led their people away into Freedomways
far away from plantations of sorrow
into the dangerous safety of maroon worlds.

Paul Cuffy and Damon and Kwamena
of Guyana of the deepest Amazon.

King Zumbi of the Brazilian Palmares

King Miguel and King Bayano of Venezuela

King Benkos Bioho of Colombia

King Tackie of St. Mary's

Ancestral Mother-Warrior Nanny of the Jamaican Hills

and all the fallen heroes and sheroes
of the various
cimarrones of Mexico
the quilombos of Brazil
the cumbes of Venezuela
the palenques of Cuba and Colombia.

Of special mention we must recall
Mythical Macandal The Black Messiah
Legendary Toussaint L'Ouverture and
General Jean Jacques Dessalines—all of Haiti
You who beat back Napoleon's proud warriors
converted them into a peace party
and on 1 January 1804 created Haiti
the first true Black Republic
of the Western Hemisphere.

So often so very often
we overlook the Eastern Hemisphere and
the many many million ancestral souls
dragged across storm sands of the Sahara
across the storm waves of the Indian Ocean.
But in this solemn hour of our Re-Membering
I must recall them all
and in recalling them all
I must make memorable mention
of a special few:

Great Warrior-Poet Antara
"of whom one half ranks with the best of A'bs
the other half (he) defends with (his) sword".

Ancestral Creative Master Alexander Pushkin
"Father of Modern Russian Poetry"

and his Great Grand-Dad General Hannibal
who gave Peter his Great Peace of Mind.

Elder Statesman John Henrik Clarke
One who recently stepped out into Twilight

You can tell I am running out of breath
but please hold my voice and guide my tongue
for just a little while longer
as I pay our final debts
to that special breed of ancestral souls
who fought and put Africa back
on the conscience of an ungrateful world
True African Ancestors of the 20th Century.

Chief Albert Sam of the Gold Coast
one who brought a shipload of Africans
Back to the MotherLand a decade before
The Great Mosaih Marcus Garvey
Launched his UNIA Movement across
StormFields of America Their America.

Ras Tafarai Haile Selase
Young Abyssinian Warrior-Prince
Who beat the glory out of Imperial Italiano.

I must invoke
The Rev Dr Martin Luther King Jr
on his Memorial Freedom March.

Eternal Brother Malcolm X
whose Voice and Spirit
Survived bullets of betrayal and hate.

Ras Makennen and Jomo Kenyatta and Nnamdi Azikiwe
Agostinho Neto CLR James and Booker T. Washington
Joseph Casely Hayford and James Kwegyir Aggrey
Nicolas Guillen Eric Williams
Walter Anthony Rodney Cheikh Anta Diop
And of course Robert Nesta Marley the Rastaman

and all the many many other Voices of Vision and Hope

I must welcome you back
to this humble but proud Ancestral Home.

Now that my task is at least half-done
I must retire to my little corner
and hand you over to a final reunion
with
Three Giants from your realm:

George Padmore of the nimble mind and sharpest soul
W. E. B. DuBois Ancestral Father of Pan-Africanism
and
The Osagyefo Dr. Kwame Nkrumah
Ancestral Founder of this House this Land
Africa's Man of the 20th Millennium.

INTRODUCTION

Back to the Future: The 1958 All Africa Peoples Conference (AAPC), the Current Conjuncture, and The Power of Optimism

Dzodzi Tsikata, Edem Adotey, and Mjiba Frehiwot[1]

The 1958 AAPC and the Current Conjuncture

Sixty-six years after the 1958 AAPC, another chapter in the unfair and unsustainable global order is unfolding, and optimism is in short supply worldwide. With more than 34,000 people dead—the majority of them women and children—and over 78,000 injured, Gaza is in ruins. After six months of relentless Israeli bombardment as retaliation for a Hamas attack, a large portion of its social infrastructure—including housing units, electricity, water, sewerage, healthcare systems, and educational institutions—was destroyed. As a result, the population faces starvation, malnutrition, and long-term damage. Wringing their hands in response

---

1 We are grateful to Prof Akilagpa Sawyerr, Prof Emerita Takyiwaa Manuh, and Dr Yao Graham for their comments on earlier drafts.

to Israeli intransigence, complicit US and other Western officials continue providing diplomatic, military, and financial support for the unfolding genocide of the Palestinian population. The Russian–Ukraine war has celebrated a second anniversary at a stalemate, but the war's negative effects are still global. The United States of America is facing the disturbing possibility of the return of Donald Trump to the White House. There are still concerns over the viability of a new international order based on multilateralism, numerous poles of power, and the plurality and diversity of choices and possibilities due to Western sabre-rattling against China's development as an economic giant.

Closer to home, there is turmoil in Sahel. Four countries have experienced military takeovers: Burkina Faso, Guinea, Mali, and Niger. The Economic Community of West African States (ECOWAS) has been shattered as a result of the years of insecurity created by the regime change in Libya by Western powers, France's ongoing political and economic dominance of its former colonies, and the massive exploitation of the mineral resources of some of the poorest nations. Sudan's year-long civil war, which has created the world's most serious humanitarian crisis—an estimated 150,000 people killed and almost nine million residents displaced—puts the country at risk of disintegrating. The majority of those displaced are from the western Darfur region. According to aid agency estimates, 25 million people are in need of urgent assistance. Across Africa, the economic fallouts from the COVID-19 pandemic and the war in Ukraine have accelerated the contraction of economies, capital flight, and collapsing currencies, which have created another cycle of debt distress and a return to austerity.

In the midst of all of this, South Africa's heroic act of referring Israel to the International Court of Justice (ICJ) and the size, courage, and persistence of vociferous global opposition to Israeli actions—across geographic, demographic, class, gender, and race divides—against repressive and punitive gag orders are concrete demonstrations of the power of optimism. It also highlights the necessity of the continuing struggles for a just world order that would allow Africa to choose its own economic, social, and political destiny. This is what makes the book timely and salient.

Ghana, under the leadership of Kwame Nkrumah and the Convention People's Party, hosted the first All-African People's Conference (AAPC) from 8 to 13 December 1958 in Accra. The conference which brought together over 300 participants from the continent, diaspora, and Global South represented a shift for the Pan-African movement. It was the first major Pan-African conference held on African soil, and the host, Ghana, was the first country south of the Sahara to attain independence. This inspired the delegates, including leaders of independence movements, political parties, labour unions, and youth organisations who were instrumental in the independence of their countries, to rededicate themselves to the liberation of their countries and the entire continent of Africa.

The sixtieth anniversary of the AAPC was commemorated globally by the Pan-Africanist movements in different forms in 2018. The commemoration which is the subject of this book was organised by the Institute of African Studies at the University of Ghana in collaboration with Lincoln University, PA, USA, the Socialist Movement of Ghana (formerly Socialist Forum of Ghana), Third World Network-Africa, and the Trade Union Congress (TUC) of Ghana, from 5 to 8 December 2018 at the University of Ghana.

These commemorations took place in a world that was quite different from that of the original conference. The year 1958 had been a time of optimism for Pan-Africanism and for the project of national liberation. Under the leadership of youthful trade unionist Tom Mboya, the AAPC mapped out a path towards national emancipation and economic transformation. Two years after the conference, which was attended by the charismatic anti-colonial leader from the Congo, Patrice Lumumba, an unprecedented number of African nations gained independence and commenced national development initiatives. Ten years later, the ideal of African emancipation had been shelved, Nkrumah toppled, and Lumumba and Mboya were killed. Sixty years after 1958, we found ourselves in a radically altered world with unfulfilled agendas from the past and even more complicated realities to deal with.

The conference therefore re-examined the vision of the founding mothers and fathers of modern African states and the Pan-Africanist movement that gathered in Accra in 1958 to discuss the liberation of Africa from colonial rule and the transformation of the entire continent into a truly liberated space.

The Unfinished Business of Liberation and Transformation is the topic of the sixtieth-anniversary commemoration, which indicates that the necessary transformation and liberation have not materialised beyond political independence. Therefore, the organisers were concerned about the necessity to evaluate the current state of the African nation, identify the headwinds that were buffeting its aspirations for emancipation, and consider seriously how to change its fortunes. This presented an additional chance to centre discussions around marginalised African constituencies. The 2018 commemoration privileged the participation of students, younger scholars, and women in honour of the women who had been largely absent from the conference in 1958 and whose contributions to the struggles for Africa's liberation had long been erased by androcentric histories.

This introduction, which draws from the work given in this book, considers the unresolved issues that spurred the meeting. It discusses Africa's incomplete decolonisation, paying attention to enduring issues such as cyclical economic crises, the failed promise of liberal democracy, and the trends and fissures in Pan-Africanist movements that have been challenging the forward movement of struggles. We also examine new and topical concerns such as environmental degradation and the climate crisis, questions of reparatory justice and repair, and the decolonialisation of knowledge. The topic of the globe since 2018 is then covered, including the COVID-19 pandemic and its aftermath, the current debt crisis, and the return to International Monetary Fund (IMF) prescriptions of neoliberal economic solutions. As we argue, these developments are taking place alongside an insurgent civil society and movements for justice across the world.

In these movements against the casual snuffing out of Black lives, police and army brutality, and the war in Gaza, we are witnessing the emergence of a new generation of activists who will continue to fight for Africa's total liberation and a world of possibilities.

The Unfinished Business of Decolonisation and Economic Liberation

Since the 1960s, Africa has experienced multiple cycles of economic crises interspersed by brief intervals of economic growth accompanying social and demographic change. Africa's subservient relationship with the Global North, which is characterised by its export commodity dependence, over-reliance on food and petty consumer imports, agrarian stagnation, and deindustrialisation, is the core cause of these cyclical crises. This is the unfinished business of decolonisation and economic liberation, which has been compounded by the failure of substantive democracy and social justice, the resilience of an unjust unipolar world order, and the financial control of transnational corporations. It was the global debt crisis in the 1970s that derailed heterodox approaches to African development and led Africa into the cul de sac of Structural Adjustment Programmes (SAPs) and the triumph of neo-liberalism (see Baah, in this book).

Each debt crisis in Africa since then has deepened the lack of policy autonomy and innovation in Africa.

The current debt crisis has been caused by a combination of old (the primary export commodity dependence and its cyclical crises of collapsing prices) and new factors (the COVID-19 pandemic's deleterious effects on economies, the high levels of government borrowing to finance the COVID-19 response, the effects of the war in Ukraine, and capital flight in response to rising interest rates in the Global North). A contributory factor is the lack of accountability and corruption in the use of borrowed money.

The current crisis is expected to have even more devastating impacts because of its size and spread,[2] who is owed (foreign private international lenders), the fact that it extends beyond sovereign debt, and the fact that it has also engulfed domestic lenders to governments. It has been accompanied by the savage devaluation of currencies in many African countries, rising interest rates, high rates of inflation (particularly in food prices, which carries the risks of intergenerational damage), and the rapidly rising costs of essential goods and services such as energy, education, health, and transportation.

Short-term solutions taken by governments across Africa include debt restructuring, reduced interest rates on government bonds, and the

---

2 In 2020, the average debt-to-GDP ratio in Africa was estimated at 71.4%. In at least twelve African countries, public external debt has doubled in the space of five years, rising from a cumulative stock of $89bn at the end of 2015 to $191bn at the end of 2020 (ADB, 2021). In 2022, twenty-two countries were either in debt distress or at high risk of debt distress (Bradlow, D. and Masamba, M., 2022).

resort to IMF bailouts and austerity measures. The situation is getting worse because governments are prioritising the repayment of external debt at unsustainable levels of government budgets and renegotiating domestic debt in ways that are creating livelihood crises for domestic government paper holders' ability to support their families. This leaves very little money in government budgets for large-scale structural transformation programmes that require huge investments in urban and rural infrastructures, social sectors, production, and social reproduction.

Even more damaging is the resort to excessive taxation of the poor. There is currently much anger and despair about the new spate of aggressive and regressive taxation, for example, in South Africa, Nigeria, Ghana, Zambia, Kenya, and Ethiopia. These taxes, amid high levels of inflation and currency depreciation, are intensifying the crisis of household debt and social reproduction in both urban and rural areas, especially among working people, and it is also beginning to affect the professional middle classes. This shift to austerity and a strengthening of neo-liberal policies will cause further depression, especially in rural areas where decades of neoliberal policies, neglect, and discrimination have resulted in a combination of agrarian stagnation, food insecurity, work precarity, and long-standing rural distress.

In addition to their economy-wide impacts, fifty years of neo-liberal policies have deepened and widened inequalities of class, gender, race, ethnicity, and generation across Africa. The social concern has been neglected for a long time, which contributes to the growing disparities. Although the social question was integral to the anti-colonial struggle in Africa and was explicitly stated in the manifestos of nationalist movements through statements about unity, economic development, and social equality, these promises were not fulfilled when independence was gained. Instead, new forms of injustice, driven by class, ethnicity, and gender, were allowed to flourish. Mkandawire has identified three factors that militated against social equality in the early independence period. They are: (a) the prioritisation of the national question and nation-building, manifested in de-racialisation and indigenisation of key positions of privilege and power; (b) policymakers embraced a linear view of history, which posited that social equality could only be achieved at much higher levels of development, and under conditions of industrialisation; and (c) the framing of the development agenda itself as either a trade-off or a sequencing action between development and social equality (Mkandawire, 2013). The neglect of the social question became even more acute in the era of economic liberalisation with its trickle-down policies and reduction of social policy to social protection programmes. Social policy has been subjected to market principles, targeting, and more recently, financialisation. As a result, issues of inequality and social cohesion are not given due consideration (Adesina, 2011) and are made worse by regressive social policy instruments (Balasubramanian, 2021).

More recent attempts to set Africa on the path to growth and structural transformation include the adoption of declarations and programmes such as the African Union's Agenda 2063, Comprehensive African Agriculture Development Programme (CAADP), and even the African Continental Free Trade Area (AfCFTA). These attempts are taking place in a situation characterised by the hegemony of economic liberalisation, which has been accompanied by the liberalisation of politics.

While this appeared to have arrested the cycle of coup d'états, one-party governments, and de facto and de jure, liberal democracy, which swept throughout Africa in the 1990s, has gradually lost its shine. Its limitations have been clear with every election cycle as citizens have become impatient with what has been characterised as "choiceless democracy" (Mkandawire, 1998, 2004). Under this scenario, political parties across the spectrum supervise the execution of comparable social and economic policies and are more successful at granting favours to their followers than enacting ground-breaking policies.

Election-related violence is spreading throughout Africa, and several regimes are manipulating political processes to extend their rule or their hold on power. The most recent examples include Emmerson Mnangagwa of Zimbabwe and Faure Gnassingbe's constitutional reform in Togo that modifies the country's presidential election process. The loss of confidence in liberal democracy coupled with economic malaise is fuelling civil unrest, insurgencies, insecurity, and banditry in countries such as Mozambique, Democratic Republic of Congo (DRC), Sudan, Nigeria, Tunisia, Egypt, and across the Sahel, where civil unrest has been described by the peasant leader Coulibaly as the peasant revolt in the Sahel (Coulibaly & Grajales, 2023).

Although the forms and the causes of disputes vary in every nation, the fundamental problems are generally the same. The disputes are really about resources, especially lack of access to resources, despite the fact that they are frequently portrayed to the outside world as religious, ethnic, and political divisions. Several of these countries such as the DRC, which is the largest producer of cobalt in the world, are heavily dependent on exporting raw materials.

West Africa is also grappling with a security crisis, mostly as a result of Boko Haram and other groups' destabilising activities. The region has witnessed a resurgence of coup d'états in Guinea, Mali, Niger, and Burkina Faso. It is striking to see popular support in Burkina Faso for a new Pan-African direction which is led by the transition president Ibrahim Traore. Nonetheless, we acknowledge that coup d'états frequently result in longer-lasting suffering for the populace. Given the existing state of some African governments, the topic of how to shift to a more people-centred government still needs to be answered. With their reaction to Niger and the expulsion of Niger, Mali, and Burkina Faso from the union, the sustainability of ECOWAS and other regional and continental organisations is coming under scrutiny.

Following the military's return to power in Guinea, Mali, Niger, and Burkina Faso, as well as the ineptitude and double standards displayed by ECOWAS's responses to this development, West Africa is set to become even more fragmented, making it more difficult to address the issue of Islamic insurgency and insecurity that has taken hold with the disintegration of Libya due to Western governments' agendas for regime change. The new military governments' anti-French position and anti-imperialist declarations allude to emancipatory politics. However, the reliance of the regimes on the Africa Corps (formerly known as the Wagner group) and Russia for securing their borders points to a complicated set of circumstances that might not advance an agenda of liberation.

Another enduring issue is the decolonisation of knowledge production (Falola, 2022; Mbembe, 2015; Ndlovu-Gatsheni, 2020; Zeleza, 2017). At the heart of Africa's development are the knowledge systems that define who we are, what we must be, and how we must be. This was not lost on Kwame Nkrumah. Thus, when he officially opened the Institute of African Studies (IAS) at the University of Ghana in 1963, decolonising knowledge production was the core mission he entrusted the institute with. Unfortunately, even in cases when higher education institutions have been successful in Africanisation after more than sixty years on, they have failed decolonising. The plethora of academic conferences, publications, podcasts, projects, and related activism on decolonising the academy such as "Rhodes Must Fall" is a testament to the growing momentum of efforts to address this issue. African knowledge systems are still marginalised and treated as less "scientific". African institutions of higher learning which are complicit in the hegemony of Western knowledge systems must work to decolonise the academy (Clark, 2023; Dzisah & Kpessa-Whyte, 2023; Poe, 2023).

From the foregoing, decolonisation and liberation are ongoing processes that go beyond achieving independence. Not all African nations have attained the legal status of decolonisation; Morocco still holds Western Sahara as a colony of Morocco, while civil wars and other crises have torn apart nations like Ethiopia, Sudan, and Libya. While social movements in Africa are resurgent and making their demands known, the Pan-African movement itself has been unable to harness these energies for the liberation of the continent. Pan-Africanism is riven by factionalism and contradictions among its parts, which has proved to be paralysing. The call to pay attention to the persistence of neo-colonialism, particularly how African economies are integrated into the global economy, is apt (Sawyerr, Closing Address). Furthermore, these longstanding issues of economic policy, politics, and the social question have now been layered over and complicated by new issues that also demand urgent attention.

New Business to Take Care of

After the 1958 AAPC, Africa has had to deal with significant new challenges, which makes the 2018 memorial meeting extremely timely. These include environmental degradation and restoration, which has taken on added global urgency in the last few years. The UN Secretary-General, António Guterres, at the UN Climate Change Conference COP28 pointed to this when he noted "The world cannot afford delays, indecision, or half measures". (https://www.un.org/sg/en/content/sg/statement/2023-12-13/secretary-generals-statement-the-closing-of-the-un-climate-change-conference-cop28). While Africa is the least producer of carbon emissions in the world, it is one of the major casualties of global warming. Africa's smallholder farmers are experiencing the most deleterious impacts of global warming (Tsikata, Welcome Address). The devastating effects of seasonal hurricanes in the Caribbean and recent cyclones in Africa such as Cyclone Idai in Mozambique, Zimbabwe, and Malawi in 2019 and the Caribbean also show the costs in human and material terms of climate change. Regretfully, research indicates that the frequency and intensity of these occurrences will increase, with the continent expected to see extreme heat waves annually by 2040 (Campbell, Closing Keynote).

The unaddressed question of reparations and restitution provides an opportunity for Global Africa to come together to demand accountability for the centuries of pillage of its human and natural resources. The campaign over the years has received a lukewarm response from many African governments as shown at the UN "World Conference Against Racism, Racial Discrimination, Xenophobia and Related Intolerance" in Durban in 2001. The campaign has been bogged down by questions of financial compensation. As a new wave of "apologies" and "reparations" from the perpetrators and beneficiaries of these heinous crimes including the Church of England takes hold, it is time to recentre this conversation beyond financial compensation to a more just world order.

Managing Africa's demographic transitions is another important challenge of the twentieth century. The UN estimates that by 2050, a quarter of the world's population will be African. This has been described as a demographic transformation that "has the potential to alter the world order" (https://www.imf.org/en/Publications/fandd/issues/2023/09/PT-african-century#:~:text=The%20United%20Nations%20projects%20that,world's%20population%20will%20be%20African). Africa's potential is also inherent in its majority youthful population. Unfortunately, high unemployment rates and the lack of credible opportunities for self-realisation arrests the transition of large numbers of young people to full adulthood and citizenship and make them susceptible to the lure of internet fraud, irregular migration, and radicalisation by armed and terrorist groups that hold some parts of the continent to ransom.

This crisis of youth unemployment was underpinned by decades of primary commodity-driven economic growth which led to celebrations of "Africa Rising". The fact that the commodity boom created little by way of employment, but instead widened disparities in many nations, highlighting the need for a different kind of growth and transformation models to address the challenges posed by Africa's demographic shifts. In the new scramble for the essential minerals for the fourth industrial revolution and green development agendas of industrialised countries, Africa is once more a target because of its mineral resources. It will be crucial for the future how Africa positions itself to reap the benefits of these resources, keeping in mind the lessons learned from the cyclical crises by its reliance on basic commodity exports.

A related challenge is the systemic character and persistence of gender inequalities that mostly affect women, youth, and LGBTQI+ groups. These are reinforced by economic arrangements and patriarchal institutions within the state and civil society. While women make up the majority in many African countries and have played instrumental and indispensable roles across time and space, many are still dispossessed and marginalised due to economic, social, and political discrimination. This has been compounded by some neoliberal policies which reinforce these inequalities. For instance, Wallace (2023) draws attention to the gender discrimination at the heart of the neoliberal policies that inform initiatives such as AfCFTA.

Finally, the rise of the right and authoritarian populism in the West poses a threat to the interests of Africans at home and abroad, as the rhetoric of these leaders has emboldened racist, xenophobic attacks, and other human rights abuses. The US-led Western intervention in Libya and its disastrous fallout, including the jihadist movements' expansion in the Sahel, which poses a threat to the stability of these governments as well as the entire region, should serve as a wake-up call to all Africans. Georges Nzongola-Ntalaja draws parallels from the DRC (Opening keynote).

Promising Signals

Despite the unfinished business and the new compounding issues notwithstanding, there are promising signs of progress with African liberation. The autocratic regimes that dominate Africa, which are also an impediment to Global Pan-Africanism, are being challenged by vibrant youth movements. The Arab Spring, which originated in Tunisia in North Africa, set the world of politics on fire in the early 2010s (Korany & El-Mahdi, 2012). It jumpstarted the most recent manifestations of popular resistance and popular protests in Africa. The #Feesmustfall, #Rhodesmustfall, *Université Populaire de L'Engagement Citoyen (UPEC), Y'en a marre, Project South, #EndSars, Filimbi,* and *Lucha* (Gueye, 2013; Ndiaye, 2023) add to the list of popular movements that are challenging the status quo in Africa. These popular movements stem from years of economic, social, and political hardships. A lot of African countries are changing to become more democratic as a result of youth-led initiatives. Macky Sall of Senegal faced challenges from large-scale demonstrations and the Constitutional Court, which resulted from the regime's over-throw through elections. Sall's recent unilateral postponement of elections caused a significant political crisis for Senegal and ECOWAS. This is an important contrast to the neighbouring countries where coups have taken place—Mali (2021), Guinea (2021), Niger (2023), and Burkina Faso (2023). While these movements have not specifically called for a united Africa, much of their discourse is reminiscent of the agenda of Pan-African leaders such as Kwame Nkrumah, Gamal Nassar, Julius Nyerere, Sekou Toure, Funmilayo Ransome-Kuti, Mabel Dove-Danquah, and Thomas Sankara. In Burkina Faso, Ibrahim Traore and the government are embracing the Pan-African spirit of Thomas Sankara by attempt-ing to nationalise natural resources. Calls for even cooperation between French-speaking countries demonstrate the relevance of Pan-Africanism in the twenty-first century. Recent moves by Mali, Niger, and Burkina Faso to establish an Association of Sahel States (AES) and their stated intention to withdraw from ECOWAS reveal that the recent wave of resistance is leading towards new configurations across the continent.

The most recent manifestations of Pan-African activity have been led by youth and forward-looking activists. Pan-African debates, pro-tests, and struggles have been at the forefront of the movement for the last twenty years. However, the demographic character of Pan-African activism has shifted. The #FeesMustFall, #RhodesMustFall, #Bringbackourgirl, #EndSars, #FreeSenegal, Movement to Free DRC, and #BlackLivesMatter movements have women and other marginalised groups, such as members of the LGBTQ+ community, at their forefront. These international Pan-African struggles which have been both local and global, as well as separate and connected moments in the Pan-African movement, are challenging capitalism, patriarchy, and dictatorial regimes. This is evidenced in the work of members of the Nigerian Feminist Forum originally organised against gender-based violence in Nigeria and later turned their sights on police brutality (Darkwah, Mohammed, Williams, & Nagarajan, 2022). This demonstrates how the Pan-African movement is inclusive. Connecting these struggles to both local reality and the broader Pan-African movements is a challenge the movement faces today.

The re-emergence of Pan-Africanism is spreading globally from the continent to the diaspora and back to the continent. The essential role that Africa plays in the movement is constant. There have been calls for unity between African people on the continent and those outside of the continent. The question of how to unify and in what form is exercising the movement at this juncture. Pan-African organisations and political bodies such as the Sankofa study group and the *Partido Africano para a Independência da Guiné e Cabo Verde*, (PAIGC) are promoting Pan-Africanism as the key to their future. While the scale, location, geography, and ideology may differ between a small local organisation and a large political party, the agendas of both are tied to the global Pan-African movement and are simultaneously interconnected. Another interesting evolution of the movement is the robust calls for unity and liberation beyond the English-speaking world. An example is the most recent summit, the *Université Populaire de L'Engagement Citoyen* (UPEC) held in 2018 in Senegal. The UPEC summit brought together fifty-five social movements that represented thirty countries (Ndiaye, 2023). This represents one of the larger Pan-African gatherings in French-speaking Africa. Additionally, in East Africa, *AfricansRising* a Pan-African collective, is promoting African unity and solidarity (https://www.africansrising.org/about/our-mission-and-vision/). The organisation's Kilimanjaro Declaration 2.0 highlights the need for a holistic approach to the Pan-African movement. The declaration contends that there is a need for actualising African unity, a borderless Africa with one currency, free movement of people, goods, and services, and the total liberation of our people (Africans Rising, 2022).

The global Pan-African movement has long been concerned with decolonising knowledge in African and African-majority universities globally. The Council for the Development of Social Science Research in Africa (CODESRIA), which was established in 1973, was a seminal event in an attempt to wrest control of knowledge production about Africa from non-African institutions and to overcome Africa's linguistic barriers. During the crisis of Africa's higher education system created by the defunding of universities in the 1990s, CODESRIA played a pivotal role in supporting generations of African scholars to undertake research on Africa's experience with economic and political liberalisation, among other critical issues, in freedom from censorship and repression. Despite the fact that academics from all over Global Africa are active in the effort to decolonise knowledge systems, the quest for epistemic justice in African universities has grown during the past 20 years as these institutions have recovered from the destructive effects of neo-liberalism. The Kwame Nkrumah Chair in African Studies established at the University of Ghana (2005) and the Mwalimu Julius Nyerere Chair in Pan-Africana Studies at the University of Dar es Salaam (2008) are two key distinguished chairs that allow for critical and nuanced debates on decolonising knowledge production. Another significant development was the establishment of the African Studies Association of Africa (ASAA) in 2013. Before its inception, all African Studies Associations were based outside Africa. In collaboration with CODESRIA, the association is facilitating candid and transparent conversations about knowledge production among Africans across the continent and in diaspora, thereby helping to bridge the linguistic gap across the continent's four main zones.[3]

Finally, the Pan-African movement may now reach a far wider audience worldwide due to the rise of virtual activism. Due to this trend, relatively local problems can now almost instantly become global ones. The Pan-African movement has advanced due to the adept utilisation of these platforms by digitally organised activists.

---

3 ASAA also hosted a six (6) series Pan-African Conversation in the USA, Martinique, Ghana, DRC, Tanzania, and one will take place in Senegal to debate, discuss and move forward questions of decolonising knowledge production in Africa (https://as-aa.org/).

Social media has been used as an avenue for political education, recruitment, as an organising tool for rallies protests, and to create global movements. This is positive in that the Pan-African message can travel and the seeds of the work done in one space can be grown in another location across the globe. The challenge is bringing these movements together to develop a comprehensive, cohesive, and effective movement that will move the anti-imperialist needle, and for Africa to gain control of the inventions it is currently mainly consuming.

The AAPC@60 Commemoration

The sixtieth Anniversary of the AAPC held in 2018 created a platform to ask critical questions about the impact of the 1958 conference and to chart a way forward for the Global Pan-African Movement to develop an agenda for its future.

The four-day international conference was attended by more than 400 participants made up of students, workers, academics, and civil society actors. The event consisted of plenary and panel presentations and a substantial artistic programme of film shows, a photo exhibition, social gatherings, and a musical concert. In keeping with the ethos of the 1958 Conference, this event was organised by an energetic group of younger scholars, supported by more established Pan-African activists. But the participation of students from the West Africa Region—Ghana, Burkina Faso, Togo, and Nigeria—who travelled by road, was especially noteworthy. Unlike the 1958 Conference, there was also a sizable representation of women among attendees as well as in the conference leadership. The conference honoured the participation of youth and women with the designation of the first day of the conference as Youth and Women's Day.

The conference was anchored on six key themes, namely (a) Peoples of Africa; (b) Neocolonialism and Imperialism; (c) The African Union and Agenda 2063; (d) Emancipation of Women; (e) Reparations and Restorative Justice; and (f) Global Warming. These themes guided the discussions, papers, plenaries, keynote speakers, artistic programmes, and resolutions. The opening keynote speaker, Georges Nzongola-Ntalaja, captivated an audience of almost 900 people with his speech that focused on the Democratic Republic of the Congo among other critical

junctures in global Pan-Africanism. The conference was closed by distinguished pan-Africanist Horace Campbell, third occupant of the Kwame
Nkrumah Chair in African Studies at the University of Ghana, who gave
a passionate summary of the proceedings, the status of the Pan-African
movement today, and a demand that Pan-Africanism be realised within
the next fifteen years. The closing occurred at a historic location on the
campus of the University of Ghana, the Kwame Nkrumah Complex of
the Institute of African Studies.

The conference organisers recognised the importance of hosting a
well-rounded and inclusive conference. Parallel artistic events, such as a
film and discussion series, photo exhibition, *Palm Wine Night*, bazaar,
and a 1 *Africa Musical Concert* were one way this was accomplished.
The six sub-themes were addressed in the film selection process, and the
discussions that followed the screenings focused on issues that were also
being discussed at the conference plenaries and parallel sessions. The
Palm Wine Night was a combination of Pan-African music, Ghanaian
food and drinks, and Pan-African networking. This night was strategically hosted at the old premises of the Institute of African Studies, where
Kwame Nkrumah officially opened the Institute of African Studies in
1963, and where the J.H. Kwabena Nketia Archive is housed. The J. H.
Kwabena Nketia archive began as the archive of the first African Director
of the Institute of African Studies. The 1 *Africa Musical Concert* featured
a long list of Pan-African artists that came from far and near. The show,
which was headlined by two internationally acclaimed forward-looking
artists M. anifest and Dr Knii-Lante, featured reggae artists, rhythm
and blues artists, a gospel artist, spoken word artists, and Temitope
Fagunwa, who was part of our Nigerian delegation and brought his
saxophone and asked to join the artists performing. His contribution
to the two main artistic programmes was a highlight of the evening
performances. Finally, there was a photo exhibit curated by Mr Allotey
Bruce-Konuah titled, *re_sisters - Emancipation of Women - Global Africa*,
which featured the contributions of Global African women to the Pan-
African Movement.

On the final day, small groups discussed each of the six themes in
order to create a thorough list of problems and suggestions. The final
day's small group structure was an afterthought added to the conference

schedule. The evolution of the conference demonstrated that participants were extremely active and wanted to play an active role in developing the path forward. Throughout the conference, there were mini conversations and outright declarations that we needed to think critically about how to ensure that the commemoration was not just another talk shop. This led to a last-minute decision to create space for the collective to engage the various themes and develop corresponding issues and recommendations. The issues and recommendations highlighted six areas for focus, namely: (a) On-Pan-Africanism Today, Tomorrow, and Building a New Politics of Substantive Democracy and Security; (b) On Pan-African Epistemologies for Knowledge Production; (c) On Ending Imperialist Domination and Transforming Africa's Economies; (d) On Climate Change and Environmental Repair; (e) On Restorative and Reparative Justice; and (f) On Youth, Workers, Progressive Women and Africa's Transformation. These issues and recommendations reflect the wide breadth of Pan-Africanists who attended the conference.

The conference was comprised of an inspired group of participants who were active in every aspect of the conference. There were calls for the conference to be held again and to serve as a springboard for interacting with the Pan-African movement on a global scale; 2018 ended on a note of optimism and renewal.

The World Since 2018

The relevance of the topics covered at the conference have been highlighted by worldwide occurrences such as the COVID-19 pandemic and the Black Lives Matter campaign that occurred since the conference was held in 2018.

The Fallouts From the COVID-19 Pandemic

The most significant of a series of unplanned and unprecedented events to shake the world since the 2018 conference was the COVID-19 pandemic. The first paper presented on the first day of the 2018 Conference was about the fallouts of the cholera epidemic in Zimbabwe. Simukai Chigudu (2020) clearly stated that epidemics are not simply health events, but rather multi-dimensional crises with deep roots in history, requiring a fundamental rethinking of society and politics. These predictions were prescient, and Africa's Ebola experiences were just a taste of what happened when COVID-19 brought the entire world to a standstill. Even though the mortality rates predicted for Africa did not materialise, the harsh responses and increasing authoritarian tendencies of African governments proved to be extremely detrimental to the continent's economies, many of which shrank as a result of taking on unmanageable debt to pay for COVID-19 measures (Sibeko, 2022).

While Africa's armies of self-employed and casual workers were the most affected by the shutdown of economic activities, the bulk of mitigation measures were directed at businesses, public sector wage workers, and households with direct access to water and electricity. By far the most egregious example of the neglect of the livelihoods of working people was the closure of land borders across Africa, long after airports had opened for business (Tsikata & Torvikey, 2021). It may be argued that if land borders had been left open allowing traders and other economic players to operate freely across borders, the brutal contraction of many African economies would have been mitigated.

Africa ought to have been seated at the table where decisions on COVID-19 responses are made globally, given its model response to the pandemic. First, the African Centre for Disease Control was established, showcasing Africa's research skills and promoting Pan-African collaboration in health and epidemiological research. In order to obtain vaccines and protective gear for Africa, the African Union (AU) assembled a group of powerful Africans. The African Union (AU) composed a team of influential Africans to secure vaccines and protective equipment for Africa. There were also innovative responses from across Africa—the indigenous medicines and cures, the prototypes of ventilators and other equipment, and the use of Information Communication Technology (ICT) for the marketing of goods and services. While these were exemplary, they exposed the continent's lack of industrial capacity and its neglect of social services and infrastructure. However, Africa's best efforts were derailed not by its limitations but by the inward-looking and supremely self-focused stance of the West to a global crisis. Africa's inability to secure vaccines it had mobilised resources to pay for because of vaccine hoarding, the vaccine apartheid represented by the refusal to recognise vaccines manufactured outside the West; and the refusal to suspend patents on vaccine technology to enable the manufacture of vaccines in Africa were only three of the stark reminders of Africa's unfinished task of liberation and transformation (Tsikata & Torvikey, 2021).

The global pandemic created a platform for technology companies to gain enormous fortune, while the digital divide brought issues of race and class to light everywhere. As a result of their adaptation to the new reality, African nations started using online platforms to organise and convene countless conversations for education, hold programmes, demand justice, and convene as a community. The IAS also shifted to working virtually, including the hosting of the Third Biennial Kwame Nkrumah Pan-African Intellectual and Cultural Festival under the leadership of Amina Mama, the fourth occupant of the Kwame Nkrumah Chair in African Studies at the IAS. The conference was curated entirely online with performances, plenary speakers, keynote speakers, a film show, and a youth day.

Global African/Black Lives Campaigns

Following the 2020 death of African American George Floyd in Minneapolis, Minnesota, at the hands of police officer Derek Chauvin, the #Black Lives Matter movement attracted international attention. The movement which started in 2013 to highlight systemic racism and police brutality against African Americans, particularly males, following the death of African American teenager Trayvon Martin and the subsequent acquittal of George Zimmerman of charges for his murder, brought to the fore the historic injustices suffered by African Americans. Like the founders of the Black Lives Matter campaign, the forebears of Pan-Africanism sought to bring freedom, liberation, and justice to black folks.

One noteworthy accomplishment of this movement was bringing racism to light not only in the United States but also in many other countries, especially among the African diaspora. Africans were dehumanised and used like chattel during the long-ago era of transatlantic slavery. There have been initiatives to alter the historical narrative of slavery and colonialism in other regions of the world, including Britain. In 2020, these movements resulted in the removal of monuments honouring slave traders like Edward Colston from Bristol. The inhumane conditions of

Brazilians of African descent in the favelas also remind us of the plight of millions of Africans in the diaspora. Haiti, the first African country to be independent in the Western hemisphere, has been taken over by violent gangs who deny the citizenry their basic human rights. Clearly, there is still work to be done to restore the dignity of Africans after centuries of abuse and disdain for African people and their cultures.

Conditions are not too different on the continent. The dignity of life that independence promised has failed to materialise for the vast majority. While many Africans live in poverty, their kleptocratic leaders enjoy lavish lifestyles. While many nations are supposedly democratic, the leaders have used the military and the police to stifle dissent. In 2020, the #EndSARS movement led by the youth in Nigeria to disband the Special Anti-Robbery Squad (SARS) accused of human rights abuses was met with police brutality which unfortunately resulted in innocent civilians being shot at by security forces at the Lekki Toll Gate in Lagos. In the Democratic Republic of Congo, the M23 rebel group and other groups have been fighting the government and the United Nations (UN) peacekeepers, leaving in their wake loss of lives and displacement. Thus, it is ironic that African governments are committing atrocities against their citizens as we organize against racism against the dehumanisation of African living abroad. Since the 2018 conference, there has been no decrease in these violations of human rights. The AU on occasion has been criticised for not forcefully protesting the treatment of Africans in the diaspora. However, one cannot be calling for reforms in policing by racist police officers while Africans are brutalised by African police in Africa. This calls for concerted efforts both on the continent and in the diaspora to address these human rights abuses.

The world has also witnessed other related human rights issues including the criminalisation of migration, especially by governments in the West. This includes Italy's Giorgia Meloni's threat to crack down on migrants including a naval blockade of the coast of North Africa, the United Kingdom (UK) bill to send migrants who arrive in the UK across the English Channel to Rwanda permanently, and the United States, the push by Republicans for the passage of a border bill that, among other things, bars migrants who pass through another country before arriving at the US-Mexico border from seeking asylum.

This perception of immigrants as criminals or undesirables, as well as the prejudice that many experience, are fostered by the propaganda of some of these governments, which holds them accountable for crimes, destroying national cultures, and displacing natives from their occupations. The Western news media is awash with images of desperate Africans and other nationals in dingy boats making the perilous journey across the Mediterranean Sea to Europe. On the US–Mexico border, the picture is no different, as people trek long distances from parts of Central and South America at the risk of violent attacks and kidnappings by criminal gangs to reach the US border. These migrants seeking refuge from wars and economic hardships have been subjected to inhumane treatment at the borders. For those who can make it across the border, this may not be the end of their woes. Some have spent years in holding camps waiting for their asylum to be processed. Others have faced arrest and deportation, thus, living a life of fear and uncertainty in a space that was to provide succour.

From the aforementioned, it is evident that the business of liberation and transformation is indeed an unfinished one. They confirm and reinforce the salience of the conference's outcome document, as well as the other material presented in this book.

The Book—Purpose, Segments, and Contents

This book interrogates the Pan-African agenda of liberation and transformation of the 1958 All-African People's Conference (AAPC-1958), which H.E. Thabo Mbeki, former president of South Africa, described as a "timely and historic conference" with "ground-breaking outcomes". It is also a document of record that curates the published articles and unpublished material—speeches, statements, an interview with one of the last surviving delegates of the 1958 conference, conference documents, resolutions, and a report on artistic activities connected with the sixtieth-anniversary commemoration of this important event (AAPC-2018). The book not only confirms the unfinished business of liberation and transformation but also the urgency and necessity of overthrowing the neocolonial yoke. It also proffers creative ways of addressing these challenges in a manner that reflects the realities of today.

The book is in three interrelated sections, beginning with an "Invocation" and ending with an "Exhortation". The "Invocation" is a poem by the renowned Ghanaian poet, Kofi Anyidoho, aptly titled "Ancestral Roll Call", which pays tribute to the forebears of Pan-Africanism, such as John Henrik Clarke, Pedro Alonzo Nino, Queen Amina of Zazzau, Queen Nzinga of Ndongo and Matamba, and Nana Yaa Asantewaa of Asanteman.

The first section contains the opening and closing keynote addresses delivered by Georges Nzongola-Ntalaja and Horace Campbell, respectively, papers previously presented by Issa Shivji, first occupant of the Julius Nyerere Professorial Chair in Pan-African Studies, University of Dar es Salaam, Tanzania and Anthony Yaw Baah, the Secretary General of the Trades Union Congress (TUC) of Ghana, and six feature articles recently published in the *Contemporary Journal of African Studies*.

Both keynotes stress the importance of lessons learned since the 1958 Conference, essentially the centrality of the unification and emancipation of Africans at home and abroad to the success of the Pan-Africanist project. Georges Nzongola-Ntalaja calls for the mobilisation of new social movements led by progressive intellectuals, a call echoed by Horace Campbell's call to mobilise the masses and for new forms of organisation and leadership.

The essay by Issa Shivji draws parallels between the Pan-African thought of Julius Nyerere and Kwame Nkrumah and urges African intellectuals to play a critical role in the development of a new Pan-Africanism. Baah outlines the development initiatives in Africa since the colonial period, distinguishing between "initiatives by Africans and initiatives for Africa". He argues for the former, that is, Africa-owned initiatives that are people-centred.

The six feature articles tackle some of the conference's key themes. In "Pan-African Epistemologies of Knowledge Production: A Deconstruction-Based Critical Reflection", James Dzisah and Michael Kpessa-Whyte challenge practices that sustain colonial knowledge structures such as indexing of journals in colonial outlets and university rankings by Western-based agencies.

In "Hip-Hop Studies as a Model for Anti-imperialist Research in Africa", Msia Kibona Clark argues the case for applying hip-hop studies methodologies to decolonise African studies. Her chapter discusses the theoretical and methodological frameworks of hip-hop studies, which emphasise an organic interaction between researchers and the communities they investigate.

Adryan Wallace turns the gaze on neoliberal approaches to development in Africa, especially economic integration, using the AfCFTA as a point of discussion. Her chapter, "Generating Inclusive and Sustainable Growth: Challenging Neoliberal Approaches to Gender Mainstreaming in Regional Economic Integration in Africa", draws attention to the inherent inequalities in these neo-liberal frameworks.

The three pieces that follow are on political liberation. D. Zizwe Poe shows how institutions of higher education can be integral to the unfinished business of liberation and transformation. In his chapter, "Ghana (1957-1966): Reflections and Lessons from a 20th Century Pan-African Liberated Nation-State", he points to their strategic roles in shaping the minds of the next generation of Africans in the liberation struggle.

In "Transnational Citizenship on the Borderlands: Towards Making (Non)Sense of National Borders in Africa", Edem Adotey examines the vexed issue of inherited colonial borders and proposes transnational citizenship on the borderlands to reflect the daily realities of life for cross-border communities.

Mjiba Frehiwot's "Looking Backwards to Run Forward: A Critical Examination of the 60th Anniversary of the 1958 All-African People's Conference", which closes the section, offers rich historical insight into both AAPC-1958 and AAPC-2018. She highlights some of the key takeaways of both conferences—the importance of African agency and the deepening of relations across Global Africa for achieving true liberation and transformation.

The second section comprises the welcome address by the Chair of the Secretariat of AAPC-2018, the then Director of the Institute of African Studies, Dzodzi Tsikata, the closing speech by Akilagpa Sawyerr, the Conference Chair of AAPC-2018, solidarity statements from two prominent Pan-Africanists, H. E. Thabo Mbeki, and the Deputy Chairperson of the African Union Commission, H. E. Kwesi Quartey, and an interview with a living delegate at the AAPC-1958. In her opening address, Dzodzi Tsikata highlights the grave challenges and immense opportunities facing the continent and underscores the focus of the conference by asking what it would take to achieve a truly liberated, united, and prosperous continent.

H. E. Thabo Mbeki's solidarity message speaks of the unfinished business of liberation and the need for a renewed commitment to this vision, while Ambassador Kwesi Quartey reminds us of the common challenges and aspirations.

Akilagpa Sawyerr stresses the importance of the networks and relationships across Global Africa established at the conference, the ideas exchanged, and their implications for the attainment of the Pan-African dream of liberation and unity.

The interview with Mr G. A. Balogun, a former Ghanaian trade unionist who participated in the 1958 AAPC, provides some historical context on the event as well as insights into Nkrumah's liberation project.

The third and last sections of the book present the conference background paper, a report on artistic activities at the conference, and the Statement of Issues and Recommendations adopted at the Conference. The background paper sheds light on the themes, while the resolutions address these themes, namely Pan-Africanism Today and Tomorrow and Building a New Politics of Substantive Democracy and Security; Pan-African Epistemologies for Knowledge Production; Ending Imperialist Domination and Transforming Africa's Economies; Climate Change and Environmental Repair; Restorative and Reparative Justice; and Youth, Workers, Progressive Women, and Africa's Transformation.

The artistic programme report examines the array of activities, which included documentary and feature films about the African experience, a photo exhibition, an evening palm wine, local music, and food event, and an international musical concert. As the report notes, the programme not only showcased the potential of the arts in mobilising people for the Pan-African cause but enabled the active participation of non-academic audiences in the Conference.

The book ends with an "Exhortation", a poetry performance by Arthur Rickydoc Flowers, in which he urges "the ancient race in deep decline" to follow an African way.

Looking Forward

This book speaks to many Pan-African, African, and Global audiences. It is especially targeted at the Pan-African movement, which is on an upward trajectory with new leadership, more inclusivity, and a rootedness in grassroots struggles. Pan-Africanism today is manifesting in pockets around Global Africa with a specific focus on youth and women in the leadership of the local movements that contribute to the larger global Pan-African movement. The sixtieth anniversary of commemorations of the AAPC demonstrated that the Pan-African movement is as popular as it was in 1958, and more widely discussed and debated in the twenty-first century than it was in the twentieth century. There are certainly historical events that have contributed to the widening appeal of Pan-Africanism today, yet this has not translated into total liberation and transformation.

The sixtieth-anniversary commemoration explained why we can have Pan-African wildfires yet still grapple with unimaginable challenges globally. The business of liberation and transformation must be at the forefront of the agenda for all Pan-African institutions, academics, and activists. The academy in Global Africa, particularly the African/Africana/Black and Pan-Africana studies departments, associations, and researchers (students and faculty) must take seriously questions of ontology and epistemology at the heart of decolonisation. These institutions must become what Kwame Nkrumah identified as liberated zones and what D. Zizwe Poe articulates as an updated way to judge if an institution is a Pan-African liberated zone or an enemy-held zone. Beyond the colonial gaze, Global Africa must grapple with economic dependency, autocratic leadership, climate change, and human rights violations against women, marginalised persons including the LGTBQI+ community, and persons with disabilities. Globalisation and imperialism have and will continue to impact Africa in ways that severely stall its people's development and thus the re-emergence of internationalism is interconnected with the way forward for the Pan-African movement.

Lastly, the next couple of years should be occupied with the recommendations that emerged from the sixtieth anniversary. The first is the development of Pan-African epistemologies. Without a new Africa-facing and African-centred knowledge base, the African revolution will be impossible. Secondly, African states must build inclusive, representative, and democratic institutions. This includes ending imperialist domination and transforming Africa's economies into ones that are controlled by Africans themselves and prioritise the needs of Africa's working people. Africa must also find pathways to achieve the renewed interest in structural transformation and industrialisation and the building of inclusive economies that guarantee the reproduction of the next generation. It also calls for Africa to resist the resurgence of austerity and the further loss of policy autonomy that will set back the continent and Global Africa for decades to come. Only then can Africa address the most pressing recommendation, that of addressing climate change and environmental repair.

No longer can we afford to disregard the damage we are doing to the planet. This must become a central concern for all Pan-Africanists. There should be an end to activities that damage the environment. Africa must also demand justice from those whose actions have brought the planet to the brink of catastrophe. Linked with this, Africa's development aspirations must not be sacrificed at the altar of environmental policies that recolonise and grab Africa's natural resources in the name of green technologies and conservation.

The Pan-African movement must also focus on restorative and reparative justice with a focus on the Global African family. Global African people must restore their ability to be the subject of their story and find the courage to look inward for solutions and to repair tears in the fabric of the movement, nations, regions, continents, and Global Africa. Lastly, the movement must be all-inclusive providing equal opportunities, and honouring the contributions and leadership of the youth, women, persons with disabilities, and LGBTQI+ communities. Only then will Africa have a future of total liberation and transformation.

References

Adesina, J. O. (2011). Beyond the social protection paradigm: Social policy in Africa's development. *Canadian Journal of Development Studies / Revue Canadienne d'études du développement*, 32(4), 454–470. https://doi.org/10.1080/02255189.2011.647441

African Development Bank. (2021). "African economic outlook 2021", Abidjan. Retrieved from https://www.afdb.org/en/documents/african-economic-outlook-2021

Africans Rising. (2022, August 31). *The Kilimanjaro Declaration 2.0.* Arusha, Tanzania: Author.

Africans Rising. (n.d.). Retrieved from https://www.africansrising.org/about/our-mission-and-vision/

Balasubramanian, P. (2021). *Debt in everyday life: AA critique on the increasing role of finance in social policy* (The Current Column). Bonn, Germany: German Development Institute / Deutsches Institut für Entwicklungspolitik (DIE).

Bouilly, E., Rillon, O., & Cross, H. (2016). African women's struggles in a gender perspective. *Review of African Political Economy, 43*(149), 338–349.

Bradlow, D., & Masamba, M. (2022). Debt distress in Africa: Biggest problems, and ways forward. *The Conversation*. Retrieved from https://theconversation.com/debt-distress-in-africa-biggest-problems -and-ways-forward-182716

Chigudu, S. (2020). *The political life of an epidemic: Cholera, crisis, and citizenship in Zimbabwe*. Cambridge, UK: Cambridge University Press.

Clark, M. K. (2023). Hip-Hop studies as a model for anti-imperialist research in Africa. *Contemporary Journal of African Studies, 10*(2), 27–46.

Coulibaly, I., & Grajales, J. (2023). Being a peasant is about resistance: West African peasant movements and the struggle for agrarian justice. *The Journal of Peasant Studies, 50*(2), 591–609. https://doi.org/10 .1080/03066150.2023.2170791

Darkwah, A. K., Mohammed, A., Williams, B., & Nagarajan, C. (2022). Women's organising in Nigeria during the COVID-19 pandemic. *Feminist Africa, 3*(1), 128–140.

Dzisah, J., & Kpessa-Whyte, M. (2023). Pan-African epistemologies of knowledge production: A deconstruction-based critical reflection. *Contemporary Journal of African Studies, 10*(2), 1–26.

Falola, T. (2022). *Decolonizing African studies: Knowledge production, agency, and voice* (Vol. 93). Woodbridge, UK: Boydell & Brewer.

Global Africa. (2022). Freedom, truth, courage! A Pan-African journal on global issues, right here, right now. *Global Africa, 1*, 8–9. https://doi. org/10.57832/ga-7d49

Gueye, M. (2013). Urban guerrilla poetry: The movement Y'en a Marre and the socio-political influences of hip hop in Senegal. *The Journal of Pan African Studies, 6*(3), 22–42.

Jesus, B. S. D. (2023). Black women activists and Pan-Africanism in the Black Atlantic diaspora: Profiles and dialogues. *Brazilian Political Science Review, 17*(2), 1–28.

Korany, B., & El-Mahdi, R. (Eds.). (2012). *Arab Spring in Egypt: Revolution and beyond.* Cairo, Egypt: American University in Cairo Press.

Mbembe, A. (2015). *Decolonizing knowledge and the question of the archive.* Retrieved from https://worldpece.org/content/mbembe-achille-2015-"decolonizing-knowledge-and-question-archive"-africa-country

Mkandawire, T. (1998). 7 crisis management and the making of "choiceless democracies". In R. Joseph (Ed.), *State, conflict, and democracy in Africa* (pp. 119–136). Boulder, CO: Lynne Rienner Publishers. https://doi.org/10.1515/9781685851828-008

Mkandawire, T. (2004). Disempowering new democracies and the persistence of poverty. In M. Spoor (Ed.), *Globalisation, poverty and conflict* (pp. 117–153). Dordrecht, The Netherlands: Springer. https://doi.org/10.1007/1-4020-2858-X_8

Mkandawire, T. (2013, April 17–19). Beyond recovery, Aggrey-Fraser-Guggisberg lectures, University of Ghana.

Ndiaye, B. (2023). African social activism and the rise of neo-Pan-Africanism: A look at the UPEC Summit. *Global Africa, 3,* 8–9. https://doi.org/10.57832/d71r-jh63

Ndlovu-Gatsheni, S. J. (2020). *Decolonization, development, and knowledge in Africa: Turning over a new leaf* (1st ed.). Routledge. https://doi.org/10.4324/9781003030423.

Poe, D. Z. (2023). Ghana (1957-1966): Reflections and lessons from a 20th century Pan-African liberated nation-state. *Contemporary Journal of African Studies, 10*(2), 47–73.

Sibeko, B. (2022). *A feminist approach to Debt.* NAWI Afrifem Macroeconomics Collective African Forum and Network on Debt and Development (AFRODAD).

Tripp, A. (2001). Women's movements and challenges to neo-patrimonial rule: Preliminary observations from Africa. *Development and Change, 32,* 33–54. https://doi.org/10.1111/1467-7660.00195

Tripp, A. M. (2018). Women's movements in Africa. In A. Basu (Ed.), *Women's movements in the global era: The power of local feminisms* (2nd ed., pp. 37–64). Routledge.

Tsikata, D., & Torvikey, D. (2021). COVID-19 and Africa: A synthesis of twelve country studies. *INCLUDE Knowledge Platform.*

Wallace, A. (2023). Generating inclusive and sustainable growth: Challenging neoliberal approaches to gender mainstreaming in regional economic integration in Africa. *Contemporary Journal of African Studies, 10*(2), 132–161.

Zeleza, P. T. (2017). The decolonization of African knowledge. Essay specially prepared for the 9th Africa Day Lecture, University of the Free State, Bloemfontein, South Africa, pp. 1–10.

Section 1

Sixty Decades after the First All-African People's Conference: Why Are Liberation and Transformation Still Lagging in Africa?*

Georges Nzongola-Ntalaja

Introduction

It is a great honour and privilege, indeed, for me to be asked to serve as the keynote speaker for the opening ceremony of this historic event. I am very grateful to Professor Dzodzi Tsikata and her colleagues on the planning committee of the conference for having bestowed this honour upon me.

When the first All-African People's Conference (AAPC) took place under the leadership of Dr Kwame Nkrumah between 5 and 13 December 1958, I was a teenager in the Belgian Congo. I was a student in the first year of a Presbyterian-Methodist Secondary School, which eventually expelled me in April 1960, two months before our independence, for my anticolonial activism. It seemed that the American missionaries had overlooked their contribution to our political awakening. Their actions had not only provoked our anger by reinforcing the racist colonial propaganda that Africans could not govern themselves but they also provided our student centre with a powerful

---

* Opening Keynote at the sixtieth anniversary commemoration of the All-African People's Conference, 5-8 December 2018.

radio which allowed us to access news from international broadcasters like the Voice of America (VOA) and the British Broadcasting Cooperation (BBC) as well as all the major newspapers published in Kinshasa (then Léopoldville), including those of the principal Congolese political parties.

Patrice Lumumba, who was just emerging as a nationalist leader following his election as president of a new and multi-ethnic political party, the *Mouvement National Congolais* (MNC) or Congolese National Movement, in October 1958, spoke to his first All-African audience on 11 December at the Accra Conference. He and two other MNC colleagues made the trip to Accra, thanks to financial support from the Pan-African Freedom Movement for East and Central Africa (PAFMECA) obtained on their behalf by A. R. Mohamed Babu of Zanzibar (Tanzania) and Tom Mboya of Kenya.[1]

The Accra Conference took place at a very propitious moment in Lumumba's life. After quitting his 12-year civil service career as a postal employee and a leader in African elite organisations that fought for better entitlements and privileges in the colony, he was hired as the publicity director of Kinshasa's second-largest brewery but he was also contemplating working full-time as a leader in the national struggle for independence. Nearly two weeks in Accra interacting with progressive heads of state and leaders of radical liberation movements involved in armed struggle solidified his *volte-face* or total rupture with the assimilationist positions of middle-class African *évolués*.[2] As Fanon has described them, these gentlemen had "a wish to identify permanently with the bourgeois representatives from the metropolis" (2004, p. 122).

The rupture with Lumumba's earlier ideas was evident in his speech to the Accra Conference. He no longer perceived colonialism as a harbinger of Western civilisation in Africa. It was, on the contrary, a system

---

1 Personal communication from Mohamed Babu, London, September 1987.
2 Kwame Nkrumah and Gamal Abdul Nasser were among the leaders who befriended Lumumba, with Nkrumah taking an active role in Congo affairs until his overthrow in 1966, and Nasser providing support to Lumumba's followers and having his children grow up in Egypt. As a member of the permanent committee of the AAPC, Lumumba used the committee's meetings in Conakry to develop a great relationship with President Ahmed Sékou Touré of Guinea, who provided support, including political advisers, to the Congolese leader. With respect to African liberation movements, the leaders he met in Accra included Amilcar Cabral of the African Party for the Independence of Guinea and Cape Verde (PAIGC), Frantz Fanon of the Algerian National Liberation Front (FNL), and Dr Felix-Roland Moumié of the Union of the Populations of Cameroon (UPC).

of exploitation and injustice. Colonial invaders like Henry Morton Stanley—the Welsh American adventurer—and their successors were no longer heroes to be admired, but racists with an idiotic superiority complex. As for the objective of the political struggle undertaken by the Congolese people, it was no longer a fight for racial equality in a Belgo-Congolese community, but for their total liberation from colonialism and the attainment of full independence.

Thanks to Accra, the notions of freedom and development that Lumumba had been wrestling with since July 1956 became very clear in December 1958. Independence did not mean the embourgeoisement of the so-called educated Africans: the assimilated of French or Portuguese colonies, the "Black Englishmen" of the newly independent Ghana, Nigeria, and other British colonies, or the Congolese *évolués*. It denoted freedom or liberation from all forms of racism, economic exploitation, political repression, and cultural oppression. This independence was not to be granted on a silver platter like Charles de Gaulle did in 1960 in repudiation of his own French Community of 1958. Africans were to rise to seize independence on their own initiative. While the ultimate aim was and still is the establishment of the United States of Africa, the most immediate task then was the implementation of a national project of democracy and development through self-determination politically, self-reliance economically, and Pan-African solidarity throughout the continent including the African diaspora worldwide.

This is the message that Lumumba brought back to Kinshasa, and he conveyed it to the populace on Sunday, 28 December 1958 during a public rally on the AAPC. An urban uprising rocked the city for four days on Sunday, 4 January 1959 following the refusal by the Belgian mayor of Kinshasa to authorise a rally organised by Joseph Kasavubu's Alliance of Bakongo (ABAKO). Kasavubu was frightened of losing the leadership of the independence struggle to Lumumba's MNC. A week later, on 13 January, both the Belgian king and his government made two separate declarations announcing that they were ready to start discussions on the independence of the Congo. The AAPC made it possible for the Congo to celebrate 4 January 1959 as Independence Martyrs' Day. Our country's national hero is Lumumba, whose own martyrdom took place on 17 January 1961, two years later. His effective tenure as prime minister lasted for two-and-a-half months, from 30 June to 14 September 1960, and he was assassinated in the Katanga province, which had declared its independence with Belgian support on 11 July 1960.

Having set the stage for understanding the connections between the 1958 AAPC and the independence of the Democratic Republic of the Congo (DRC), I would like to address the general issues affecting the continent and the Black world in general as identified by the organisers of this conference. I completely agree with their framing of our deliberations around the theme, "The unfinished business of liberation and transformation from colonialism and neo-colonialism", as well as their thesis that this unfinished business is linked to at least four key factors, namely: (a) the unending crisis of the DRC; (b) the assassination of Patrice Lumumba; (c) the coup d'état of 1966 against Kwame Nkrumah; and (d) the destabilisation of the liberation agenda all over the continent by imperialism in collaboration with the enemies of the African revolution, both national and foreign. I will limit myself to the first two factors and draw from the lessons of the Congo to illustrate some of the major reasons for the failure of our continent to implement the All-African project of democracy and development.

Pan-Africanism was born as a belief that Africans on the continent and in the diaspora must unite in resistance to their dehumanisation and oppression anywhere in the world. African agency and unity are indispensable for this political movement for self-determination, liberation, and prosperity. In his brilliant essay entitled *Expectations of Independence*, the distinguished Nigerian historian Jacob Ade Ajayi states that freedom and prosperity were the two major expectations of ordinary Africans from independence. He describes these people's expectations as follows:

> Insofar as they fully appreciated what was involved in the independence movements, their basic expectation was to see an end to the unpredictability and irrationality of the white man's world. Without the dubious advantage of Western education, they rejected the white man's culture, and for as long and as much as possible, stuck to what they knew. This did not mean that they wanted to re-create the past in its entirety. Their notion of freedom was not an abstract ideal, but a catalogue of specific wants: freedom from unjust and incomprehensible laws and directives; return of their land; and freedom to

be left alone to live their lives and seek their own goals, especially in regard to land tenure and local government groupings that affected historical relationships. These wants developed and became more specific with each new hope and each disastrous frustration. Soon, expectations came to include improved standards of living in housing and clothing, greater returns for their labour, better transportation for exporting and marketing their surpluses, education as a means to the social mobility that would ensure a better life for their children, and an adequate water supply, electricity, health care facilities, and other such amenities of life (Ajayi, 1982 p. 5).

These goals of freedom and material prosperity were strongly endorsed by Pan-Africanists like W. E. B. Du Bois, C. L. R. James, Kwame Nkrumah, Frantz Fanon, Amilcar Cabral, Patrice Lumumba, Julius Nyerere, Malcolm X, Mariama Bâ, Walter Rodney, Thomas Sankara, Wangari Maathai, and others, who also saw Pan-African solidarity as an indispensable foundation for political self-determination with democratic governance, plus economic self-reliance, and development. Although some progress has been made towards the realisation of these goals on the continent, the business of liberation, development, and solidarity is still unfinished. What went wrong, and what can be done to resurrect and implement the Pan-African project? There is no better place to start the diagnosis of the failure to promote and realise the Pan-African project than in the DRC.

The Unending Crisis of the Congo

The central and catalytic role of the crisis of national construction in the DRC in the general crisis of the African continent was underlined by Fanon in his essay on Lumumba's assassination, which first appeared in the Algerian National Liberation Front (FNL) publication *El Moudjahid* and is reproduced in the posthumous collection of some of his political essays entitled *Toward the African Revolution* (1998, pp. 191–197). Like Nkrumah (1967), who entitled his own excellent book on the DRC *Challenge of the Congo*, Fanon (1998, p. 197) urged all Africans "never to forget" that "the fate of all of us is at stake in the Congo". This is because the Congo has been the principal site of the struggle for Africa's survival as a continent of free and proud people since the 1880s. It is the second largest country in Africa (after Algeria) with an area of 2,345,409 km² and endowed with enormous wealth in natural resources. Strategically situated in the centre of the continent, it shares borders with nine other countries. All this makes it the envy of the world's predators, big and small. At the dawn of the era of capitalist imperialism, a recurrent concern of the major powers then, like today, was the question of *who should not control* this vast, rich, and beautiful land. Each of the major Western powers (Britain, France, Germany) did not want to see one of its adversaries acquire the territory. All three were pleased to see the Congo fall into the hands of King Leopold II of the much smaller country of Belgium.

The Congo was the focus of the first-ever intergovernmental conference on Africa because it was so prominent in the European competition for African territory. Formally known as the "Berlin Conference on West Africa", this gathering of thirteen European countries plus the United States was referred to in much of the European press as the "Congo Conference" since two of its three agenda items dealt with freedom of navigation on the Congo and Niger rivers and freedom of trade in the Congo basin. If the conference did not draw up the continent's borders, as it is widely believed, it did play a key role in starting the process of acquiring new territory, which became known as the "scramble for Africa". This was made possible through Chapter VI of the Berlin Act on "effective occupation", the solution to the third agenda item, on the rules of the game for territorial claims in Africa.

On 1 July 1885, the Congo entered colonial history as an independent country, the Congo Free State (CFS), with its own flag, its own army, and with Leopold II as king of both Belgium and the Congo. He was a constitutional monarch in Belgium, but in his African concession, he was referred to as "King Sovereign". The CFS was a unique kind of independent state. Its king never stepped foot in the region, preferring to give orders from afar and to read reports on what was basically a very lucrative business venture. As one Belgian historian has written, King Leopold owned the Congo just as John Rockefeller owned Standard Oil (Slade, 1962, p. 527). The key question was whether the property was profitable. Thus, the independence of this state did not mean freedom for its inhabitants, who were subjects living under slave labour, and not citizens with human and democratic rights. As African-American journalist and historian George Washington Williams noted in a public letter to the king in 1890, the real independence in this state resided in the licence of the king's internationally recruited murderous cast of administrators and security forces to subject the Congolese to a system of primitive accumulation that resulted in a reign of terror involving "crimes against humanity".[3] According to Adam Hochschild, author of the 1998 best-seller *King Leopold's Ghost*, the violence, starvation, and diseases resulting from this reign of terror amounted to a holocaust of approximately 10 million deaths (pp. 225–234 and 292–294).

As the jewel in the crown of European imperialism in Africa, the Congo also became a country of strategic importance to the United States. As an emerging world power in the nineteenth century, the United States was the first country in the world to recognise King Leopold's claims to the Congo in April 1884, seven months before the Berlin Conference. This was due to the lobbying work of Henry Shelton Sanford, the king's lobbyist in the United States and a friend of US President Chester Arthur and influential senators. Through the Rockefeller and Guggenheim fortunes, the US maintained stakes in plantation agriculture, diamond mining, and other sectors of the Congo's economy but to a lesser extent than Britain and France.

However, U.S. stakes in the Congo were cemented a century later when President Harry Truman used uranium from the Congo to develop the first nuclear weapons, which were dropped on Hiroshima and Nagasaki in 1945. In her very entertaining and superbly written book, *Spies in the Congo: The Race for the Ore that Built the Atomic Bomb*, the British historian Susan Williams (2016) describes how American, Belgian, British, and French spies were running into each other in their attempts to prevent the Nazi regime of Adolf Hitler from getting its hands on the very powerful uranium of the Shinkolobwe mine in Congo's Katanga province. Following the defeat of the Nazis and the outbreak of the Cold War, the U.S. ruling class saw its primary mission in the Congo as that of denying the Soviet Union access to Congo's uranium and other strategic minerals. This is the mission that eventually served as a pretext for US

---

3   On the role of George Washington Williams and other African Americans in the struggle for freedom in Africa, see Elliott Skinner (1992) (Skinner, 1992).

involvement in the assassination of Patrice Lumumba in the interest of Western hegemony in Central Africa.

Today, major powers prefer puppets or weak leaders rather than patriotic and progressive leaders who are likely to promote the interests of their people rather than serve foreign interests in return for wealth and protection. In the footsteps of Nkrumah, who had declared at Ghanaian independence in March 1957 that the independence of Ghana would be meaningless if much of Africa were to remain under colonial bondage, Lumumba stated in his now famous Independence Day speech that the liberation of the Congo was the first phase of the complete emancipation of Africa. This revolutionary Pan-Africanism was anathema to the major imperialist powers—the United States, Britain, and France—who did not, and do not, want to see a country like the DRC, whose enormous wealth in mineral resources, hydroelectricity, water, forests, and arable land can light up and nourish our entire African continent, raise the banner of African self-determination, self-reliance, and unity. For his memoirs, Jacques Foccart, the *éminence grise* of Charles de Gaulle and other Gaullist leaders on African policy, gave the following answer to a question about the DRC by his interviewer, Philippe Gaillard, in 1994:

You asked me what was France's interest. On this matter, there is no ambiguity. Congo-Léopoldville, Zaire today, is the largest country in Francophone Africa. It has considerable natural resources. It has the means of being a regional power. The long-term interest of France and its African allies is evident.[4]

What is evident to Congolese democrats and patriots is that France did not want their country to develop into a regional power in Central Africa, and thus become France's rival for influence in the latter's *chasse gardée* (or private hunting ground) of resource-rich countries. Foccart's statement shows that revolutionary Pan-Africanists are not the only people to be aware of the enormous leadership potential of resource-rich countries like the DRC in the promotion of African unity and development. As noted by Cabral, Fanon and Nkrumah regarding the ability

---

4 Foccart, J. and Gaillard, P. (1995). p. 310. My own translation. In October 1971, the Congolese dictator Joseph-Désiré Mobutu (Mobutu Sese Seko from February 1972) unilaterally renamed the DRC "Zaire", a Portuguese corruption of the Kongo word "*Nzadi*" (big river), by which this mighty river was known in the Kongo kingdom.

of developed countries to manipulate decolonisation to serve their own interests, the imperialists and their think tanks never pause to consider and devise strategies to undermine the developmental potential of the African continent.

Over the years, Western intelligence agencies and think tanks have developed several strategies of destabilisation for the Congo, one of them being the brilliant idea, according to French journalist Jean-Pierre Alaux (1979), "*That for Western interests, the ruin of Zaire is preferable to a strong and indispensable state, capable of supporting the struggle against white Southern Africa.*" [emphasis added]. We know what role President Mobutu played against the liberation movements of Southern Africa, particularly against the Popular Movement for the Liberation of Angola (MPLA), and the strong support he gave to political groups supported by the U.S. Central Intelligence Agency (CIA) like Holden Roberto's National Front for the Liberation of Angola (FNLA) and Jonas Savimbi's Union for the Total Independence of Angola (UNITA).

The second strategy is the despicable and laughable idea of the balkanisation of the Congo in cooperation with some of its neighbours, on the false assumption that our country is too big and ungovernable. It is despicable because it adds insult to injury, as the former colonial powers had already dismantled some of the largest territorial entities in balkanising Africa at decolonisation. Unfortunately, many African leaders participated in this process for reasons to be discussed later. In the case of the Congo, Belgium engineered the secessions of Katanga and South Kasai as a means of undermining Lumumba and retaining control over the Congo, but this attempt at the balkanisation of our country did fail.

The strategy of balkanisation is preposterous because it has no future in our continent. Africa has made a firm commitment never to recognise a secessionist state except when the breakup is made in exceptional circumstances and with the approval of the central government. As a member of the United Nations Observer Mission to Verify the Referendum in Eritrea (UNOVER) in April 1993, I heard Dr Salim Ahmed Salim, then Secretary General of the Organisation of African Unity (OAU), made the following statement in a hotel lobby in Asmara: "We have now accepted Eritrea, and maybe in the near future we might accept South Sudan. And then we draw the line". What a prophetic statement!

Although Eritrea was not really a case of secession, it was viewed that way by many African states. Balkanisation will not succeed, but its attempt has resulted in the death of too many innocent civilians, which ought to be constantly denounced by all the relevant social forces on the continent.

The Assassination of Patrice Lumumba

The strategic importance of the Congo to the Western powers was such that, unlike other martyrs of the liberation struggle who were assassinated directly by their respective colonial powers, the demise of Patrice Lumumba, like that of Muammar Qaddafi 50 years later, had to involve the leader of these powers, the United States of America. In the Congo case, what was at stake in 1960 concerned more than the interests of the former colonial power. Lumumba became a victim of a counterrevolution involving the whole African subcontinent from Katanga to the Cape of Good Hope. Mining companies and white settlers in this region were reluctant to cede their political power and economic privileges to the forces of Pan-Africanism and African nationalism. For as long as they could, they retained power with the support of Western powers, most of whom were convinced that Europeans and their descendants were better protectors of Western economic and strategic interests than Africans.

Geographically and economically, the Katanga area of the Copperbelt has long been an integral part of the Southern African economic complex—a relatively interdependent region of world capitalism with a highly developed industrial structure in South Africa and an abundance of mineral resources in all major countries. Through businesses like the British South African Company (BSAC), Tanganyika Concessions Ltd. (also known as Tanks or TCL), Anglo-American, Consolidated Gold Fields, and De Beers, South African capital had been invested in almost all of the region's nations. In addition to offering cheap migrant labour and markets for South African goods and services, such as marketing and transportation, the poorer nations in the region supported the apartheid economy. The development of mining and related industries in Katanga attracted white South Africans and Rhodesians to the Belgian Congo. With these hardcore racists as their reference groups, Belgian settlers sought to create a colonial settler system comparable to the apartheid and other white minority systems of Southern Africa. They were repulsed in their quest for state power by both the colonial state and the Belgian corporate elite, who did not want to concede a higher portion of the surplus to the settlers.

However, the prospects of independence under a radical nationalist government led by Lumumba brought a rapprochement between the corporate leaders, led by the top management of the *Union Minière du Haut-Katanga* (UMHK), the largest corporation in the colony and a subsidiary of the Belgian corporate giant, the *Société Générale de Belgique* (SGB). With the support of the Belgian government and its North Atlantic Treaty Organisation (NATO) allies, plus lobbying efforts of right-wing circles in Western countries, particularly the United States and Britain, mining companies and white settlers felt that their time to seize power had come.

Since Brussels was not willing to set up a government of white settlers on the models of South Africa and Rhodesia and Nyasaland (now Malawi, Zambia, and Zimbabwe), the solution was to set up a fake government with Black politicians, but one run by Belgian civil servants and military officers. The first Belgian shadow government was known as the Belgian Technical Mission in Katanga (Mistebel), which administered the province from 22 July to 26 August 1960. It was led by Count Harold Aspermont Lynden, a nephew of Count Gobert d'Aspremont Lynden, the grand marshal of the royal court or chief of staff of the Belgian King Baudouin I. Following his departure from Katanga to become the Belgian minister of African Affairs, the younger d'Aspremont Lynden took on the role of overseer for his successor, Dr René Clemens, a sociology professor at the University of Liège, who headed the Katanga Advisory Office, the second Belgian shadow government operating in Katanga. As Ludo De Witte, the Belgian sociologist and author of the best book on the assassination of Lumumba writes, Katanga under Moise Tshombe and Godefroid Munongo was nothing but a caricature of a state (*un État d'opérette*) (De Witte, 2000, p. 83).

As it is widely known today, Lumumba was assassinated on orders from U.S. President Dwight Eisenhower and the Belgian government, acting mostly through Minister of African Affairs Harold d'Aspremont Lynden and his "advisory" team in Katanga. Both the Americans and the Belgians abandoned their earlier assassination plots—the CIA plan to have cobra venom injected in Lumumba's food or toothpaste, and the

Belgian's Barracuda Plan of hiring a European crocodile hunter to shoot Lumumba. The two countries decided to go along with a more practical idea from Lawrence Devlin, then CIA station chief in the Congo, who thought that collaborating with the moderate Congolese leaders who were against Lumumba and associating them to the crime would yield the desired result quickly. With the approval of the U.S. National Security Council, the CIA mounted Project Wizard, by which Congo President Joseph Kasavubu, Military Chief Joseph Mobutu, Security Police Chief Victor Nendaka, and others took unknown quantities of U.S. dollars to sacrifice the life of their former comrade in the fight for independence.

Like Kwame Nkrumah five years later, Lumumba was the victim of a crime of betrayal by his own compatriots. This is the verdict of Amilcar Cabral—who would be later eliminated in the same way—as stated in his eulogy of Nkrumah in Conakry in 1972. Like the French writer Émile Zola in the Dreyfus Affair, Cabral had the courage to express before Africa and the world his *J'accuse* moment against all African traitors. Didn't many other notable African leaders, including Mehdi Ben Barka of Morocco, Tom Mboya of Kenya, and Chairperson of the Conference we are commemorating today, and Thomas Sankara of Burkina Faso fall victim to the same fate? Other participants in the abduction and murder of Lumumba, either directly or indirectly, include the Tshombe government and the United Nations, whose Secretary General Dag Hammarskjöld had *"given de facto protection to the Katanga secession";* [emphasis added] (De Witte, 2000, p. 83) and MI6, the British foreign intelligence service. Baroness Daphne Park, who served as the MI6 officer in Kinshasa between 1959 and 1961, admitted to a fellow House of Lords peer that she had "organised" the British role in the assassination of Lumumba (Corera, 2013; Shaoul, 2013). While the exact nature of this role is not clear, it might include some assistance in the pursuit and abduction of Lumumba when he left Kinshasa on 27 November 1960, with the aim of returning to his political fief of Kisangani (then Stanleyville).

Lumumba was captured on 1 December 1960 at Lodi, on the left bank of the Sankuru River, and denied UN protection by the Ghanaian contingent under British military officers at Mweka the next morning. Here is an additional fallout from the errors committed by postcolonial regimes, to be added to the ones Fanon already identified following Lumumba's 1961 assassination and explained below. It was erroneous to believe that senior British military personnel would remain politically impartial in a crisis such as the one in the Congo, regardless of the motivations for President Nkrumah's decision to keep them in top command roles within the Ghanaian army for over three years following the country's independence. One of the senior officers in the UN force whose anti-Lumumba sentiments were well-known was Major General Henry Alexander, the Chief of Defence Staff of the Ghanaian army, who did not get along with the country's ambassador in the Congo. Nkrumah did dismiss all the British officers in September 1961, but the damage was already done.

Likewise, the head of the Moroccan contingent, General Ben Hammou Kettani, was also the deputy commander of the UN force in the Congo. He is alleged to have entertained close contacts with American officials in Kinshasa and to have coached Mobutu in staging his first coup d'état of 14 September 1960, against Lumumba. Like Alexander, Kettani was undermining the authority of a person to whom the regime of King Mohammed V gave strong support. This disconnect between progressive regimes and the military serving them is another example of African governments' inability to control the institutional structures inherited from the colonial past. A major objective of Pan-Africanism was to destroy them or, at the very least, to place them under individuals committed to transforming them to defend African interests instead of those of the former colonial powers.

From Mweka, Lumumba was taken to Ilebo (then Port Francqui) and flown to Kinshasa where, after enduring more humiliation and torture at the Binza parachutist camp in Mobutu's presence, he spent a miserable night in Nendaka's garage. The next day, he was transferred to the élite armoured brigade garrison at Mbanza-Ngungu (then Thysville). Even in prison, Lumumba continued to pose a threat to the moderate leadership in Kinshasa, as the Lumumbist government in Kisangani began expanding its control and authority in the eastern part of the Congo and encouraged Lumumba's followers all over the country to continue the struggle for genuine independence, national unity, and territorial integrity. US and Belgian officials were greatly alarmed by these developments, with the U.S. embassy in Kinshasa preoccupied with rumours of a pro-Lumumba coup d'état and the moderate Congolese leaders worrying that the soldiers guarding Lumumba at Mbanza-Ngungu might free him. For Washington and Brussels, the time to get rid of Lumumba physically had arrived. Brussels ordered his transfer to Katanga, where it was certain that he would be killed.

Lumumba and his two companions, Youth and Sports Minister Maurice Mpolo and Senate Vice-President Joseph Okito, were severely beaten by Mobutu's soldiers on the plane ride to Katanga, in the presence of two members of the College of General Commissioners: Defence Commissioner Ferdinand Kazadi and Internal Affairs Commissioner Jonas Mukamba. The three prisoners were subjected to torture at the Brouwez villa, about 8 km from downtown, not far from Luano airport in Lubumbashi (then Elisabethville). Munongo and other Katanga leaders also personally assaulted them. Lumumba and his companions were shot by a Belgian execution squad of police officers and soldiers led by Captain Jules Gat. The next day, Police Commissioner Gerard Soete and his brother removed the bodies from the burial site, cut them into small pieces, and dissolved them in sulphuric acid.

What are the lessons of the Congo crisis and Lumumba's assassination for the African continent? Frantz Fanon has noted two mistakes: Lumumba's request for UN intervention in his attempt to expel Belgian troops from Katanga, and the willingness of African countries to send peacekeeping troops under UN cover. While Fanon is correct about the first mistake, it is ironic that Lumumba's first inclination was to appeal to the United States for support. When he and the ceremonial president Kasavubu made this request through U.S. Ambassador Clare Timberlake, he advised them to appeal instead to the UN, where UN Secretary General Dag Hammarskjöld had already planned the UN intervention before it was authorized by the UN Security Council. With his deputy Ralph Bunch already in Kinshasa before the Independence ceremony, American leaders were already happy in directing the Congolese leaders to Mr. H and Professor Bunch, given their confidence that the UN is the most effective tool for safeguarding Western interests in the former colonial territories. The UN Secretary-General and his chief collaborators shared a common Cold War outlook with Western policymakers and saw their mission in the Congo as that of preserving the then-existing balance of forces in the world.

For this reason, it was largely forgotten that the first shipment of military supplies and equipment to the Congo was part of the Soviet contribution to the UN operation, which included the ferrying of Ghanaian troops from Accra to Kinshasa. Dag Hammarskjöld also raised a fuss about Soviet planes, trucks, and supplies sent to Lumumba to fight the colonial Belgians and racist white mercenaries establishing the secession in Katanga. Dag Hammarskjöld had refused to use force against these forces, his main preoccupation being a little assistance to Lumumba by the Soviet Union. In a note to Hammarskjöld, Moscow replied that "the sending by the Soviet Union to the government of the Republic of the Congo—in the form of civil aircraft and motor vehicles—was not contrary to the terms of the resolutions of 14 and 22 July 1960, since the said resolutions set no limit on the right of the government to ask for or be given direct bilateral aid" (Weissman, 1974, p. 147). Meanwhile, the so-called Katanga government was getting all the military assistance it needed from Belgium, under Hammarskjöld's watch.

Even now, after the Cold War, Fanon (1998, p. 195) is correct in asserting that "the UN is the legal card used by the imperialist interests when the card of brute force has failed". As a former UN employee, I have a lot of respect for the organisation and the many wonderful things that its specialised agencies have accomplished and continue to do every day. However, peacekeeping tied to promoting the interests of some countries at the expense of millions of innocent people who are starving or dying for the benefit of the former is contrary to the lofty ideals of the United Nations. The lesson learned here, according to Fanon, is Nkrumah's well-known dictum: *Africa must unite*. Instead of relying on the United Nations and remaining blind in the face of the hidden agendas of the major powers, progressive Africans must rely on their own resources and organisations to meet the challenges of peace and security.

As for the willingness of African governments to place their troops under UN command, it is not so much a mistake as the realisation of the realities of power relations in today's world. The United States, for example, is seldom willing to place its own troops under UN command.

Limitations of capacity force many of our countries to rely on developed countries for logistical and expert assistance in peacekeeping operations. For example, when the Southern African Development Community (SADC) resolved to send an Intervention Brigade to eastern Congo to expel the M23 militia back to Rwanda and Uganda, major powers insisted that this force be integrated with the United Nations Organization Stabilization Mission in the Democratic Republic of the Congo (MONUSCO). As things turned out, since the Force Intervention Brigade (FIB) defeated the M23 in 2013, nothing spectacular has happened. The FIB's integration into the UN force served the purpose of controlling and limiting its peacebuilding actions. In more than 20 years, the UN presence in the DRC has not improved the security situation in the region. What SADC and other Regional Economic Communities (RECs) need is greater political will to use the enormous natural wealth of Africa to develop their own capacity to deal with threats to peace and security on their own. As the peacekeeping mechanisms of the African Union (AU) and building blocks for African political and economic integration, the RECs must increase their capacity for conflict prevention as well as for peacekeeping and peacebuilding. Realising the twin objectives of freedom and material prosperity for ordinary Africans requires peace and security.

The Unfinished Business of Liberation and Transformation

The preceding analysis of the unending crisis of the DRC and the trauma that hangs over this country since the assassination of Patrice Lumumba has revealed a few issues that contribute to the general crisis of the state and society in Africa today. To conclude the discussion on Pan-Africanism today and tomorrow, I have chosen the following four critical questions raised by the organisers of this conference in connection with these issues.

1. How do we repair the betrayal of the cardinal principles of Pan-Africanism: the unity and indivisibility of the African continent, and solidarity with oppressed Africans everywhere?
2. Why have African states failed to manage their affairs in such a way as to satisfy the people's expectations of independence: freedom and material prosperity?

3. Why is the neocolonial state incapable of dealing effectively with catastrophes such as droughts and famines?
4. Is the current African leadership an obstacle to further development of the revolution?

Issue #1: Repairing the Betrayal of Pan-Africanism

According to Walter Rodney, by accepting the neocolonial strategy of imperialism, which sought to establish a multitude of dependent mini-states that could readily be ruled by the former colonial masters and other major powers—and by largely ignoring solidarity with oppressed Africans everywhere in the world, the African petty bourgeoisie betrayed the cardinal principles of Pan-Africanism. With respect to the first principle, most of the nationalist leaders accepted the neocolonial strategy for two major reasons. In the first place, it was in their immediate interest for the most part because it involved gaining independence more or less on a silver platter and without armed struggle. Those who gave this any serious thought accepted Nkrumah's dictum of seeking the political kingdom as a prerequisite for building a democratic developmental state. However, this was difficult, if not impossible, in a neocolonial context.

In the second place, and more importantly, the neocolonial strategy of balkanisation was favourable to the narrow class interests of the nationalist petty bourgeoisie. They, too, preferred smaller states to larger entities for purposes of occupying senior state positions like president and minister. The more states, the more such positions would be available. Thus, the nine territories of French West Africa (including the French-run part of the UN Trust Territory (TT) of Togo), the five territories of French Equatorial Africa (including the larger part of the UN TT of Cameroon), and the three territories of Belgian Africa (the Congo and the UN TTs of Rwanda and Burundi) became independent as separate states, when they used to be governed from Dakar, Brazzaville, and Kinshasa, respectively. Instead of three solid and economically viable states, we now have seventeen. Mwalimu Julius Nyerere's proposal to wait for Tanganyika to gain independence with its sister nations in a single federation was rejected by British colonialists and African leaders in Kenya and Uganda, leading to the independence of the three territories of British East Africa, which already shared common services in railways, ports and harbours, air transport, higher education (the Makerere University), posts, and telecommunications, among other areas. The British granted independence to Tanganyika in 1961, Uganda in 1962, and Kenya in 1963.

What can be done to repair this betrayal of the Pan-African principle of the unity and indivisibility of the African continent? The most practical thing that can be done today is to implement the Abuja Treaty on African economic and political integration with the RECs as building blocks towards African unity. Each of these groupings has precolonial and colonial roots on which greater economic and political integration can be built. While the 1964 Cairo resolution of the OAU sought to prevent interstate conflicts by declaring colonial boundaries inviolable, these can be made less rigid through the free circulation of persons, goods, and ideas, as is the case in much of Europe today.

One major step in this regard ought to be the suppression of visa requirements for travel by Africans across the continent of their ancestors. It is a shame that foreigners have less difficulty travelling in Mother Africa than their own daughters and sons. Moreover, the expulsion of African refugees and migrants by African states is a violation of the spirit of Pan-Africanism. However, justified states might be in expelling undocumented migrants, they ought to examine the root causes of the migrations and try to find humane and long-term solutions in accordance with Pan-African solidarity. Isn't it shocking that Black South Africans would lynch Black people from countries north of the Limpopo, but have no problem with Europeans and Asians residing in their country, despite all the efforts and sacrifices made by African countries for the liberation of South Africa?

This relates to Pan-African solidarity in general and with regard to oppressed Africans specifically, which is the second cardinal premise of Pan-Africanism. If the OAU was successful as a Pan-African organisation in one area, it was in its unrelenting pursuit of the complete decolonisation of Africa, with the exception of Morocco's ongoing and illegal occupation of the Western Sahara and the annexation of numerous islands by Britain, France, and Spain, as well as the Moroccan cities of Ceuta and Melilla by Spain.[5] Not only did the OAU succeed in mobilising

---

5 Britain has also leased to the United States the island of Diego Garcia in the Indian Ocean for military purposes.

world public opinion against Portugal for its ultra-colonialism in Africa and the colonial-settler states of Zimbabwe, Namibia, and South Africa for their racist autocracies, it spearheaded the worldwide ostracism of apartheid South Africa, including its exclusion from some international organisations and major events such as the Olympic Games. Moreover, the OAU Liberation Committee did an outstanding job in providing both moral and material support to liberation movements engaged in the armed struggle in Guinea-Bissau and in Southern Africa.

TransAfrica, the African American lobby for Africa and the Caribbean, played a key role in the struggle against apartheid. Founded in 1977 on the initiative of the Congressional Black Caucus, its educational, lobbying, and mobilisation work culminated in the passage by the US Congress of the Comprehensive Anti-Apartheid Act of 1986 over President Ronald Reagan's veto. The ramifications of this act on South Africa's military-industrial complex were so severe that a combined force of Cuban, Angolan, ANC, and SWAPO troops defeated the apartheid state in the 1988 Battle of Cuito Cuanavale, Angola, paving the way for Namibian independence, the release of Nelson Mandela (1918–2013) from jail in 1990, and the establishment of non-racial democracy in South Africa in 1994.[6] It should be noted that many of the Cuban troops in Angola were Afro-Cubans, who serve as admirable examples of Pan-African solidarity. These troops include those who trained Laurent Kabila's guerrillas in the Democratic Republic of the Congo (DRC) in 1965 under Ernesto Che Guevara's command, and those who provided military advice to Amilcar Cabral's African Party for the Independence of Guinea and Cape Verde (PAIGC) in Guinea-Bissau.

Today, Global Africa has expanded beyond North America, the Caribbean, and South America to include Europe and Asia, with an ever-growing number of Africans in the former colonial metropoles and in China. Given this reality, the AU, which succeeded the OAU in 2002, has decreed that Global Africa or the diaspora is now the sixth region of Africa after the five geographical regions of the continent (North, East, West, Central, and Southern). However, the manner in which the various overseas African communities are to participate in AU activities as

---

6   For details on the Battle of Cuito Cuanavale, see the brilliant analysis by Campbell (2013).

an integral part of its institutional framework remains unclear. On the other hand, there is a recognition that the growing numbers of Africans and peoples of African descent around the world can play a major role in the African Renaissance through both solidarity with African states and investments in Africa. Having given solid support to the anti-colonial and liberation struggles, Global Africa is now called upon to contribute to Africa's renewal and prosperity while continuing to engage in advocacy for African interests internationally.

While benefiting from this support to strengthen Africa's independence and position in the world system, the AU and African states must remain vigilant in promoting and defending the fundamental rights and the interests of Global Africa. In this regard, it is a shame that the AU and African states generally have remained mostly silent in the face of growing police brutality in the United States, where unarmed persons of African descent, mostly young men but including all categories of Black people, are wantonly killed by the police for the simple reason of being Black. In nearly all cases, the murderers go scot-free, and this impunity continues to encourage more killing. In Brazil, where 51% of citizens declared themselves to be of African ancestry in the 2010 census, people of African descent are still struggling for equal opportunity.

Africa must also condemn in the strongest terms the killing of thousands of innocent civilians in the resource wars that the continent has endured since the 1990s in places like Angola, the DRC, Liberia, and Sierra Leone—wars that gave rise to terms such as "blood diamonds" and "conflict minerals". Documentation from the DRC included in multiple reports published by the I UN Panel of Experts on the Illegal Exploitation of the Natural Resources and Other Forms of Wealth of the DRC since 2000 has given conclusive proof of the looting of the country by well-known transnationals, including tech and mining companies, airlines, and international banks. This criminal endeavour also involves high government officials, members of the security services, Congolese militia, and militia groups sponsored and controlled by Rwanda, Uganda, and Burundi, among other neighbouring governments.

All of these reports, and the death of over six million Congolese resulting from violence and insecurity since 1998, have yet to galvanise a sustained and appropriate African response in addition to the SADC

FIB. Even more shocking was the silence of the international community following the release in 2010 of the *Mapping Report on the Most Serious Crimes Committed on the Territory of the Democratic Republic of the Congo between 1993 and 2003* by Navi Pillay, then UN High Commissioner for Human Rights. A major aspect of this war is the horrific prevalence of sexual violence against women and girls, for which the exemplary healing work of Dr Denis Mukwege has made him one of the two Nobel Peace Prize laureates of 2018, along with the brave Yazidi human rights activist, Nadia Murad.

One form of violence that has not been studied rigorously by scholars is the violence unleashed by the state against its own citizens. An excellent contribution in this regard is Professor Lloyd Sachikonye's analysis of Robert Mugabe's Zimbabwe in his book *When a State Turns on its Citizens* (2011). This is the violence unleashed by an authoritarian state and its agencies of repression (the security forces, the intelligence organisation, and the youth branch of the ruling party) against unarmed civilians, who are simply attempting to exercise their constitutional rights, such as voting for candidates of their choice or defending their democratic rights. Except for Botswana, African states did not openly denounce the horrific acts of violence committed by the state against its own citizens, including the late Morgan Tsvangirai, leader of the opposition Movement for Democratic Change (MDC).

Issue #2: Satisfying the People's Expectations of Independence

The reasons why African states have failed to manage their affairs in such a way as to satisfy the people's expectations of independence are evident from the descriptions of these expectations by Ade Ajayi, the radical diagnosis of the postcolonial state by Frantz Fanon, and the outline of the democratic developmental state by Amilcar Cabral. In fighting for independence, the people wanted to exchange the arbitrariness and despotism of colonial rule for a regime of freedom and fundamental human rights, including access to the basic amenities of modern life such as running and clean water, electricity, decent housing, affordable health care, and free education, at least at the primary and secondary levels, for a better future for their children. These expectations have not been met in most African countries, including in places where one would expect such a realisation, as in Nigeria, South Africa, and the DRC.

The two major reasons for this failure are: (*a*) the failure to implement the Pan-African project of political self-determination with national sovereignty and democratic governance, economic self-reliance and development, and Pan-African solidarity; and (*b*) the failure to transform the inherited structures of the state and the economy, which were not established to benefit Africans but their colonisers and European settlers. Self-determination does not simply mean flag independence and the coming to power of African rulers. As an emancipatory and genuine process of freedom and self-rule, it ought to include ordinary people in the policy-making process. It must include the following changes from the colonial state.

- People's human rights and fundamental freedoms are respected, thus allowing everyone to live with dignity.
- People have a say in decisions that affect their lives, not only nationally through free, fair, and transparent elections but also through participation in local governance structures.
- People can hold decision-makers accountable not only through regularly held elections but also in recall elections and peaceful protests.
- A vibrant civil society and free, independent media are indispensable for articulating alternative solutions to public issues.
- A system of checks and balances based on the separation of powers with independent judicial and legislative branches of government capable of limiting executive authority and preventing authoritarianism and despotism.
- Effective civilian control of the military and other security forces.
- Women are equal partners with men in private and public spheres of life and decision-making.
- People are free from discrimination based on race, ethnicity, class, gender, or any other attribute.
- Economic and social policies are responsive to people's needs and aspirations and mindful of the needs of future generations.

Consistent with Fanon's critique of the postcolonial African state as a dictatorship of the state or bureaucratic bourgeoisie, Cabral advocates for the transformation of this state from its exploitative and repressive colonial form to a democratic developmental state. In an informal talk with representatives of some 120 African American organisations in New York City on 20 October 1972, Cabral has this to say about the state in Africa:

> We are not interested in the preservation of any of the structures of the colonial state. It is our opinion that it is necessary to totally destroy, to break, to reduce to ash all aspects of the colonial state in our country in order to make everything possible for our people. … Some independent African states preserved the structures of the colonial state. In some countries they only replaced a white man with a black man, but for the people it is the same. … The nature of the state we have to create in our country is a very good question for it is a fundamental one. … *It is the most important problem in the liberation movement. The problem of the nature of the state created after independence is perhaps the secret of the failure of African independence* (1973, pp. 83–84).

This is the fundamental issue for postcolonial Africa with respect to democratic governance: whether the colonial state is destroyed or survives in a neocolonial garb under African rulers. The colonial state was incompatible with democracy. Colonised peoples were *subjects* with obligations to their distant rulers in imperial capitals and their immediate European masters in the colony and not *citizens* with human and democratic rights. In the Congo, the brutality and naked violence of the colonial state were captured under the term "*Bula Matari*", which literally means "the crusher of rocks". This was the nickname given to Henry Morton Stanley, King Leopold's colonial agent, for the wanton brutality to which he subjected Africans and the terror provoked by the dynamite he used to blow up mountains in building a wagon road from Matadi near the Atlantic Ocean to Kinshasa. Eventually, the term became used to refer to the colonial state and Belgian colonial officers and continues to be used today to refer to "government". As Crawford Young points out, although the term "*Bula Matari*" was particular to the Belgian Congo, "its evocative imagery can be projected onto the much larger domain" of the African colonial state (Young, 1994, p. 2).

In the economic field, as in politics, Cabral's starting point is the same: "Destroy the economy of the enemy and build our own economy" (1979, pp. 239–242). This is one of the eight directives on theoretical and practical guidance that he sent in his capacity as PAIGC Secretary-General to his party cadres in 1965 on the implementation of the decisions of the First Party Conference held at Cassaca in February 1964. This sixth directive is the one that contains one of the best-known and most profound passages from Cabral's writings:

> Always remember that people do not struggle for ideas, for things in the heads of individuals. The people struggle and accept sacrifices demanded by the struggle, but in order to gain material advantages, to be able to live a better life in peace, to see their lives progress and to ensure their children's future. National liberation, the struggle against colonialism, working for peace and progress—independence—all these are empty words without meaning for the people, unless they are translated into a real improvement in standards of living. It is useless to liberate an area, if the people of that area are left without the basic necessities of life (1979, p. 241).

I have heard in my own country, the DRC, and there are testimonies from elsewhere in Africa of old people asking their younger relatives when this "independence of yours" is going to end so they could go back to the political order, economic stability, and social benefits of the 1950s. Although this may represent a minority opinion, it is nonetheless a powerful critique of the postcolonial state's inability to provide the bare necessities of life, such as food and clean drinking water; maternities, health centres, and schools with adequate equipment, furniture, and supplies; and good roads and transportation infrastructure to facilitate the transportation of produce from rural to urban areas for peasant farmers.

For Cabral, liberation from colonial domination is meaningful only when it goes beyond the political realm to involve the development of "production, education, health facilities, and trade (1970, p. 165)". With respect to property rights, four types of property were to be recognised:

personal, private, cooperative, and state. Priority was to be given to the development, modernisation, and transformation of agriculture, with a view to ensuring prosperity and preventing agricultural crises, drought, and famine. Here again, as in the political sphere, the liberated areas were to serve as a prefiguration of the postcolonial state. There, and later on in the postcolonial state, the ruling party was to focus on the following tasks:

> [D]evelop agricultural production both by extending the culti-vated areas and by improving farming methods, with more care in farming and by increasing the range of crops. Pay special attention to the development of food crops (rice, maize, manioc, potato, beans, vegetables, bananas, cashew nuts, oranges and other fruit trees). Pay special attention to the care of cattle and breeding livestock (pigs, chickens, sheep, etc.) to cattle fodder and to the preservation of grazing land. Demand an effective control over fires, to avoid the destruction of our forest and bush. Employ all spare time of the armed forces with help to farmers, above all at harvest time. ... Help the smiths to carry on developing their skill, notably in the making and repair of farm tools. Intensify the production of coconut, palm oil and other oils, the manufac-ture of 'homemade soap' and all the other products of use to the population and traditionally made in our country. Make prepara-tions to bring back into operation soon the sawmills abandoned by the settlers. Develop exchange (mutual aid) between families in one village and between villages. Establish collective farming areas for some crops such as the banana, pineapple and fruit trees. Form through experience and whenever conditions are favourable simple co-operatives for farm production. Hand over properties (orchards, cattle) abandoned by their owners to a local committee to use and manage them (1979, p. 240).

The transformative agenda of reconstruction and development outlined here is ambitious but doable. It is consistent with the view of the late Samir Amin, the most prominent African economist of the last 60 years that the continent cannot develop without an industrialisation strategy based on the modernisation of agriculture and the production of capital goods in Africa.[7] The greatest challenge for African countries is to be able to conceive and execute development strategies that are likely to satisfy the deepest aspirations of the popular masses for economic development and material prosperity. The question that Cabral raises is a simple one: Are African leaders going to make common cause with their people by opting for those policies likely to meet the latter's needs, or are they going to side with the international bourgeoisie and accept the antisocial development strategies and policies imposed by the IMF and the World Bank?

Beyond the choice of economic policy by African governments, there is an even more fundamental question that Cabral has raised, i.e. can an independent state based on the same system of economic exploitation as the colonial state satisfy the needs of African workers and peasants? Since the answer to this question is obviously negative, the reality is that the African postcolonial state has a choice to make between the interests of its own people and the constraints of the world system. This is why Cabral calls on African revolutionaries to destroy the colonial economy and build a new and more people-friendly economy.

Issue #3: Dealing Effectively With Catastrophes Such as Droughts and Famines

In 1985, the Ugandan government revoked the citizenship of Professor Mahmood Mamdani following a public speech he made in Kampala stating that droughts do not automatically bring about famines, for the two are not necessarily related. Droughts, he pointed out, are natural phenomena, while famines are social phenomena. If a drought is an act of nature, a famine is a manifestation of the failure of public authorities to make provisions for catastrophes or to have an adequate disaster prevention system established with food reserves and personnel to distribute it in case of famines or other emergencies. Being a Ugandan of Indian origin, Mamdani was being punished for pointing out the government's weaknesses on the false premise that he had not sworn allegiance to Uganda, when in fact he had done so twice: first when he became an

---

7   Amin has published numerous books and articles. Among the most relevant for this paper are *Maldevelopment* (2011) and *Africa and the Challenge of Development* (1998).

adult, and then when he returned home following the overthrow of the dictator Idi Amin Dada.

The stance adopted by the Ugandan government at the time is still maintained throughout the African continent, where governments typically attribute famines to droughts. There are no famines in the United States, where there are severe cases of malnourishment in children, such as inflated tummies and yellow hair, even though the country has droughts almost annually in some regions. Even when agencies of disaster prevention, management, and relief do exist in Africa, they are too poorly equipped and financed to be able to do their job well without external assistance. Sometimes, our governments are not even ashamed of blaming international organisations and NGOs for coming too late to the rescue, as though it is the responsibility of these groups to take over what should be the tasks of national agencies.

Moreover, like other African countries in which boats and ferries are usually overloaded, the DRC government exercises little or no control over transportation on rivers and lakes, roads, and roads. Ineffective responses to disasters such as famines, brush and forest fires, traffic safety, and other issues are indicative of the postcolonial state's incapacity to fulfil its basic responsibilities in protecting citizens from disasters. The sorry state of hospitals and health clinics in fragile states like the DRC is a good indicator of how low the people's plight is considered by governments whose senior officials have no shame letting the health infrastructure deteriorate at home while they go abroad for their own medical needs. The only way this weakness can be corrected is to cleanse the government and the administration of irresponsible leaders and all the deadwood in government agencies, and to replace them with real patriots or men and women who are committed to serving their compatriots with devotion to duty.

Issue #4: Leadership Needed for the African Revolution

That reconstruction and development are yet to take place in much of postcolonial Africa is an indication of the fact that most of our leaders have refused to follow *the revolutionary path* advocated by Fanon, instead of opting for the easier road of enrichment within neocolonial structures (2004, pp. 97–144). The major consequences of this option include the emergence of an African oligarchy whose main aim is to use state power as a means of personal enrichment, the deepening of underdevelopment in most of our countries, and the impoverishment of the popular masses. Instead of establishing democratic developmental states, we are faced with predatory states and their political economies of plunder.

The first and second generations of African leaders have failed to deliver on the people's expectations of independence. We need new leaders, and these should come from social movements of women, workers, and the youth. Such movements ought to be people-centred, and not elite organisations in which ordinary members are simply cheerleaders for ambitious leaders. Their agenda is crystal clear: (*a*) repair the betrayal of Pan-Africanism by pursuing the goal of Pan-African unity and solidarity in Africa and the diaspora; (*b*) transform the structures of the state and the economy in order to meet the people's expectations of independence, which were and still are freedom and material prosperity; (*c*) improve the administration of our states to provide more peace and security to our people; and (*d*) follow the revolutionary path advocated by Fanon to free our continent from neocolonialism and to strengthen ties with Africans in the diaspora.

References

Ade Ajayi, J. F. (1982). Expectations of independence. *Daedalus, III*, 2, 1–9.

Alaux, J.-P. (1979, April). L'étonnante longévité du régime Amin Dada. *Le Monde diplomatique*. Retrieved from https://www.monde-diplomatique.fr/1979/04/ALAUX/35075

Amin, S. (1998). *Africa and the challenge of development: Essays*. Ibadan, Nigeria: Hope Publications.

Amin, S. (2011). *Maldevelopment: Anatomy of a global failure* (2nd ed.) Cape Town, South Africa: Pambazuka Press.

Cabral, A. 1970). *Revolution in Guinea: Selected texts*. New York, NY: Monthly Review Press.

Cabral, A. (1973). *Return to the source: Selected speeches*. New York, NY: Monthly Review Press.

Cabral, A. (1979). *Unity and struggle: Speeches and writings*. New York, NY: Monthly Review Press.

Campbell, H. (2013, April 1). The military defeat of the South Africans in Angola. *Monthly Review*. Retrieved from https://monthlyreview. org/2013/04/01/the-military-defeat-of-the-south-africans-in-angola/

Corera, G. (2013, April 2). MI6 and the death of Patrice Lumumba. *BBC News*.

De Witte, L. (2000). *L'assassinat de Lumumba*. Paris, France: Karthala.

De Witte, L. (2001). *The assassination of Lumumba*. London, UK: Verso.

Fanon, F. (2004). *The wretched of the earth*. New York, NY: Grove Press.

Fanon, F. (1988). *Toward the African revolution*. New York, NY: Grove Press.

Foccart, J., & Gaillard, P. (1995). *Foccart parle: entretiens avec Philippe Gaillard* (Vol. 1). Paris, France: Fayard/Jeune Afrique.

Hochschild, A. (1998). *King Leopold's ghost: A story of greed, terror, and heroism in colonial Africa*. Boston, MA: Houghton Mifflin.

Nkrumah, K. (1967). *Challenge of the Congo*. London, UK: Nelson.

Office of the United Nations High Commissioner for Human Rights. (2010). *Report of the mapping exercise documenting the most serious violations of human rights and international humanitarian law committed in the territory of the Democratic Republic of the Congo between March 1993 and June 2003*. Geneva, Switzerland: Author.

Rodney, W. (1974). Towards the sixth Pan-African Congress: Aspects of the international class struggle in Africa, the Caribbean, and America. In H. Campbell (Ed.,), *Pan-Africanism: The struggle against imperialism and neo-colonialism* (pp. 18–41). Toronto, ON, Canada: Afro-Carib Publications.

Sachikonye, L. (2011). *When a state turns on its citizens: 60 years of institutionalized violence in Zimbabwe*. Harare, Zimbabwe: Weaver Press.

Shaoul, J. (2013, April 18). Britain's involvement in assassination of Congo's Lumumba confirmed. *Africa and the World*. Retrieved from https://www.wsws.org/en/articles/2013/04/18/lumu-a18.html

Skinner, E. P. (1992). *African Americans and U.S. policy toward Africa, 1850-1924: In defense of Black nationality*. Washington, DC: Howard University Press.

Slade, R. (1962). *King Leopold's Congo: Aspects of the development of race relations in the Congo Independent State*. London, UK: Oxford University Press.

Weissman, S. R. (1974). *American foreign policy in the Congo 1960-1964.* Ithaca, NY: Cornell University Press.

Williams, S. (2016). *Spies in the Congo: The race for the ore that built the atomic bomb.* London, UK: C. Hurst & Co.

Young, C. (1994). *The African colonial state in comparative perspective.* New Haven, CT: Yale University Press.

Closing Presentation at the All-African Peoples Conference*

Horace G. Campbell

Good afternoon, everybody. What a marathon week! Even after four exhausting days and nights, in this marathon week, we are still here. It gives me great pleasure to be making the closing statements at this historic All-African Peoples Conference (AAPC) meeting: Thinking back sixty years since the inaugural conference was held in Accra, Ghana. It has been a week full of energy and positive vibrations of Pan-African liberation. We gathered to discuss the unfinished business of liberation and transformation. Despite the punishing schedule, we are still here after four days of debates and nights of African cultural renewal. We must express our heartfelt appreciation for the work done by the team that enabled us to work collectively to pull this conference off. I would like all of you here to give a big round of applause to the chairperson of our conference, Professor Akilagpa Sawyerr, who, at his young age,[1] continues to work hard to build the work for the Pan-African cause of freedom. We will aim at the global progressive Pan-African movement to distinguish individuals like Aki Sawyerr from those who use Pan-Africanism for opportunistic reasons.

---

* Closing Keynote at the sixtieth anniversary commemoration of the All-African People's Conference, 5-8 December 2018.

1 This was a joke about the agility of Professor Aki Sawyerr who was about to turn 80 years old.

Professor Dzodzi Tsikata, the Director of the Institute of African Studies, must be commended. Kindly stand on my behalf. Her leadership within the organising committee, placing the resources of her brains, her intellect, and her determination to pull together the resources of the Institute of African Studies at the University of Ghana to register this historic event in Ghana at this moment is commendable. We want to show our appreciation to her and the Institute of African Studies.

The leaders of the many committees deserve our praise, particularly the teams that have contributed to the success of this conference. However, above all, we must commend those who came by road and spent hours on the road; we salute their perseverance. We must commend all delegates who travelled from near and far, especially those who came at their own expense, at their own costs, and their determination to attend, realizing the significance of this momentous occasion.

At the opening, there were more than 600 persons present, and, in large part, our mobilisation for this meeting was enhanced by the work of the workers of Ghana. The Trade Union Congress (TUC) of Ghana proved to be a valuable ally for this enterprise. In order to discuss the unfinished business of liberation and unification, we would like to thank the working people of Ghana, both those who attended and those who did not for their solidarity in supporting us on the occasion of the AAPC's sixtieth anniversary. It was especially important that hundreds of youths and students from across this region of West Africa participate in this meeting.

It is important to note that imperialism is not waiting for this conference to be over before it starts its mischief. When a different conference was called for the same location and name as our gathering, we were able to observe the misunderstanding surrounding the AAPC 2018 goals and objectives right in front of our eyes. As if by provocation, there were those who have called another AAPC, in the very same university grounds, at the Bank of Ghana Auditorium. The clear differences between the agenda of this gathering organised by the Institute of African Studies and the TUC, and that other gathering, are stamped in those who are headlining that other meeting: the current President of Ghana and the current President of Senegal. These two presidents are among those who are trying to deny the historical importance of Kwame Nkrumah and the AAPC.

They understand the power of the ideas of Pan-African unity and so they will pay lip service to unity, but every day work against African unity.

From the outset and planning, and in the organisation of this meeting, it was clear that this meeting was organised with the understanding that the workers, the women, students, and progressive Pan-Africanists would be the core anchors for the next phase of Pan-African liberation. The invitations that were sent out to delegates in all parts of the Pan-African world (along with the digital call posted on the website of the IAS) were sent with the expectation that this was the meeting to celebrate the struggles for liberation and chart the course for the next round.

During the course of this conference, one participant asked why the Pan-African movement was divided in this way throughout the summit. Why did the AAPC have two ceremonies to commemorate its sixtieth anniversary? I replied that there were significant divides during Nkrumah's period. The Casablanca group and the Monrovia group were the two groups that were present. The lesson from that period was that there were members of the Monrovia group who actively worked with external forces to undermine the Pan-African project. Similarly, throughout the struggles for national liberation, there were those states and leaders who aligned with the apartheid regime and called for dialogue. We cannot have unity for the sake of togetherness; we must base our unity on the freedom of African peoples.

Lessons From the 1958 Conference

At the opening of the AAPC in 1958, Nkrumah summed up the goals of that conference as follows.

Remember always that you have four stages to make:

1. the attainment of freedom and independence;
2. the consolidation of that freedom and independence;
3. the creation of unity and community between free African states; and
4. the economic and social reconstruction of Africa.[2]

---

2 Speech by the then Prime Minister of Ghana, Kwame Nkrumah at the opening session of the AAPC, on Monday, 8 December 1958. http://www.columbia.edu/itc/history/mann/w3005/nkrumba.html

One will note that Nkrumah made a clear link between the material and spiritual freedom of Africans when he said,

And here we must stress that the ethical and humanistic side of our people must not be ignored. We do not want a simple materialistic civilisation which disregards the spiritual side of the human personality and man's need of something beyond the filling of his stomach and the satisfaction of his outward needs. We want a society in which human beings will have the opportunity of flowering and where the humanistic and creative side of our people can be fostered, and their genius allowed to its full expression (Nkrumah, 1958).

With respect to the four goals that were outlined by Nkrumah in 1958, the goal of independence has been achieved through long struggles. The other three, consolidating independence, unity and community, and the economic reconstruction of Africa, have not been achieved. This matter of the unification of Africa was evident back then; it is more evident now: except where in 1958 and 1963, Kwame Nkrumah was speaking of the unity of states, the present emancipation project requires the liberation and unification of the peoples who can transform Africa in the twenty-first century. The rejection of the colonial borders had been articulated in the resolution on "Frontiers, Boundaries and Federations" of the AAPC in 1958. Between the time of the two important AAPC conferences and the formation of the OAU in 1963, there had been the compromise in the clause of the "non-interference in the internal affairs of member states". After acrimonious border disputes in differing parts of Africa in the first years after independence, during the Cairo Summit Conference in July 1964, there was another compromise with a new doctrine, according to which existing borders should be accepted.

The people's liberation is now necessary for African liberation. It is on the question of the unification of the peoples across the current borders that there is big difference in where we are today and what Nkrumah stated in 1958 and 1963 at the opening of the OAU, when he called for a federated state of Africa. Kwame Nkrumah was calling for the unification of states in 1963, and throughout this conference, the deliberations reinforced what we have painfully learned over the past 50 years: the states as they are constituted as present are not the states that originated from African peoples and societies. The current states were established based on the borders at the infamous Berlin Conference. The OAU decided in 1964 to accept the then-existing borders as a compromise during a critical time in the struggles against white settler colonialism. Fifty-four years later, one cannot proclaim "federalism" as the basis for African unity because this kind of federalism will seek to give legitimacy to the existing borders in Africa. In this conference, we have clearly stated that one of the things that we have to do is break down these borders to allow African people travel freely around the continent.

Intergenerational Energies

The vigorous discussion among the youth on the first day brought many of the youths in touch with veterans of some of the liberation struggles in Africa. What a joy for us in this meeting was the first day with the presence of Elder Balogun. Balogun was present at the 1958 conference. Can you stand, my brother, so that all present can see you?

One of the joys for us, my elder, was your presence in this meeting because you offered an intergenerational conception of what Pan-Africanism meant. In your presentation, you said the people who came to the AAPC in 1958 were coming from movements. So, on the whole, they were speaking for and representing workers, students, farmers, and traders. When they went back, they could go back to carry forward the tasks of liberation. As someone who has been in the movement for over 70 years, we commend you for your strength and consistency. We pray that the ancestors will give you a long life so that you can continue the work that you have been doing.

During the invocation of our own poet, Kofi Anyidoho, many of the youths were reminded of their ancestors who fought for independence and freedom. Those who did not know of Toussaint Louverture, Harriet Tubman, Marcus Garvey, Patrice Lumumba, Amilcar Cabral, Frantz Fanon, Thomas Sankara, Wangari Maathai, and Walter Rodney, heard of the hundreds of freedom fighters whose footsteps we are continuing. I was wondering to myself how many of us here knew all of the ancestors that Kofi called on to bless this conference. This invocation brought home to me the reality of the task of organisations such as the Institute of African Studies to ensure that, in primary schools, we will teach about these heroes and heroines of the Pan-African movement. Because, in the education system, they want to overthrow Pan-Africanism: they want to ensure that primary school children do not know of the contributions of Patrice Lumumba and Kwame Nkrumah. We know that the propaganda against Kwame Nkrumah has been unrelenting. The coup d'état against Nkrumah, the killing of Felix Moumié, the assassination of Muamar Gaddafi, and the assassination of Thomas Sankara, were all efforts to assassinate the Pan-African liberation project. But you cannot assassinate the Pan-African liberation project. As the resolution of this meeting has made clear, we have seen how the so-called "leaders" of Africa have become accomplices in the neo-liberal domination and exploitation of Africa.

If there was any doubt about these ancestors, the exhibition of women freedom fighters throughout the conference hammered home this point about the centrality of women in the liberation of Africa. The photo exhibition (entitled *re-sisters*), highlighting the emancipation of women in global Africa, brought home this point in addition to the dynamic intervention of our sisters in struggle throughout this conference.

Health and Liberation

The goals and objectives of this conference were clear from the opening plenary of the youth. The very first paper was a statement of the limitations of those who fought for liberation and failed to work for the upliftment of the standards of living of the people. The paper, *"State of emergency": the politics of Zimbabwe's cholera outbreak, 2008/09* by Simukai Chigudu brought to light the tremendous suffering of the peoples of Zimbabwe under a leadership that had been proclaiming its liberation credentials as defending the African peoples.[3] In a country with trained health professionals, there had been the horrific circumstance of an unprecedented 98,000 cases of cholera with over 4,000 deaths.[4] The outbreak could be explained by the breakdown of the country's water and sanitation systems. In their tradition of manipulation, the government of Robert

---

3   Paper presented by Simukai Chigudu, "State of Emergency: The politics of Zimbabwe's cholera outbreak", 2008–2009.

4   For one scientific explanation of the cholera outbreak, see C. Nicholas Cuneo, corresponding author Richard Sollom and Chris Beyrer (2017), The Cholera Epidemic in Zimbabwe, 2008–2009: A Review and Critique of the Evidence, *Health and Human Rights Journal,* 19(2).

Mugabe and the ZANU-PF blamed the deaths on biological warfare unleashed by the West against Zimbabwe.[5]

I want to thank those panellists who started off this conference by making it clear that leaders like Robert Mugabe of Zimbabwe cannot use the old discourse about liberation, when those discourses are not in the interests of the majority of the working people of Africa. The opening discussion was a clear signal to the working peoples of other former settler colonies. The message was simply this: the reclamation of the land was one of the central platforms of African liberation. But the transfer of land must go to the people who work on the land. Importantly, in this conference, there were deliberations on the new forms of property relationships beyond private property that must be nurtured in the transition to a new social system.

It was at this opening plenary that the issues of urban spaces and the pathways for youth to become meaningful citizens in the world were raised. The question of education for the youth of Africa at home and abroad, along with the forms of reconstruction for urban spaces, were deliberated. There was clear objection to the nature of current planning for cities, where the children of global Africa are relegated to slums. The paper on gentrification registered clarity on the relationships between class power and gentrification. A similar lucid clarification was provided with respect to the evolving urban non-plan for Africa. African liberation now requires town planning for African peoples. The current cities of Africa were not planned for Africans. These were planned as spaces for the extraction of capital from Africa. The liberation of urban spaces; the building of new towns and cities; and the reconstruction of Africa are tasks linked to the reversal of global warming and reparative justice.

The conference had provided the mandate to deliberate on contemporary imperialism, neo-liberalism, Global Africa, Pan-Africanism, the emancipation of women, reparative and restorative justice, and Global

---

5 On 12 December 2008, Dr Sikhanyiso Ndlovu accused the West of biological warfare against Africa, and claimed that the cholera outbreak was actually a "serious biological-chemical weapon" attack by the United Kingdom, which Ndlovu asserted was trying to commit genocide. He said, "Cholera is a calculated, racist, terrorist attack on Zimbabwe by the unrepentant former colonial power, which has enlisted support from its American and Western allies so that they can invade the country". See UK caused cholera, says Zimbabwe. BBC. 12 December 2008.

warming. In every discussion, it became clear that none of the tasks could be fulfilled outside of the context of the unification and emancipation of the African peoples at home and abroad. From the opening plenary to this morning's deliberations, it was very clear that what was needed was a new push to mobilise the masses of the peoples in new organisations and new forms of leadership, ideologically prepared, so that the AU Agenda for a prosperous, free, and integrated Africa could be made real. What became clear throughout the discussion this week was that we cannot wait until 2063 for the unification of the peoples of Africa.

Over the week, it became evident that Agenda 2063, which sets a projected period for the unification of Africa, is an unrealistic goal. Unrealistic, in so far as the conditions of global warming will drive the necessity for collaboration and cooperation beyond borders to reverse global warming.

What became clear through this discussion this week was that we cannot wait until 2063 to achieve the unification of Africa. The evidence of environmental degradation and destruction of natural environment ensures that the entire African continent will experience extreme heat waves every single year by 2040 (Russo et al., 2016). Many current communities will not exist. The Caribbean islands have seen massive hurricanes, where hundreds of thousands of persons have been displaced. The current meeting in Poland on global warming (2018 United Nations Climate Change Conference) has sent the message that the commitments made in 2015 at the Paris Accords are now meaningless in the face of the continuing emissions and accompanying disasters.

The neoliberal theories of how to combat global warming of mitigation and adaption were thoroughly critiqued.

During the destruction of the environment and massive hurricanes, Africans will have to plan for the repair of the environment. There will have to be the re-greening of Africa, the planting of trees, the storage of water, the transfer of water, the restoration of many communities, and, as was said in the case of cities, the building of new cities. In this regard, the current plans for the large water transfer schemes to replenish Lake Chad have emerged as central to the reversal of global warming. African youths will have to engage the plans in so far as this is about their future. Our engineers, hydrologists, and policymakers cannot afford to allow

France and the European Union to dictate the terms of reference for research and the rejuvenation of Africa.

There were sessions on industrialization during the rebuilding talks, but the evidence indicates that we cannot pursue industrialization in the old forms that destroy the environment. Africans can learn valuable lessons from industrialisation in China. They have been so successful at industrialisation that they have polluted the air, land, and water, and the pollution levels are among the highest in the world. We have to talk about green industrialisation that can unleash renewable energies and use the vast wealth of solar energy all across Africa so that we can build a new society. A deeper comprehension of reparations and reparative justice will be necessary for the restoration of the natural environment.

Therefore, this conference did not come up with narrow understanding of reparations, because the restoration of the natural environment is most crucial and urgent. You cannot restore the natural environment without repairing the human spirit. The repair of the natural environment and the repair of the human spirit bring together that principal task to transcend the capitalist mode of production that destroys humans and nature.

The Continuing Importance of the Congo

It was most fitting that the keynote presentation at the official opening of this conference was on the unfinished business of the liberation of the Congo along with the potential of the Congolese peoples. Patrice Lumumba had been introduced to the Global Pan-African World at the AAPC 1958 Conference. The machinations of the empire to derail the independence and self-determination of the Congolese people represent one of the top criminal actions of imperialism against the African redemption process. Similar to how Patrice Lumumba was killed for mobilising the people for genuine independence, the President of Libya was killed in 2011, when he gesticulated towards the support for the common currency to unite Africa. The overthrow of Kwame Nkrumah, the assassination of leaders all across Africa, reminded everyone that the path towards the unification and emancipation of Africa will not be smooth.

The experiences over the past twenty years of seeking to transcend Mobutism in the Congo have cured many of us of the idea that liberation in this period must involve armed struggle. The disaster that we have seen from what happened in the Congo with the armed forces of Rwanda and Uganda was the wake-up call about military engagements without clear political and ideological mobilisations. That was the very clear lesson communicated at the opening ceremony by Dr Georges Nzongola Ntalaja. This lesson is evident not only in the Congo but in Liberia, Nigeria, and Somalia, where groups like Charles Taylor, Boko Haram, and Al-Shabaab have used the language of armed struggle to further create misery for peoples. In Liberia and Sierra Leone, Charles Taylor and Foday Sankoh, respectively, were two leaders who declared themselves to be revolutionaries. These are good examples of individuals and movements who sought to use weapons to fight for liberation, only to bring the nightmare to the people in the society.

We have seen other organisations that have not been so pretentions as to declare themselves revolutionaries but have taken up arms in the name of religion. Youth unemployment, absence of social security safety nets, and general alienation from the oppressive states have ensnared many youths of Africa, who have been persuaded to join organisations such as Al-Shabaab and Boko Haram. One of the urgent tasks of this moment is to politically neutralise those who have mobilised the youth into anti-people militias as in Al-Shabaab and Boko Haram. The AU adopted the platform of Silencing Guns by 2020. In this platform, the AU has committed itself to "ending all wars, civil conflicts, gender-based violence, and violent conflicts and preventing genocide in the continent by 2020". Progressives must hold the AU to this pledge and dishonour those leaders and forces within the African Union that sit on the Peace and Security Council of the AU but actively undermine this pledge. It must be made clear on all platforms that we cannot achieve Pan-African unity without peace in Africa.

At this meeting, it became clear that, although the current leaders signed on to the support for unity and for an Africa whose development is people-driven, relying on the potential offered by people, especially its women and youth and caring for children in practice, the current leaders of the AU are afraid of unity and are ideologically and intellectually submissive to the neoliberal agenda of the imperial states. Hence, there is no understanding of the current imperialist onslaught against Africans;

instead, these leaders speak of "reforms" and "development partners". They are so steeped in the structural adjustment "reforms" of the Bretton Woods system that there can be no consideration of the complete transformation of Africa by the current leaders. Yesterday, Farmers' Day, I was in the radio station and the interviewer asked me what I thought of Ghana beyond aid. I said, "Beyond which aid? Who is aiding who? I will talk about the aid that Ghana gives Britain and Europe. There are many wrong conceptions about the billions of dollars that are taken out of Africa by the African ruling classes".

As the resolutions of this conference have made clear, the weaknesses of the African states are not a result of the failures of the African peoples, but of the slavish alliance between the current leaders and global capitalism. The evidence shows that the illicit flight of capital from Africa is not just the actions of some corrupt leaders but a direct result of the institutions and policies of the International Monetary Fund. A June 2018 report by the Political Economy Research Institute (PERI) at the University of Massachusetts Amherst examined capital flight from 30 African countries between 1970 and 2015 and documented losses of approximately $1.4 trillion over the 46-year period ($1.8 trillion if lost interest is taken into account). This amount far outweighs both the stock of debt owed by these countries as of 2015 ($496.9 billion), as well as the combined amount of foreign aid all the countries received over this period ($991.8 billion). The direction of capital flows actually makes the group of African countries a "net creditor" to the rest of the world—a startling conclusion when contrasted against common perceptions about Africa (Ndikumana & Boyce, 2018).

The manifestations of imperialist plunder were spelt out in many of the plenary sessions and on the all-day sessions and panels organised by the TUC of Ghana. In these presentations, the day-to-day battles for decent wages, safety at work, and health benefits were spelt out. It was made very clear that the quality of the lives of the African workers and small farmers cannot change as long as the governments enter into agreements that facilitate the licit and illicit outflows of capital from Africa. It was clear that Africa did not need foreign investments but merely the return of the assets that were held outside of Africa by the African ruling circles. In order to be protected by their imperial masters, these ruling circles have entered into military agreements. These agreements tie the African ruling class to the most backward branches of international capital.

The International Crisis of Capitalism

We are living in a very delicate moment, and the delicacy is made all the more urgent because of the international capitalism crisis. We cannot speak lightly about this crisis. In 2008, the depth of the crisis and the band-aid measures to prop up capitalism with measures such as quantitative easing led some sectors of Global Capital to believe that the reconstitution and recomposition of capitalism can be carried through on the backs and bodies of African peoples, and the peoples of the Global South. We have with us at the present moment, these currency wars, trade wars, sanctions, cyber warfare, and the process of the diminution of the US dollar as the currency of world trade. We have this conflict now between the Society for Worldwide Interbank Financial Telecommunication (SWIFT) and the China International Payment System (CIPS) where the question of which international payment system will replace the current dollar standards is debated. The weaponisation of finance by the US Treasury is only one other manifestation that the Bretton Woods system of 1944 has come to an end. The US dollar is now a fiat currency and military management of international systems means that the United States believe that they can maintain their supremacy by military means. So, Africans have to be prepared to understand the meaning of the crisis of capitalism. Neither the Chinese, nor the Europeans, nor the Americans should believe that their currency can be supported based on African labour and African resources. In the midst of this current economic war, the urgency of the African common currency has been very evident.

Strengthening our Understanding of Pan-Africanism

Now it is imperative to teach our youths about the crisis of capitalism. At this meeting, we must register, at this meeting, our condemnation of the NATO destruction of Libya. The countries of NATO that unleashed the destruction of Libya continue to hold on to the resources of Libya against the wishes of the Libyan peoples. We need students and researchers today in Africa to understand that the new slave trade is being carried out through the ports in Libya. We must oppose and condemn this new slavery as we condemn the old slavery. In this crisis of capitalism, we have witnessed the most extreme forms of promulgation of white racism, chauvinism, and white nationalism. From the beginning of the development of the capitalist system, white supremacy has always served as a prop for this system, especially in Western Europe and North America. White supremacy is not only about the colour of one's skin, it is about maintaining a certain kind of economic system in the world today. Donald Trump is only one manifestation of rallying around white nationalism. What about Bolsonaro and the neo-fascists who have come to power in Brazil? Bolsonaro has promised to physically eliminate a lot of Black people in Brazil. One of the limitations of our meeting is that we did not have enough resources to reach out to our brothers and sisters in Brazil so that they could have participated in this meeting.

We know, very clearly, that struggles for Black freedom and dignity in Latin America will be defining spaces in the Pan-African struggle. All of Latin America and the Caribbean will be spaces where we will have to intensify our work in the next phase. The execution of the activist Marielle Franco in the streets of Rio de Janeiro earlier this year was one indication of the war against Black women who are progressive activists.

Why do fascists afraid of progressive Black women? Why are they afraid of women organising? Black women in the US were fighting against sexual harassment, sexual abuse, and sexual exploitation long before the #MeToo movement emerged Thus, we have the rising up of Black women. It is not by accident that in the "Black Lives Matter" movement, the emergent leadership has been Black women and transgender women, offering a new perspective of leadership in the Black liberation and Pan-Africa movement. I was pleased, yesterday, when our sisters spoke on the new struggles for democracy in Africa. They made it clear that we must denounce the leaders of Uganda, Tanzania, Kenya, and those leaders who use homophobic language to divide the working people of Africa. There are some places where it is a no-no to discuss the question of the rights of LGBTQ persons in the Pan-African movement. Well, progressive women in the Pan-African movement have made it clear that you cannot fight for freedom for one group of people and oppress another group of people. Thus, from the AAPC, we are going to send a message, which comes from "Black Lives Matter", to Mr Museveni in Uganda, that this homophobic rhetoric, this violation, and harassment of women that we have in the Ugandan society, must stop.

Pan-African Memories

So, whose memory do we have, when we go forward, when we discuss the next round? All of the questions that were discussed in the six points of this conference brought the question back to restoring ourselves as human beings. The reparations question is misunderstood precisely because there is a lack of education on reparations. Some people say that reparations are about money, but the reparations movement is divided. There are some who have made a claim for monetary compensation. But what if you get money? Then what? We always refer to the reparative claims of the state of Israel. The state of Israel received compensation for what happened in the holocaust against the Jewish people, but the money was used to stabilise international capitalism, and as a result, they turned around and continued to exploit and harass the Palestinian people.

Has our reparations movement got to be different? Yes, or No? I did not hear you? (Yes).

So, the ten-point programme of the Caribbean Reparations Plan is a minimum programme, because it was very difficult to get all the governments of the region to agree. What we are calling for from this AAPC is that the knowledge gap that exists about enslavement, about Pan-Africanism, and Pan-African liberation, must be closed, and we must close the gap by looking at the international capitalism system and deciding whose memory we must validate.

The point was made that part of reparations is the return of cultural artefacts stolen from Africa. This morning, I read a newspaper article about the opening of a museum that was rebuilt in Belgium. There are over 10,000 artefacts from Africa in that museum. When people from the Congo demanded the return of the artefacts, the Belgian authorities said to the Congolese, "You do not have the capability to look after the artefacts, so, let us keep them for you". The reparations question must be upheld, and we want to uphold it as the educational process for systemic change. Let me try to conclude by looking at the lessons of liberation and unification.

Conclusion

Last Sunday, while I was in Johannesburg, there was a major concert. The concert was called the Global Citizen Concert. The headliners for this concert were Beyoncé and Jay-Z. There were tens of thousands of young people who came out to the concert to listen to Beyoncé and Jay-Z. But who was sponsoring this concert? It was the World Bank that had organised this concert in the name of Global Citizens, which does not challenge global capitalism. Oprah Winfrey, the president of South Africa, Cyril Ramaphosa, and other luminaries were present to piggyback on the popularity of Beyoncé. Therefore, our movement has to be strong enough to teach Beyoncé that, when we celebrate Nelson Mandela at 100 years old, Global Capitalism cannot separate Nelson Mandela from the black liberation struggle of Africa. Nelson Mandela cannot be separated from Winnie Mandela and those who carried out the struggle within Africa.

Madame Chairperson, please permit me to ask the audience, how many of you in the audience know about Cuito Cuanavale? (Campbell, 2013). Please put up your hands for me. So, there are 200 persons in the room, but only ten persons know about Cuito Cuanavale. What is Cuito Cuanavale? It is one of the most important expressions of the fight for liberation by African peoples that came from the organisation of the peoples of frontline states and the organisation of peoples of Southern Africa along with the Cuban revolutionary forces. Why is it that our youth do not know about Cuito Cuanavale? Because they want us to think that liberation was a gift granted by foreigners to Africa, and in the process, we will not see Nelson Mandala as a figure that came from struggle but the figure who came from compromise and negotiations. Now, we cannot stop at Cuito Cuanavale, although we must teach about Cuito Cuanavale. Because in Angola, the generals who fought the battles for liberation have turned their leadership in the military to the leadership in the accumulation of capital. There are billions of dollars overseas and that money is going back to Angola. The same thing can be said about

South Africa, Namibia, Mozambique, and all the former settler colonies. So, the liberation that we are embarking on, that is to say for the next fifteen years (because we cannot wait 60 years for the unification of Africa), must be a liberation that is grounded in the workers and peasants of Africa. We must mobilise the scientific and technological knowledge that exists among the African people as we train the African youths. As Walter Rodney said,

> We must go back to the underlying movement of history and have confidence in the capacity of our people; if they could have breached the gates of colonialism through their own effort, then it seems to me they have brought into the neo-colonial period a capacity to breach the walls of imperialism (Rodney, 1990).

We cannot breach the walls of imperialism with an NGO-isation of politics. We cannot breach the walls of imperialism with the idea that we are going to get handouts from the West. The West is looking for the brightest of the African youth to mobilise in the service of imperialism. There is something called the Young African Leadership Initiative (YALI), that was established by former United States President Barack Obama.[6] They have a database of over 50,000 of those they consider to be among the brightest youth in Africa. This networking among the African youth is to mobilise the brightest to go to the United States of America for six weeks to teach them neo-liberalism. But guess what? When they get to the United States of America, they are afraid they would be infected by people fighting for Black liberation—by the scientific and technological work of Black people who are fighting for their rights. And we know that, in the current struggle, the youths have the creativity and wherewithal to create a new society.

The film *Black Panther* told us that, in this mythical future Wakanda, we could mobilise all of the scientific resources, and there was one

---

6 YALI is a United States government programme, started in 2010, aimed at mobilising and networking young African leaders with activities including a fellowship to study in the United States for six weeks, follow-up resources, and student exchange programs. In 2014, the program was expanded to include four regional "leadership centres" in Ghana, Kenya, Senegal, and South Africa.

mineral which was an abstraction of the great mineral wealth of Africa, which could be used for the wealth and reconstruction of Africa. And you notice that Wakanda centralised the scientific skills of women in the mobilisation for the unification of Africa. As a result, we will need new forms of mobilisation and organisation. Fortunately, we don't need to go far because from the fight against colonialism, the fight against enslavement, the organising to fight against Mubarak, the organising to fight against apartheid, we know that all the ideas of vanguardism cannot free us. And we must build and hold.

I was very pleased when there was discussion about property relations. We must explore new property relations in Africa for the unification of Africa, so we have to catch up with the cultural artists, we have to catch up with the Fela Ransome Kutis and the Bob Marleys of the world. Because the ideas of *Ubuntu* ("I am a person because you are a person") are central to how we will be human beings in the twenty-first century. Kurzweil (2005) wrote a book called *The Singularity is Near.* The thesis of the book is that, by 2045, humanity will break out in two, and we will have those who are humans and those who are cyborgs. So, we are struggling to be humans in the twenty-first century. We are struggling so that planet Earth will be a place for human beings.

The Pan-African movement for the unification and emancipation of Africa is the struggle for the emancipation of human beings.

Forward ever, backward never.

References

Campbell, H. (2013). The military defeat of the South Africans in Angola. *Monthly Review, 64*(11).

Kurzweil, R. (2005). *The singularity is near: When humans transcend biology.* London, UK: Gerald Duckworth.

Ndikumana, L., & Boyce, J. K. (2018). *Capital flight from Africa: Updated methodology and new estimates.* Political Economy Research Institute. Retrieved from https://www.peri.umass.edu/publication/item/1083-capital-flight-from-africa-updated-methodology-and-new-estimates

Rodney, W. (1990). *Walter Rodney speaks: The making of an African intellectual.* Trenton, NJ: Africa World Press.

Russo, S., Marchese, A. F., Sillmann, J., & Immé, G. (2016). When will unusual heat waves become normal in a warming Africa? *Environmental Research Letters, 11*(4). Retrieved from https://iopscience.iop.org/article/10.1088/1748-9326/11/5/054016/meta;jsessionid=1BE487D4E-C4957E4F0B0B3B7D08D51A3.c2.iopscience.cld.iop.org

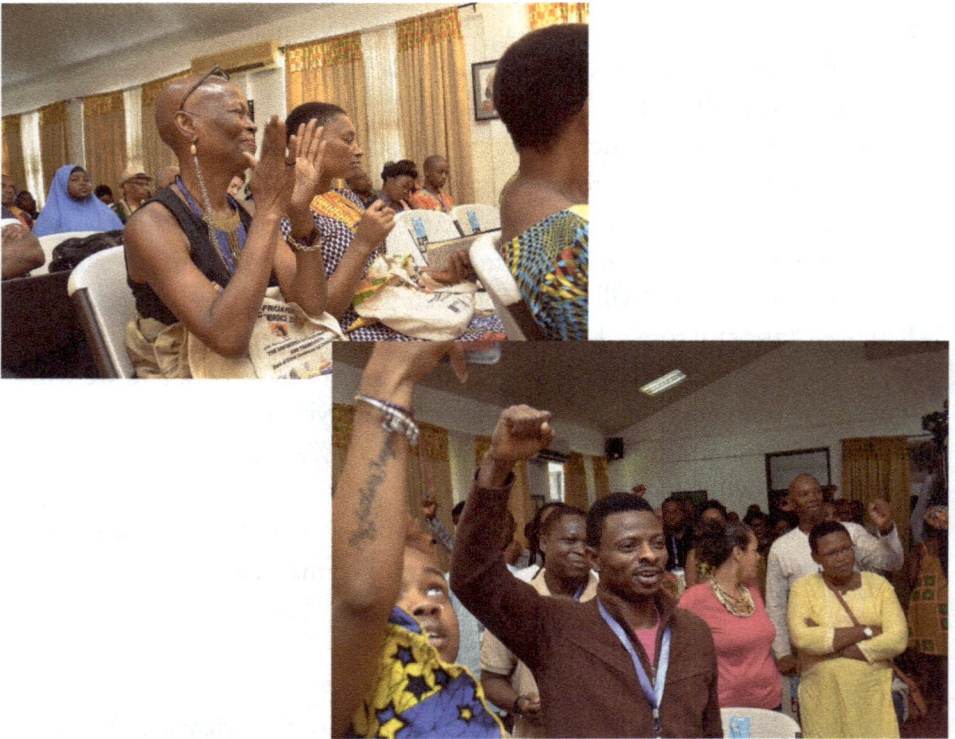

Participants at the closing ceremony held on 8th December 2018 at the J. H. Kwabena Nketia Conference Room at the Institute of African Studies, Kwame Nkrumah Complex

Pan-Africanism in Mwalimu Nyerere's Thought—Being Both King and Philosopher*

Issa Shivji

The inauguration of the Mwalimu Nyerere chair in Nkrumah Hall is neither accidental nor coincidental. It has historical significance. Julius Nyerere and Kwame Nkrumah were iconic figures of Pan-Africanism. They arrived at Pan-Africanism through different intellectual and political routes. Nyerere discovered Pan-Africanism through Tanganyikan nationalism, and Nkrumah discovered Ghanaian nationalism through Pan-Africanism. Mwalimu's intellectual formation was steeped in missionary influence. He had political contacts with the Labour Party and the Fabian Colonial Bureau while he was in England. He took a gradualist stance towards transformation and was a moderate opponent of colonialism (See Shivji et al, 2020). Nkrumah went to Lincoln University in the US. It was a black college. He had first-hand experience of racial discrimination, lived in Harlem during summer vacations, and was mentored by great African-American Pan-Africanists like W. E. B. Du Bois, George Padmore, and C. L. R. James (See Sherwood, 1996). Nkrumah's extreme approach to independence was based on his understanding of

---

* Lecture delivered on the installation of the author as the first Professor of Mwalimu Julius Nyerere Professorial Chair in Pan-African Studies at University of Dar es Salaam on 23 April 2008. It was first published in *Pambazuka News*, Issue 431 (2009) and is revised and reproduced here with permission.

the political economy of imperialism, which informed his anti-colonialist stance. Nkrumah ended up writing a great treatise, *Neo-Colonialism: The Last Stage of Imperialism* (1965). Mwalimu authored the *Arusha Declaration: Socialism and Self-Reliance* (1968). If the *Arusha Declaration* had had a sub-title in the stagiest language of Nkrumah, it would have been something like—to borrow from the words of C. L. R. James— *Socialism and Self-Reliance: The Highest Stage of African Resistance* (C. L. R. James once described the Arusha Declaration as "the highest stage of resistance ever reached by revolting blacks").

Nkrumah did not survive. Imperialism overthrew him in a CIA-engineered coup only a year after the publication of *Neo-Colonialism*. Mwalimu survived, but the *Arusha Declaration* did not. Neoliberalism discredited and buried "socialism and self-reliance" in a Reaganite counter-revolution against development and national self-determination (Shivji et al, 2020).

Despite these differences in the intellectual and political formation of the two men, they were both unreservedly great Pan-Africanists and fighters for African unity. They differed in their approach. Nkrumah wanted the United States of Africa "now, now", whereas Nyerere counselled gradualism. Several decades later, Mwalimu paid a wholesome tribute to Nkrumah for his single-minded crusade for African unity. In the process, he acknowledged their different intellectual backgrounds and even admitted that Nkrumah had a point. Some 40 years of "state nationalism" has made African unity even harder to achieve, just when Africa needs it most. On the fortieth anniversary of Ghana's independence in March 1997, Mwalimu said:

> Africa must unite! That was the title of one of Kwame Nkrumah's books. That call is more urgent today than ever before. Together we the peoples of Africa will be incomparably stronger internationally than we are now with our multiplicity of unviable states. The needs of our separate countries can be, and are being, ignored by the rich and powerful. The result is that Africa is marginalised when international decisions affecting our vital interests are made.
>
> Unity will not make us rich, but it can make it difficult for Africa and the African peoples to be disregarded and humiliated (Nyerere, 1997).

A year later, in his reflections with Ikaweba Bunting, Mwalimu recalled his encounter with Nkrumah and their different perspectives on Pan-Africanism. Mwalimu described Nkrumah's perspective as the "aggressive Pan-Africanism of W. E. B. Du Bois and Marcus Garvey. The colonialists were against this and frightened of it". Mwalimu continued:

> Kwame and I met in 1963 and discussed African unity. We differed on how to achieve the United States of Africa. But we both agreed on the United States of Africa as necessary. Kwame went to Lincoln University, a black college in the US. He perceived things from the perspective of US history, where 13 colonies that revolted against the British formed a union. That is what he thought the Organisation of African Unity (OAU) should do.
>
> I tried to get East Africa to unite before independence. When we failed in this, I was wary about Kwame's continental approach. We corresponded profusely on this. Kwame said my idea of "region-alisation" was only balkanisation on a larger scale. Later African historians will have to study our correspondence on this issue of uniting Africa (Nyerere, 1997).

We are the latter-day African historians who need to study this because Pan-Africanism is not only historical. It is the present. Only Pan-Africanism can be true African nationalism under globalisation. However, it is not my intention to discuss the comparative perspective of these two paragons of Pan-Africanism, fascinating as it is. My purpose is to engage critically with Pan-Africanism in Mwalimu's thought. That is the task of an intellectual.

I propose to isolate two strands in Mwalimu's thought. One relates to the rationale or justification for the unity of Africa, the other to the agency that would bring it about. Mwalimu deployed three interrelated elements in his argument for unity. For a lack of better words, I sum them up as identity, non-viability, and sovereignty.

Identity

There is constant assertion and argument in Mwalimu's speeches and writings on the African-ness of the African people. Unlike other people,

Mwalimu said, our identity is African, not Tanzanian, Ghanaian, or Gabonese. Not only is our own perception of ourselves African but even outsiders also recognise us as Africans. In his Ghana speech, he summed up this position in his usual simple but graphic fashion:

> When I travel outside Africa the description of me as former President of Tanzania is a fleeting affair. It does not stick. Apart from the ignorant who sometimes asked me whether Tanzania was Johannesburg, even to those who knew better, what stuck in the minds of my hosts was the fact of my African-ness. So I had to answer questions about the atrocities of the Amins and the Bokassas of Africa.
>
> Mrs Gandhi did not have to answer questions about the atrocities of the Marcosses of Asia. Nor does Fidel Castro have to answer questions about the atrocities of the Samozas of Latin America. But when I travel or meet foreigners, I have to answer questions about Somalia, Liberia, Rwanda, Burundi and Zaire, as in the past I used to answer questions about Mozambique, Angola, Zimbabwe, Namibia or South Africa.

Although I have used the post-modernist phrase "identity", it is clear that Mwalimu's argument was political rather than post-modernist. The commonness of Africans lay in their common experience as Africans, rather than their common identity. As he put it, "For centuries, we had been oppressed and humiliated as Africans. We were hunted and enslaved as Africans, and we were colonised as Africans... Since we were humiliated as Africans, we had to be liberated as Africans" (Nyerere, 1997).

Undoubtedly, Mwalimu is talking about common interests, but his notion of "interest" is individual, personal, and embedded in political theories of enlightened individualism. Unlike Nkrumah, Mwalimu's characterisation of interest is not social or class, grounded in political economy. This is one of the interesting and significant differences in the philosophical formation and outlook of the two men, which informed their political prognosis. If I were to use the language of Marxist classics, I would say Mwalimu understood Leninist politics better than Marx's political economy. Nkrumah's politics was not particularly astute, but he had a better understanding of political economy.

Mwalimu's was a consistent anti-colonialism; Nkrumah's a militant anti-imperialism. Mwalimu sneered at imperialists; Nkrumah stung them. Mwalimu saw African unity as a goal, which could be achieved by small steps. For Mwalimu, any number of African states uniting in any form— economically or politically, regionally or otherwise—was a step forward. For Nkrumah, national liberation and African unity were two sides of the same coin, the coin being an anti-imperialist, Pan-Africanist struggle. Mwalimu conceptualised the task of the first generation of African nationalists as twofold: national liberation (meaning independence) and unity. By 1994, when South Africa formally ended apartheid, the first task was complete. In Mwalimu's assessment, the first-generation African nationalists succeeded in the task of national liberation but failed in the task of African unity. To an extent, a kind of stagiest approach is implied here—independence first, then unity. Within unity, too, there is a stagiest notion, regional unity leading to continental unity. To be fair, Mwalimu recognised the difficulty of his stagiest theory. He forcefully argued, for example, that the proposed East African Federation should precede the independence of individual countries; otherwise, unity would become difficult. History has shown that he was correct in his powerful argument. However, Nkrumah's argument for immediate continental federation and his own for regional unity before independence had a similar foundation and line of reasoning. Nkrumah's position was that regional unities would make continental unity even more difficult. He viewed "regionalisation" as being balkanisation on a larger scale.

Fifty years later, we are less regionalised and even more balkanised. In his *Reflections* on his seventy-fifth birthday, Mwalimu once again returned to the theme of the balkanisation of Africa. He said the Balkans themselves are being Africanised as they are absorbed in the larger European Union, while we, Africans, are being tribalised! Mwalimu said:

> ...these powerful European states are moving towards unity, and you people are talking about the atavism of the tribe, this is non-sense! I am telling you people. How can anybody think of the tribe as the unity of the future, *hakuna*! (Othman, 2000, p. 22)

I believe there is another underlying difference between the gradualist and radical approaches of Nyerere and Nkrumah, which has not been sufficiently analysed. I will only hint at it. In my opinion, Nkrumah saw unity and emancipation as anti-imperialist movements rather than as a formal process of dissolving state sovereignty. Amílcar Cabral captured the national liberation struggle as an anti-imperialist struggle well when he said, "[S]o long as imperialism is in existence, an independent African state must be a liberation movement in power, or it will not be independent". The notion of an independent African state being a "national liberation movement in power", I suggest, gives us the core of the ideology and politics of Pan-Africanism as a vision of not only unity but liberation. African liberation is not complete with the independence of single entities called countries. "Territorial nationalism" is not African nationalism. African nationalism can only be Pan-Africanism or else, as Mwalimu characterised it, it is "the equivalent of tribalism within the context of our separate nation-states". Pan-Africanism gave birth to nationalism, not the other way round. This is a powerful argument implied in Mwalimu's ideas on African unity. This brings me to the second element of his justification for African unity, the non-viability of African states.

Non-Viability

Mwalimu spent a lot of time demonstrating the irrationality and non-viability of African states. He used the Kiswahili diminutive *vinchi* to describe them. Without intending to offend linguists, I would translate *vinchi* as "statelets" (as in islets). These statelets had neither geographical nor ethnic rationality. There are fifty-three independent African states, all members of the United Nations. "If numbers were horses", Mwalimu quipped, "Africa would be riding high!" Yet Africa is the weakest continent. World councils make decisions without regard to the interests of Africa. "Let us not glorify nation-states inherited from colonialism", Mwalimu used to tell his fellow state leaders. He admonished the new generation of African leaders to reject the "return to tribe". He characterised the current upsurge of ethnic, racial, and other forms of narrow nationalisms (which we are witnessing all over Africa, including in our own country) as fossilising "Africa into the wounds inflicted upon it by the vultures of imperialism" (Nyerere, 1997).

Colonial boundaries were artificially carved up by the colonialists, of the colonialists and for the colonialists. They have little to do with the history or cultures of Africa. The map of Africa is full of straight-line boundaries, compared to other continents. It is as if someone sat with a geometrical set to draw them. That is what, more or less, happened when colonial powers met at the Berlin Conference in 1885 to slice up their newly acquired booty. Teaching us the map of Tanzania, I remember my geography teacher telling us to start by drawing a hexagonal tilted at the bottom and then modify it to get the map. The greatest modification would of course be the shores of the Indian Ocean—the only side of the boundary the colonialists could not get straight!

Related to the argument on non-viability was the third element of sovereignty or self-determination.

Sovereignty

Mwalimu argued that the mini-states of Africa could not, on their own, exercise their sovereign right to make their own decisions in the global world dominated by the powerful. He emphasised, particularly in his early writings, that our erstwhile colonial masters would divide us based on our sovereignties to continue ruling us. There is no doubt that in his political outlook, Mwalimu placed a great premium on the right of the people to make their own decisions. That was the fundamental meaning of independence—the right to make our own decisions ourselves.

However, Mwalimu was a political leader and ruler of state. His underlying premise of state sovereignty served as the foundation for his view on the right of the people to make their own decisions. People make their decisions through their states. In fact, the dichotomy and the contradiction between people's sovereignty and state sovereignty were pretty fudged in Mwalimu's thought and much more so in his political practice. I won't get into his political practices other than to state that they are closely related to his second main line of thinking, which is the agency question.

Agency

Having forcefully argued for African unity, the basic questions of history arise: Who will bring it about? Which social agency will be the carrier of this great historical task? Neither Nyerere nor Nkrumah raised these questions in this form, at least not while they were in power. However, it was evident from their stance that the state was the entity responsible for bringing about unification. This was realpolitik in part, and awareness of the state's historical genesis in colonial Africa in part. The state in Africa was a colonial imposition. It did not develop organically through social struggles within the African formation. Thus, when we raised the flag of independence, sang our national anthem, and proclaimed sovereignty, it was the sovereignty of the state inherited from colonialism. In that sense, it was not our state; we took over the colonial state. There was no internal social class to shoulder the task of nation-building and economic development. The only available organised force was the state. The colonial heritage thus left the first generation of African nationalists with no option. The state was virtually automatically given the mission of transformation. The real contradiction lay in this. Because the state, which was meant to be in charge of creating nations, was in reality a colonial state—the very antithesis of a national state.

When it came to the task of building African unity, the contradiction was even more blatant. First, independence meant attaining state sovereignty. Independence before unity meant recognising and reinforcing colonial boundaries. Ironically, the man who condemned colonial boundaries most was the same man who moved the motion on the sanctity of colonial boundaries at the 1964 (OAU) summit in Cairo. Even more ironically, it was the same man who recognised secessionist Biafra and marched into Uganda without regard to borders. That man was Mwalimu Nyerere. As intellectuals and historians, we may say it was ironic. But Mwalimu was not simply an intellectual. The king and the philosopher combined in him, and they could not always sit together comfortably.

So, ironic or not, he could not escape making pragmatic political decisions. Mwalimu cites two examples which made him move the resolution on boundaries. Just after independence, Hastings Kamuzu Banda of Malawi paid a visit to Mwalimu with some old book of maps. He tried to persuade Mwalimu that part of Mozambique belonged to Malawi and another part belonged to Tanganyika. Mwalimu, of course, was disgusted at this proposal of swallowing up Mozambique, just like that! Another example is that of Somalia publicly claiming the Ogaden province of

Ethiopia, while Ethiopia whispered that the whole of Somalia belonged to Ethiopia. To prevent border wars among Africans, Mwalimu moved his resolution on the inviolability of colonial boundaries. Man proposes, history disposes. With the benefit of hindsight, we now know that what Mwalimu feared came to pass, regardless of the resolution. The Ogaden war is still with us. History cannot be re-made, but it can be re-read and re-learnt.

Second in the way of unity were the vested interests of the political class. Unity meant dissolving, even if partially, the sovereignty of the newly independent states. This meant depriving the new political class, which had been landed with state power, of their power, privileges, and the accompanying possibilities of acquiring wealth. No wonder the new rulers of Africa were nervous and resistant to Nkrumah's call for African unity. Mwalimu alludes, with some amusement, to the situation of the African heads of state at the 1965 Accra summit, during which Nkrumah wanted to establish a union government. I cannot resist quoting him again (he was a captivating storyteller, and no one could tell stories of African heads of state as effectively as Mwalimu):

> Once you multiply national anthems, national flags and national passports, seats of the United Nations, and individuals entitled to a 21-gun salute, not to speak of a host of ministers, prime ministers, and envoys, you would have a whole army of powerful people with vested interests in keeping Africa balkanised. That was what Nkrumah encountered in 1965.
>
> After the failure to establish the union government at the Accra summit, I heard one head of state express with relief that he was happy to be returning home to his country still head of state. To this day, I cannot tell whether he was serious or joking. But he may well have been serious, because Kwame Nkrumah was very serious and the fear of a number of us to lose our precious status was quite palpable.

Forty years later, I believe, the state has become more than simply a site of accumulating power and privileges. It has become the site of accumulating wealth and capital. This class, which uses state positions to acquire wealth and accumulate property, is not a productive class. It does not accumulate and invest in production. It is an underdeveloped "middle-class", as Frantz Fanon described it on the eve of independence. As he said, it is a "little greedy caste, avid and voracious, with the mind of a huckster, only too glad to accept dividends that the former colonial power hands out to it" (Fanon, 1963, p. 175). In any case, the social character of the African state and its role in the process of worldwide capitalist accumulation is an issue which our research, analysis, and debates will have to address. Without understanding issues of state, class, and accumulation, we cannot identify and assess the agency of the Pan-Africanist struggle.

These are very general and broad strokes on the Pan-Africanist discourse of the first generation of African nationalists, as encapsulated in Mwalimu's thought. I have no doubt that the "mischievous" among you would want me to explore not only Mwalimu's thought but also his political practice as a Pan-Africanist, specifically in relation to the Zanzibar question. I will not oblige—not because time does not permit. That would be an intellectually lazy and dishonest excuse! I will not do so because I have done a book-length study on the union question (See Shivji, 2008).

Insurrection of Pan-Africanist Ideas

I believe Pan-Africanism is making a comeback. I believe African nationalism is at the crossroads. It can either degenerate into narrow chauvinistic nationalisms—ethnic, racial, cultural—or climb the continental heights of Pan-Africanism. Do not glorify the nation-state, Mwalimu admonished. Rise to the challenge of being Africans first and Africans last, rather than "fossilise Africa into the wounds inflicted upon it by the vultures of imperialism". We, as intellectuals, have to develop a new Pan-Africanist discourse. It will undoubtedly be a different discourse from the Pan-Africanist discourse of the first-generation nationalism. But I have no doubt in my mind that it will be a discourse of national liberation and anti-imperialism—the nation this time around being the African nation. The new Pan-Africanist discourse will have to take account of the failure of the national project and its implication for African nationalism. It will have to question the first-generation nationalism, which was essentially "state nationalism". It will need to investigate, examine, and evaluate the social character of the African state as well as its agency. Examining and analysing the neoliberal project in all of its guises, including the New Partnership for Africa's Development (NEPAD), will be necessary. It will have to investigate and reveal fresh instances of global hegemony and imperialism. It will need to accomplish a lot of tasks, all towards the one goal of emancipating the African people.

What is the role of an African intellectual in the development of a new Pan-Africanism? I do not have a complete answer. I hope that the work of the Mwalimu Nyerere chair will begin to give us some answers. Meanwhile, let me simply assert that we need a new nationalist insurrection—an insurrection of Pan-Africanist ideas in the era of globalisation. In his speech at the inauguration of Kenneth Kaunda as the Chancellor of the University of Zambia in 1966, Mwalimu agonised over "the dilemma of a Pan-Africanist" (Nyerere, 1968, pp. 2007-17). The dilemma that he was talking about was that of a Pan-Africanist state leader. On the one hand, his conviction and philosophy pull him to Pan-Africanism; on the other, as a head of state, he presides over building and nurturing "territorial nationalism".

Mwalimu could not resolve the dilemma, nor did he pretend to do so! Whatever the case, he said, "African unity does not have to be a dream; it can be a vision which inspires us". I agree. Pan-Africanism is beyond our control and exists solely in our subconscious if it is merely a fantasy. It is within the realm of possibility if it is a vision. It requires deliberate nurturing and effort on our part. It is up to us African intellectuals to instil Pan-Africanism in the collective consciousness of our people. Professor Souleymane Bachir Diagne, the chairman of CODESRIA's scientific committee, says we have to make Pan-Africanism a category of intellectual thought. The task of converting the Pan-Africanist vision into a category of intellectual thought squarely falls on the shoulders of African intellectuals. We do it by engaging critically with Pan-Africanist ideas; many ideas, varied ideas. Let us form Pan-African organisations and Pan-African movements—the Pan-African youth movement, the Pan-African student movement, the Pan-African women's movement, the Pan-African trade unions, and so on. This time around, we have to invert the relationship. Let us work from the civil society to the state. We have to work towards building an African civil society. From the vantage point of the African civil society, we have to cajole, persuade, pressurise, criticise, even satirise, the African state. Don't demonise the

State; de-legitimise it by engaging with it, not in it. That would be the beginning of building the hegemony of Pan-Africanism within African civil society. In short, let a hundred flowers of Pan-Africanist thought blossom.

"New Pan-Africanism must be anchored in democracy", says Thandika Mkandawire. "Africa needs some kind of social democracy", argued Archie Mafeje, whom we lost recently. On Mwalimu's seventy-fifth birthday, I argued that Africa needs a new democracy built around popular livelihoods, popular participation and popular power. But in this day and age of militarised hegemonies and despotic democracies, from Iraq to Somalia, we need to question the very concept of democracy. Where ideas are commodities, manufactured on order by ideas-traders, we need to return to the ideas of commitment and the commitment to the ideas of human emancipation. We need committed Pan-Africanist intellectuals. The question before us is: Who are we—Pan-Africanist intellectuals committed to African liberation and human emancipation, or neoliberal impostors serving "imperialist vultures"? In her poem, *Intellectuals and Impostors*, Micere Githae Mugo sings:

> Tell me
> tell me whether
> their theories are
> active volcanoes
> erupting with fertilizing lava
> on which to plant
> seeds that will
> cross-fertilize
> into collective being
>
> Knowledge became
> action theory
> Knowledge became
> living testimony
> of our people's
> affirmative history
> liberated herstory

Actioned theory

Inscribed as protest
Manifesto
Re-aligning our people's
averted humanity

Yes tell me this
and I will tell you
whether they are
intellectuals
or impostors.

References

Afari-Gyan, K. (1991). Kwame Nkrumah, George Padmore and W. E. B. Du Bois. *Research Review NS*, 7(1 & 2).

Fanon F. (1963) The Wretched of the Earth, New York: Grove Press. Available at https://monoskop.org/images/6/6b/Fanon_Frantz_The_Wretched_of_the_Earth_1963.pdf

Furedi, F. (1994). *The new ideology of imperialism*. London, UK: Pluto.

Grimshaw, A. (Ed.). (1992). *The C.L.R. James Reader*. Oxford: Blackwell.

Landsberg, C., & Kornegay, F. (1998). *The African Renaissance: A quest for Pax Africana and Pan-Africanism* (Foundation for Global Dialogue Occasional Paper, no. 17).

Legum, C. (1965). *Pan-Africanism: A short political guide* (Rev. ed.) London, UK: Pall Mall Press.

Legum, C., & Mmari, G. (Eds.). (1995). *Mwalimu: The influence of Nyerere*. Dar es Salaam, Tanzania: Mkuki na Nyota.

Luthuli, A., Kaunda, K., Chisiza, D. K., Mboya, T., & Nyerere, J. K. (1964). *Africa's freedom*. London, UK: Unwin Books.

Nkrumah, K. (1965). *Neo-colonialism, the last stage of imperialism*. London, UK: Heinemann.

Nnoli, O. (1985). External constraints of Pan-African economic integration. In W. A. Ndongko (Ed.), *Economic co-operation and integration in Africa* (pp. 125–152). Dakar, Senegal: CODESRIA.

Nyerere, J. K. (1967). *Freedom and unity: A selection from writings and speeches.* Dar es salaam, Tanzania: Oxford University Press.

Nyerere, J. K. (1968). *Freedom and socialism.* London, UK: Oxford University Press.

Nyerere, J. K. (1997). *Africa must unite.* Edited excerpts from a public lecture delivered in Accra to mark Ghana's fortieth Independence Day anniversary celebrations. Retrieved from http://www.unitednewafrica.com/Africa%20Unite.htm. Also in the New African, February 2006.

Nyerere, J. K., & Bunting, I. (1999, January–February). The heart of Africa: Interview with Julius Nyerere on anti-colonialism. *New Internationalist Magazine,* no. 309.

Nyong'o, P. A., Ghirmazion, A., & Lamba, D. (Eds.). (2002). *New partnership for Africa's development, NEPAD: A new path?* Nairobi, Kenya: Heinrich Boll Foundation.

Othman, H. (Ed.). (2000). *Reflections on leadership in Africa: Forty years after independence, essays in honour of Mwalimu Julius K. Nyerere, on the occasion of his 75th birthday.* Brussels, Belgium: VUB University Press.

Pannikar, K. M. (1961). *Revolution in Africa.* Mumbai, India: Asia Publishing House.

Sathyamurthy, T. V. (1981). Tanzania's non-aligned role on international relations. *India Quarterly.*

Sherwood, M. (1996). *Kwame Nkrumah: The years abroad, 1935-1947.* Legon, Ghana: Freedom Publications.

Shivji, I. G. (2005a). The rise, the fall and the insurrection of nationalism in Africa. In F. A. Yieke (Ed.), *East Africa: In search of national and regional renewal.* Dakar, Senegal: CODESRIA.

Shivji, I. G. (2005b). *Pan-Africanism or imperialism? Unity and struggle towards a new democratic Africa* (Bill Dudley Memorial Lecture Series No. 2). The Nigerian Political Science Association.

Shivji, I. G. (2008). *Pan-Africanism or pragmatism? Lessons of Tanganyika-Zanzibar Union.* Dar es Salaam, Tanzania: Mkuki na Nyota.

Shivji, Issa G., Saida Yahya-Othman & Ng'wanza Kamata, 2020, Development as Rebellion: the biography of Julius Nyerere, Dar es Salaam: Mkuku na Nyota.

Ghana (1957–1966): Reflections and Lessons From a Twentieth Century Pan-African Liberated Nation-State*

D. Zizwe Poe

Introduction

The inspiration for this paper comes from Kwame Nkrumah's brain-child, the All-African People's Revolutionary Party (Nkrumah, 1969) (A-APRP), and its commitment to creating the much-needed Pan-African Interdependence Movement *(PAIM)*[1]—a movement in which "liberated" African nation-states and "liberation organisations" collectively depend on each other to improve the lives of the African masses. The inspiration to write was rekindled after participating in the All-African Peoples' Conference at 60 (2018-AAPC1),[2] held in Accra, Ghana, and collaboratively sponsored by the Institute of African Studies, University of Ghana

---

* This chapter is a slightly edited version of an article first published in *Contemporary Journal of African Studies*, Vol. 10, No. 2 (2023) and is reproduced here with permission.

1 This term is a refinement of the popular term, "African unity movement". The PAIM embraces Nkrumah's announcement that Ghana's independence meant nothing if it was not connected to the total liberation of the African continent (Nkrumah, 1973, p. 121). Spokespersons of Pan-African Nationalism (Poe, 2015a) often indicated that African independence required the interdependence of African persons and people. See also the original mission and vision statement of the African Union Commission (2004, pp. 20–27).

2 The number "1" is attached to distinguish this conference from a second conference held in Accra, Ghana, of a similar name, sponsored by the Pan-African Federalist Movement.

at Legon; the Trades Union Congress (TUC) of Ghana; the Socialist Forum of Ghana (SFG); Third World Network-Africa; and Lincoln University, PA, USA. The conference was a 2018 commemoration of the 1958 All-African People's Conference (1958-AAPC1).

The 2018-AAPC1 reflected on contemporary issues that Africans are facing worldwide. Participation was multigenerational and attendees were from all geographical regions of the world. There were numerous formal and *ad hoc* discussions held over the unfinished goals of the 1958-AAPC. It was reaffirmed that a formidable PAIM is required for real African independence to successfully complete the decolonisation of Africa. Nkrumah (1969)[3] suggested the organisational form of this type of movement to be a committee of political coordination, aptly called the "All-African Committee for Political Co-ordination (AACPC)" (p. 58). His published theories on "positive action(s)", in relation to "liberated zones", and "optimal levels of Pan-African agency" undergird the concepts presented in this paper. Additionally, the study is supported by the author's Pan-African experiences and initiatives that span a period of 50 years, 25 of which have seen him participating in the political education institutions of the A-APRP. Given this background as context, the paper's content uses Nkrumah's strategic zonal analysis theory along with other pertinent statements about empowering the African masses from his co-president, Ahmed Sékou Touré (1922–1984).[4] The relationship between Nkrumah, as the head of state and Pan-Africanist liberation leader, and Touré, as the head of state and a sibling Pan-African liberation leader, accelerated a Pan-African thrust towards material support for continental decolonisation. This was an important lesson that ought to be included in all political science curriculum throughout African secondary educational institutions and higher. Nkrumah and Touré became an symbolic exemplars of what was possible between

---

3   The authoritative voice of Kwame Nkrumah is validated by his service as the founder and chairperson of the CPP; the founder of the A-APRP; first prime minister and president of Ghana (1957–1966); co-president of PALZ Guinea (1966–1972) with President Sekou Touré; African of the Millennium as voted by the British Broadcasting Company's African listenership.

4   Significant books of note, published by Republic of Guinea's state press, were *Strategy and Tactics of the Revolution* (1976); *United States of Africa* (1980); *Revolution, Culture, and Panafricanism* (1976); and *Enhancing the People's Power* (1983).

liberated nation-states and liberation parties. After the overthrow of the Convention People's Party (CPP), it was Guinea-Conakry, led by the Democratic Party of Guinea (PDG), that allowed and encouraged Co-President Nkrumah to continue collaborating with and advising liberation organisations such as the Partido Africano da Independencia da Guine e Cabo Verde (PAIGC), the Cuban Communist Party, along with the creation of the A-APRP. Some contemporary authors repeat the imperialist narrative that Nkrumah stopped working for the elimination of colonialism and neo-colonialism after being forced out of the presidency of Ghana by foreign sponsors and internal collaborators. These authors, who frequently serve as academicians promoting imperialist narratives through the official educational institutions that employ them, have not looked carefully at the strategy and tactics of the Pan-African revolution.

Sékou Touré's dialectical approach to culture, with his recognition of the tension between tradition and innovation, and his elucidation of the "People's Class", "Anti-People's Class", and the "Party-State" concepts added to the toolkit of liberation organisations concerned with consolidating victories against internal agents of recolonisation and neo-colonisation. Touré's (1978) book, *Strategy and Tactics of the Revolution* (pp. 183–199), is a classic addition to the scholarship on class struggle. The book titled, *Revolution, Culture, and Panafricanism* expounded that "Revolutionary Panafricanism having for fundamental reference Africa of Peoples must lean on Peoples in front of States" (Touré, 1976, p. 175). Even as Touré headed a nation-state, he clearly understood that the struggle for Pan-African unity had to be prosecuted by the collective agency of the mass population. In published texts of the le Parti Democratique de Guinée (PDG), class struggle is described as a battle between the People's class and the anti-People's class. This required a cultural revolution that was to be linked to an intellectual revolution. The members of the Pan-African Intelligentsia (PAI) were tasked with sparking the revolutionary mass consciousness needed to reignite mass movements for power and improvement. This was accomplished by academics and artists, and history has repeatedly demonstrated that merely controlling the state apparatus of a nation is insufficient to make fundamental changes on a global scale.

During the first ten years of independence, Pan-African liberation zones (PALZs) became more prevalent on the continent. The concept of "liberated zones" was introduced by Nkrumah (1969) in the *Handbook of Revolutionary Warfare: A Guide to the Armed Phase of the African Revolution*.[5] During this period, Ghana, Guinea-Conkary, and Tanzania (formerly known as Tanganyika) should all be considered liberated zones. Following its independence, Tanzania was considered a Pan-African liberated zone primarily due to the nation's internal and external Pan-African and decolonial policies.

Tanzania, under the leadership of Julius Nyerere's Tanganyika African National Union (TANU), later renamed the Chama Cha Mapenduzi (CCM), promoted the Ujamaa project which aimed to delink Tanzania from its former coloniser and position the Tanzanian people at the centre of their own liberation and development (Otunnu, 2015; Pallotti, 2009). Guinea-Conakry, under the leadership of Sékou Touré's PDG, can also be described as a liberated zone, particularly for their delinking from French political control and their Pan-African policies that aimed at liberating African People's class. Their role in the Guinea-Ghana-Mali union further indicates their liberated status. Ghana served as a PALZ that was central to the Pan-African movement between 1957 and 1966. Kwame Nkrumah's CPP declared Ghana as a PALZ after declaring that Ghana's independence was meaningless without the liberation of the rest of Africa. Ghana instituted Pan-African policies in its development plans, internal and external policies, and the nexus of this activity was the creation of the Bureau of African Affairs (Grilli, 2017).

Ghana, as a PALZ in the twentieth century, serves as an exemplar for institutions across Global Africa. However, non-state institutions

---

5   Kwame Nkrumah identified three zones in this text. The zones are described as follows: (*a*) liberated areas are zones organised by an anti-capitalist and radical political party. These political parties seek to decolonise the zone and extend the decolonisation across Africa; (*b*) zones under enemy control are zones that are heavily controlled by imperialists. These zones are economically and politically controlled by foreigners and/or puppet governments; and (*c*) contested zones are zones that are in transition and can be the staging group to organise liberation movements for a neighbouring country or to be transformed to liberated zones by liberation leaders (Nkrumah, 1969). The above-described zones were based in a war-like setting and as such some of the characteristics will change when transferring this analysis to different spaces.

can also incorporate the strategies employed by Ghana to develop liberated spaces inside or outside of neo-colonial states. Institutions of higher education in Global Africa are poised to become PALZ with a specific focus on those institutions located at historic sites of resistance, such as the Dar es Salaam School, the Dakar School, and the Institute of African Studies of the University of Ghana. Nkrumahist and People's class-oriented curricula development is one of the first steps towards the creation of PALZs

This paper intends to engage Kwame Nkrumah's zonal analysis and the exemplar of Ghana under the leadership of the CPP as a model for institutions of higher education in Global Africa. These institutions could provide better assistance to the Pan-African movement if they were indeed liberated spaces promoting Pan-African agency, in conversation with Pan-Africanist organisations concerned with Africa's liberation and unification. However, most institutions of higher education in these spaces embrace and model Eurocentric education in their features and curriculum. In order to properly situate Global African institutions of higher education, it is important to develop liberatory language that can guide the assessment of existing institutions and organisations that are yet to be developed. The use of liberatory language is needed to appreciate what Ghana became from the mid-1950s through the mid-1960s and is paramount to extracting the lessons of Ghana for contemporary Pan-African application. A language that has restored agency[6] will enable learners and educators to understand the magnitude of the Pan-African initiatives launched (Masaka, 2021; wa Thiong'o, 2018). The new terminology introduced contributes to scholarship that challenges Eurocentric ways of knowing, explaining, and interpreting.

Transforming terminology to embrace a liberatory approach to education is at the heart of restoring agency to Global Africa. Colonial and neo-colonial mentalities, paradigms, and assumptions are recipes for making unsuspecting subjects colonial slaves again. These mental frameworks, therefore, must be mitigated until they can be avoided and replaced. The liberating terminology recommended in this paper

---

6 Restored agency in this context speaks to the presentation of the Pan-African personality as a key enriching factor of liberation education.

seeks to reduce the debilitating effects of the colonial mentality embedded in the social climates and curricula of today's colonised and neocolonised institutions. "Global Africans" is a popular term used in the report from the 2018-AAPC1 (Organising Committee of the 60th Anniversary Commemoration of the All-African Peoples' Conference, 2019), contributing to the expansion of Pan-Africanists' identity. The following new terms are used in this paper: "African ascendants", "Pan-African Interdependence Movement (PAIM)", "Communal Nations", "Pan-African Liberated Zone (PALZ)", "Pan-African Personality", "Pan-African Intelligentsia (PAI)", "The People's class", "African Unity Movement (AUM)", and the "Pan-African Nationalist Movement (PANM)". These terms will be defined in detail to provide an epistemological grounding to examine Ghana during the tenure of the study and to transpose the definitions to research on Pan-Africanism.

Separate from the introduction and conclusion, this paper is divided into four equally important sections. The first section addresses needed Pan-African epistemological concepts. The next section addresses the relationship between Pan-Africanism and class struggle. The second to last section engages with reflections and some lessons on PALZs and the next steps to consider in building liberated spaces. Finally, the last substantive section recommends a criterion for an applied zonal analysis for Institutions of Higher Education in the following zones: (*a*) retarding zone—anti-African academic space; (*b*) contested zone—multinational-centred space; (*c*) forwarding zone—African liberated space; and (*d*) optimal zone—space in support of Pan-African unity; this is followed by a conclusion.

Pan-African Epistemological Concepts

This section will introduce the reader to Pan-African terms that have been introduced by the author. These terms are not widely used or are new to the discourse on Pan-African epistemology. Research and discussion about the Pan-African movement are often rooted in an epistemologically Eurocentric view of Africa. The Pan-African movement has given rise to the "African ascendant". This is an individual or organisation that identifies ideologically and programmatically with the political choice to commit one's life to the achievement of Pan-African power for the African People's class. This identity indicates an affinity for Pan-African nationalism (Poe, 2015b). African ascendancy is an active identity adding purpose to the life of the claimant. This concept is derived from the realisation that identities are dialectical, indicating not only one's place of origin but also one's destination of commitment. The term "African descendant" describes a person or a collective agent that has African ancestry or African origin. It is a passive term that tells little about the entity claiming it. The term reveals little information about political leanings or national allegiance. The term "African ascendant" has a greater potential for energising African agency than a passive descriptor. The need for a movement for Pan-African interdependence today is a requirement for African independence on a macrolevel. "Independent" micro-nations that exist on the African continent are losing their gained independence to neocolonial forces by not being able to protect their economies or their populations (Rahaman, Yeazdani, & Mahmud, 2017).

Now, more than at any time in the recent past, the clarion call for the PAIM must be mobilised to push the continental African nation-state into functional operations. The PAIM, a natural development of the African Unity and African Liberation movements (ALMs), includes the collection of African organisations and key personnel who worked together to bring a cessation to European classical colonialism in Africa. Tactical unity within the movement existed on the ideas of socialism and unity. Only those territories and organisations that favoured the option of socialism and unity should be seen as Pan-African nationalists and should more appropriately be recognised as the PAIM, a distinct Pan-African nationalist subset of the ALM (Nkrumah, 1969).

Authoritative organisations of the collective agency have far too often been pejoratively classified as "tribes" and their leadership structures as "chieftaincies" by most Eurocentric literature attempting to categorise Africa's social order. This is terminology that obscures the existence of the myriad of "communal nations" that have existed on the African continent along with their governing nation-states that they gave rise to. The centralised Nile Valley government of Kemet (KMt), now called ancient Egypt, reveals the debilitating lens of colonial nomenclature. KMt, if properly understood as a unitary organisation of 44 communal nations connected naturally through the shared cultural experience of managing the Nile flood, would add heft to the historic record of African governance (King, 2015). The point is that the existence of African nations did not begin in the twentieth century. In fact, there were numerous communal nations and confederations that fought against foreign encroachments and occasionally against each other (Shillington, 2019).

There were, and continue to be, multiple communities across Ghana many of which should be recognised as communal nations according to their population sizes, geographic expanse, and influential political-economic resources (Izuagie & Sado, 2015). Historically, each of the communal nations had distinguishing customs, traditions, and local authoritative organisations. Occasionally, these communal entities would be organised into broader federations and empires. Structural rigidity was often the approach of tradition, but fluidity became a cultural/social technique when confronting natural and social obstacles threatening the healthy living of community members (Shillington, 2019).

Academically trained historians tend to illuminate commercial empires or military empires when surveying the nation-state developments that arose in West Africa. Nevertheless, diverse organisational models in this part of Africa shared a similar goal, i.e. to improve the members' lives within their communal nations. These communal nations had people in powerful positions as monarchs and/or presidents and other titular executives of their own that Eurocentric academies and other imperial agents have categorised as "chiefs". For centuries and millennia, these communal nations of various sizes collaborated with each other. They united into federations or general unions covering large geographic areas, and at times, formed small groups that anthropologists would later refer to as clans.

The 1958 All-African People's Conference

Nkrumah (1969), the founder of both the CPP and the A-APRP, wrote his book titled, *Handbook of Revolutionary Warfare* from his PALZ base in Guinea-Conakry while serving as its co-president. In that book, he identified three zones, as noted earlier, namely: (*a*) liberated areas; (*b*) zones under enemy control; and (*c*) contested zones (i.e. hot points) (p.

43). Nkrumah's zonal analysis included a historical and contemporary (at the time) perspective of geopolitics and the state of African people world-wide. Embedded in the ideas and writings of Nkrumah, one can find the African personality which is closely related to the zonal analysis. The Pan-African personality, which at minimum assumes the identification of Africa as a homeland for people of African descent globally, was a central component of the class struggle in Ghana and Guinea (Poe, 2015a).

The Pan-African personality looks not only in the traditions of culture but actively employs a forward-looking vision of uniting Africa into a powerful continent-wide nation that will help to improve the human condition. Contemporary struggles against xenophobia among various African collectives have shown that the broader African personality does not exclude such relationships (Asuelime, Okem, & Asuelime, 2015). The Pan-African personality assumes a composite culture and Pan-African identity. It seeks the African personality in its global redemptive manifestation. Historically rooted in the millennia of social evolution, the Pan-African personality is enriched with the refinement of African cultural innovations created outside of Africa to ensure the well-being of "All-Africans", not merely the residential inhabitants of the African continent nor limited to the inhabitants of the Africans outside of the African homeland (Dei, 2012). Projecting the identifying elements of the Pan-African personality, as distinctly narrower than the African personality, is a contemporary exigency of the PAI, as identity debates are primarily within the purview of that sector of African society.

The PAI is distinct from the African intelligentsia because of its focus on devoting its resources towards the establishment of continental Pan-African institutions and a continental nation-state in the service of the African People's class (Mkhwanazi, 2017). In this regard, the PAI uses its access to vetted information sources and related resources to update and apply Nkrumah's zonal analysis to the living spaces that Africans inhabit. Additionally, the PAI should develop strategies to impact all institutions they influence in the interest of humanity, especially those of the African masses. In short, those members of the PAI are duty-bound to assist in the victory of the People's class by assisting in the Pan-African revolution.

For Pan-Africanists, it is clear that continental development requires continental unity. This assumption requires a brief introduction to those not familiar with the "People's class" concept, a term made popular through the African liberation experience. Osagyefo Dr Kwame Nkrumah (1909–1972), founder of the CPP, summarised this concept and declared the CPP as a mass-based political party. He defined classes succinctly in his book titled, *Class Struggle in Africa* (1970) by stating:

> For in the final analysis, a class is nothing more than the sum total of individuals bound together by certain interests which as a class they try to preserve and protect.
>
> Every form of political power, whether parliamentary multiparty, one-party or open military dictatorship, reflects the interest of a certain class or classes in society. (pp. 17–18)

The straitjacket of Marxist dogmatists, who provided excellent details of class evolutions in European history but failed to grasp the peculiarities of the economic and political class formations within African historical evolution, and therefore, too often, have ignored the class struggle concepts in Nkrumah's works. Nkrumah did, however, acknowledge the inevitability of class struggle (Nkrumah, 1970b). The concept of the class embodied by the African masses was further clarified by Ahmed Sékou Touré the leader of PDG, the CPP's sibling organisation. In Touré's (1978) book titled, *Strategy and Tactics of the Revolution*, he stated:

> The most reliable, the infallible operational bases of the Revolution remain the masses, the exploited classes, the disinherited who are working, toiling and hoping. It is those of the **People's class** [emphasis mine] who have acquired through class struggles, an acute class awareness. That is why, it is always advisable, in analysing [*sic*] the revolutionary process, to define clearly the dynamic contour of the classes that are truly apt to undertake, pursue and continuously radicalize the Revolution. At this level, an error of appreciation may be fatal to the revolutionary movement. (p. 307)

At first glance, the "People's class" may seem like an alternative title for "the masses" but the class designation reminds one of the class interests that animates the purposeful agency of the masses. The People's class is a wilful entity that is in opposition to the anti-People's class, which is described by both Nkrumah and Touré as those actors blocking the socialist development of the masses and promoting the interest of imperialism. Classes compete for the control of nation-states and related institutions of power. This is precisely what makes the concept of the People's class germane to this narrative.

The AUM and PANM are monikers for that association of African agents committed to the rapid evolution and revolution of a continent-wide autochthonous government and cultural institutions. These continental nationalists are to be distinguished from regionalists and micro-nationalists opposed to a politically organised African continental nation as a minimum requirement to ensure decolonisation (Nkrumah, 1970). The ALM was subsumed for a while under the oversight of the Organisation of African Unity (OAU). With the refurbishing and resurrection of an African Union (AU), the PANM was brought into clearer focus and distinguished from African liberators that sought irredentists or nationalisms wedded to colonial borders. In this work, the PANM speaks to those who promoted the establishment of Africa as one nation under scientific socialism similar to Nkrumah's (1969) description of Pan-Africanism. The AUM was a broader movement that included the PANM and federalists ranging from those in favour of a centralised union to those that would rather have loosely federated forms of continental unity not subject to a central authority.

Some of the participants of the Casablanca Group were a part of this movement for a union, while the latter group formed the Monrovia Group (Thompson, 1969). One distinguishing factor between these collectives was the concept of sovereignty. The Casablanca Group sought the sovereignty of the African masses, while the Monrovia Group considered the sovereignty of the national borders they inherited from the colonial experience as sacred (Ifidon, 2011; Poe, 2005). The explanation of these terms was extensive but necessary. Without the use of these terms, certain important lessons for establishing a liberated territory committed to Pan-Africanism might escape an activist/scholar.

Nkrumah's territorial analysis was written while the African liberation struggle was being assessed by using "units of measure" comprising geopolitical territories and the human inhabitants transforming the social relations within those territories.[7] The philosophic formula that undergirded the transformation was graphically presented in the last chapter of Nkrumah's (1964) book *Consciencism: Philosophy and Ideology for De-colonization*. The PALZ qualifies the positive action by including the trajectory of Pan-African Nationalism and policies consistent with the achievement of the African Interdependence Movement (AIM). Liberated territories described in the book, *Consciencism: Philosophy and Ideology for Decolonization*, are summed up in the *Encyclopedia of Black Studies* as follows:

1. Revolutionary African ideology requires the positive synthesis of the traditional African base culture with the Islamic and Euro-Christian impact.
2. When a foreign philosophy is studied, it should be seen in the context of the intellectual history to which it belongs and the context of the milieu in which it was born.
3. Most African traditional societies see humans as essentially spiritual beings.
4. Positive action leads to liberated territories while negative action supports various forms of foreign domination.
5. In order for a country to apply socialism, it must be liberated, be unified, and embrace philosophical materialism. It also needs a philosophical consciencism to hold to its general nature while allowing for its individuality in the family of nations. It does this through its response to the material conditions of the territory, its generation of dialectical moments, and its employment of "positive action" through a mass party. (Poe, 2005, p. 197)

---

7 It is important to note, at this point in the paper, that Nkrumah's presentation of zones was written as a description of social spaces under conflict with oppressive and exploitative organisations of tyrannical hegemony. In fact, it is clearly war terminology. Nkrumah wrote while attempting to liberate and defend a national territory and the institutions within it. This paper will apply this warrior approach specifically to educational institutions that the PAI inhabit.

The above criteria are compiled primarily from Nkrumah's (1969) *Handbook of Revolutionary Warfare* but include a few salient points from Touré's (1980) *United States of Africa*. Touré's points are important because of his hindsight as leader of the PDG and as a witness to the weaknesses of the African nation-states that comprised the OAU. The PDG's organisation of the party-state of Guinea, as a PALZ, lasted for 18 years beyond the termination of the CPP's control of the Ghanaian PALZ. After the 1984 death of Sékou Touré, the PDG was ousted through a military seizure of the government in the same manner the CPP had been, by some of the same imperialist collaborators.

Nkrumah's (1969) *Handbook of Revolutionary Warfare: A Guide to the Armed Phase of the African Revolution* was published while he served as the co-president of Guinea-Conakry. In that book, he openly spoke about his preferred Pan-African nationalism, rather than the limitations of his Ghanaian micro-national identity. He saw the more limited identity as an insufficient anachronism for the final development of the African masses. Sékou Touré, one of the kindred spirits of the Ghanaian PALZ and a co-founder of the Union of African States (UAS), would increasingly agree as evidenced in the publications of the PDG. Two books specifically address these themes: *Revolution, Culture, and Panafricanism* (1976) and the *United States of Africa* (1980).

Reflections and Some Lessons on Pan-African Liberated Zones

PALZs had minimal requirements to be considered as such. PALZs, at the time of the CPP rule in Ghana, were expected to support all ALMs and sibling organisations fighting against imperialism and for Pan-African unity. They were also expected to support revolutionary liberation movements in contested and enemy-held zones of Africa. In addition, the CPP constructed organic linkages and liaisons that focused on political and economic lives with the other liberated zones of the African nation.[8] To perform the above expectations, the PALZ must continuously bring

---

8 African nation refers to the global African nation. It does not presuppose that Africa is one
   country or that there is no diversity in Global Africa. It is a political designation signifying
   the unity of African people globally and the power that will ensure with this unity.

in objective and up-to-date analyses of both popular progress of mass empowerment and alternatively of enemy aggression. The Bureau of African Affairs took on this task as the foundation for Ghana's Pan-African liberated research (Ahlman, 2012). PALZs, by definition, are not expected to be passive or neutral in the face of regressive challenges. They take sides and take action to recapture territories and other zones lost to the enemy and rectify mistakes that enabled enemy victories such as any renewed form of colonialism or other forms of oppression. "The main criterion for judging liberated zones is the actual direction in which they are moving since our assessment is of changing and not static phenomenon" (Nkrumah, 1969, p. 48).

Touré (1980) wrote in his book, *United States of Africa*, that a liberated society (zone) was one that practised national unity in the support of the working masses. The governing organisation had to work with weak members of the society and develop a strong cadre to become the destroyers of imperialism. Such a society had to ensure that power was placed in the hands of the People's class and that power would grow proportionately as the members of that class mastered politics, science, techniques, and technology to ensure that the masses were no longer manipulated by so-called smart persons and elite cliques. Finally, as an organisational tool of mass governance, similar to the PDG's local revolutionary authorities, pouvoir révolutionnaire local (PRLs) were established throughout the liberated zone at various territorial levels (Touré, 1978).

The PRLs were essentially the local manifestation of the PDG. Guinea was not the only PALZ to implement such an organisation of the masses. During its time as a PALZ, the Libyan Jamahiriya followed the edicts of *The Green Book* (Al-Gaddafi, 2016), which described a similar organisation of "direct democracy", to consolidate the organisation of mass governance at various levels throughout the nation-state. Other revolutionary organisations in Algeria, Guinea, Bissau, especially those that had to use armed struggle to liberate territories, relied on mass mobilisation which was best done through mass organisation. The CPP learned these requirements and expectations early on in their rise to political success, which is described further in the next section of this paper.

Ghana, the Vital Nexus, and the Pan-Africanist Victory

When Ghana became a PALZ in 1957, it unveiled a powerful collab-oration of social movements that overcame a colonial administration, organised a mass-based nation-state, and launched the ALM. There were territories in Africa, prior to 1957, that had won political independence from imperial overlords, and many more would follow in the decade of the 1960s, yet only a few made the same significant impact on Africa's ending of "classical colonialism" as the Ghanian PALZ. The abnormal establishment of a PALZ was at least a decade in the works prior to the official 1957 date (Allman, 2008).

The nexus of African social movements that led to Ghana's PALZ status shared a common cause: to transform the relationship of African nation-states with each other and with the rest of the world. This paper provides a brief overview of three significant African collective agencies: communal nations in the Gold Coast colony; African ascendants in the Pan-Africanist movement; and budding African liberation organisations. This served as the essential component of the nexus, content, and agency of the collective movement. What follows is the context of the imperial-ist internal rupture.

The catastrophic death and destruction of capital that appear to be endemic to competitive capitalist relations destabilised the colonial metropolises of Europe from 1914 through 1949. The disorder caused by the warring governments revealed the societal frailty of the empire which had propagated itself as the citadel of civilization. During the same period, two gigantic socialist nation-states emerged as rising options to the capitalist powers in global international relations.

Africans, at home and abroad (in Africa and elsewhere), were active participants in the shaping of this global context. Imperial destabilisation provided opportunities for liberation activities to mature in a variety of African collective agencies (Bush, 2011). It was the nexus of organised activity among these collective agencies which sped the rupture in the capitalist world order and allowed the world a preview of a PALZ. That PALZ would eventually come to control the hearts and minds of mil-lions along with the economic reserves of a former prosperous colony. Each of the collective agents that comprised the nexus was rewarded with significant, albeit brief, victories. Each is briefly reviewed along with their role in establishing the premiere Pan-African victory. Who specifically were those critical African social movements that collaborated and gained control of the resources of an ex-colonial nation-state? They were the communal nations of the Gold Coast Colony, the Pan-African ascendants abroad, and the ALM (Botchway, 2018). Each social movement sought an end to the exploitative and oppressive relationship between European colonial imperialism and Africa. They agreed on what they were against but not necessarily on what they were for. The CPP discovered this in the process of organising the communal nations in the Gold Coast Colony.

The push for the liberation of various African territories is as old as the colonisation of African persons and African communal nations. Movements that established communal "maroon" nations and "quilombo nations" along with colonial resistance movements on the African continent were the predecessors of entities like the Universal Negro Improvement Association and African Community Leagues (UNIA-ACL) as well as the Pan-African Conference and Congress movements (Whitfield, 2018).

The 1945 Pan-African Congress meeting held in Manchester, England, gave another impetus to the ALM with a specific plan for Africans abroad to return to their home territories to liberate them while uniting the liberation organisations and movements (Nkrumah, 1973; Sherwood, 2012). Upon the victory of the CPP's control of the nation-state of Ghana, resources were immediately deployed to serve other liberation organisations. These actions sped up the political decolonisation of African territories (or so it seemed).

When used by the CPP, the term "All-African" was essentially interchangeable with "Pan-African". Neither term was an adjective describing geographical spaces. Both phrases are nominal terms of socio-cultural movements concerned with "optimal" African agency. Both phrases also signified the Pan-African movement's entry into the competitive formal arena of nation-state politics in the African homeland during the colonial-era. The 1958 AAPC was a conference committed to advancing the Pan-African revolution along with a four-stage strategy (Campbell, 1996; Grilli, 2018).

Each of the Gold Coast-controlled communal nations had a history of interrelationships, and the CPP understood that bringing the masses together under a new collective nationalistic identity required a proliferation of its organisational work to transform the variety of micronationalist identities into the collective identity of the new nation of Ghana.

Even prior to independence, the CPP started using state offices to improve the lives of Ghanaian residents by qualifying their education and skill levels (Frehiwot, 2015). The transformation of the CPP from a vanguard party to a mass party took place during the implementation of its positive action campaign, which required the participation of most segments of society in the Gold Coast colony (Mensah, 2016). The campaign became a movement that politically empowered the CPP and enabled the party to rapidly seize control of the colony's internal governance until complete control of the nation-state was achieved. All of this happened in less than a decade. True to the CPP's pledge and plans, the masses were immediately gifted with initiatives to improve the economic and cultural well-being of all living within the former colony.

Halfway through the twentieth century, the one-year-old CPP experienced a nexus of historic opportunities which it took advantage of to initiate a "beachhead" of Pan-African unity and support for the ALM. The CPP was launched in 1949 and was a child of the Pan-African movement and the youth wing of the United Gold Coast Convention (UGCC) (Thompson, 2015). The nationalistic enthusiasm of that youth wing along with the militant consciousness that was rising among soldiers, trade union workers, farmers, and market women in the Gold Coast colony forced Kwame Nkrumah, then the secretary of the UGCC, to resign from that organisation to lead the transformation of the Convention Youth Organisation of the UGCC into a political party seeking immediate liberation from British colonial control.

The protracted wars between competing European empires weakened the Gold Coast colony's zone of governance. By 1945, there was a different attitude towards the colonial masters amongst the colonial subjects. Challenges to alien economic and political control were growing from different segments of African communities, including trade unions, market associations, students, and professionals. Even lawyers and traditional leaders were resisting against colonial domination. A sense of militancy had risen for the soldiers who fought in the European wars that were supposed to end fascist rule, only to return to places where their families were still victims of colonial fascism. The militant attitude of righteousness came along with the realisation that the colonial powers were fallible. This shifted the psychological balance in the Gold Coast colony such that Ghana was emerging on the horizon. The veterans' battle experiences taught them that colonists could be hurt and, if necessary, killed.

The Gold Coast intelligentsia and professionals of privilege could not see the raging hurricane on the horizon that would turn the zone of governance into an intensified "hotly" contested zone. Proclamations and declarations to the colonial metropoles were no longer satisfactory means of protest. Liberty was no longer limited to legal battles among lawyers and the colonial apparatus.

The uniting of the rebellious spirit of the masses into a unified liberation movement awaited the rise of the CPP into a mass party. "Freedom Now" became the demand of the powerful CPP and all its affiliates. The goal of the CPP was to liberate the Africans in Africa generally and in West Africa particularly (Mensah, 2007). Their task was never to provide liberty just for Africans living in the Gold Coast colony. In order to do this, the Gold Coast colony had to be liberated from the British Empire and rebuilt according to the ideals of the Pan-African personality.

The CPP organised a plenum of social forces in the Gold Coast colony to mould them into an effective national union able to defeat the British colonial project. The British Empire refused to consider the demands of the CPP (White, 2003). In response, the CPP launched the weapon of "non-violent" non-cooperation. The so-called Positive Action campaign was an unavoidably violent campaign in the sense that the CPP threatened to use it as a weapon to encourage the working population of the Gold Coast colony to withhold labour from employers and to boycott goods (Nimako, 2010). The CPP's leadership spoke of positive action as a moral alternative to armed struggle. To the imperial order, this was a violent ultimatum that the colonial subjects had no right to demand.

Pan-African Intelligentsia

Another special ingredient was added to the activity and ideology of the CPP. That ingredient was the PAI, a growing contingent of "African ascendants" from the European portion of the Asian continent and the Americas. PAI special forces shared a uniform idea of making the new Ghana the base of a Pan-African-inspired liberation movement that would work to liberate the entire mother continent (Frehiwot, 2015). These special forces included Pan-Africanist personalities and their organisations committed to the Pan-African movement during this period. The PAI in Ghana at the time embraced the idea from that point forward that:

1. Pan-African evolution of the African political and social order has a protracted rhythm with ebbs and flows.
2. Pan-Africanism required the revolutionary modification of national boundaries from the colonial ones that limited the agency of the African masses.
3. Pan-Africanism advocated that the African continent was the ideal geographic homeland for the African nation.

The new nation of Ghana ushered in a period when the CPP and the PAI established a symbiotic relationship that would enhance the ALM (Gyamfi, 2021). The powerful relationship between these two entities was not an accident. In fact, it was called for by the 1945 Pan-African Congress meeting held in Manchester, England, when African ascendants met to plan a future strategy of African decolonisation. That meeting was a nexus of Pan-Africanists from various countries across four continents. It was also a nexus of the Universal Negro Improvement Association and African Communities League (UNIA-ACL), the Garvey movement, and the Pan-African Congress movement, often attributed to W. E. B. DuBois' inspiration (Fergus, 2010). The real inspiration behind both historic movements was the committed multitude of the cadre that was organised for mass African empowerment. As in the case of the CPP, it is important to emphasise that there was a long list of women and men that made up the PAI from all over the world (Allman, 2013). The success of the CPP's organisation of the Ghanaian masses now gave the PAI the tool of a nation-state in the African motherland with ample resources to electrify the liberation movements throughout the African continent. Securing the Ghanaian masses was the first strategic step.

The CPP were exemplars of the Pan-African personality, which linked Ghana's nationalism to the PANM. Several of the CPP leaders studied and made connections with the Pan-African movement in Europe and the USA. Nkrumah was admittedly the most notable articulator of the CPP ideology and that of the PANM. There were, however, other CPP leaders who maintained interdependent relationships with both the PAI and international workers employed in shipping and related types of mobile employment in Europe and the Americas, as well as with Africans from all parts of Africa (Padmore, 1953).

General plans were made by these Africans to unite and liberate various home territories prior to the formation of the CPP. Proposals were launched among participants of the 1945 Pan-African Congress along with organisations such as the African Student Association of North America, the West African Student Union, the West African National Secretariat, and the Circle (Nkrumah, 1973; Sherwood, 1996). The Gold Coast colony would soon become the outstanding praxis of these proposals.

The CPP used political education and propaganda as weapons to etch awareness of the Pan-African agency on another level with the December 1958 All-African People's Conference. Sixty-two liberation organisations attended with invited observers interested in the furtherance of the Pan-African revolution. The amazing thing about this conference was that it formally launched the ALM and activated a formal organisational base in the PALZ of Ghana. Both activities as well as their follow-up actions impregnated the Ghanaian social environment with a sense of continental leadership.

The overwhelming majority of Ghanaians, for the time in which they accepted CPP leadership, merged their nationalist interest with that of

Pan-African nationalism. Ghanaian nationalism was the progeny of Pan-African nationalism for the former without the latter was fragile and prone to fissures from retrograde irredentist identities.

Lessons From the Pan-African Liberated Zone

There are several very important lessons to learn from the era of twentieth-century PALZs, especially from the Ghanaian nation-state from 1957 to 1966. The first and maybe the most important of these lessons is that PALZs must immediately commit to building additional PALZs as soon as possible. It was because of this awareness that Kwame Nkrumah, the leader of the CPP, was able to survive the 1966 coup d'état of Ghana. Nkrumah was immediately accorded respect and acknowledged as a co-president of the Guinean nation-state by the PDG of Guinea (Conakry) PALZ. In this role, Nkrumah remained tasked to continue supporting other liberation organisations and leaders. These were important years for the CPP founder as he was able to produce and publish works that allowed him to share his experiences with future liberation organisations and budding nation-states. During this time, he was also able to set the groundwork for his second political party: the A-APRP.

The task of this second political party launched by Nkrumah was not designed to run for any nation-state office on the African continent but was to be a propaganda organisation that would qualify the ALM by uniting the African liberation organisations into two formations: one called the All-African Committee for Political Coordination (AACPC) and the other called the All-African People's Revolutionary Army (AAPRA) to unite the fighting forces against imperialism and their African collaborators. His entire plan was sketched out in his book titled *Handbook of Revolutionary Warfare* published in 1969. This book should be considered a required reading for all PALZs and PALZ architects.

Another lesson that should become painfully clear is that imperialism will resort to assassinating the leadership of PALZs. Those assassinations are usually physical but are sometimes imagined. Physical assassination is easy to understand but imagined assassinations are equally effective as they attempt to remove the voices of the liberation leaders from the ears of the masses. Physical assassinations, like that of Patrice Lumumba or Thomas Sankara, turn the assassinated leaders into martyrs immediately.

Assassinations of imagination delay martyrdom and are equally effective as a damper on activity, if not more so, than physical assassination. Consider the propaganda of the imperialist forces after Nkrumah relocated to Guinea (Conakry). Western media news agencies broadcasted that Nkrumah was spending his final years in exile. Even now, some well-respected African history scholars make that claim. This was a propaganda theme that was used to disparage the PANM and the ALM.

That lesson helps us to recognise that the first stages of liberation involve a war of propaganda and education. The military component of liberation wars is secondary. The goal of these types of wars is the acquisition of the hearts and minds of the masses. This is what the PALZs, the colonial and neo-colonial zones (enemy-held zones), compete for. The task of the PAI is made ever clearer with the realisation that territory is only one realm of the zones to be liberated. The educational zones, especially the institutions of higher education, remain battlefields that influence upcoming generations, and for that reason, the intelligentsia is duty-bound to apply zonal analysis to the environments in which they operate.

Currently, the PAI, at a minimum, should use its access to information and related resources to update and apply Nkrumah's zonal analysis to the living spaces in which they inhabit. If at all possible, a strategy should be developed to impact all institutions they influence in the interest of the African masses and humanity in general. In short, those members of the PAI are duty-bound to assist in the victory of the People's class by assisting in the Pan-African revolution.

What follows is an applied zonal analysis designed for institutions where Africans and the PAI find themselves. This rubric will help organisers to assess which academic institutions engender, develop, and fortify optimal Pan-African agency, or which academic institutions neuter, maldevelop, and make self-destructive African agency. The utility of these organised institutions spans a "goal-affirmation" range. The categorical names within the range are inspired by Nkrumah's (1969) zonal analysis. They include the terms from the *Handbook* but are adjusted to the specific context of the intelligentsia. As such, three additional zones are added to the tool kit of the PAI's social environment assessment: (*a*) optimal zone, (*b*) forwarding zone, and (*c*) retarding zone.

The utility of these zonal indicators is that they clarify parameters and offer recommendations to create safe and nurturing spaces for the PAI in educational institutions. This is done by identifying the following parameters:

- Available institutional supporters of Pan-African agencies at all levels
- Educational institutions that celebrate Africanity
- Educational institutions that contribute to the African Renaissance
- Educational institutions that uphold and advocate the principles of Maat.

Retarding Zone: Anti-African Academic Space

- Administrative sponsorship of xenophobic (especially Anti-Pan-African) activity
- No institutional resources for instruction on Pan-African agency
- Lethargic students and faculty around the world and African affairs
- An area where there is an allowance for anti-African pedagogy and curriculum
- Sustained absence of African presence in the faculty, administration, and student body
- Placement of openly racist and/or imperialist personnel in prominent positions.

Contested Zone: Multinational-Centred Zone

- Encouragement of multi-cultural education
- Growing diversity in a previously European social environment
- Diversity of culture-based patriotisms
- Administrative sponsorship of multicultural activity inclusive of Africanisms
- Balanced allocation of resources reflecting multicultural "parity" approach
- Debate of students and faculty concerning social, political, and economic *status quo.*

Forwarding Zone: African Liberation Zone
- Celebrates diversity without coercion
- Growing presence of pro-African and indigenous personnel
- Abandonment of imperialist patriotism
- Administrative sponsorship of research in 'traditional' African cultures and communal nations
- Allocation of resources in a (non-Eurocentric) fair and transparent contest
- Debate among students and faculty around the direction of the campus in terms of national policy, especially towards Africa.

Optimal Zone: Zone in Support of Pan-African Unity
- Supports the transmission of Maatian ethics and the "African aesthetic"
- Growing indigenisation and Pan-Africanisation
- Support for Pan-African and anti-imperial patriotism
- Administrative sponsorship of multicultural activity inclusive of Pan-Africanism
- Allocation of resources for African nation-building
- Debate among students and faculty concerning Pan-African Nationalism.

Finally, the contemporary thought that the military and the police should stay out of politics does not work for PALZs. Rather, the ideological training of the military and the police is a requirement to sustain their cooperation with liberation work. During the current era of neo-colonialism in Africa, only the ideologically trained armed forces will defeat the zombies of colonialism and neocolonialism. They must have a working knowledge of the political line asserted by the liberating organisation and the goals of the revolution. This knowledge must not depend on the dictates of the so-called superior officers. They must remain true to the hopes and aspirations of the masses. In fact, in finality, they must be the same as the masses with whom they will remain loyal. This is the required vaccine against the spike in neo-colonial, retrogressive, coup d'états.

Conclusion

The most powerful Pan-African agential form in the post-WW2 era was the Pan-African liberated nation-state. Ghana, the penultimate leader in the PALZ formations, and as Malcolm X accurately declared, it became "the fountainhead of Pan-Africanism" (Breitman, 1965), and it led the way to the creation of the UAS. The UAS, as the initiating core of the liberated African territories, was dedicated to the immediate establishment of a Pan-African nation-state that would be the central organising force of a continental-wide African government.

Cognisant of the fact that liberated zones are achievable at various levels, this paper has stressed the need for more PALZs to be created. The paper calls for consistent "zonal" assessments of these institutions, categorised within a range of 'liberatory' to 'enemy-held' institutions for the Pan-African personality and Pan-African Nationalism. The ideal institution will be moving in the direction of the liberated zone. The identification of higher education institutions supporting Pan-Africanism will help with the fortification of the PAI, an exigency for the successful prosecution of the All-African People's War.

The PAI was tasked to remain as a change agent and assist the African masses by recommending appropriate parameters to reach optimal African agency. The PAI should provide specialised skills that multiply the power of the African masses. The Pan-African Nation is the optimal form of the Pan-African personality in this century. The PAI, at this particular time, is the heart (in the Kemetic sense of being the seat of conception) of the Pan-African personality. The People's class is the body and spirit of the Pan-African personality. The All-African People's War is this class's assertion of coming of age.

References

African Union Commission. (2004). *Strategic plan of the African Union Commission* (Vol. 1). Retrieved from http://www.foresight-fordevelopment.org/sobipro/55/731-strategic-plan-of-the-african-union-commission

Al-Gaddafi, M. (2016). *Gaddafi's "The Green Book."* North Charleston, SC: CreateSpace Independent Publishing Platform.

Ahlman, J. S. (2012). Managing the Pan-African workplace: Discipline, ideology, and the cultural politics of the Ghanaian Bureau of African Affairs, 1959–1966. *Ghana Studies, 15–16*, 337–371.

Allman, J. (2008). Nuclear imperialism and the Pan-African struggle for peace and freedom: Ghana, 1959–1962. *Souls, 10*(2), 83–102. https://doi.org/10.1080/10999940802115419

Allman, J. (2013). Kwame Nkrumah, African studies, and the politics of knowledge production in the Black Star of Africa. *The International Journal of African Historical Studies, 46*(2), 181–203.

Asuelime, L. L. E., Okem, A., & Asuelime, R. A. (2015). Re-visiting xenophobia in South Africa and its impact on Africa's integration. *Africa Insight, 45*(2), 75–85.

Botchway, D.-V. N. Y. M. (2018). "There is a New African in the World!"—Kwame Nkrumah and the making of a "New African (Wo)Man" in Ghana 1957–1966. *Comparativ, 28*(5), 60–76.

Breitman, G. (1965). *Malcolm X speaks*. New York, NY: Grove Weidenfeld Press.

Bush, R. (2011). Black internationalism and transnational Africa. In O. Vaughan & M. O. Okome (Eds.), *Transnational Africa and globalization* (pp. 39–69). New York, NY: Palgrave Macmillan US.

Campbell, H. (1996). Pan African renewal in the 21st century. *African Journal of Political Science, 1*(1), 84–98.

Dei, G. J. S. (2012). Reclaiming our Africanness in the diasporized context: The challenge of asserting a critical African personality. *The Journal of Pan African Studies, 4*(10), 42–57.

Fergus, C. (2010). From prophecy to policy: Marcus Garvey and the evolution of Pan-African Citizenship. *The Global South, 4*(2), 29–48. https://doi.org/10.2979/globalsouth.4.2.29

Frehiwot, M. J. I. B. A. (2015). Pan-African education: A case study of the Kwame Nkrumah Ideological Institute, print media and the Ghana young pioneer. In C. Quit-Adade & V. Dodoo (Eds.), *Africa's many divides and Africa's future: Pursuing Nkrumah's vision of Pan-Africanism in an era of globalization* (p. 296). Newcastle upon Tyne, UK: Cambridge Scholars Publishing.

Grilli, M. (2017). Nkrumah, nationalism, and Pan-Africanism: The Bureau of African Affairs Collection. *History in Africa, 44*, 295–307.

Grilli, M. (2018). From Manchester to the All-African People's Conference (1945–1958): Ghana's Pan-African foreign policy in the age of decolonization. In M. Grilli (Ed.), *Nkrumaism and African nationalism* (pp. 33–108). Cham, Switzerland: Palgrave Macmillan. https://doi.org/10.1007/978-3-319-91325-4_2

Gyamfi, B. (2021). From Nkrumah's black star to the African diaspora: Ghanaian intellectual activists and the development of Black studies in the Americas. *The Journal of African American History, 106*(4), 682–705. https://doi.org/10.1086/716492

Ifidon, E. (2011). Africa's political groupings and voting on cold war issues in the United Nations General Assembly, 1960-1962. *Journal of Intra-African Studies, 5*, 15–33.

Izuagie, L., & Sado, A. A. (2015). Communalism in Pan Africanism: A retrospect. *Journal of African Union Studies, 4*(2), 101–124. Retrieved from https://hdl.handle.net/10520/EJC179291

King, L. D. (2015). The nation in antiquity: Unification, civil war, and national liberation in Ancient Kemet. *Journal of Black Studies, 46*(3), 239–257.

Masaka, D. (2021). Knowledge, power, and the search for epistemic liberation in Africa. *Social Epistemology, 35*(3), 258–269. https://doi.org/10.1080/02691728.2021.1882607

Mensah, K. (2007). Kwame Nkrumah and political marketing: Locating campaign strategy in modern political campaigning. *Journal of Pan African Studies, 1*(8), 93–114.

Mensah, E. O. (2016). Collective memory, merging enemies, consistency of word and place: Nkrumah's rhetorical artefacts in the "Positive Action" protest. *African Yearbook of Rhetoric, 7*(1), 21–32.

Mkhwanazi, E. S. (2017). The challenges faced by contemporary Pan-African intelligentsia in the re-building of Africa: A Nkrumahist perspective. *Theoria, 64*(153), 144–164. https://doi.org/10.3167/th.2017.6415309

Nimako, K. (2010). Nkrumah, African awakening and neo-colonialism: How Black America awakened Nkrumah and Nkrumah awakened Black America. *The Black Scholar, 40*(2), 54–70.

Nkrumah, K. (1964). *Consciencism: Philosophy and ideology for de-colonization.* New York, NY: Monthly Review Press.

Nkrumah, K. (1969). *Handbook of revolutionary warfare: A guide to the armed phase of the African revolution* (1st ed.). New York, NY: International Publishers.

Nkrumah, K. (1970). *Africa must unite.* New York, NY: International Publishers.

Nkrumah, K. (1970b). *Class struggle in Africa.* New York, NY: International Publishers.

Nkrumah, K. (1973). *Revolutionary path.* New York, NY: International Publishers.

Nyerere, J. K. (1968). *Freedom and socialism.* Dar es Salaam, Tanzania: Oxford University Press.

Otunnu, O. (2015). Mwalimu Julius Kambarage Nyerere's philosophy, contribution, and legacies. *African Identities, 13*(1), 18–33. https://doi.org/10.1080/14725843.2014.961278

Organising Committee of the 60th Anniversary Commemoration of the All-African Peoples' Conference. (2019, February). *Statement of issues and recommendations.* Accra, Ghana: Institute of African Studies, University of Ghana. Retrieved from https://ias.ug.edu.gh/iasnew/content/conference-report

Padmore, G. (1953). *The Gold Coast Revolution: The struggle of an African people from slavery to freedom.* London, UK: Dennis Dobson.

Pallotti, A. (2009). Post-colonial nation-building and Southern African liberation: Tanzania and the break of diplomatic relations with the United Kingdom, 1965–1968. *African Historical Review, 41*(2), 60–84. https://doi.org/10.1080/17532521003607393

Poe, D. Z. (2005). Consciencism. In M. K. Asante & M. A. Mazama (Eds.), *Encyclopaedia of black studies* (1st ed., pp. 195–197). Thousand Oaks, CA: SAGE Publications.

Poe, D. Z. (2015a). Pan-African nationalism. In M. J. Shujaa & K. J. Shujaa (Eds.), *The SAGE encyclopedia of African cultural heritage in North America* (Vol. 2, pp. 686–689). Thousand Oaks, CA: SAGE Publications.

Poe, D. Z. (2015b). Perspectives on African independence: Perennial challenges to African independence and the nagging essentials of African liberation. In C. Quist-Adade & V. Dodoo (Eds.), *Africa's many divides and Africa's future: Pursuing Nkrumah's vision of*

Pan-Africanism in an era of globalization (pp. 14–33). Newcastle upon Tyne, UK: Cambridge Scholars Publishing.

Poe, D. Z. (2016). Perspectives on African independence: Designing a dynamic Nkrumahist evaluation. In C. Quist-Adade & W. Royal (Eds.), *Re-engaging the African diasporas: Pan-Africanism in the age of globalization* (pp. 44–58). Newcastle upon Tyne, UK: Cambridge Scholars Publishing.

Rahaman, S., Yeazdani, R., & Mahmud, R. (2017). The untold history of neocolonialism in Africa (1960-2011). *History Research, 5*(1), 9–16. https://doi.org/10.11648/j.history.20170501.12

Sherwood, M. (1996). *Kwame Nkrumah: The years abroad 1935–1947.* Legon, Ghana: Freedom Publications.

Shillington, K. (2019). *History of Africa.* London, UK: Red Globe Press.

Thompson, V. B. (1969). *Africa and unity: The evolution of PanAfricanism.* London, UK: Longmans Green.

Thompson, W. S. (2015). *Ghana's Foreign Policy, 1957-1966: Diplomacy, ideology, and the new state.* Princeton, NJ: Princeton University Press.

Touré, A. S. (1976). *Revolution, culture, and panafricanism.* Conakry, Guinea: Patrice-Lumumba National Printing Press.

Touré, A. S. (1978). *Strategy and tactics of the revolution.* Conakry, Guinea: Press Office.

Touré, A. S. (1980). *United States of Africa* (Vol. XXV). Conakry, Guinea: Patrice-Lumumba National Printing Press.

wa Thiong'o, N. (2018). The politics of translation: Notes towards an African language policy. *Journal of African Cultural Studies, 30*(2), 124–132.

Whitfield, E. (2018). What must we do to be free? On the building of Liberated Zones. *Prabuddha: Journal of Social Equality, 2*(1), 45–58.

White, E. (2003). Kwame Nkrumah: Cold War modernity, PanAfrican ideology and the geopolitics of development. *Geopolitics, 8*(2), 99–124. https://doi.org/10.1080/714001035

Transnational Citizenship on the Borderlands: Towards Making (Non) Sense of National Borders in Africa[*]

Edem Adotey

Introduction

On the sixtieth anniversary of the historic 1958 All-African People's Conference (AAPC), at which demands were made for the abolition or adjustment of the borders, this paper revisits the subject of decolonising the colonially imposed borders. This paper seeks to examine the legacies of these borders with a particular interest in citizenship on the borderlands. What meanings have post-colonial governments attached to the borders? What are the concepts and constructions of citizenship by the borderlanders? How can territorial sovereignty be reconciled with citizenship as the African Union (AU) seeks to integrate the continent ultimately? This paper problematises concepts such as sovereignty and citizenship vis-à-vis lived experiences of borderlanders to highlight the crisis of citizenship on the borderlands.

This study suggests transnational citizenship, a flexible type of citizenship, built on cross-border cultural and historical relations that

---

[*] This chapter is a slightly edited version of an article first published in *Contemporary Journal of African Studies*, Vol. 10, No. 2 (2023) and is reproduced here with permission.

reflects life on the borderlands to decolonise the borders, based on the lived experiences of borderlanders. In other words, it proposes an adjustment to the meaning of national borders as they operate in the African context, rather than the abolishment of the borders.[1] This paper posits that, although abolishing the borders is desirable, the existence of a border per se may not necessarily be a problem. Rather, what matters is the system for controlling or managing borders, as borders are more than just physical or cadastral lines on maps; they are also politically, economically, socially, and culturally constructed (Lamb, 2014; Lybecker, McBeth, Brewer, & Sy, 2018; Newman, 2006; Rumford, 2008).

A border control or management regime is imperative to decolonising borders in the twenty-first century. This is more so as most of the political leadership of the various countries has been averse to the idea of dismantling colonial borders as they are religiously perceived as markers of sovereignty (Ajala, 1983; Herbst, 1989; Mutua, 1995; Ndlovu-Gatsheni, 2018; Touval, 1967). Interestingly, none of the post-colonial leaders in the twenty-first century is calling for the abolishment of borders. The closest we have is Julius Malema, the leader of South Africa's Economic Freedom Fighters (EFF), who declared before the 2019 South African elections that he would abolish the borders if his party came to power. According to him, "Borders were imposed on us by colonisers and we are unwittingly supporting the colonizers" (Isilow, 2019).

More importantly, the AU, the Pan-African continental body, not only accepted the colonial borders but, like its predecessor body the Organisation of African Unity (OAU), also forges ahead with completing the enforcement of these borders. While its border programme, which was adopted in 2007, seeks to develop Cross-Border Cooperation (CBC), it is engaged in demarcating the borders as well as developing the capacity of states to manage the borders.[2] It is within this context that this paper leans towards a more creative approach to the border challenges.

---

1   In this paper, abolishing the borders means literally erasing or redrawing the inherited colonial borders.
2   According to the AU of its 109 terrestrial international boundaries covering the length of about 170,000 km2, only 35% are demarcated (AUBGS, 2020. p. 6).

The debates on borders, boundaries, and borderlands in Africa, their coloniality, and decolonisation have been topics of intense debates, discussions, policies, and interactions since the era of African independence (Moyo, 2020; Moyo & Nshimbi, 2020; Ndlovu-Gatsheni, 2018; Nshimbi, 2018).[3] Before transitioning to the AU, the OAU established several bodies with the aim of addressing the limitations of artificial borders in Africa. With a particular focus on economics, the OAU founded an African Economic Community (AEC) that seeks the political, economic, social, and cultural integration of the continent by 2028.[4] Later, the AU would establish the African Continental Free Trade Area (AfCFTA). Nevertheless, regardless of the AU's attempts to unify borders, nations cling to the colonially imposed borders.

One school of thought on addressing Africa's borders is to abolish them altogether. Arthur Mutambara, speaking at the Oxford Debating Union in 2019, argued that:

> For a start, we need the United States of Africa—a country—and not a union of sovereign states. We need to abolish national sovereignty and embrace continental sovereignty. We must pool our individual national sovereignties into one indivisible and all-inclusive Pan-African sovereignty (Mutambara, 2021).

Others, in calling for the abolishment of the borders, have recommended political units based on pre-colonial political entities, ethnic identities, or some other configuration. Ayittey (2010) advocates a confederation of African states; Mutua (1995), for instance, envisages collapsing the existing states into fourteen larger states, while Gakwandi proposes seven states (Ramutsindela, 1999).

---

3 There are conflicting and overlapping definitions of border and boundary. According to the UN Development Programme, "'Border' refers to the lines used to distinguish between states according to international law", while "'Boundary' is a less specific term, used to refer to nonterritorial lines of distinction" (UNDP Africa Borderland Unit, June 2020, p. 2). However, for this paper, borders and boundaries are used interchangeably to mean the border as defined above.

4 In 1991, the OAU adopted the Treaty Establishing the AEC (Abuja Treaty) which is aimed at the integration of the economies of the various states as the bedrock for the development of the continent. For details, see the Treaty.

However, some, in rejecting the borders, have suggested creative approaches to the border to address the challenges of the twenty-first century. Ndlovu-Gatsheni (2018) suggests rethinking citizenship to deal with the realities of African mobilities, while Nshimbi (2018) proposes transforming the borderlands into amorphous spaces to make the borders functional bridges between neighbouring states. Moyo (2020) highlights the plight of non-state actors within regional integration approaches such as the Southern African Development Community (SADC) and suggests border passes to ease the cumbersome border formalities.

This debate may appear outdated; however, its relevance is validated in the "issues and recommendations" of the 2018 Anniversary Conference organised by the Institute of African Studies of the University of Ghana, under the theme, "Revisiting The 1958 All-African People's Conference—The Unfinished Business of Liberation and Transformation". The conference was in commemoration of the sixtieth anniversary of the first AAPC held in Accra from 5 to 15 December 1958.

The AAPC, held under the auspices of Ghana's prime minister Kwame Nkrumah, emphasised the importance of engaging with questions of borders, frontiers, and federations both in the sessions and in the issues and recommendations. In its resolution on "Frontiers, Boundaries and Federations", it noted that:

> WHEREAS artificial barriers and frontiers drawn by imperialists to divide African peoples operate to the detriment of Africans and should therefore be abolished or adjusted;

> WHEREAS frontiers which cut across ethnic groups or divide peoples of the same stock are unnatural and are not conducive to peace and stability;

> WHEREAS leaders of neighbouring countries should co-operate towards a permanent solution of such problems which accords with the best interests of the people affected and enhances the prospects of realisation of the ideal of a Pan-African Commonwealth of Free States; ...

BE IT RESOLVED and it is hereby resolved by the All-African People's Conference that the Conference:

(a) denounces artificial frontiers drawn by imperialist Powers to divide the peoples of Africa, particularly those which cut across ethnic groups and divide people of the same stock
(b) calls for the abolition or adjustment of such frontiers at an early date
(c) calls upon the Independent States of Africa to support permanent solution to this problem founded upon the true wishes of the people. (*Resolutions of the all-African people's conference*, 1959, p. 46)

The call for the borders to be abolished or adjusted was premised on their artificiality and arbitrariness primarily because they cut across families, communities, and ethnic groups. This division had led to petitions before the conference from groups such as the All-Ewe Conference (AEC) to the United Nations (UN) in the 1940s to address the "Ewe Problem", that is, the division of the Ewe-speaking people between the British and the French colonial territories (Amenumey, 1989).

This paper contributes to this discussion. It utilises published works on borders, continental, and regional integration in Africa as well as some blogs which are vibrant sites about abolishing borders. Primary data are sourced from continental and regional legal instruments as well as ethnographic studies in communities on the Ghana–Togo border. The ethnographic study on the borderlands provides important insights into how sovereignty and citizenship intersect. Information was derived from interviews with chiefs and elders, opinion leaders, security agents, and commercial transporters. This was complemented by participant observation in rites such as enstoolments of chiefs, funerals, and festivals.

This paper is structured as follows: this introductory section is followed by a discussion of the conceptual framework that underpins the study. It then examines the historical context of Africa's international borders to appreciate its current configurations and related challenges.

This is followed by an examination of border control or management regimes in post-colonial Africa to understand the meanings that governments have attached to the borders and the weaknesses inherent therein. The final section addresses the question of abolishing Africa's borders.

Conceptual Framework

This section engages with orthodox notions of sovereignty and citizenship vis-à-vis borders. Examining the abolition of the borders through the perspective of sovereignty and citizenship not only helps in understanding the position of post-colonial states on the inherited colonial borders but also provides alternative approaches to a borderless Africa. These interrelated concepts provide the foundation for transnational citizenship.

Sovereignty

Sovereignty is defined as "the authority of a state to govern itself—the ability to operate free from external control" (Davies, 2016, p. 5). Humphrey (2007) notes that "If we accept the common definition of sovereignty as the capacity to determine conduct within the territory of a polity without external legal constraint, then the 'polity' in question is normally considered to be the nation-state and the 'territory' a geographical space bounded by state frontiers" (p. 418).

This orthodox notion of sovereignty is based on Westphalian concepts of a territorially circumscribed state with states controlling their borders. According to Foucher (2020), "Modern state-building is based on and achieved through a country controlling its territory, which is meant to act as a marker of identity and a tie between the government and its citizens" (p. 301). He further notes that "Borders define the state, which cannot exist without linear boundaries" (Foucher, 2020, p. 301). However, as some scholarly works on sovereignty point out, there is tension between the ideal and practice in the post-colonial state. Like the colonial state, the post-colonial state is not as hegemonic as it is made to seem (Hansen & Stepputat, 2006). Statehood, as Hagmann and Péclard (2010) argue, is negotiated between the local, national, and transnational state and non-state actors. Cooper (2014) also points to the divisibility of sovereignty that made it possible for both French and African leaders to envision dismantling the French colonial empire not as a choice between assimilation and separation or independence and colonialism. Several studies point to multiple sites of sovereignty, thus proving the misconception of absolute sovereignty purely on power and political economy grounds. Ray (1996), for instance, contends that there is "divided sovereignty" in Ghana because the chieftaincy institution forms a parallel power to the post-colonial state. This is further complicated on the borderlands where chiefs straddle the border (Adotey, 2018a, 2018b). In other words, the authority and jurisdiction of these chiefs may not be limited to one nation-state. This segues into the relationship between the state and its people.

Citizenship

Citizenship, according to Marshall, is "a status bestowed on those who are full members of a community. All who possess that status are equal with respect to the rights and duties with which the status is endowed ...." (cited in Turner, 2022, p. 703). It also "represents a relationship between the individual and the state, in which the two are bound together by reciprocal rights and obligations" (Heywood, 1994, p. 155). These ideas are based on territorially bounded states. It neglects communities that may not belong to only one state. Thus, on the borderlands, one may find a discrepancy between this conception of a citizen held by the state and those held by borderlanders who transcend the borders. As Turner (2022) notes, "The contemporary problems of citizenship both as theory and as a socio-political framework are related to national sovereignty and the idea of integrated communities and common cultures based on an underlying notion of solidarity and sameness" (p. 709). These assumptions have been challenged by cross-border communities that, though culturally integrated, have been split by the borders, as this study shows. Diouf and Fredericks (2014) also show the uneven and contested nature of citizenship in the urban landscape.

Ong (2022) points to symbolic and social meanings of citizenship and shows how spaces of citizenship formation have moved from national to transnational spaces. As she notes on the waning significance of liberal citizenship, "In an age of interconnected crises and information flows, citizenship as a state-protected status has become fragile and uncertain for too many people. Citizenship, as we conventionally understood it, is waning as a central identity for the powerful as well as the marginalized and displaced" (p. 604). Nyamnjoh (2007) also highlights the limits of bounded citizenship in contemporary times and suggests reconceptualising citizenship to make it flexible

> There is a clear need to reconceptualize citizenship in ways that create political, cultural, social and economic space for excluded nationals and non-nationals alike, as individuals and collectivities. Such inclusion is best guaranteed by a flexible citizenship unbounded by race, ethnicity, class, gender or geography, and that is both conscious and critical of hierarchies that make a mockery of the juridico-political regime of citizenship provided by the coercive illusion of the "nation-state" (p. 80).

It is interesting to note that, in addition to border tightening, some leaders have deployed citizenship as a political tool in the wake of the COVID-19 pandemic, excessive nationalism in Western nations, and an increase in terrorist acts, especially in the West African sub-region. However, evidence also suggests changes in contemporary conceptions and constructions of citizenship. A recent British Broadcasting Corporation (BBC) documentary on citizenship underlines these complexities by highlighting how citizenship transcends just belonging and community to convenience and affordability. It shows how states such as Malta and the Comoros Islands are offering citizenship for sale to outsiders. Notably, the government of the United Arab Emirates (UAE) purchased citizenship from the Comoros to award it to Bedouins who had been refused citizenship in the UAE (BBC, The Documentary Podcast, "The Price of Citizenship", 14 January 2023). This is what Ong (2022) refers to as "mutations in citizenship" where there is a "shifting articulation of key elements that make up citizenship, as certain rights, duties, and entitlements are dropped, and other emphases such as economic productivity, military service, and human rights are added" (p. 600).

In light of the multi-faceted and multi-layered nature of citizenship, it could be said that it is not just about passports issued by states but also about how people feel and what they do with borders. This is particularly so if one takes a performative approach that views borders not only as geographical lines that demarcate territories but also as concepts that are socially and culturally produced and reproduced by the state and other actors. Besides, as Cooper (2014) shows, historically, citizenship was a "permeable barrier" noting that "the question of who would pass through it was not simply a juridical but a political question" (p. 18). This opens new vistas to transnational citizenship, to which we now turn.

Transnational Citizenship

There are multiple dimensions to transnational citizenship which include rights claims, belonging or identity performance, and ascribed status (Bauböck & Faist, 2010; Belloni, 2021; Fox, 2005; Hörschelmann & Refaie, 2014; Owen, 2011; Smith, 2007; Stokes, 2004). Transnational citizenship here refers to the legal status of borderlanders as recognised citizens of the nations they straddle. In other words, it means binational or multinational belonging that entails full membership and rights that are institutionally guaranteed in the countries that divide families, communities, and ethnic groups on the borderlands. These rights include but are not limited to civil and political rights such as cross-border electoral participation, that is, the right to vote and be voted for, amongst others.

The paper diverges from contemporary scholarship on transnational citizenship that is often based on migration and a globalised understanding of transnationality. This paper contends that transnational citizenship can exist on the borderlands in African countries where communities have not had the opportunity to travel outside of the continent but who have transnational citizenship due to their cultural, geographical, and political relations across the borderlands.

Borderlands are contested spaces that disrupt the lives, livelihood, and way of life of many communities living there. This transnational citizenship reimagines both sovereignty and citizenship in new ways that challenge the coloniality of these borders by centring the rich social, cultural, political, and economic relations that have long characterised African life, especially at the borderlands. It contributes to the transformation and decolonisation of citizenship in Africa as it is used in a pragmatic sense which derives from de facto citizenship rights claimed by borderlanders through their everyday practices on the borderlands.

Transnational citizenship focuses on the borderlands because they are important sites where rights and membership intersect. But beyond that, taking a borderlands-centred perspective makes it possible to focus on partitioned peoples and stress the concepts of citizenship held by the borderlanders and how that interfaces with the dominant notions of citizenship. Besides, it is in line with Resolution 3 of the 1958 AAPC noted above, which stresses the abolition or adjustment of borders that "cut across ethnic groups and divide people of the same stock" (*Resolutions of the all-African people's conference*, 1959, p. 46).

This kind of transnational citizenship, while limited to communities divided by these borders, is more comprehensive than the Economic Community of West African States (ECOWAS) or AU citizenship as it is not limited by the mutual respect for national sovereignty, as I describe in later sections. It illuminates flexible citizenship on the borderlands and points to its practical viability and meaningful significance not only on the borderlands but for regional and continental integration.

Africa's Borders in Historical Context

The concept of a border was not unknown in parts of Africa before the colonial partition. These borders varied and were delimited using natural features such as hills, rivers, and plants. They were fluid in many cases influenced largely by the kind of relationship that existed between states, socio-political conditions, as well as the geographical nature of the area (Asiwaju, 1983). This has been categorised into frontiers of contact separating distinct cultural groups living side by side; frontiers of separation, which usually were buffer zones like forests that neither community claimed; and frontiers of transition with overlapping diverse communities (Ajala, 1983; Asiwaju, 1983).

In essence, many African states did not consider borders as fixed lines of separation. Mbembe (2017) notes that in pre-colonial Africa, mobility was the defining principle in delimiting space. As he points out, "Networks, flows, and crossroads were more important than borders. What mattered the most was the extent to which flows intersected with other flows." Nugent (1996), on the other hand, makes a distinction between closed frontiers which were "zones of warfare", and open frontiers, which were directed towards "corridors of trade" and hence qualify an African conception of the border that "placed more emphasis on its role as a link or bond rather than as a point of separation" (Nugent, 1996, p. 38). Nevertheless, pre-colonial concepts of political space in some communities, such as the Ewe, moved beyond bounded territories to include membership in clans and cults (Greene, 1996).

European colonial rule largely defined the present borders of many African states based on European concepts of borders. Unlike pre-colonial African borders that were fluid, as states expanded or contracted or even relocated due to ecological or military factors, there was an element of fixity attached to it by the Europeans. These borders, too, ignored the fact that peoples and states did not necessarily coincide. Besides, the European conception of state sovereignty as absolute failed to consider the limits of direct rule and shared sovereignty (Nugent, 1996).

The making of African borders also took very little account of the pre-existing social, cultural, political, and economic relations. This was compounded by European ignorance of the places they purported to own. For example, as Peter J. Yearwood notes regarding the partition of Cameroon between the British and the French, "The Picot line was casually drawn with a heavy pencil by a diplomat who knew nothing of the lands and peoples he was dividing" (Yearwood, 1993, p. 235). This arbitrariness is evident in the many straight lines and watersheds used as border markers; about 30% of Africa's borders are straight lines (Ajala, 1983).

An important event in defining Africa's borders was the Berlin Conference of 1884–85. Although it is commonly misrepresented as where African borders were drawn, this conference played a significant role in the division of Africa by the European powers. (Katzenellenbogen, 1996). It is worth noting that by 1884 several European nations had acquired "colonies" and "protectorates" in Africa. For example, parts of the Gold Coast (Ghana) were declared a British colony in 1874, that is, ten years before the Berlin conference. Nonetheless, most of the borders of modern African states were drawn after the Berlin Conference (Griffiths, 1986). The conference shaped the "scramble for Africa" as provisions in the Berlin Act, such as "effective occupation", which were agreed upon for acquiring these territories, were used by the European nations to justify their claims when it suited them.

Later, some of these borders were changed to account for regional factors like traditional polities (Bening, 1983; Foucher, 2020; Nugent, 1996, 2002; Zeller, 2010). It is, however, worth noting that these adjustments were largely informed by European rather than local interests. The effect of these borders was the division of families, communities, and ethnic groups between various European colonies. For instance, the Ewe, Konkomba, Dagomba, and Dangme were divided between the British and the Germans; the Ovambo or the Kwanyama between the Germans and the Portuguese; the Kakwa, Baka, Mundu, and Arukaiya between the French and British (Asiwaju, 1985, pp. 256–258; Bening, 1983; Brambilla, 2007; Griffiths, 1986; Nugent, 2002; Taha, 1977).

Besides splitting ethnic groups, families, and communities, the borders impacted mobility as people could not move freely across these borders and participate in the political, social, and economic activities that they had hitherto partaken in. These restrictions, in turn, affected people's livelihoods. For example, nomadic peoples such as the Somali and Maasai could not freely move their cattle to graze as they had previously done (Ajala, 1983).

President Julius Nyerere described these borders as "ethnological and geographical nonsense" because of the way they cut across ethnic groups and disregarded physical divisions (*Evening News*, 1 February 1963, p. 9). The leaders began debating vehemently what to do with this colonial heritage at independence. The notions of sovereignty and citizenship are used to explore the meanings post-colonial African states and organisations have attached to these borders in the next section.

Sovereignty, Citizenship, and Africa's Borders

Post-colonial African states have privileged orthodox definitions of a state, which inevitably prioritises calcified borders. Unlike the position adopted at the 1958 AAPC meeting of the "masses" to abolish or adjust the borders, many African leaders, such as Sir Abubakar Tafawa Balewa, the prime minister of Nigeria, and Modibo Keita, the president of Mali, spoke in favour of maintaining the borders. While they agreed that the borders were artificial, they argued that adjusting them would create more problems than would be solved (Ajala, 1983; Herbst, 1989; Touval, 1967).

The continental body formed in 1963, the OAU, affirmed these borders. Article III of its charter appealed to member states to respect "the sovereignty and territorial integrity of each state and for its inalienable right to independent existence" (Paragraph 3, Article III, Charter of the Organisation of African Unity, 1963). This was subsequently affirmed at the first Ordinary Session of the Assembly of Heads of State and Government of the OAU in 1964 as Resolution AHG/Res. 16(1). In addressing border disputes, members pledged to respect the borders that existed at independence.

In 2002, the OAU was formally replaced by the AU, and it maintained the same position on respecting inherited colonial borders. Article IV(b) of its Constitutive Act (African Union, 2000) states that it shall function per "respect of borders existing on achievement of independence". Following these positions, the post-colonial states have sought to protect their territorial integrity and sovereignty by jealously guarding their borders. Although there have been efforts at the national, regional, or continental level to ease the restrictions on movements, residence, and establishment for non-citizens, they have been cast in the mould of citizenship in a territorially bounded sovereign state. For instance, in Ghana, the Immigration Act of 2000 (Act 573) recognises people it describes as "border-residents".[5] Section 3(4) states that "Regulations may be made under this Act to provide for free movement across the border of a border-resident for the purpose of attending to his routine economic or social matters". While this is usually the case, this has not been without challenges to border-residents because the onus lies on them to prove that they are indeed border-residents which is not always an easy task. Other countries, too, have introduced visa-on-arrival for non-citizens or scrapped the need for visa altogether. Seychelles and Benin are visa-free for all African citizens, while Rwanda and Ghana have visa-on-arrival for all AU citizens (N. A., 2017). Zimbabwe has no visa for citizens of members of the SADC, while ECOWAS has 90-day visa-free entry for citizens of member states (Mukeredzi, 2016).

---

5 A border-resident is defined in Act 573 (Section 56) as "a national of a neighbouring country who ordinarily resides within five kilometres radius of either side of Ghana's territorial frontiers with the Republics of Togo, Burkina Faso and Cote d'Ivoire".

Yet, despite the easing of visa restrictions by several African countries, studies show that it is still very difficult to travel within the continent. According to the latest Africa Visa Openness Report 2022, 27%
of African countries do not require visas, 27% offer visas on arrival, and
47% of African countries require visas (African Development Bank and
African Development Bank Group, 2022). In effect, despite upward progress, there is less freedom of movement for Africans in African countries.

At the regional level, Regional Economic Communities (RECs) such as
ECOWAS, established in 1975, endorsed the freedom of movement, residence, and establishment in the fifteen member states in the treaty establishing it (ECOWAS Treaty, Article XXVII). In 1979, it introduced the Protocol
Relating to Free Movement of Persons, Residence, and Establishment,
which spelt out the rights and obligations of citizens as well as member states
(Protocol A/P.1/5/79 relating to Free Movement of Persons, Residence, and
Establishment). The revised ECOWAS Treaty of 1993 (Article LIX) reiter-
ates the right of free movement, residence, and establishment, and enjoins
members to eliminate all obstacles to its implementation. Similar provisions
are captured in the SADC Treaty (Moyo & Nshimbi, 2020).

The ECOWAS passport for citizens of the community, introduced
in 2000, makes a move towards transnational citizenship. However, the
ECOWAS transnational citizenship, as noted earlier, is fundamentally
grounded in national citizenship and limited by mutual respect for state
sovereignty. For example, ECOWAS members have visa-free stay in a host
country for only 90 days (ECOWAS Protocol on Free Movement of Persons,
Right of Residence and Right of Establishment, Article III (2)). In addition,
a host country may prohibit persons it deems "inadmissible" from entering
its country under its laws (Article IV). Similar conditions are contained in
the AU Protocol on Free Movement of Persons, Right of Residence and
Right of Establishment,(2018b Article VI (4,5); Article VII (1c)).

At the continental level, several initiatives have been implemented by
the OAU and the AU to facilitate the integration of the continent and
its people. The Abuja Treaty (1991) is one such initiative. This has been
followed by others such as the AU's (2018a) Migration Policy Framework
for Africa (MPFA).[6]

---

6 This has been replaced by a revised version, *The Migration Policy Framework for Africa (2018
   –2030) and its Plan of Action.*

In 2007, the AU instituted the African Union Border Programme (AUBP), which aimed at not only resolving border disputes but also facilitating regional and continental integration. This has been marked since 2011 by the African Border Day on 7 June (African Union Border Programme, 2017). Its primary objective revolves around the delimitation and demarcation of the borders of the sovereign state. In the same vein, the AU Convention on CBC (Niamey Convention) envisions "an integrated Africa with borders serving as bridges for peace, growth, and development". Its main aim is the peaceful resolution of cross-border disputes.

The AU's African Passport and Free Movement of People is one of the flagship projects under its blueprint programme for transforming the continent, *Agenda 2063: The Africa We Want*. Agenda 2063 was aimed at, among other things, abolishing visas for all African nationals by 2018 and introducing AU passports for African nationals to move freely on the continent by 2020 (Njoroge, 2022). This is yet to materialise as just a handful of African countries have ratified the AU protocol on the free movement of persons (Phillip, 2021). As can be seen from the above, these laws and customs that support citizenship within a state are influenced by statist border control or management systems. These legal tools disregard the fact that, despite state restrictions, borderlanders enjoy flexible citizenship. What this entails for citizenship on the borders is examined in the next section.

Africa Beyond Borders

The national borders on the continent, as several scholarly studies show, have not prevented multiple belongingness to different states expressed in cross-border cultural, social, economic, and political interactions. These cross-border relations are expressed through joint traditional festivals and ceremonies, rotating markets, joint participation in birth, marriage, and burial rites, and chiefly jurisdiction across borders (Adotey, 2018a, 2018b, 2020, 2021; Asiwaju, 1985; Bensassi, Jarreau, & Mitaritonna, 2019; Chalfin, 2001; Lawrance, 2003; Lentz, 2003; Moyo, 2016, 2020; Nshimbi, 2019; Nugent, 2019, 2002).

On the Ghana–Togo border, the Ewe-speaking people of Ghana and Togo celebrate festivals to cement their cultural and historical links. The

Leklebi of Ghana and Lavie of Togo celebrate the *Agbonutoza* (Adotey, 2021); this festival is rotated between the Leklebi in Ghana and the Lavie in Togo. On such occasions, families on both sides lodge with each other. It is interesting to note that families on both sides share the same surname, for example, Deh, Adoboe, and Biaku. Both groups, according to oral traditions, are of the same stock who migrated from Notsie in present-day Togo in the famous escape of the Ewe-speaking people from the tyrannical rule of their ruler Agorkoli (Amenumey, 1989; Mamattah, 1978; Spieth, 2011). Another cross-border festival that also commemorates the exodus from Notsie is the *Komabu Dukoza* (Adotey, 2021). This is celebrated by the Wli and Liati of Ghana and Danyi-Kakpa, Danyi-Atigba, and Atti of Togo. It is rotated between the towns in Ghana and Togo.

Similarly, the Ga-Dangme people of Agotime in Ghana and Togo celebrate *Agbamevoza* to strengthen historic family and cultural connections between both groups (Nugent, 2019). The Chewa-speaking people of Zambia, Malawi, and Mozambique celebrate the *Kulamba*, during which period they cross the national borders to be with their kith and kin (Nshimbi, 2019).

Jurisdiction in the borderlands is mainly international in dimension, with chiefs wielding authority and jurisdiction across borders. Chiefs are involved in adjudicating cases across some borders. As the chief of Ave-Atanve in Ghana notes, the court of the paramount chief of Edzi in Togo is their "supreme court", meaning cases from his court in Ghana can be appealed against in that in Togo (Adotey, 2018b).

Cross-border involvement in installation rites and allegiances to chiefs are two ways that relationships are expressed. For example, in Ghana-Nyive and Togo-Nyive, chiefs have participated in the chief installation and funeral ceremonies on both sides of the border. The Ave-Dzalele people of Ghana and their mother polity, Edzi, in Togo, have similar customs (Adotey, 2018b). It is important to state that these chiefs will not be considered legitimate if these rites are not performed by the ritual officiants on the other side of the border. Likewise, in the case of the Mandara who are astride the Nigeria–Cameroon boundary, the Sultan of Mandara, located in Cameroon, is deemed the legitimate authority to bestow titles on both sides of the border (Barkindo, 1984).

Besides, ritual objects such as drums are moved across the borders to be used in the performance of rites during events such as funerals. It is important to state that drums are not just musical instruments for entertainment but are used to invoke the spirits of the ancestors and deities on such occasions. There are also special drums reserved for some categories of chiefs, such as paramount chiefs and war chiefs. At the funeral of the *Avafia* of Ghana-Nyive, one such drum had to be brought from Togo to perform the rites of the late chief (Adotey, 2018b). This shows the shared ancestry of these people.

These continuing cross-border relationships can even be discerned from contemporary funerary practices such as funeral posters. Funeral posters are important places where kin and other relations are recognised. Names are arranged in a particular order to indicate the nature of the relationships, particularly in the case of chieftaincy. A case in point is the funeral poster of the *Avafia* of Ghana-Nyive where the position of the chiefs of Togo-Nyive on the poster was an indication of their seniority in the relationship (Adotey, 2018a).

Despite the challenges that many borderlanders face in navigating borders, they go about their daily lives as if the borders that separate them into different countries do not exist. People cross the border daily to visit family and partake in events such as naming ceremonies, marriages, funerals, and family meetings on either side of the border. For instance, the mother and siblings of the *Mankralo* of Ghana-Nyive lives in Togo-Nyive and he visits them regularly. In many of these borderland communities, such as Wli-Todzi and Leklebi-Kame in Ghana, where peoples' farms straddle the border, it is common to find people going to their farms in Togo in the morning and returning to Ghana in the evening with their harvest. People buy goods in the Ghanaian currency, the cedi, on the Togo side, and receive their change in the Togolese currency, the CFA franc, and vice versa.

In effect, juxtaposed against the meanings attached to these borders by post-colonial governments, the sanctity of the border so prized by post-colonial governments, which underpins the sovereignty of the state, means very little to many of those directly affected by these borders. As some put it so succinctly, the border is "an imaginary line" (Adotey, 2021).

These everyday practices bring to the fore the question of citizenship on the borderlands. Many in these places have developed what is termed "border citizenship" (Adotey, 2020; Moyo, 2016). A border citizen is defined as:

> a category co-produced between states and citizens, where people, who are often perceived as marginal, enact alternative forms of citizenship, using its mechanisms to make strategic claims on both of the states whose overlapping sovereignty constitutes the non-post-colonial third space... (cited in Moyo, 2016, pp. 5–6).

These claims on the part of the borderlanders include, amongst others, multiple citizenships of countries that they straddle. As many noted on the Ghana-Togo border, "*mi nye Ghanatɔwo kple Togotɔwo*" (we are Ghanaian and Togolese) (personal communication, 27 October 2012; 16 February 2018). These "citizenship rights" include possession of national identification cards, voter identification cards, national health insurance cards, access to social amenities such as schools and hospitals, and involvement in the governance of these countries. On the Ghana-Togo border, this includes cross-border participation in political activities such as elections in Ghana (Adotey, 2020; Nugent, 2019; Robert-Nicoud, 2019).

Defining citizenship is not the sole preserve of the state as Dorman, Hammett, and Nugent (2007) point out, "States may seek to claim the exclusive right to define citizenship, but when their coercive and persuasive power is equally limited it may be easier to defer to 'local' agendas" (p. 22).

For instance, in 2016, the New Patriotic Party (NPP) launched "Operation Eagle Eye" to prevent "Togolese" voters from voting in Ghana's elections, while the National Democratic Congress (NDC), on the other hand, encouraged "Ghanaians" in Togo to vote (Adotey, 2020). On the Ghana-Togo border, people also define their citizenship based on the divided traditional states. According to a borderlander, "we are one people, my father is here, and my mother is on the other side" (Adotey, 2020, p. 11).

In this vein, reconceptualising citizenship, as this paper suggests, is to be informed from below by how those on the borderlands define their citizenship. This border citizenship is based on historical and cultural ties to communities that straddle the border and is in contrast to those defined based on colonial borders. As some argue, they did not ask anyone to come and divide them and place them in different countries hence belonging to communities in both countries makes them citizens of both countries. These multiple and conflicting claims to citizenship by both the state and the borderlanders have created a crisis of citizenship on the borderlands. It highlights the need for more flexible citizenship which rejects "the status quo of colonially crafted borders together with its logics of exclusion and fragmenting African people" (Ndlovu-Gatsheni, 2017, p. 32) as the continent strives for political, economic, social, and cultural integration. The paradigm shift proposed is a form of flexible citizenship—transnational citizenship. This transnational citizenship is a veritable heterodox phenomenon. It is built on historical and cultural relations and reconciles contemporary notions of sovereignty with the everyday realities of the border for borderlanders. In essence, it is making de jure what is a de facto practice.

Transnational citizenship captures the AU and the RECs' push towards flexible citizenship. In 2020, the AU introduced the African Union Border Governance Strategy (AUBGS) to complement and clarify earlier arrangements and modalities for border governance. The document acknowledges that in Africa:

> state borders are often not identical to peoples' borders and hence have been known to foster three kinds of tensions: between neighbouring states, between states and their people and between states and violent actors, including international criminal cartels and terrorist groups" (AUGBS, 2020, p. 6).

It thus implores members that "political, economic and strategic choices made in asserting its sovereignty implies that the state's definition of a border regime is capable of reconciling national, regional and continental interests" (AUBGS, 2020, p. 18). Similarly, the revised ECOWAS

Treaty notes that for the integration to be viable, there is the need for "partial and gradual pooling of national sovereignties to the Community within the context of a collective political will" (Preamble, 1993).

Transnational citizenship is a form of CBC envisaged by the AU that builds on geographical proximity, kinship, history, and culture to transform border areas as catalysts of political integration (Niamey Convention, Article II (6)).

Conclusion

Africa's international borders are one of the intractable legacies of colonial rule. Despite the challenges to Africa's liberation and transformation resulting from this arbitrary division of this continent and its peoples, and calls for their abolishment, these inherited colonial borders remain largely intact. Mbembe (2017) reflects on the effect of a state-centric model which jealously guards borders and obstructs migration with its disastrous impact on Africa when he notes that

> the fetishization of the nation-state has done untold damage to Africa's destiny in the world. The human, economic, cultural and intellectual cost of the existing border regime in the continent has been colossal. It is time to bring it to closure.

While it is true that African states are not unique in their state-centred border management regimes (Sassen, 2013), contemporary sovereignties and citizenship challenge mutually exclusive bounded territories and bounded citizenship (Hagmann & Péclard, 2010; Nyamnjoh, 2007) and hence the need to explore more creative approaches to the borders. Through the analysis of the concepts of sovereignty and citizenship vis-à-vis the lived experiences of borderlanders, this work shows a crisis of citizenship in the borderlands. The central proposition of this paper is a call for a form of flexible citizenship—transnational citizenship—built on cross-border cultural and historical relations that reflects life on the borderlands in order to decolonise the borders.

References

Adotey, E. (2018a). Where is my name? – Contemporary funeral posters as an arena of contestation and (re)negotiation of chiefly relations among the Ewe of Ghana and Togo. *History in Africa, 45*, 59–69. https://doi.org/10.1017/hia.2018.4

Adotey, E. (2018b). "International Chiefs": Chieftaincy, rituals and the reproduction of transborder Ewe ethnic communities on the Ghana–Togo boundary. *Africa, 88*(3), 560–578. https://doi.org/10.1017/S0001972018000220

Adotey, E. (2020). "Operation Eagle Eye": Border citizenship and cross-border voting in Ghana's Fourth Republic. *Journal of Borderlands Studies, 38*(1), 21–38. https://doi.org/10.1080/08865655.2020.1861551

Adotey, E. (2021). An imaginary line? Decolonisation, bordering and borderscapes on the Ghana–Togo border. *Third World Quarterly, 42*(5), 1069–1086. https://doi.org/10.1080/01436597.2020.1813019

African Development Bank & African Development Bank Group. (2022, December 13). *Africa visa openness report 2022*. African Development Bank Group - Making a Difference. Retrieved from https://www.afdb.org/en/documents/africa-visa-openness-report-2022#:~:text=The%202022%20report%20reflects%20on,peak%20score%20achieved%20in%202020

African Union. (2000). *Constitutive Act*. Retrieved from https://au.int/en/constitutive-act

African Union. (2013). *Agenda 2063: The Africa we want*. Retrieved from https://au.int/en/agenda2063

African Union. (2014). *Convention on Cross-Border Cooperation (Niamey Convention)*. Retrieved from https://au.int/en/treaties/african-union-convention-cross-border-cooperation-niamey-convention

African Union. (2017). *African Union Border Programme (AUBP)*. Retrieved from https://www.peaceau.org/en/page/85-au-border-programme-aubp

African Union. (2018a). *Migration policy framework for Africa and plan of action (2018 – 2030)*. Retrieved from https://au.int/en/documents/20181206/migration-policy-framework-africa-mpfa

African Union. (2018b). *Protocol to the treaty establishing the African Economic Community relating to free movement of persons, right of residence and right of establishment.* Retrieved from https://au.int/en/treaties/protocol-treaty-establishing-african-economic-community-relating-free-movement-persons

African Union. (2020). *African Union Border Governance Strategy.* Retrieved from https://archives.au.int/handle/123456789/8851

Ajala. A. (1983). The nature of African boundaries. *Africa Spectrum, 18*(2), 177–189.

Amenumey, D. E. K. (1989). *The Ewe unification movement: A political history.* Accra, Ghana: Ghana Universities Press.

Asiwaju, A. I. (1983). The concept of frontier in the setting of states in pre-colonial Africa. *Présence Africaine, 127/128*, 43–49. https://doi.org/10.3917/presa.127.0043

Asiwaju, A. I. (Ed.). (1985). *Partitioned Africans: Ethnic relations across Africa's international boundaries, 1884–1984.* London, UK: C. Hurst & Co.

Ayittey, G. B. N. (2010). The United States of Africa: A revisit. *The Annals of the American Academy of Political and Social Science (Perspectives on Africa and the World), 632*, 86–102.

Barkindo, B. M. (1984). The Mandara astride the Nigeria-Cameroon boundary. In A. I. Asiwaju (Ed.), *Partitioned Africans: Ethnic relations across Africa's international boundaries, 1884-1984* (pp. 29–50). London, UK: C. Hurst & Co.; Lagos, Nigeria: University of Lagos Press.

Bauböck, R., & Faist, T. (2010). *Diaspora and transnationalism: Concepts, theories and methods.* Amsterdam, The Netherlands: Amsterdam University Press. https://doi.org/10.1111/cag.12101

Belloni, M. (2021). Remittance houses and transnational citizenship: Mapping Eritrea's diaspora–state relationships. *Africa Spectrum, 56*(1), 59–80. https://doi.org/10.1177/00020397211003101

Bening, R. B. (1983). The Ghana-Togo Boundary, 1914-1982. *Africa Spectrum, 18*(2), 191–209.

Bensassi, S., Jarreau, J., & Mitaritonna, C. (2019). Regional integration and informal trade in Africa: Evidence from Benin's borders. *Journal of African Economies, 28*(1), 89–118. https://doi.org/10.1093/jae/ejy016

Brambilla, C. (2007). Borders and identities/border identities: The Angola-Namibia border and the plurivocality of the Kwanyama identity. *Journal of Borderlands Studies, 22*(2), 21–38. https://doi.org/10.1080/08865655.2007.9695675

Chalfin, B. (2001). Border zone trade and the economic boundaries of the state in north-east Ghana. *Africa, 71*(2), 202–224. https://doi.org/10.3366/afr.2001.71.2.202

Cooper, F. (2014). *Citizenship between empire and nation: Remaking France and French Africa, 1945-1960.* Princeton, NJ: Princeton University Press.

Davies, G. (2016). *Sovereignty and collaboration: Affordable strategies in times of austerity?* Montgomery, AL: Air University Press.

Diouf, M., & Fredericks, R. (Eds.). (2014). *The arts of citizenship in African cities: Infrastructures and spaces of belonging.* London, UK: Palgrave Macmillan.

Dorman, S., Hammett, D., & Nugent, P. (Eds.). (2007). *Making nations, creating strangers: States and Citizenship in Africa.* Leiden, The Netherlands: Brill.

Economic Community of West African States. (1975). *Treaty.* Retrieved from https://ecowas.int/wp-content/uploads/2022/06/THE-1975-TREATY-OF-ECOWAS.pdf

Economic Community of West African States. (1979). *Protocol relating to free movement of Persons, Residence and Establishment, A/P 1/5/79.* Retrieved from https://www.refworld.org/docid/492187502.html

Economic Community of West African States. (1993). *Revised treaty.* Retrieved from https://ecowas.int/wp-content/uploads/2022/08/Revised-treaty-1.pdf

Foucher, M. (2020). African borders: Putting paid to a myth. *Journal of Borderlands Studies, 35*(2), 287–306. https://doi.org/10.1080/0886565.2019.1671213

Fox, J. (2005). Unpacking transnational citizenship. *Annual Review of Political Science, 8*, 171–201. https://doi.org/10.1146/annurev.polisci.7.012003.104851

Ghana Immigration Service. (2000). *Immigration Act, 2000 (Act 573).* Retrieved from https://www.gis.gov.gh/ACTS%20AND%20REGULATIONS/ACT%20573.pdf

Greene, S. E. (1996). *Gender, ethnicity and social change on the upper slave coast: A history of the Anlo-Ewe.* Portsmouth, NH: Heinemann.

Griffiths, I. (1986). The scramble for Africa: Inherited political boundaries. *Geographical Journal, 152*(2), 204–216.

Hagmann, T., & Péclard, D. (2010). Negotiating statehood: Dynamics of power and domination in Africa. *Development and Change, 41*(4), 539–562. https://doi.org/10.1111/j.1467-7660.2010.01656.x

Hansen, T. B., & Stepputat, F. (2006). Sovereignty revisited. *Annual Review of Anthropology, 35*(1), 295–315. https://doi.org/10.1146/annurev.anthro.35.081705.123317

Herbst, J. (1989). The creation and maintenance of national boundaries in Africa. *International Organization, 43*(4), 673–692.

Heywood, A. (1994). *Political ideas and concepts: An introduction.* New York, NY: St. Martin's Press.

Hörschelmann, K., & Refaie, E. E. (2013). Transnational citizenship, dissent and the political geographies of youth. *Transactions of the Institute of British Geographers, 39*(3), 444–456. https://doi.org/10.1111/tran.12033

Humphrey, C. (2007). Sovereignty. In D. Nugent & J. Vincent (Eds.), *A companion to the anthropology of politics* (pp. 418–436). Malden, MA: Blackwell Publishing Ltd. https://doi.org/10.1002/9780470693681.ch26

Isilow, H. (2019, April 18). S. Africa opposition party pledges to abolish borders. *AA.* Retrieved from https://www.aa.com.tr/en/africa/safrica-opposition-party-pledges-to-abolish-borders-/1457154

Katzenellenbogen, S. (1996). Arcs and line – Myths and realities: It didn't happen at Berlin: Politics, economics and ignorance in the setting of Africa's colonial boundaries. In P. Nugent & A. I. Asiwaju (Eds.), *African boundaries: Barriers, conduits and opportunities* (pp. 21–34). London, UK: Pinter.

Lamb, V. (2014). "Where is the border?" Villagers, environmental consultants and the "work" of the Thai Burma border. *Political Geography, 40*, 1–12. https://doi.org/10.1016/j.polgeo.2014.02.001

Lawrance, B. N. (2003). "En Proie à la Fièvre du Cacao": Land and resource conflict on an Ewe frontier, 1922-1939. *African Economic History, 31*, 135–181.

Lentz, C. (2003). "This is Ghanaian territory!": Land conflicts on a West African border. *American Ethnologist, 30*(2), 273–289. https://doi.org/10.1525/ae.2003.30.2.273

Lybecker, D. L., McBeth, M. K., Brewer, A. M., & Sy, C. D. (2018). The social construction of a border: The US–Canada border. *Journal of Borderlands Studies, 33*(4), 529–547. https://doi.org/10.1080/08865655.2016.1247652

Mamattah, C. M. K. (1978). *The history of the Eves: The E[w]es of West Africa. Vol. 1, Oral traditions: The A[n]l[o]-E[w]es and their immediate neighbours.* Accra, Ghana: Volta Research Publications.

Mbembe, A. (2017). Scrap the borders that divide Africans. *The Mail & Guardian.* Retrieved from https://mg.co.za/article/2017-03-17-00-scrap-the-borders-that-divide-africans/

Moyo, I. (2016). The Beitbridge–Mussina interface: Towards flexible citizenship, sovereignty and territoriality at the border. *Journal of Borderlands Studies, 31*(4), 427–440. https://doi.org/10.1080/08865655.2016.1188666

Moyo, I. (2020). On decolonising borders and regional integration in the Southern African Development Community (SADC) region. *Social Sciences, 9*(4), 2–12. https://doi.org/10.3390/socsci9040032

Moyo, I., & Nshimbi, C. C. (2020). Of borders and fortresses: Attitudes towards immigrants from the SADC region in South Africa as a critical factor in the integration of Southern Africa. *Journal of Borderlands Studies, 35*(1), 131–146. https://doi.org/10.1080/08865655.2017.1402198

Mutambara, A. (2021, March 14). Excerpt: Professor Arthur Mutambara upcoming book: *In search of the elusive Zimbabwean dream* (Vol. 3). *The News Hawks.* Retrieved from https://zwnews.com/excerpt-professor-arthur-mutambara-upcoming-book-in-search-of-the-elusive-zimbabwean-dream-volume-3/

Mukeredzi, T. (2016). Pan-Africa passport to open up borders. *Africa Renewal.* Retrieved from https://www.un.org/africarenewal/magazine/august-2016/pan-africa-passport-open-borders

Mutua, M. W. (1995). Why redraw the map of Africa: A moral and legal inquiry. *Michigan Journal of International Law, 16*(4), 1113–1176.

N. A. (2017, December 7). Africa with open borders: A possibility or a pipe dream. *Africa Portal*. Retrieved from https://www.africa-portal.org/features/africa-open-borders-possibility-or-pipe-dream/ (accessed October 11, 2022).

Ndlovu-Gatsheni, J. S. (2018). Decolonising borders, decriminalising migration and rethinking citizenship. In H. H. Magidimisha, N. E. Khalema, L. Chipungu, T. C. Chirimambowa, & T. L. Chimedza (Eds.), *Crisis, identity and migration in post-colonial Southern Africa* (pp. 23–37). Cham, Switzerland: Springer. http://doi:10.1007/978-3-319-59235-0_2

Newman, D. (2006). Borders and bordering: Towards an interdisciplinary dialogue. *European Journal of Social Theory, 9*(2), 171–186. https://doi:10.1177/1368431006063331

Njoroge, J. (2022). Africa: Era of the African passport – A mixed bag of opportunities? *allAfrica.com*. Retrieved from https://allafrica.com/stories/202207030068.html

Nshimbi, C. C. (2018). Issues in African informality – What is the relevance for regional or continental integration? *Africa Insight, 48*(1), 41–61.

Nshimbi, C. C. (2019). Life in the fringes: Economic and sociocultural practices in the Zambia–Malawi–Mozambique borderlands in comparative perspective. *Journal of Borderlands Studies, 34*(1), 47–70. https://doi.org/10.1080/08865655.2017.1300780

Nugent, P. (1996). Arbitrary lines and the people's minds: A dissenting view on colonial boundaries in West Africa. In P. Nugent & A. I. Asiwaju (Eds.), *African boundaries barriers, conduits and opportunities* (pp. 35–67). London, UK: Pinter.

Nugent, P. (2019). *Boundaries, communities and state-making in West Africa: The Centrality of the margins.* Cambridge, UK: Cambridge University Press.

Nugent, P. (2002). *Smugglers, secessionists and loyal citizens on the Ghana–Togo frontier: The lie of the borderlands since 1914.* Athens, USA: Ohio University Press.

Nyamnjoh, F. B. (2007). From bounded to flexible citizenship: Lessons from Africa. *Citizenship Studies, 11*(1), 73–82. https://doi.org/10.1080/13621020601099880

Ong, A. (2022). Citizenship: flexible, fungible, fragile. *Citizenship Studies,* *26*(4–5), 599–607. https://doi.org/10.1080/13621025.2022.2091244

Organisation of African Unity. (1963). *OAU Charter.* Retrieved from https://au.int/en/treaties/oau-charter-addis-ababa-25-may-1963

Organisation of African Unity. (1964). *Border disputes among African States* (Resolution AHG/Res. 16(1)). Retrieved from https://www.peaceau.org/uploads/ahg-res-16-i-en.pdf

Organisation of African Unity. (1991). *Treaty establishing the African Economic Community.* Retrieved from https://au.int/en/treaties/treaty-establishing-african-economic-community

Owen, D. (2011). Transnational citizenship and the democratic state: Modes of membership and voting rights. *Critical Review of International Social and Political Philosophy, 14*(5), 641–663. https://doi.org/10.1080/13698230.2011.617123

Phillip, X. (2021, November 25). AU's failure to ratify African passport protocol stalls free movement for citizens. *The Africa Report.* Retrieved from https://www.theafricareport.com/150265/aus-failure-to-ratify-protocol-for-african-passport-stalls-free-movement-for-citizens/

Ray, D. I. (1996). Divided sovereignty: Traditional authority and the state in Ghana. *Journal of Legal Pluralism and Unofficial Law, 28*(37–38), 181–202. https://doi.org/10.1080/07329113.1996.10756479

Resolutions of the all-African people's conference. (1959). *Current History, 37*(215), 41–46. Retrieved from http://www.jstor.org/stable/45313673

Robert-Nicoud, N. R. (2019). Elections and borderlands in Ghana. *African Affairs, 118*(473), 672–691. https://doi.org/10.1093/afraf/adz002

Rumford, C. (2008). Introduction: Citizens and borderwork in Europe. *Space and Polity, 12*(1), 1–12. https://doi.org/10.1080/13562570801969333

Sassen, S. (2013). When territory deborders territoriality. *Territory, Politics, Governance, 1*(1), 21–45. https://doi.org/10.1080/21622671.2013.769895

Smith, M. P. (2007). The two faces of transnational citizenship. *Ethnic and Racial Studies, 30*(6), 1096–1116. https://doi.org/10.1080/01419870701599523

Spieth. J. (2011). *The Ewe people: A study of the Ewe people in German Togo* (E. F. Tsaku et al., Trans.). Accra, Ghana: Sub-Saharan Publishers (Original work published 1906)

Stokes, G. (2004). Transnational citizenship: Problems of definition, culture and democracy. *Cambridge Review of International Affairs, 17*(1), 119–135. https://doi.org/10.1080/0955757042000203687

Taha, F. A. R. A. (1977). The Sudan-Zaire boundary. *Sudan Notes and Records, 58*, 73–84.

Touval, S. (1967). The Organization of African Unity and African borders. *International Organization, 21*(1), 102–127.

Turner, B. S. (2022). Marshall and Dahrendorf: Theories of citizenship 1945-2022. *Citizenship Studies, 26*(4–5), 702–711. https://doi.org/10.1080/13621025.2022.2091254

Yearwood, P. J. (1993). "In a casual way with a blue pencil": British policy and the partition of Kamerun, 1914–1919. *Canadian Journal of African Studies / La Revue Canadienne des études Africaines, 27*(2), 218–244.

Zeller, W. (2010). Neither arbitrary nor artificial: Chiefs and the making of the Namibia-Zambia borderland. *Journal of Borderlands Studies, 25*(2), 6–21. https://doi.org/10.1080/08865655.2010.9695758

Looking Backwards to Run Forward: A Critical Examination of the Sixtieth Anniversary of the 1958 All-African People's Conference*

Mjiba Frehiwot[1]

Introduction

The 1900 Pan-African Conference in London marked the beginning of decades of organised Pan-African activism, which culminated in the creation of the All-African People's Conference (AAPC). The organised nature of the Pan-African Movement (PAM) continues to evolve between the 1900 conference and the 1958 AAPC.[2] Pan-Africanists, during this period, were tackling questions related to improved conditions

* This chapter is a slightly edited version of an article first published in *Contemporary Journal of African Studies*, Vol. 10, No. 2 (2023) and is reproduced here with permission.

1 This author acknowledges the support of the Institute of African Studies, Professor Dzodzi Tsikata, Dr Edem Adotey, Dr Zizwe Poe, Professor Horace Campbell, Malaika Aryee-Boi, and all colleagues on the AAPC planning committee and at the Pan-Africana Studies Programme at Lincoln University. The project on which the paper is based benefitted from the support of the Andrew W. Mellon Foundation Afro-Asian Futures Past, Mellon Foundation grant.

2 This statement does not negate Pan-African activity that occurred prior to the 1900 conference. The author contends that Pan-African activity occurred in Global Africa leading to this organised manifestation of Pan-Africanism.

for Africans under colonial rule and an end to racism in the African
Diaspora. Organizations that helped pave the way for Pan-Africanism
to spread throughout Africa were part of the PAM at the time. The
African Association was one such organisation that was founded in 1897
(Sherwood, 2012a) and transformed into the Pan-African Association
(responsible for organising Pan-African conferences forthwith) at the
1900 Pan-African Conference. The Pan-African Association recommended that a Pan-African Congresses be held every two years, according
to a letter written by W. E. B. Du Bois to the permanent committee of
the association in 1923 (Du Bois, 1923). However, due to global political
events, the conference did not occur every two years.[3] Nonetheless, other
congresses, like the 1919 congress in Paris, were placed during this period
and attracted less attention. Although the Pan-African Association did
not have a long life, its formation set in motion a series of events that
would transform the nature of the PAM.

Over the next several decades, Europe housed many Pan-African
organisations. The West African Student Union (WASU), founded in 1925
(Adi, 2000), served as a space for West African students to consider ways
to liberate their respective countries. The International African Friends
of Abyssinia (IAFA), formed in 1934, and replaced by the International
African Service Bureau (IASB), (Adi, 2012), served as forerunners to Pan-
African institutions in Ghana. The West African National Secretariat,
another critical institution, focused on the unification of West Africa
through Pan-African work in Britain (Adi, 2000; Sherwood, 2012a).

Kwame Nkrumah joined George Padmore, W. E. B. Du Bois, and
other vital Pan-Africanists in 1945 as organisers for the fifth Pan-African
Congress (fifth PAC) (Sherwood, 2012b). The hub of Pan-African activity was not only geographically rooted in Europe but was also situated
within organisations that were promoting Pan-African solutions to the
problems of African people. These organisations and institutions, particularly the fifth PAC, catapulted Ghana into the centre of the PAM when
Kwame Nkrumah returned home to the then-Gold Coast from the US
and the UK in 1948 (Adi, 2000; Poe, 2003; Sherwood, 2012a; Valera,

---

3 Historical events such as the onslaught of colonialism across the continent, the repression
   of Pan-African socialists in the USA and World War I may have impacted the ability of the
   Pan-African Congress to occur every two years.

2017). During this time, the PAM was also concerned with the global anti-imperialist internationalist movement, in particular the Afro-Asian Solidarity Movement. The Asian–African Conference (Bandung) held in Indonesia in 1955 called for the immediate end of colonialism in Africa and Asia. The Gold Coast (Ghana) sent a small delegation to the conference. The conference attempted to build anti-imperial bridges among African and Asian nations (Farid, 2016; Hongoh, 2016). This collaboration extended to the AAPC as the Afro-Asian Solidarity Organisation (a permanent institution to organise the conferences) based in Egypt is among the fraternal delegates.

The AAPC, a rallying point for freedom fighters, independent African governments, members of the African Diaspora, and anti-imperialists, is arguably the most groundbreaking Pan-African gathering held on the continent. An expansion of the Pan-African activity that Kwame Nkrumah and his allies had been involved in for more than ten years prior was the inaugural AAPC, which was held in 1958. The AAPC's resemblance to the previous Pan-African Congresses and institutions demonstrates that the activities in Ghana were a continuation of the Pan-African organisations that existed in Europe (Aniche, 2020). Kwame Nkrumah inherited the historical and contemporary legacy of Pan-Africanists during his period in Europe. His interactions with Pan-Africanists and Pan-African organisations sharpened his forward-looking view of Pan-Africanism and his practical interactions with future leaders of independent African nations and members of the Diaspora. (Poe, 2003; Biney, 2011).

The 1958 AAPC had two main objectives: the total liberation and unification of Africa and the independence of the African continent from foreign domination ("All-African People's Conference. All African People's Conference Leaflet", 1958). The AAPC (1958) provided an opportunity for Pan-Africanists to meet on the continent and build collaborations across space and time to advance the PAM. It allowed them to concretise the thoughts, ideas, and principles of the PAM as a complement to the raging independence movement. These ideas saturated the minds of many of the participants at this historic conference and dominated the speeches. It seemed plausible that a unified Africa would come to fruition in their lifetime. Nkrumah's speech at the conference reinforced his commitment to the Pan-African project. He said, "This mid-twentieth century is Africa's. This decade is the decade of African independence. Forward then to independence—to independence now—tomorrow, the United States of Africa…" (Nyumbani, 2007). The Pan-African nature of the conference and the establishment of the Bureau of African Affairs cemented Ghana as a strategic base for leading the Pan-African charge on the continent (Poe, 2003; Grilli, 2018). The Bureau of African Affairs was the main organ responsible for researching, coordinating, and promoting Pan-Africanism (Ahlman, 2012). The bureau was also tasked with planning and executing the All-African Conference Series and liaising with freedom fighters who had not achieved independence, as well as governments of independent African nations, scholars, activists, and anti-imperialist organisations, particularly those that embraced Socialism.

The sixtieth anniversary of the AAPC (1958) was celebrated globally throughout 2018. In Ghana, there were two commemorations held in December on the University of Ghana campus. One of the commemorations was organised by the Nkrumah Pan-African Centre (KNAC) and the Pan-African Federalist Movement, while the other was hosted jointly by the University of Ghana's Institute of African Studies (IAS), Lincoln University (PA), the Trade Union Congress (TUC) of Ghana, the Socialist Forum of Ghana (Socialist Movement Ghana), and Third World Network Africa. This paper will focus on the commemoration hosted by the IAS and partners from 5 to 8 December 2018. The holistic and Pan-African make-up of the institutions planning this conference and the positionality of the author are the primary reasons why this conference is the centre of this paper. The sixtieth-anniversary commemoration held by IAS replicated the original format of the 1958 conference, with a contemporary approach to examining the PAM and the challenges and Pan-African prospects that affect Global Africa today. My role in the sixtieth-anniversary celebration as the convenor of the conference secretariat ensured that I was intimately involved in all components of the conference. This insider knowledge informed my analysis of the resolutions of the 1958 and 2018 conferences. Additionally, my activism and participation in the PAM undergirded my interrogation of the resolutions of the 1958 conference and the statement of issues and recommendations (IARs) of the 2018 conference. My political and academic experience brings a depth of experience and knowledge to the analysis that positions the paper at the crossroads between the academy and Pan-African activism. To accommodate the positionality of the author, the project employed an auto-methodological approach to examining primary and secondary source materials.

This paper analyses the outputs of the 1958 AAPC and 2018 sixtieth anniversary conference—specifically, the resolutions of the 1958 conference and the statement of IARs of the 2018 anniversary conference. The essay incorporates primary and secondary data from the conferences, including memos, reports, speeches, and plenary presentations, to examine the auxiliary conditions that impact the 1958 and 2018 conferences. This essay contributes to research and debates about the impact of the AAPC as an institution on the global PAM. The paper has four main interconnected sections. The introduction is followed by a section that examines the conceptual and methodological considerations. The third section focuses on the 1958 AAPC; the fourth tackles the 2018 AAPC anniversary; and the final section interrogates the way forward for Pan-Africanism and includes a conclusion.

Conceptual and Methodological Considerations

Conceptually, this project leans on three inter-related concepts, namely national liberation, Africa-nation, and decolonisation to interrogate the impact of the 1958 AAPC and the 2018 sixtieth anniversary of the AAPC. These three concepts are part of the resolutions, statement of issues, and recommendations of the 1958 AAPC and the 2018 sixtieth-anniversary celebration. The concept of national liberation stems from the African liberation movement in which African nations fought for their liberation against colonialism. This paper adopts Amilcar Cabral's definition of national liberation in his text *National Liberation and Culture* (1974); he identifies its objective thus:

> The objective of national liberation is, therefore, to reclaim the right, usurped by imperialist domination, namely: the liberation of the process of development of national productive forces. Therefore, national liberation takes place when, and only when, national productive forces are completely free of all kinds of foreign domination (Cabral, 1974, p. 39).

Cabral's concept of national liberation extends beyond political independence but incorporates the independence of the economy, particularly the productive forces. This concept is being used because of the revolutionary nature of national liberation. The 1958 AAPC and its 2018 sixtieth anniversary were founded on the need to revolutionise the African liberation movement and PAM.

Muchie (2004) contends that the African-nation is the key to African unity and liberation. Muchie argues, "We propose the thesis that efforts to free and unite Africa should integrate the idea of the African with the idea of making Africa-nation; both with Pan-Africanism and African Renaissance" (Muchie, 2004, p. 148). The concept of African-nation does not explicitly identify the United States of Africa or an integrated States of Africa. However, this paper embraces the idea of a United States of Africa when referring to African nations. This concept is not a new concept; it was repackaged from the calls for African unity by influential Pan-Africanists like Kwame Nkrumah, Sékou Touré, and Julius Nyerere. It transcends debates about colonial borders and individual African states' sovereignty. This concept grounds the analysis of this paper as it interrogates the resolutions and statements of IARs of these historic conferences.

The final concept, decolonisation, has roots in the anti-colonial struggle in Global Africa. Decolonisation in this paper refers to the complete de-linking of Global Africa from slavery, colonialism, and neo-colonialism physically, spiritually, politically, and economically. Decolonisation is a concept that, as Ogba Adejoh and Okpanachi Idoko assert, is and has been intertwined with Pan-Africanism. They contend that organisation contributed to the loss of African values, shared ideals, and customs (Sylvester & Anthony, 2014). The decolonisation movement includes efforts to combat this loss through the philosophical and practical decolonial activities of Frantz Fanon of Algeria, Julius Nyerere of Tanzania, Kwame Nkrumah of Ghana, Sékou Touré of Guinea, and Gamal Nassar of Egypt. These three concepts weave in and out of the resolutions of the 1958 AAPC and the sixtieth anniversary of the AAPC in 2018.

Methodologically, this is a qualitative study that uses historical and insider research methods to examine primary and secondary source materials. The historical method will be employed through the examination of the available primary source materials of the 1958 AAPC and the 2018 anniversary conference. Insider research will be employed to account for the inner knowledge and association of the author with the 2018 sixtieth anniversary and the IAS. Greene defines insider research as "that which is conducted within a social group, organization or culture of which the researcher is also a member" (2014, p. 1). This methodological approach was chosen because of the role of the author in the planning of the sixtieth anniversary of the AAPC. As a member of the planning committee, and convenor of the Conference secretariat, I have both firsthand knowledge of the scope of the conference and the themes the conference sought to address. Insider researchers share identity, language, and organisational culture and provide access to people and resources more difficult to obtain (Dwyer & Buckle, 2009). Additionally, the author identifies as a Pan-Africanist and is using this experience to identify the most pressing IARs presented by the 2018 commemoration. The primary source materials represent memos, official records, and resolutions of the 1958 AAPC and information from the Bureau of African Affairs. The primary data bank for the sixtieth anniversary stems from the sixtieth-anniversary background, issues, and recommendations of the sixtieth anniversary and video recordings of the plenary sessions of the 2018 commemoration.

The 1958 All-African Peoples Conference

The AAPC held in 1958 in Accra (8–13 December), Ghana, was attended by 300 participants who represented liberation movements, independent governments, and members of the PAM. Anti-imperialist friends, comrades, and observers were also present, although they may not have represented an African country or liberation struggle (Varela, 2017). The theme for the conference was *Hands off Africa! Africa Must Be Free.*

The conference was promoted to potential delegates using a brochure that identified potential participants, the conference theme, objectives, and aims. The leaflet outlined four critical areas that the conference would develop as the strategy and tactics of the "African Non-Violent Revolution" (All-African People's Leaflet, 1958). The four critical areas cited were as follows.

1. Colonialism and Imperialism.
2. Racialism and Discriminatory Laws and Practices.

3. Tribalism and Religious Separatism.
4. The position of Chieftaincy under Colonial Rule and a Free
   Democratic Society.

The mass character of the conference was underscored in the leaflet. It highlights that participants would include representatives from the following institutions.

- African states at the non-governmental level.
- Nationalists.
- Trade union activists.
- Women's and youth groups (All-African People's Leaflet, 1958).

The AAPC marked the first time the Diaspora was invited to a Pan-African conference held on the continent. Delegates at the conference generally represented political parties fighting for independence and anti-imperialist movements. There were diverse delegates who had varying experiences with and responses to colonialism. Several delegations from selected nations were represented by more than one political institution. For example, the group from Sierra Leone had members of the People's Party and the Progressive Party (Daily Graphic, 1958a). The Nigerian delegation was composed of eight different entities, including the Action Group, All-Nigeria Trade Union Federation, Dynamic Party, Dynamic Party (East Branch), National Council of Nigeria & Cameroons, Northern Element Progressive Party, Zikist National Vanguard, and the Northern Elements Progressive Party (Daily Graphic, 1958a). A five-person delegation arrived at the AAPC from Ethiopia with a donation of £400 from Emperor Haile Selassie. The delegation was headed by Mr G. Mekasha (Daily Graphic, 1958b). Paramount Chief Undi, Mr Nkumbula, and Chief Shakunbula represented Northern Rhodesia (Zimbabwe) at the AAPC. A few of the documents lacked information on the jobs held or the organizations they were affiliated with. Tunisia sent a six-person delegation of which two women, Mrs Ferida Cherif and Mrs Stein Benghazi, were listed as members (Daily Graphic, 1958b). Sending women to the AAPC was a bold and revolutionary act as women were generally heavily underrepresented in such gatherings.

Patrice Lumumba's attendance at the conference and his delivery of a powerful address accentuating the peculiar political situation in the Congo and the importance of African unity reinforces the theme of "Hands Off Africa and African Unity". He stated:

> This historical conference, which puts us in contact with experienced political figures from all the African countries and from all over the world, reveals one thing to us: despite the boundaries that separate us, despite our ethnic differences, we have the same awareness, the same soul plunged day and night in anguish, the same anxious desire to make this African continent a free and happy continent that has rid itself of unrest and of fear and of any sort of colonialist domination (Lumumba, Sartre, & Van Lierde, 1972, p. 58).

Members of the African Diaspora were also present at the meeting; however, most were fraternal delegates or observers. These members did not have the right to vote as official delegates but observed the proceedings. The official registry recorded Mr Horace Bond,[4] Mrs Paul Robeson,[5] and Mrs Shirley Graham Du Bois[6] of the United States as fraternal delegates. The invitation to and attendance by the African Diaspora at the AAPC signified a move to embrace global Pan-Africanism. This showed the Diaspora that they had a role in developing the continent and the Pan-African vision immediately after independence. There were also representatives of the Afro-Asian Solidarity Movement on the conference list. Yang Shuo[7] represented the Afro-Asian Solidarity Council. The presence of the Afro-Asian Solidarity Council conveys solidarity between Africa and Asia and ties to internationalism. Among the organizations in attendance were the Afro-Asian Secretariat from the United Arab Republic and the Society of African Culture, which is headquartered in Paris. (AAPC Bulletin, ACC, no. 848,

---

4 Horace Bond is a person of African descent born in the United States. He was also a graduate of Lincoln University, PA, and a social activist.
5 Mrs Paul Robeson is the wife of Paul Robeson but, more significantly, she was an active member of the Sojourners for Truth and many other movements of the period.
6 Mrs Shirley Graham Du Bois is a Pan-African socialist who was a playwright and wrote a significant play titled "Tom Tom" challenging slavery and colonialism. She also was an international figure who was the first Director of Television in Ghana during the first republic.
7 Yang Shuo represented the Afro-Asian Solidarity Movement based in Egypt.

58, 1958). Official delegates represented 30 countries across Africa with 62 political parties, associations, trade unions, and movements.

Kwame Nkrumah's opening remarks charged delegates to prioritise the liberation and unity of Africa. He contended that unity was needed for African nations to obtain complete independence. He specified four stages the continent needed to pass through to achieve political and economic independence: (*a*) the attainment of freedom and independence; (*b*) the consolidation of that freedom and independence; (*c*) the creation of unity and community between free African states; and (*d*) the economic and social reconstruction of Africa (Nyumbani, 2007). According to Nkrumah, these stages were necessary for African nations to gain and maintain independence. Nkrumah's four phases of economic and political freedom are especially important because, in 1958, the majority of African countries lacked independence. The AAPC aimed to develop a more extensive network of independent nations to build the PAM. The tone of the meeting shifted between Pan-African jubilance and confronting the long road ahead for Africa. W. E. B. Du Bois's address, read by Shirley Graham Du Bois, provides a sober history of his life and the evolution of the Pan-African Congresses as a precursor to the first Pan-African conference hosted in Africa. He concluded his speech with a futurist rally call, "Africa, awake! Put on the beautiful robes of Pan-African socialism" (Du Bois, 1958, p. 5). The conference chair, Tom Mboya of Kenya, voted in by delegates, symbolised Pan-Africanism. In an interview, he reverberated the Pan-African spirit that echoed throughout the conference halls. He remarked,

> This is the first conference of all-African political and Trade Union leaders to ever be held in Africa. The purpose of it is to try to get all these leaders to come together and discuss African problems. With a view of course to find out means and ways to collectively trying to fight against things like imperialism and colonialism, racialism, tribalism and of course questions of boundaries between states (Adeyinka, 2022).

The format of the conference included plenary sessions tackling high-level questions of unity and liberation and smaller committees that engaged in the intellectual work of the conference. The committees focused on five key themes: (*a*) imperialism and colonialism; (*b*) frontiers and federation;

(c) racialism; (d) tribalism and traditional institutions; and (e) establishment of a permanent organisation (*International Organization*, 1962, p. 430). The conference was organised through a committee structure where delegates were divided into groups to work on the resolutions. The names of these committees are difficult to unearth due to a loss of records. These broad resolutions would serve as the basis for the liberation struggle as delegates returned home. The conference committee developed a pamphlet to outline resolutions and how they could be implemented across Africa.

Sixtieth Anniversary of the AAPC

In the 60 years since the 1958 AAPC, the economic and political landscape in Global Africa has been significantly transformed. The political environment has been influenced by five decades of economic organization, global financial crises, the fall of the Soviet Union, and the rise of the unipolar world. These global events influenced the economies and political systems of African states and prevented them from engaging Pan-African organisation activity. Additionally, the disappointments with independence, the rise of concepts like good governance and how they are employed, and multi-party constitutional rule and its limitations have also impacted the PAM. It is with this backdrop that the sixtieth anniversary of the AAPC was organised by the IAS at the University of Ghana, Socialist Forum of Ghana (now Socialist Movement of Ghana), Third World Network Africa, Trades Union Congress of Ghana, and Lincoln University (Pennsylvania). The Lincoln University delegation represented the President of the University and included four faculties and two students. This Pan-African conference and cultural celebration occurred from 5 to 8 December 2018, at the University of Ghana Conference facility and the Kwame Nkrumah Complex—IAS. The conference served two purposes: the first and most immediate was to commemorate and celebrate the 1958 AAPC. The second was to gather Pan-African academics, activists, community members, and students to converge to examine the most pressing questions facing Global Africa in the twenty-first century.

Since its inception, the IAS has been one of the centres of Pan-African academic and activist activity in Ghana and Global Africa. The IAS is well-placed to convene key Pan-African stakeholders because of its central role in researching, teaching, and advocating for Pan-Africanism

(Allman, 2013, Adomako Ampofo, 2016). When the IAS was formally established by Dr. Kwame Nkrumah in 1963, he urged the professors and personnel to see the institution's mission as a liberating force dedicated to advancing Pan-Africanism and Internationalism. In his opening address, which has come to be known as "The African Genius", he states:

> And in Ghana the fact that we are committed to the construction of a socialist society makes it especially necessary that this Institute of African Studies should work closely with the people—and should be constantly improving upon its methods for serving the needs of the people of Ghana, of Africa and of the world. Teachers and students in our universities should clearly understand this (Nkrumah, 1964, p. 7).

This charge from Kwame Nkrumah revibrates through the research, teaching, and community engagement of the IAS. The theme for the conference, "*Revisiting the 1958 AAPC—The Unfinished Business of Liberation and Transformation*", called for a historic review of the 1958 conference and a forward-looking engagement of Global Africa's liberation and transformation. The AAPC secretariat invited participants from Global Africa, some of whom represented political, economic, and academic institutions[8] and ensured that women played a leading role in each of the plenary sessions. Women were central in the sixtieth anniversary of the AAPC in planning, debates, speakers, and participants. Participants of the conference consisted of individuals representing 34 countries across Global Africa and all six regions of the African Union. Participants hailed from Algeria, Belgium, Cameroon, Costa Rica, Egypt, Ghana, Haiti, India, Japan, Namibia, Tanzania, and St. Lucia (Tsikata, 2018). The conference was organised around six sub-themes to engage the current conjuncture in Global Africa and renew our collective commitment to Pan-Africanism. The themes: (*a*) Peoples

---

8   Some of the organisations that participants were affiliated with and members of include: The All-African People's Revolutionary Party, African Studies Association of Africa, Lake Chad Basin Commission, the Orature Collective, Mwalimu Nyerere Foundation, Network for Women's Rights in Ghana, PANAFEST Foundation, Convention People's Party, Economic League, and many more. The Pan-African Women's Organization was not officially invited to the conference; however, the conference promoted African feminism through the participation of key African feminists.

of Africa; (*b*) Neo-Colonialism & Imperialism; (*c*) African Union and *Agenda 2063*; (*d*) Emancipation of Women; (*e*) Reparations and Restorative Justice; and (*f*) Global Warming anchored the conference theoretically and practically.

The central institutions of the conference were seven plenary sessions (based on the six sub-themes), 120-panel presentations, sub-committees that tackled the key conference themes, and an IARs committee. The seven plenaries focused on: (*a*) Being Youth in Africa Today; (*b*) The Youth, Transformation and African Futures; (*c*) Neoliberalism: Africa's Economies and the Living Conditions of Africans;(*d*) Ending Imperialist Domination and Transforming Africa's Economies; (*e*) Pan-African Epistemologies for Knowledge Production; (*f*) Building a New Politics for Substantive Democracy and Security; and (*g*) Where do we go from here: The Future of Pan-Africanism.[9]

The conference published a list of IARs which can be found on the IAS website,[10] corresponding to the six sub-themes. All six IARs are comprehensive and merit a thorough examination. This paper investigates four of the six IARs. These IARs were chosen due to their close alignment with the resolutions of the 1958 AAPC and their representation of contemporary issues facing Global Africa. They correspond with the three resolutions reviewed from the 1958 AAPC and one forward-looking issue and recommendation. The four main IARs that this paper will examine are as follows.

1. On Pan-Africanism Today, Tomorrow and Building a New Politics of Substantive Democracy and Security.
2. On Pan-African Epistemologies for Knowledge Production.
3. Ending Imperialist Domination and Transforming Africa's Economies.
4. On Restorative and Reparative Justice (AAPC Statement of IARs, 2018).

---

9 The conference programme for the sixtieth anniversary of the AAPC can be accessed here: https://ias.ug.edu.gh/content/conference-programme
10 Statement of IARs: https://ias.ug.edu.gh/sites/ias.ug.edu.gh/files/ AAPC%20 2018-Issues%20%26%20Recommendations_Feb%202019_.pdf

The above IARs highlight contemporary matters that Pan-African academics and activists are tackling in the twenty-first century. They demonstrate the evolution of the PAM and the issues that African people have been facing globally, despite the victories of the independence era. Technological advances, extractive economies, environmental concerns, and global racial capitalism all impact Africa and African people globally. Horace Campbell, the fourth occupant of the Kwame Nkrumah Chair in African Studies at the University of Ghana, outlined the essence of these four IARs in his fiery closing speech. He said:

> The conference provided a mandate to deliberate on contemporary imperialism, neoliberalism, global Africa, Pan-Africanism, the emancipation of woman, reparative and restorative justice, and global warming. In every discussion, it became absolutely clear that none of the tasks could be fulfilled outside of the context of the unification and emancipation of the African peoples at home and abroad (University of Ghana, 2018).

Looking Backwards to Run Forward

This section draws connections between the 1958 AAPC and the 2018 sixtieth anniversary. The two conferences occurred in different centuries with unique markers based on the global geo-politics of the respective period. The sixty years that separated the two conferences witnessed monumental historical and political changes on the continent. Most notable is the political independence of most African nations (Western Sahara remains the exception), the establishment of the Organisation of African Unity (now African Union), several Pan-African Congresses, the creation of regional economic and political blocs in Africa, a decrease in the number of socialist and communist nations, and the end of the Cold War. These global political and economic manifestations impacted the issues that each conference tackled. The political landscape in Africa over the period impacted the resolutions at the 1958 AAPC and 2018 sixtieth anniversary.

1958 All-African Peoples Conference: Selected Resolutions

Imperialism and Colonialism

The resolution on imperialism and colonialism begins with defining the two types of colonial projects and characteristics of colonialism in Africa. According to the resolution, *Indirect rule* is categorised as "territories where indigenous Africans are dominated by foreigners who have their seats of authority in foreign lands". *Settler colonialism* is defined as "those where indigenous Africans are dominated and oppressed by foreigners who have settled permanently in Africa and who regard the position of Africa under their sway..." (University of California Press, 1959, p. 43). The resolution highlighted the human rights violations that were occurring on the continent. With a particular focus on racialism, the resolution contended that subjection of one race by another is unacceptable and violates fundamental human rights. African people's economic, political, and social oppression was indicated as central to colonialism and imperialism. The resolution strongly condemned the "militarization of Africans and the use of African soldiers in a nefarious global game against their brethren" (University of California Press, 1959, p. 43). The importance of human rights appeared in the resolution, focusing on freedom of speech, association, movement, worship, and the freedom to live full lives. The most significant section of the resolution demanded "that independent African states should pursue in their international policy principles which will expedite and accelerate the Independence and sovereignty of all dependent and colonial African Territories" (University of California Press, 1959, p. 44).

Frontiers, Boundaries, and Federation

This resolution addresses the impact of frontiers and boundaries on the unification of African people across the continent. The first preambular clause sets the tone for the remainder of the resolution. It proclaims that:

> Whereas the great mass of African peoples are animated by a desire for unity; Whereas the unity of Africa will be vital to the independence of its component units and essential to the security and general well-being of African peoples..." (University of California Press, 1959, p. 45).

The belief in African unity expressed in this declaration is widespread among African people. This is particularly significant in light of the ideological rift between African leaders that emerged in the few years after the AAPC. The AAPC recognised the importance of African people being at the forefront of the struggle for Pan-Africanism. The resolution's language supports African unity being driven by the larger African masses rather than from an elite group of vanguard Pan-Africanists. The creation of the Commonwealth of Free African States was a focal point of speeches, particularly that of Kwame Nkrumah, Tom Mboya, and Patrice Lumumba. The resolution called for existing independent African states to organise groups based on geography, economic interdependence, and cultural and linguistic similarities (University of California Press, 1959). These groupings would hasten the liberation of African states and the continent's unification. The resolution stressed that only independent and free states should collaborate with other independent states and must not engage with colonial states. The question of regional groupings being permanent structures was addressed it stated:

> WHEREAS regional federation or groups should be regarded as a means to amend and should not be prejudicial to the ultimate objective of a Pan-African Commonwealth by hardening as separate entities and thereby impending progress towards a continental Commonwealth... (University of California Press, 1959, p. 45).

The immediate abandonment of artificial barriers and frontiers drawn by colonialists and the need to embrace continental unity closed the resolution.

Racialism and Discriminatory Laws and Practices

The resolution on Racialism and Discriminatory laws practiced had a particular focus on settler colonialism. The resolution violently opposed colonialism in general but identified the rather egregious examples of settler colonialism in the Union of South Africa, the Rhodesia's (Zambia and Zimbabwe), and Nyasaland (Malawi). It demanded the immediate withdrawal of colonial governments and the independence of nations under the yoke of settler colonialism. The resolution condemned the act of settler colonialism as a violation of the United Nations Declaration of Human Rights established ten years earlier. Little had changed in these "territories" since the declaration was born, and the international community's silence on this gross oversight was a focus of the resolution.

Additionally, the resolution addressed the deficiency of educational facilities, racial segregation, forced labour, minority rule, and land grabbing by colonialists (University of California Press, 1959, p. 41). The resolution demanded that all African countries that supplied labour to South Africa withdraw and withhold workers for use in their country's development. It provides practical ways of supporting liberation struggles beyond individual borders. It contends that: (*a*) African states should have no diplomatic relations with any country that has race discrimination; (*b*) April fifteenth should be established as Africa Day as a rally point for freedom; (*c*) the permanent Secretariat will create a bureau of information to serve as the nucleus of information on liberation movements; and (*d*) independent states should form an "African Legion" (University of California Press, 1959, p. 42). These recommendations focused on intensifying the pressure on settler colonial states. This resolution also calls on the British Government to end the state of emergency in Kenya and release all political prisoners.

The AAPC's 1958 resolutions addressed concerns that African people faced on a national and continental level. The resolutions and the meeting were anchored by the appeal for liberation and unification. The resolutions provided a futuristic understanding of the need for African unity and the immediate need for freedom in countries still under the yoke of colonialism. The resolutions are comprehensive and representative of the tenor of the conference and the period in which Ghana served as a strategic base for Pan-African activity.

2018 Sixtieth Anniversary of the AAPC: IARs

Pan-Africanism Today, Tomorrow, and Building a New Politics of Substantive Democracy and Security

The foundation of this IAR is rooted in the belief that decolonisation is incomplete. This IAR challenged the claims that Global Africa is independent and contended that the European and American hegemonic construct governs Global Africa. With a specific focus on the impact of economic systems, the IAR contends that weak economies and political systems affect nations' ability to advance democracy, security, and autonomy. The statement asserted that the unification and liberation of Africa are thwarted by the state of African national economies propelled by these Euro-American hegemonic paradigms. The lack of political parties with a Pan-African orientation and national borders that embrace a colonial tradition is a significant barrier to achieving Pan- Africanism (IAS-UG, 2019). This issue recognised that official Pan-African organisations such as the African Union are not effectively reflecting Global Pan-African aspirations.

The recommendations for this section focus on an immediate end to all forms of colonial rule of African people. The conference immediately calls for the Moroccan government to withdraw from Western Sahara. The statement of IARs highlights the need for inclusive democracy in Africa, including equity and fairness for all in Global Africa (Africa and African descendants outside of Africa). The statement contends that inclusive democracy is key to developing democratic economies. This democracy must be inclusive of Pan-African ideals. The replacement of the dominant elite political class with formations representing cultural workers, peasants, farmers, youth, labour, and traders was accentuated as an option to achieve inclusive democracy (IAS-UG, 2019). The recommendation calls for the widening and deepening of the relationship across Global Africa using African languages on social media, development, and control of technology and media outlets. Support for global movements like #BlackLivesMatter on the continent and globally was underscored as particularly significant.

On Pan-African Epistemologies for Knowledge Production

Epistemology is defined in this IAR *as how we know what we know*. The power of knowledge and knowledge production as a political project is emphasised as key to developing Pan-African epistemologies. According to the IAR, "knowledge products" can be manipulated to meet the objectives of their manufacturer. "Their collective intellectual capabilities have been undermined to facilitate subjugation and marginalization"

(IAS-UG, 2019, p. 3). This suppression occurs in formal education institutions in Global Africa, as reported by the plenary on Pan-African epistemologies. The issue contends that contemporary African higher education institutions are not conducive to addressing Africa's pressing needs. The African intelligentsia is complicit in elevating Western and colonial knowledge over African-based knowledge. Neo-colonial education is juxtaposed by the Dakar School, the Dar es Salaam School, and the Ibadan School,[11] which were considered liberated spaces during the initial phases of independence in Africa (Campbell, 1991; Thioub, 2007). Today, the IAS is considered to be what Kwame Nkrumah identified as a liberated zone (Nkrumah, 1968) inside the academy in the twenty-first century.

The creation of Pan-African institutions independent from neo-colonial educational institutions is a primary recommendation of this IAR. There was a focus on the necessity of embracing decolonised and liberatory knowledge and self-knowledge. Recognising that many Pan-Africanists must operate in neo-colonial higher education institutions, it was suggested that there must be a union between academic scholarship and Pan-African activism. In addition, to calls to bridge the gap between Pan-African academics and community activists, the IAR recommended the development of a curriculum (the level was not specified but one could assume this was for all education levels) to expand the Pan-African personality. This curriculum would have the bandwidth to be employed in formal and non-formal systems. The development of (an) African languages (s) that can be used universally across the continent to communicate was a focus of this recommendation (IAS-UG, 2019). Pan-African knowledge producers were tasked with engaging policymakers to influence African-centred scholarship and general Pan-African policies. This recommendation suggested that the AAPC should be organised every two years henceforth. Unfortunately, this was not realised due to the global COVID-19 pandemic and its disruption of academic and activist gatherings.

---

11 The Dakar School, Ibadan School, and the Dar es Salaam School were institutions of higher education that were pivotal immediately after independence. These spaces engaged in developing African intellectuals and ideas that would challenge the contemporary research and thinking on Africa, African people, and intellectualism in Africa.

On Ending Imperialist Domination and Transforming Africa's Economies

This IAR issue on ending imperialist domination and transforming Africa's economies outlines the key economic challenges facing the African continent in the twenty-first century. The most significant challenge to Africa's economies according to the IAR is that they are "structurally dependent on the production and export of raw material commodities which feed industrial production, job creation and incomes in other economies" (IAS-UG, 2019, p. 4). The issue discusses the fact that African foreign investors are protected and supported by African state actors. The issue contends that the most important internal sectors across Africa are dominated by Western transnational capital. The IAR suggests that Africa's ruling elites are, "largely comfortable overseeing realities within which there is widespread unemployment, a crisis of livelihoods in rural areas, and urbanization amidst deindustrialization" (IAS-UG, 2019, p. 4). The issue highlights the impact of increased precarious working conditions that impact the livelihoods of workers who are part of the "informal" economy. High unemployment, coupled with a larger percentage of youth who have never had a relationship with formal employment, further crippled the living conditions in many African countries (IAS-UG, 2019).

The recommendations for this section highlight the importance of stemming and returning the illicit outflows of capital from Africa. This recommendation suggests that African states must be redesigned to facilitate the self-reliance and self-sufficiency of African states and people (IAS-UG, 2019, p. 4). This includes the redesign of the banking sectors to ensure that they are people-centric and focus on financial cooperatives such as credit unions as a model to house the people's resources. On the educational front, the issue suggests that "Global Africans develop and disseminate analysis that promotes the understanding that neoliberalism and the neoliberal economic system are anti-people, anti-solidarity, anti-collective, and bolstered by the expansion of debt and numerous debt cycles" (IAS-UG, 2019, p. 4). Lastly, this issue recommends that Global Africans confront the power that foreign states, financial capital, and transnational corporations (TNCs) have over African economies. This recommendation outlines the steps that African nations must use to shed their economic colonial legacies. It contends that African nations must take their economies into their own hands to chart a new economic path for Global Africans.

On Restorative and Reparative Justice

Restorative and reparative justice (IAR) focuses on reparations as central to Global Africa's development. Reparations in this context are not a call for financial compensation but speak to the dignity of Africa and African people. The section is based on the assertion that "we cannot wait for external reparations before we repair ourselves and our environment" (IAS-UG, 2019, p. 6). This recommendation called for a new paradigm to examine the global economy beyond 1492 and to engage African history for lessons for reparative justice. The 2011 U.N. Conference Against Racism was referenced as a pivotal moment in the fight against slavery (Zaki, 2011). Slavery is a crime against humanity; however, most African states do not incorporate slavery as a crime into their international policies. The recommendation calls for the creation of a global education programme focusing on reparations and restorative justice. It also calls on the AAPC@60 to "organise to secure recognition of the historic ecological debt and reparations owed to Africa's people for slavery and colonial plunder" (IAS-UG, 2019, p. 6). The recommendation encourages Africa, Caribbean nations, and other African-majority nations to participate in self-reparations. Self-reparations include, but are not limited to, resource and land reclamation and restoration, return of lost populations (return of people of African descent to the continent, knowledge by African people and African agency), and removal of colonial legacies (images, nationalism of African assets in the name of working people, and correction of legal frameworks).

Global African solidarity foregrounds this section of the recommendations, with a particular focus on developing tangible connections between Caribbean communities (CARICOM) and African states. There was also a call for African nations to support CARICOM's ten-point[12] plan and the Global Africa Congress' twelve-point plan. Finally, this recommendation strongly condemns the occupation of Palestine and calls

12 For more information about CARICOM's Ten-point plan visit-https:// caricomreparations. org/caricom/

for all African people to support the Boycott, Divestment, and Sanctions (BDSs) campaign against the State of Israel until the state recognises the social and political rights of the Palestinian people (IAS-UG, 2019).

Looking Backwards to Run Forward

The 1958 AAPC was a pivotal conference for African independence. Two short years after the conference, over one-third of the continent had gained independence. The 1958 conference promoted liberation, unity, and African agency to those present and those in conversation with the conference. The 1958 conference resolutions targeted broadly the eradication of any form of colonial control on the continent, including settler colonialism and an immediate need for African unity. Interestingly, the 2018 sixtieth anniversary of the AAPC's focus was like the 1958 conference in that the strands tackled issues of neo-colonialism and African unity. Both conferences promoted African agencies as pivotal components of the PAM. The African nation served as the centre of both conferences. Resolutions and speeches advocating for the independence of African nations in line with African unity in 1958 raised issues related to the African continent. All African people and nations were essentially affected by the oppression or colonization of one African. The 2018 sixtieth anniversary called on the African nation to centre the contemporary issues facing African people globally in the PAM. An assessment of these two conferences reveals that some topics were still pertinent for the 2018 conference and that there were still unresolved liberation and transformational concerns in some sectors.

Unfinished Business of the PAM

The 1958 AAPC conference resolutions and the 2018 sixtieth anniversary IARs overlap primarily on the question of imperialism and colonialism. These topics were raised through debates, discussions, resolutions, and IARs. In 1958, AAPC resolutions focused on the impact of imperialism and colonialism on Africa. The geopolitical moment necessitated the conference's focus on the liberation and unification of African nations and the eradication of racialism. The sixtieth-anniversary issue and recommendation *On Ending Imperialist Domination and Transforming African Economies and Building a New Politics of Substantive Democracy and Security* focused on the effects of imperialism and neo-colonialism economically, politically, and socially. The recommendations and issues highlight the impact these systems have on the everyday lives of African people globally. The question of human rights emerged in both the 1958 and 2018 conferences. The 1958 and 2018 conferences incorporated the importance of human rights as a vital component of African people's liberation. In 1958, the resolutions contended that the very nature of colonialism is a human rights violation. This theme was picked up again in the 2018 conference in calls for international recognition of human rights violations in Africa and the Global South with a particular focus on Western Sahara and Palestine.

The 2018 conference advanced its view on African political systems and contends that they are rooted in a Euro-American hegemonic construct. These economic models promote neo-liberal policies that demonstrate a departure from indirect and direct colonial rule to imperial domination. The plenary on Ending Imperialist Domination and Transforming Africa's Economies tackles questions of economic imperialism, including land and ocean grabbing, exploitation of natural resources, and its impact on Africa's development. This panel raises critical questions about the impact of global capitalism and provides solutions for African nations and people as they develop alternative economic models. Dr Yao Graham, the coordinator of Third World Network Africa, raises critical questions about economic sovereignty and the ownership of natural resources in communities across the continent. Dr Adotey Bing-Pappoe, a professor of International Business, suggests that cooperatives can combat the imperialist domination of economic governance in Global Africa[13] (Bing-Pappoe, 2018).

Frontiers, Boundaries, and Federation emerges in both conferences with an emphasis on eliminating colonial (neo-colonial) borders. Borders during the immediate post-colonial era became a fiercely contested concept and practical exercise. Some leaders adopted the domestication approach of solidifying their borders, which expanded their national

---

13 Yao Graham is the Coordinator of Third World Network Africa, which is a Pan-African research and advocacy organisation that works on economic and social equity within Africa. (TWNAFRICA—to Deliver a Better World!). Dr Addotey Bing-Pappoe is a Professor at the University of Greenwich.

territory (Khadiagala, 2010). This approach further cements colonial borders, which plague African nations today. The 2018 commemoration concentrated on the impact of embracing inherited colonial borders as a threat to Pan-Africanism and the decolonisation project. The influence of colonial borders on the political and economic well-being across the continent has been a topic of debate since independence. Adotey defines the border as an imaginary line that borderland residents do not acknowledge and, simultaneously, a political tool used by colonialists and the political elite (Adotey, 2021). The 2018 conference did not have a plenary session or keynote address dedicated to frontiers and federations; nevertheless, several speakers, panelists, and cultural performances referred to the dangers of enforcing and embracing colonial inherited borders. The cross section of discussions and debates on the question of eradicating colonial borders in the 2018 conference (physical and mental) speaks to the central place that borders play in the political and economic challenges faced by Global Africa. Economic sovereignty is only possible by addressing the barriers inherited from colonial borders.

Settler colonialism and occupation based on racialism features in the 1958 resolutions and the IARs of 2018. The resolutions for the 1958 conference include the immediate withdrawal of settlers in Southern Africa and the total liberation of the people of Azania, South Africa. The 2018 IAR concentrated on freeing Palestine, Western Sahara, and West Papua New Guinea. Interestingly, the 2018 commemoration lacked content on Palestine; however, the occupation of Palestine was included in the IAR. This inclusion may be credited to the political orientation of the key organisers of the conference. The 1958 conference was silent on the occupation of Palestine despite the attendance of several representatives from the Afro-Asian Solidarity Movement. This is even more curious since, only seven years later, Ghana hosted the Afro-Asian Solidarity Conference in 1965 in Winneba (Dai, 1966; Goddeeris, 2022).

Business of the Twenty-First Century PAM

The contemporary decolonisation debate is centred around academics, economists, and Pan-African activists. These debates began during the anti-colonial movement and have been more prominent at various moments in the last sixty years. These prime actors in the movement for the decolonisation of the continent are concentrated in intellectual and activist spaces, while the political elite in Africa generally embraces methodological and theoretical direction from the Global North (American and European models of governance). This divide between the intellectual and activist spaces and the cohort of African leaders occupying government positions limits the possibility of decolonisation occurring in the twenty-first century.

The 2018 sixtieth anniversary of the AAPC offered Pan-African institutions, organisations, and individuals the opportunity to dream about a future where African people could embrace their agency and manage their own affairs. The IARs are both reflective of the impact of colonialism and neo-colonialism on Global Africa and are forward- and inward-looking. The IAR on restorative and reparative justice was featured in 2018 as a vital element of the PAM. Participants debated the necessity of addressing reparations, restorative justice, and World Racism in a neo-colonial Global Africa. Debates raised at the World Conference Against Racism (WACR) supported the importance of having an All-African dialogue on reparations. The IAR boldly stated, "African, Caribbean and African majority states in other parts of Global Africa should engage in self-reparation…" (AACP 2018 Statement of IARs, 2019, p. 7). Turning inward is part of the call by organisations such as the Caribbean Community (CARICOM), which has a ten-point plan for reparations and restoration (McKeown, 2021). Concentrating on internal reparations allows Global African people to exercise agency in their redemption and liberation. This recommendation focuses on exploiting internal African resources as the basis for Africa's liberation and unification. Universal African citizenship and the free movement of African labour across Global Africa are at the core of this recommendation. This recommendation is quite similar to the 1958 resolution on frontiers, boundaries, and federation. The movement of African people across Global Africa for labour has the potential to reduce unemployment, address forced migration, strengthen economies, and increase internal trade. The top-down approach of Pan-African activity across the continent that prevailed since the original conference has not been as successful as initially envisaged (Ayittey, 2010). This can be attributed to historical and political events, including the divide between the African leaders that held varying views on African unity.[14] The relationship between African states and former colonisers, particularly embracing capitalism and Western democracy sidelined debates about Pan-Africanism.

The 2018 recommendations focused on the role of women and youth in Africa's transformation. The recommendation titled *Youth, Workers, Progressive Women, and Africa's Transformation* included tackling issues faced by women, LGBTQI+ persons and African workers. The 2018 commemoration intentionally invited youth, students, activists, scholars, and the community as the main actors of the conference. Two of the seven plenaries focused on youth, and the opening plenary invited panelists to address the theme of Being Youth in Africa Today.[15] Over 300 people attended the opening plenary with representatives from across Global Africa, including a large contingent of youth who traveled from Benin, Côte d'Ivoire, and Burkina Fâso.

There was a particular focus on African workers losing their rights to decent work and quality of life (IAS-UG, 2019, p. 7). The loss of decent work impacts the daily lives of Africans globally. With a focus on the lives of African people, the organisers embrace mass-based Pan-Africanism. Decent work as a manifestation of a Pan-African vision emerged strongly in the statement of IARs. Debates on decent work are occurring across Global Africa, for example, Atitsogbe et al. (2021) examine the psychological impact of the lack of decent work on Togolese primary school teachers (Atitsogbe et al., 2021). They contend that decent work is necessary for individual and collective development with a particular focus on primary school teachers. The recommendations of the 2018 conference suggest that focusing on decent work was a priority of the AAPC.

Many of the presentations underscored the failures of Pan-African bodies such as the African Union, ECOWAS, and other regional

---

14 The African independence era produced African leaders who embraced Pan-African unity immediately and those who preferred to have national independence as the priority. The Casablanca Bloc promoted an immediate unified Africa and was endorsed by the leaders of Morocco, Egypt, Libya, Ghana, Guinea, and Mali, while the Monrovia Bloc, which included Liberia, Nigeria, and most of Francophone Africa, promoted an approach to African unity that privileged independence at the national level over continental unity.

15 The programme and conference website for the AAPC @ 2018 can be found here: https://ias.ug.edu.gh/

groupings across Global Africa. Lastly, a bottom-up approach to building Pan-African institutions and the global movement was emphasised in this final resolution. The lessons gleaned from the 1958 AAPC strengthened the composition, structure, and issues raised and debated at the 2018 sixtieth anniversary conference. The similarities speak to the continued nature of the struggle against imperialism, colonialism, and neo-colonialism. The 2018 sixtieth anniversary renewed the primary questions raised at the 1958 conference. With a focus on new and old challenges, the 2018 commemoration provides contemporary Pan-African scholars and activists with a diverse and multi-faceted blueprint that also includes varying opinions on the struggle for Pan-Africanism in the twenty-first century.

Conclusion

This essay examines the contributions and outcomes of the 1958 AAPC and the sixtieth anniversary of the AAPC celebrated in Accra, Ghana. The significant contributions of the 1958 AAPC and 2018 anniversary cannot be discussed or debated outside of the larger Pan-African project. During the 1958 conference, Africa was mired in a fight for independence and liberation from colonial regimes. Delegates and fraternal delegates represented political parties, liberation struggles, and anti-colonial organisations. The call for immediate independence and liberation was at the core of speeches, committees, and resolutions. Resolutions were wide-sweeping and focused on the immediate issue of independence and Pan-Africanism as short- and long-term strategies for Africa. The 2018 commemoration boasted a diverse gathering of Pan-Africanists representing students, academics, activists, labour leaders, and the community. The format of the conference mirrored that of the original 1958 conference but embraced a twenty-first-century reality. The plenaries, themes, and committees addressed the history of the PAM, including the 1958 conference, and sought to imagine a new Pan-African world. The sixty years that separated the 1958 and 2018 conferences showed promise of transformation and, sadly, a re-emergence of colonialism (neo-colonialism). The effects of neo-colonialism and imperialism were addressed throughout most plenaries and sessions.

The opening and closing sessions in the 2018 commemoration raised questions about the impact of imperialism and neo-colonialism on Global Africa's development. The 2018 commemoration addressed vital issues relevant in the twenty-first century, such as reparations and restorative justice, climate change, and recognition of women, the LGBTQI+ community, and persons displaced from decent work. The 2018 IAR suggests that Pan-Africanism must be driven by mass-based organisations that embody Pan-Africanism. The state apparatus in its current state is no longer a viable institution to lead this charge. The 2018 commemoration hosted by the University of Ghana's IAS, Lincoln University, the TUC of Ghana, the Socialist Forum of Ghana (Socialist Movement Ghana), and Third World Network Africa will undoubtedly be discussed and debated in the years to come.

References

AAPC Bulletin, ACC, no. 848, 58. (1958). Public Records and Archives, Administration Department.

Adi, H. (2000). Pan-Africanism and West African Nationalism in Britain. *African Studies Review, 43*(1), 69–82. https://doi.org/10.2307/524721

Adi, H. (2012). African political thinkers, Pan-Africanism and the politics of exile, c.1850–1970. *Immigrants & Minorities, 30*(2–3), 263–291. https://doi.org/10.1080/02619288.2010.502718

Adomako Ampofo, A. (2016). Re-viewing studies on Africa, #Black Lives Matter, and envisioning the future of African studies. *African Studies Review, 59*(2), 7–29.

Adotey, E. (2021). An imaginary line? Decolonisation, bordering and borderscapes on the Ghana–Togo border. *Third World Quarterly, 42*(5), 1069–1086. https://doi.org/10.1080/01436597.2020.1813019

Ahlman, J. S. (2012). Managing the Pan-African workplace: Discipline, ideology, and the cultural politics of the Ghanaian Bureau of African Affairs, 1959-1966. *Ghana Studies, 15*(16), 337–371.

All-African People's Conference. All African People's Conference leaflet. (1958). W. E. B. Du Bois Papers (MS 312). Special Collections and University Archives, University of Massachusetts Amherst Libraries.

All-African People's Conference 60th Anniversary Opening Ceremony. (n.d.). Retrieved from https://www.youtube.com/live/5IiD-zyCLaU?feature=share

Allman, J. (2013). Kwame Nkrumah, African studies, and the politics of knowledge production in the Black Star of Africa. *The International Journal of African Historical Studies, 46*(2), 181–203.

Aniche, E. T. (2020). From Pan-Africanism to African regionalism: A chronicle. *African Studies, 79*(1), 70–87. https://doi.org/10.1080/000 20184.2020.1740974

Atitsogbe, K. A., Kossi, E. Y., Pari, P., & Rossier, J. (2021). Decent work in Sub-Saharan Africa: An application of psychology of working theory in a sample of Togolese primary school teachers. *Journal of Career Assessment, 29*(1), 36–53. https://doi.org/10.1177/1069072720928255

Ayittey, G. B. N. (2010). The United States of Africa: A revisit. *The Annals of the American Academy of Political and Social Science, 632*(1), 86–102. https://doi.org/10.1177/0002716210378988

Biney, A. (2011). *The political and social thought of Kwame Nkrumah*. Cham, Switzerland: Springer.

Bing-Pappoe, A. (2018, December 6). *All-African People's Conference 60th anniversary neoliberalism, Africa's economies and the living conditions of Africans*. Retrieved from https://www.youtube.com/live/-lhWERtvT7o?feature=share

Cabral, A. (1974). *Return to the source*. New York, NY: NYU Press.

Campbell, H. (1991). The impact of Walter Rodney and progressive scholars on the Dar Es Salaam School. *Social and Economic Studies, 40*(2), 99–135.

Dai, S. Y. (1966). Asia unity and disunity: Impressions and reflections (1964-1965). *Asian Studies: Journal of Critical Perspectives on Asia, 4*(1), 135–148.

Daily Graphic. (1958a, December 4). Sierra Leone delegates for the big talks.

Daily Graphic. (1958b, December 5). All-African talks, H. Selassie sends £400 to the conference.

Du Bois, W. E. B. (1923, August 13). Circular letter from W. E. B. Du Bois to Pan African Association Permanent Committee. W. E. B. Du

Bois Papers (MS 312). Special Collections and University Archives, University of Massachusetts Amherst Libraries.

Du Bois, W. E. B. (1958, December 9). Address by W. E. B. Du Bois delivered at All African Peoples' Conference, Accra, Ghana. W. E. B. Du Bois Papers (MS 312). Special Collections and University Archives, University of Massachusetts Amherst Libraries.

Dwyer, S. C., & Buckle, J. L. (2009). The space between: On being an insider-outsider in qualitative research. *International Journal of Qualitative Methods*, *8*(1), 54–63. https://doi.org/10.1080/17531055.2010.487337

Greene, M. J. (2014). On the inside looking in: Methodological insights and challenges in conducting qualitative insider research. *The Qualitative Report*, *19*(29), 1–13. https://doi.org/10.46743/2160-3715/2014.1106

Goddeeris, I. (2022). Between anti-imperialism and anti-communism: Poland and international solidarity with Vietnam. In A. Sedlmaier (Ed.), *Protest in the Vietnam War era. Palgrave Studies in the History of Social Movements* (pp. 113–139). London, UK: Palgrave Macmillan. https://doi.org/10.1007/978-3-030-81050-4_5

Grilli, M. (2018). From Manchester to the All-African People's Conference (1945–1958). In *Nkrumaism and African nationalism: Ghana's Pan-African foreign policy in the age of decolonization. African Histories and Modernities* (pp. 33–108). London, UK: Palgrave Macmillan. https://doi.org/10.1007/978-3-319-91325-4_2

Hongoh, J. (2016). The Asian-African Conference (Bandung) and Pan-Africanism: The challenge of reconciling continental solidarity with national sovereignty. *Australian Journal of International Affairs*, *70*(4), 374–390. https://doi.org/10.1080/10357718.2016.1168773

International Organization. (1962). Africa and International Organization. *International Organization*, *16*(2), 429–434.

Institute of African Studies-UG. (2019). *Statement of issues and recommendations-All-African People's Conference-05-08, December 2018*.

Khadiagala, G. M. (2010). Boundaries in Eastern Africa. *Journal of Eastern African Studies*, *4*(2), 266–278.

Lumumba, P., Sartre, J. P., & Van Lierde, J. (1972). *Lumumba speaks: The speeches and writings of Patrice Lumumba, 1958-1961*. Boston, MA: Little, Brown & Company.

McKeown, M. (2021). Backward-looking reparations and structural injustice. *Contemporary Political Theory, 20*(4), 771–794.

Muchie, M. (2004). A theory of an Africa as a unification nation: A re-thinking of the structural transformation of Africa. *African Sociological Review / Revue Africaine de Sociologie, 8*(2), 136–157. https://doi.org/10.4314/asr.v8i2.23255

Nkrumah, K. (1964). *The African genius: Speech delivered at the opening of the Institute of African Studies on 25th October 1963.* Ministry of Information and Broadcasting.

Nkrumah, K. (1968). *Handbook of revolutionary warfare: A guide to the armed phase of the African revolution.* International Publishers.

Nyumbani. (2007). *The United States of Africa, Kwame Nkrumah Speaks!* Retrieved from https://youtu.be/foDlCCudcsE

Poe, D. Z. (2003). *Kwame Nkrumah's contribution to Pan-African agency: An Afrocentric analysis.* New York, NY: Routledge.

Sherwood, M. (2012a). *Origins of Pan-Africanism: Henry Sylvester Williams, Africa, and the African Diaspora.* New York, NY: Routledge.

Sherwood, M. (2012b). Pan-African conferences, 1900-1953: What did "Pan-Africanism" mean? *Journal of Pan African Studies, 4*(10), 106–126.

Thioub, I. (2007). Writing national and transnational history in Africa: The example of the "Dakar School". In S. Berger (Ed.), *Writing the nation: A global perspective* (pp. 197–212). London, UK: Palgrave Macmillan. https://doi.org/10.1057/9780230223059_9

Tsikata, D. (2018, December 8). All-African Peoples' Conference 2018 – Closing Ceremony [Video]. *YouTube.* Retrieved from https://www.youtube.com/watch?v=3p_T2efjCCY&t=2400s

Varela, C. (2017). Africa finds its voice in the Halls of Manchester. *History in the Making, 10*(6). Retrieved from https://scholarworks.lib.csusb.edu/history-in-the-making/vol10/iss1/6

University of California Press. (1959). Resolutions of the All-African People's Conference. *Current History, 37*(215), 41–46.

University of Ghana. (2018). *Horace Campbell closing speech. All-African People's Conference 60th Anniversary Closing Ceremony.* Retrieved from https://www.youtube.com/live/3p_T2efjCCY?feature=share

Zaki, H. (2011, October 30). *The perils and promise of transnational activism on racial discrimination: The World Conference Against Racism, the Durban Review and the Durban Plus Ten Conferences.* Retrieved from https://ssrn.com/abstract=1951437

Generating Inclusive and Sustainable Growth: Challenging Neoliberal Approaches to Gender Mainstreaming in Regional Economic Integration in Africa[*]

Adryan Wallace

Introduction

Immediately post-independence, new heads of state recognised that securing economic stability and maintaining political sovereignty were mutually reinforcing goals (Nkrumah, 1963; Nyerere, 1987; Nzewi, 2009). In reality, political leaders and activists contended that if self-determination and autonomy were not established and maintained, it was unlikely that the institutional legacies of colonialism would be reversed (Gibb 2009; Nkrumah, 1963). These ideologies were a central feature of Pan-African movements around decolonisation and resistance to neo-colonialism (Gumede, 2019). Regional integration was touted as a way forward by Nkrumah, Nyerere, and other newly elected heads of state (Gumede, 2019). They believed that cultivating integration at the continental level

---

[*] This chapter is a slightly edited version of an article first published in *Contemporary Journal of African Studies*, Vol. 10, No. 2 (2023) and is reproduced here with permission.

could yield the following: (*a*) fiscal autonomy, (*b*) prioritisation of the needs of the most excluded groups, (*c*) collective bargaining around trade and tariffs and protectionist policies for domestic and local industries, (*d*) labour that is free from exploitation, and (*e*) the cultivation of states that are responsive to the needs of all citizens (Hailu, 2015). General agreement on the outcomes shifted the focus to outlining strategies most likely to attain and institutionalise integration (Ofori et al., 2021). The main areas of disagreement between the Casablanca Group and Monrovia Group concerned whether incremental efforts through Regional Economic Communities (RECs) or continent-wide approaches which included political integration would achieve the type of fiscal security which prioritised the interests of all populations, in particular those groups that had been marginalised by the colonial state (Abbas & Mama, 2014). Ultimately and with much consternation, the establishment of geographically based RECs became the way forward. Over eight RECs were established between 1967 and 1998: the East African Community (EAC), the Economic Community of West African States (ECOWAS), the Southern African Development Community (SADC), the Economic Community of Central African States (ECCAS), the Intergovernmental Authority on Development (IGAD), the Arab Maghreb Union (AMU), the Common Market for East and Southern Africa (COMESA), and the Community of Sahel-Saharan States (CEN-SAD). Despite having active RECs in place for over fifty-six years, regional integration remains elusive for a host of reasons including lack of institutional capacity, failure to protect economically vulnerable groups, the reinforcement of existing structural and gender inequalities, and the presence of neoliberal frameworks.

The creation of the African Continental Free Trade Agreement (AfCFTA),[1] which entered into force on 30 May 2019, represents another attempt to attain integration, this time using a continent-wide approach. There is a clear need for regional integration. Trade within East, West, and Southern African RECs remains higher on average than within other groups (UNECA, 2023). The African Development Bank (ADB) designates East Africa as the region with one of the fastest-growing economies.[2]

---

1 https://au-afcfta.org/wp-content/uploads/2022/06/AfCFTA-Agreement-legally-scrubbed-signed-16-May-2018.pdf
2 https://www.afdb.org/en/countries/east-africa/east-africa-overview

East Africa is poised to be a key economic hub in the areas of information technology and agricultural commodities markets (UNECA, 2023). The deepening of trade networks through the EAC is responsible in part for the high rates of growth among member states.[3] At the aggregate level, estimations of intra-regional trade breakdown are as follows: Africa 13%, Europe 69%, and Asia 59%.[4] These patterns are significant because increasing trade within the region can help strengthen domestic and local economies, bolster collective trade agreements, facilitate the sharing of intellectual and technological resources, and provide the infrastructure required to diversify economies (Jiboku, 2015). The ability of regional cooperation to support political stability, and at times human rights, through institutional support and norms is another benefit (Jiboku, 2015).

The passage of the AfCFTA[5] and the African Union's (AU) 2063 Agenda[6] both emphasise the critical role of regional economic integration in accomplishing their goals. The AfCFTA seeks to attain sustainable growth on the continent by increasing trade, the mobility of labour, and technology exchanges. According to the agreement, this is the best approach to use the region's fiscal, natural, and intellectual riches in support of a collective economic agenda. Some of the top policy priorities include integrating the "informal" economy into the "formal" economy, developing more robust small- and medium-sized firms, altering the place of African countries in global value chains, and addressing gender inequalities. These goals and strategies promoted by the AfCFTA are consistent with those undertaken by the existing RECs and Regional Integration Organisations (RIOs) on the continent. These initiatives by the AU also indicate that gender equality is essential and must be mainstreamed into all policy frameworks.

The primary focus of this work is to determine if the gender equality components of regional integration policies are transformative or perpetuate the status quo. The rest of the study examines the broader

---

3   https://repository.uneca.org/bitstream/handle/10855/49729/b12032669
     pdf?sequence=1&isAllowed=y
4   https://hbs.unctad.org/trade-structure-by-partner/#:~:text=Intra%2Dregional%20trade%20
     was%20most,most%20trade%20was%20extra%2Dregional
5   https://au-afcfta.org/wp-content/uploads/2022/06/AfCFTA-Agreement-Legally- scrubbed-
     signed-16-May-2018.pdf
6   https://au.int/sites/default/files/documents/36204-doc-agenda2063_popular_version

theoretical justifications for promoting regional economic integration in general and in the African region specifically. Pan-Africanism is used to analyze integration initiatives in order to determine how much the goals of more neoliberal policies or the ideologies of post-independence movements are reflected in present operations. Neoliberalism is defined as an ideology that promotes "obscuring practices that serve to entrench inequalities based on both gender and class, both oppressions being mutually constitutive" (Ossome, 2015). In this study, neoliberalism refers to both the economic model and how it is used to govern decisions and policy frameworks (governmentality) (Foucault, 1991; Ong, 2006). This study explores the ways in which these neoliberal approaches are translated into policies for economic growth and are used to measure their effectiveness. The efforts to decolonise these frameworks using African feminist critiques of the uneven effects of globalisation are also included. The implications of neoliberalism as a policy implementation method are discussed. Next, the methodological approach including the ways in which I am operationalising neoliberal gender mainstreaming in the regional integration policies is explained. The evaluation of the AfCFTA, ECOWAS, and SADC provisions is outlined and analysed. I conclude by making recommendations for rejecting neoliberal logics in regional integration efforts and gender mainstreaming and suggest some future directions for research.

Pan-Africanist Approaches to Regional Economic Integration

There is an extensive history of efforts towards regional integration on the continent, including the following key trade agreements: the 1977 Kinshasa Declaration and the Monrovia Declaration,[7] which focused on national and regional self-reliance through social and economic development; the Lagos Plan of Action[8] in 1980; the Abuja Treaty[9] 1991

---

7   https://au.int/sites/default/files/decisions/9526- assembly_en_17_20_july_1979_assembly_
    heads_state_government_sixteenth_ordinary_session.pdf
8   Provided the logistical policy steps for implementing the socio-economic provisions of the
    Monrovia Declaration among all member states of the Organisation of African Unity. The
    plan detailed domestic policy frameworks to be adopted and harmonised them with efforts
    to integrate economies in mutual networks of economic and social support across the Africa
    region.
9   https://au.int/sites/default/files/treaties/37636-treaty-0016_-_treaty_establishing_the_
    african_economic_community_e.pdf

which established the African Economic Community – including the Pan-African Parliament; Economic and Social Commission, the Court of Justice, and the Tripartite Free Trade Area (TFTA)[10] Agreement signed in June 2015. The RECs are viewed as a preliminary step in integrating the economies across the continent (Hailu, 2015). The benefits of regional integration include strengthening the capacity of countries with different economies of scale to engage in collective bargaining and pool resources to increase their competitiveness in global markets (Geda & Kebret, 2008). It also allows the states to capture sub-regional and regional markets and creates the infrastructure required to strengthen domestic private sectors (Hailu, 2015). Integration can reflect and further entrench existing hierarchies in the global economy if not undertaken in ways that place control in the hands of workers equally across economic sectors and labour categories (Ofori et al., 2021). One of the main objectives of integration must be to address the domestic inequalities, especially the disparities in access to resources and revenue that women experience at an aggregate level, which is a central goal of integration (Abbas & Mama, 2014).

Post-independence arguments for regional economic integration had both political and economic dimensions (Gibb, 2009; Nkrumah, 1963; Nyerere, 1987; Nzewi, 2009). Nkrumah and Nyerere agreed that the last remnants of neocolonial control had to be eradicated from modern African political systems, notwithstanding their stark differences regarding the nature of governing structures that should represent the interests of the people. Newly independent states sought to change a global system of extraction and exploitation by using collective bargaining, harmonising economic sectors for regional and global trade, protecting labour, and investing in social institutions of the state; however, without considering gender equality, these goals were unable to be attained Abbas & Mama, 2014). Nkrumah acknowledged that engagement with the global economy was necessary albeit under specific conditions. The following conditions are most relevant to this work and explain his vision of a single governing authority for the continent that: (*a*) African states retained sovereignty and control over their economic agenda and goals;

---

10 Established to provide a free trade area from Cape Town to Cairo including members of
  three RECs in East, North, and Southern Africa, COMESA, EAC, SADC.

(*b*) exploitation was prevented; and (*c*) the African state entered into equal partnerships with external actors (Nkrumah, 1963). Nyerere's emphasis on retaining power within institutions to determine how accumulated wealth was distributed was a central component of how he envisioned integration which included a slower-paced sub-regional approach (1987).

Over time, regional integration became less of a political project and more of an exclusively economic one emphasising participation in the global economy instead of fighting to reshape it (Gumede, 2019; Nzewi, 2009). The adoption of Western models of regional economic integration emphasised market integration to the exclusion of other political and social justice components and the transformation of institutions (Gibb, 2009). The role of RECs and continent-wide trade agreements in perpetuating neoliberal approaches to micro-credit and the financialisation of micro-finance has been heavily criticised (DeMartino, 2000; Korolczuk, 2016; Waller & Wrenn, 2021). The current frameworks and metrics for integration outlined in the AfCFTA represent another departure from the political aims outlined in Pan-African intellectual traditions of conceptualising integration (Gumede, 2019). The AfCFTA largely keeps the decision-making authority in the hands of state governments who do not always represent the interests of civil society, scholars, and the most vulnerable and socially diverse groups (Tsikata, 2014). Although creating architecture across the entire region instead of relying primarily on the sub-regional hubs represents a structural shift, it will also require an ideological one to be successful. The sheer scale of investments via fiscal and political capital that has been placed in creating and implementing the AfCFTA and render it something we cannot afford to ignore or fail to engage with directly. Much of the gender mainstreaming endeavours to date have not prioritised the democratisation of integration processes; they have just emphasised having more women participate in economic sectors with their embedded power imbalances (Ofori et al., 2021). Examining the strategies of contemporary Pan-African movements can provide critical new approaches for addressing gender equality and integration.

During the 1960s, Pan-Africanism was both a site of grassroots organising and included the participation of political leaders. In a contemporary sense, the movements remain strong; however, there are few, if any, presidents and prime ministers in the region who are members of Pan-African organisations (Gumede, 2019). The term "Pan-Africanism", while used rhetorically when referencing AU integration initiatives, has largely been decoupled from the implicit neocolonial critiques that formed its inception (Gumede, 2019). The work of Pan-African organisations like the All-African Peoples' Revolutionary Party provides conceptual approaches and practical metrics for attaining regional integration consistent with the themes of post-independence movements (2018). More specifically, the recommendations from their Sixtieth Anniversary All-African Peoples' Conference (AAPC) identify policy prescriptions that can be implemented. The plenary sessions of the AAPC panels on "Ending Imperialist Domination and Transforming Africa's Economies", "On Pan Africanism Today, Tomorrow and Building a New Politics of Substantive Democracy and Security", and "On Youth, Workers, Progressive Women, and Africa's Transformation" have critical insights on effective integration (2018). The economic panel emphasises the importance of changing the position of African countries in global value chains from being mere sources of commodities for extraction into producers of manufactured goods that can be sold in the global markets (All-African Peoples' Revolutionary Party, 2018). The need to reclaim and strengthen the capacity of the state to protect labour and industries from neoliberal markets which are seen as "anti-people, anti-solidarity, anti-collective, and bolstered by the expansion of debt and numerous debt cycles which perpetuate crisis and undermine sovereignty and autonomy of African states as well as the control of their political economy" (All-African Peoples' Revolutionary Party, 2018, p. 4). The AAPC posits that regional integration is based on Pan-African constructions of development, which uses collective bargaining to safeguard African economies (2018). The second panel focuses on the importance of creating democracies that are inclusive and capable of addressing inequalities stemming from "weak economic institutions" (2018, 2). The panel on youth, women, and workers discusses the important role of stopping economic, social, and physical violence against socially diverse groups as part of attaining development based on the principles of Pan-Africanism (2018). All three of these panels from the AAPC conference provide a roadmap for generating the institutional architecture required to integrate economies with the original political aims of autonomy, sovereignty, self-determination, and inclusion.

Regional Blocs and Integration: Feminist Critiques

The recognition of the critical role women play in the economy is one of the key reasons why this study focuses on the gender equality provisions of the agreements (Chen 2005; Dzisi, 2008; Harper et al., 2013; Naidu & Ossome, 2018; Ossome, 2015; Ossome & Naidu, 2021; Spring, 2009; UNECA, 2010; UNCTAD, 2022). More specifically, I examine how gender equality and women's empowerment are framed in the AfCFTA and the agreements of two sub-RECs: ECOWAS and SADC. The work assesses the role of RECs and continent-wide trade agreements in perpetuating or challenging neoliberal approaches to sustainable growth specifically through the application of African feminist and Pan-African theoretical frameworks. The conceptualisation of gender equality and women's empowerment in these regional integration policies focuses primarily on increasing women's descriptive representation in the marketplace. These gender equality frameworks do not reflect African feminist conceptualisations (Mbiliny & Shechambo, 2009; Naidu & Ossome, 2018; Osome, 2015; Tsikata, 2014). This study relies on a qualitative study that provides a detailed examination of the structural foundations in the AfCFTA, ECOWAS, and SADC to assess their adoption of neoliberal principles. ECOWAS [the 1993 revision of the original agreement] and SADC [original agreement] were included for two reasons. First, the AfCFTA is still in the process of finalising some of the trade protocols to include phase one—trade in goods, trade in services, dispute settlement mechanisms, and customs and trade facilitation; and phase two—intellectual property rights, investment, competition policy, and digital trade. ECOWAS and SADC have been in force longer than the AfCFTA, and the support they will lend to the continent-wide trade agreement, including harmonisation of policies, makes them appropriate case studies to evaluate the relationships among inequalities, neoliberalism, and institutionalised regional trade.

These relationships among gender, economic growth, neoliberalism, and inequality must be contextualised domestically to identify the types of structural changes that need to occur regionally and globally for gender equality to be attained. The assumption that increasing women's economic participation alone will address disparities and generate domestic growth needs to be re-examined (Ofori et al., 2021). The sources of state revenue stem from a combination of the private sector (national, multinational) and development agencies (regional, bilateral, and international). International financial institutions, foreign direct investment, and development funding largely operate under and promote neoliberalism (Mkandawire, 2014). This includes domestic, sub-regional, regional, and global governing institutions. Therefore, gender mainstreaming by these organisations should be further scrutinised to determine if their approach provides descriptive inclusion (increasing the number of women) rather than substantive inclusion (increasing the presence of women as policy decision-makers). Gender mainstreaming refers to targeted policy interventions to increase the participation of more women in the "formal" economy (Ofori et al., 2021). The role of women in governance is often untheorised in neoliberal integration approaches which can undermine the efficacy of their economic participation (Ofori et al., 2021). The ability of women to have control over supranational governing institutions and the capacity to negotiate to protect the different interests of groups of women are essential to ensuring that everyone benefits from integration. Regional integration and the AfCFTA will not be successful if we do not include African feminists' conceptualisations of gender analyses in our understanding of work, trade, development, and econometrics. We run the risk of strengthening the very systems of economic oppression that regional economic integration should attempt to challenge. African feminist theories answer the political questions. Examining how gender equality is defined and gender mainstreaming is approached in economic cooperation can help identify the presence of neoliberal agendas. The gender equality provisions of agreements and documents outlining the strategic vision of organisations are ideal policy components to use in assessing and identifying the presence of neoliberal logics for three reasons. First, gender equality provisions are mainstreamed into each dimension of the macro- and micro-economic trade agreements underpinning the regional integration policies. Second, they target the populations with the least amount of decision-making power within institutions. Third, gender inclusion within organisations often prioritises descriptive representation over institutional transformation.

There are several ways that neoliberal frameworks underpin gender mainstreaming in the agreements. Since women constitute the larger portion of the informal sector labour force, the primary ways in which women are framed within these policy frameworks are through the prioritisation of private sector growth and development coupled with an integration of "informal" and "formal" economic activities. The "formal" and "informal" distinctions represent a false dichotomy that has been extensively critiqued (Alter, 2005; Dzisi, 2008; Niger-Thomas, 2003; Spring, 2009). As previously mentioned, the false delineation between "informal and formal" economic activity is well documented. Many micro-sized enterprises and economic activities will take their place in businesses that are not registered due to the associated costs. If the registration process becomes mandatory, not only should those issues be addressed but there should be some material and institutional benefits for the owners of those firms, the majority of whom are women. Participating in the formal economy comes with tax liabilities, among others, which if not carefully regulated, can place women-owned and women-headed firms at a continued disadvantage (Spring, 2009). For example, women involved in small-scale fishing are integral to the local economies, and the underestimation of their contributions in econometric data can result in miscalculating the costs associated with formalising their economic role (Harper et al., 2013). Altering the recognition of women-owned firms necessitates that the AfCFTA and other regional agreements carefully account for the associated bureaucratic costs and collaborate in partnerships with owners to develop the processes that work. The normative approaches to gender mainstreaming within trade and development policy frameworks do not address the substantive impacts on fiscal security (True, 2008). Women are treated as a monolithic group in many attempts to address gender inequalities which do not address fundamental issues of power within which the same groups of women set the broader mainstreaming agenda. Feminist economists have been pushing these critiques further to highlight how feminist movements in the West often ignore national privilege and exclude the interests of other groups of women. Scholars argue that one of the greatest impacts of regional organisations is that they can help facilitate the adoption of democratic practices and progressive political positions within the governments of their member states (Nwogu, 2007; Ryu & Ortuoste, 2014; Spring, 2009; Tsikata & Amanor-Wilks, 2009). It is important to acknowledge tensions between various women groups. Groups occasionally have conflicting political and economic interests as well as disagreements on social concerns; one such example is the support for and mobilization of LGBTQIA+ communities. The complexities on the ground which reflect the ways in which the intersections of different socially constructed identity categories, for example, gender, socio-economic status, and ethnolinguistic heritage, necessitate that multiple women's groups need to be in positions to make decisions. Although the gains of integration are ideal, the existing political, economic, and social realities that women face every day must be accounted for; otherwise, these presumed gains can be lost or worse can lead to an entrenchment of marginalisation. Therefore, it is important to determine if regional and sub-regional integration, which uses collective bargaining, will protect women from the violence and exploitation that undermines the economic security of neoliberal economic approaches and governing mechanisms. Centring the experiences and priorities of different groups of women, such as Muslim women, is crucial as their important economic contributions are often not reflected in econometric data (Wallace, 2014). The diverse experiences of women leading firms of various sizes such as micro, small, medium, and large, as well as those engaged in agriculture work, fishing, textiles, and development work can aid in identifying the key gender equality aspects of trade and cooperative agreements. It can also help assess the direct effect of these agreements on women's economic security and development.

Development is another concept that has been extensively critiqued for perpetuating neocolonial control and definitions of economic growth which prioritises profit over safeguarding people and preferences of the private sector and market in ways that weaken state capacity (Apusigah, 2009; Tsikata, 2009; Tsikata & Amanor-Wilks, 2009). Development in the context of this work refers to a holistic Pan-African framework that includes economic, social, and political equality with an emphasis on access to education and health care as defined by African scholars and activists (All-African Peoples' Revolutionary Party, 2018; Hendricks, 2015). To address gender inequality, economic, political, and social institutions that restrict women and have a disproportionally negative impact on them need to be transformed. This is essential for regional integration because biases present in national domestic structures are scaled up and replicated within regional groups and comprehensive continent-wide trade agreements. The critical role of African women in economic contributions across sectors is substantial (Naidu & Ossome, 2018; Ossome & Naidu, 2021). The over-representation of women in micro-enterprises and other activities that do not receive full remuneration or are inaccurately reflected in econometric data makes them a group of workers that need protection, support, and institutional cover (Naidu & Ossome, 2018; Ossome & Naidu, 2021; Spring, 2009). Often, the very social and economic inequalities that collectively marginalise women's aggregate participation need to be addressed; this will make the political and economic systems accountable to those that need the greatest safeguarding. When these elements are missing from gender equality-focused components of protocols and agreements, there is a focus on participation rather than changing power dynamics which is the very definition of neoliberalism. For example, when policies are designed to support women's micro-enterprises, the women that own these businesses need to be at the table defining the provisions and detailing what they need. It is important to have direct communication channels with the authorities who have the power to make necessary changes.

> Given the merging of African Feminist and Pan-African integration frameworks, I need to outline the four core features of persistent neoliberal and neocolonial logics, which are measured in the AfCFTA, ECOWAS, and SADC agreements as described in the methods section below: (*a*) success measured as increasing the presence of women in economic industries (descriptive inclusion only), (*b*) women are centred as decision-makers setting priorities, (*c*) absence of a formal monitoring role for women, and (*d*) constraints on the negotiating power of workers through supranational economic institutions.

Research Background and Methodology

In terms of methodology, I use qualitative content analysis to assess the relative resistance to and/or accommodation of neoliberal frameworks in the gender equality provisions specified in the protocols of the AfCFTA, ECOWAS, and SADC. I selected ECOWAS and SADC because they are two economic and political communities with members that have some of the largest economies (GDPs) in the region as measured by GDP. They also have a long institutional history of implementing economic cooperative agreements, 1975 and 1980, respectively. Nigeria, the largest economy in the region by GDP, and South Africa, the second largest economy by GDP, have signed the AfCFTA and deposited their instruments for ratification with the AU. The members of their organisations are critical actors in the AfCFTA and will continue to retain a pivotal leadership role. The underlying AfCFTA provisions must include accommodations that are also made at the REC levels.

The ability of the AfCFTA, ECOWAS, and SADC to cultivate regional economic integration strategies that undermine neoliberal institutions, protect labour, and generate inclusive and sustainable growth are analysed in this study. The creation of collective policy frameworks around gender mainstreaming that are regional should be an important outcome of these regional economic integration efforts. The impact of gender equality mainstreaming and women's empowerment targets in regional integration policies on economic security for women is a fundamental metric to determine the efficacy of the approaches to regional economic integration. The institutions that undermine the participation, economic security, and decision-making capacities of women have yet to undergo transformation. The adoption of neoliberal policies involves several aspects, including: (*a*) the use of quantitative measures to gauge successful integration, with a focus on the number of women in the workforce; (*b*) giving decision-making authority to the elite; (*c*) limitations in monitoring and holding member states accountable for institutional practices; and (*d*) failing to provide workers across various sectors with the ability to negotiate terms and conditions.

I begin with a content analysis using the conceptualisations of the terms "gender equality" and "gender mainstreaming" developed in the preceding theory sections to ensure they are contextualised properly.

The legal texts that are examined in this analysis include: (*a*) the original governing agreements (ECOWAS revised agreement 1993), (*b*) the strategic vision 2050, and (*c*) the presence or absence of institutional mechanisms to include offices designated to examine issues of gender equality mainstreaming. I provide a detailed examination of the regional cooperative agreements to see if they reproduce economic disparities within member states and across sub-regional groups and sectors of the economy. There are three key areas that I assess the degree to which AfCFTA, ECOWAS, and SADC: (*a*) destabilise neoliberal institutions, (*b*) protect labour, and (*c*) generate inclusive and sustainable growth. The definition of gender equality reflected in the regional and sub-regional trade and cooperative agreements will outline other metrics that should be operationalised to have an impact on women's economic security. I used my African Feminist Pan-African theoretical frame to evaluate how gender equality mainstreaming either accommodates or resists neoliberalism. These metrics were selected because they are necessary to make sure that the process of integration is democratised and diverse, and that it secures the autonomy of individuals and African states, which are two critical components of Pan-African feminist integration goals. Moreover, I have distilled my theoretical framework into six categories of analysis detailed in each table as follows: first, the explicit goals of economic agreements explicitly specified; second, the conceptualisation of gender equality in the provisions; third, the participation of local women's organisations and activists in the formation of diverse gender equality mainstreaming policies; fourth, the adoption of primarily quantitative measures such as participation and absorption into markets measured to determine if integration has been successfully attained; fifth, the stakeholders responsible for monitoring policy outcomes and holding institutions accountable; and sixth, the existence of units or agencies designated to be part of the gender mainstreaming implementation processes.

Summary and Description of Data

This section provides a separate table for each of the three agreements to depict the critical data points. The tables depict the original agreements of the AfCFTA, ECOWAS (1993 revision), and SADC. A description of any units or specially designated agencies that have been created to further monitor the institutionalisation of gender mainstreaming in regional integration is one of the metrics of evaluation. The existence or absence of such features is significant because if they retain neoliberal biases, then the most public-facing components of the integration efforts, the governmental arm that everyday citizens might access to address their concerns, will have their ability to resolve issues severely mitigated. For example, if there is a gender desk, it is important to know if individual people may contact the office or if women and other groups are required to go through their state to gain access. Having the potential for direct contact can help people navigate around other issues of biases that may be extended through reliance on domestic governance structures. Additionally, even when departments work with civil society groups, those groups are not always representative and can speak more to the social capital of the heads of those groups rather than the variations in the needs of different women from all echelons of society. Therefore, understanding a bit about the levels of accessibility and selection criteria for grassroots participation is key.

African Continental Free Trade Agreement (AfCFTA)

The AfCFTA components examined include the original articles of formation,[11] compiled annexes to the agreement, and the organisational components for gender mainstreaming. Figure 1 summarises the key findings for the AfCFTA. The AfCFTA is still in the process of finalising several components of the agreement; therefore, the description is limited to the existing data available at the time of publication of this piece. The massive undertaking of harmonising multiple economic sectors, the needs of different member states, the role of RECs, and other stakeholders on this scale is unprecedented, post-independence. The data below serve to potentially help avoid replicating the steps of previous Western neoliberal approaches to integration.[INSERT FIG]

The overarching goals of the AfCFTA agreement include gender equality, informal, and formal market integration as well as increasing access to regional and global markets as depicted in Fig. 1. The commitment to securing a single market to facilitate the movement of goods,

---

11 https://au-afcfta.org

FIG. 1: Neoliberal approaches to gender equality mainstreaming in the AfCFTA.

Broader Goals of Economic Agreements	Conceptualisation of Gender Equality	Policy Decision Making Authority	Measuring of Successful Gender Equality Mainstreaming	Monitoring & Institutional Accountability	Presence of Unit/Division to Implement Gender Mainstreaming
➤ Establishing single market (good, services, people) ➤ Continental customs union ➤ Sustainable and inclusive socio-economic development ➤ Promote gender equality ➤ Structural transformation of the State Parties ➤ Competitiveness of the economies of State Parties- continent & global market ➤ Informal formal economic integration ➤ Addressing multiple and overlapping REC memberships ➤ Substantial liberalization ➤ Protectionist policies of some infant industries	➤ Liberal human rights language tied to economic participation ➤ Economic participation ➤ No specific definition or target areas ➤ Not fully integrated into policy in detail ➤ Interests & experiences of women & men in the design, monitoring, implementation	➤ Domestic political officials ➤ REC representatives ➤ Stakeholder meeting planned not clear selection criterion for participation ➤ Limited representative civil society participation ➤ Limited professorial or trade association participation	➤ Descriptive inclusion ➤ Full integration of women into global, regional economies ➤ Quantitative metrics ➤ Efficiency ➤ Increase women's participation in local markets ➤ Promote "progressive liberalization" ➤ General increase in women's economic activities ➤ Market integration	➤ To member states ➤ No explicit role for women's groups ➤ No explicit role of civil society ➤ No explicit role for workers associations or unions	➤ No ➤ Depending on existing state structures ➤ Mentions transforming state structures, accountability mechanism unclear ➤ Drafting protocol women and youth

services, and people is consistent with the growth aims of integration in general. The creation of a continent-wide customs union would be extremely helpful for small- and medium-sized firms and consumers allowing for the quick calculation of any import duties and could make calculating payment for goods or services more standardised and easier to complete. The other issues outlined in the first column of Fig. 1 could help build the capacity of firms to trade and work across borders. The areas of concern centre around the objective to substantially increase liberalisation which prioritises profit maximisation. When liberalisation is combined with incorporating "informal" economic activity within the "formal" economy, the additional regulation and taxation that will be experienced by firms where women are over-represented can further produce gender disparities. Women may be able to access the markets; however, the chances that they benefit at the same rate as their male counterparts are severely reduced. The structural transformation of state parties into government structures that can implement the agreement is not the same as changing them to be more democratic representative structures. The power shift required to augment domestic state institutions at each level (national, subnational, and local) needs to be part of the conceptualisation of transformation.

The second column in Fig. 1 specifies that gender equality is defined as economic participation. Even the human rights' language used ties those provisions to the increased economic engagement of women. For example, addressing gender inequalities in political participation is connected to the ability of women to use these efforts to help facilitate participation in markets. There are other political issues on the agenda, for example, addressing gender-based violence, gaps in education, and limited access to health care, all of which are important in their own right. Connecting political agendas to external labour force participation should be a foundational component of how we theorise gender equality in the context of politics to avoid being overly reductionist.

The third component described in Fig. 1, which focuses on decision-making authority given to stakeholders, shows that women's organisations ranging from non-governmental organisations to community-based groups and other civil society organisations were not substantively included in the drafting of the original articles or agreements. It also indicates that there will be a stakeholder meeting of women-led and youth organisations to design a protocol for women and youth. The format and frequency of these meetings and selection criteria for participation will have a direct impact on the ability of the AfCFTA to materially improve the lives of citizens equally across and within member states. Clearly, the variations in economies of scale mean that the amount of revenue streams may vary; however, they should be proportional rather than skewed in favour of groups and individuals already well positioned within political and social systems.

The ways in which gender equality is measured consist of descriptive metrics, that is, the presence of women participating in regional and global markets as summarised in the fourth section of Fig. 1. The commitment to "progressive liberalisation" requires women to be active agents in these systems. The market integration preoccupation can obscure the ways in which it may lower wages and incomes, come with hidden costs not necessarily absorbed by the state, and be accompanied by additional management by political and economic systems that already have biases. The lack of inclusion of women's organisations in the creation of the

AfCFTA across levels of privilege makes it difficult to represent and monitor the protection of the interests of multiple groups of women.

FIG. 2: Neoliberal approaches to gender equality mainstreaming in ECOWAS.

Broader Goals of Economic Agreements	Conceptualisation of Gender Equality	Policy Decision Making Authority	Measuring of Successful Gender Equality Mainstreaming	Monitoring & Institutional Accountability	Presence of Unit/Division to Implement Gender Mainstreaming
➤ Regional economic integration ➤ Increased flow (goods, services, people) ➤ Common currency ➤ Harmonization for protection of the environment ➤ Common market (liberalization) ➤ Harmonization of standards and measures ➤ Increase information flows women, youth, professional sectors ➤ Development fund	➤ Human rights ➤ Economic participation ➤ Gender equality and equity ➤ Enhance economic, social and cultural conditions of women ➤ Identify impediments to women making maximum contribution to integration ➤ Dialogue on projects and programmes for women ➤ Framework to incorporate women's concerns	➤ Resides among member states ➤ Limited representative civil society participation ➤ Limited professorial or trade association participation	➤ Descriptive inclusion ➤ Full integration of women into sub-regional economies ➤ Quantitative metrics ➤ Efficiency ➤ Increasing women's SMEs ➤ Capacity building institutions and organizations ➤ Equal access to basic services ➤ Economic empowerment ➤ Human rights, conflict, governance, peace and stability	➤ To member states ➤ No explicit role for women's groups ➤ No explicit role of civil society ➤ No explicit role for workers associations or unions	➤ Gender Development Centre, emphasis on existing approaches (network with women's civil society organisations)

[INSERT FIG] The goals of the economic agreement include full integration of labour markets and local markets plus goods and services being offered as described in the first section of Fig. 2. There is a commitment to the development of a common sub-regional currency. The increased flow of goods, services, and people is a part of the liberalisation processes used to create a common market. The interest in harmonising the standards and measures across industries and member states is important and can become part of the fiscal costs of expanding bureaucratic measures. Specifying how these additional expenditures will be covered is very important because of the different capacities of member states. Delays in developing the capacities of states can lengthen the process of integration for some states making it more difficult for those members and their populations to benefit. The prioritisation of increasing information flows among women, youth, and a range of professional sectors could be beneficial in terms of sharing best practices and lessons learned for groups that are often excluded. The net positive benefits of establishing a development fund are contingent on whether the definition of development is Pan-African or neoliberal.

The last section of the figure illustrates that to date the AfCFTA lacks the type of institutional mechanisms for oversight that are present in the ECOWAS and the SADC. The AfCFTA is still in the process of developing those organisational capacities, and there are plans to hold stakeholder meetings for women's civil society groups and women entrepreneurs. The selection criteria for participation of those groups have not been publicly released. The AfCFTA does rely on member state structures and discusses the importance of transforming them. There is no mechanism designed or specified for monitoring the progress of that transformation. The capacity building of the state is focused on the economic goals rather than the political or social justice aims of inclusion. The development of a monitoring arm for gender mainstreaming could be established later.

Economic Community of West African States (ECOWAS)

The ECOWAS components that are examined include the 1993 revision of the original articles of formation. Figure 2 summarises the key findings for ECOWAS. Each of the six metrics for assessing the presence of neoliberal frameworks is described in detail below. The presence of any institutional mechanisms for implementation is outlined to determine if they have the capacity to challenge or resist the presence of neoliberal ideologies present in the agreements themselves. The conceptualisation of gender equality in the second section of Fig. 2 links the social justice dimensions of equality directly to the ways they support economic engagement. The enhancement of the cultural, economic, and social conditions for women in member states could provide key insights if the diverse perspectives of these groups are used to determine if constraints have been adequately remedied. Even though gender equality and equity are included in the language of the articles of agreement, the terms are not very clearly defined. The proposed dialogue on programmatic issues listed in this column could be essential depending on who is included or excluded from the conversation. In order to create a collective set of interests for women, frameworks must include a method for addressing points of contention without distorting the experiences of the most vulnerable groups of women.

The absence of women's civil society groups in initial advocacy efforts to create the economic community has implications for how gender equality is being operationalised. Section 3 of Fig. 2 depicts the limited decision-making power given to women's groups. The overreliance on member states and limited participation of civil society groups with varying levels of privilege is problematic. A revolutionary shift in the consolidation of institutional power among marginalized people occurs when groups that normally inhabit spaces outside of institutions decide when policies are effective and ineffective.

According to the fourth section of Fig. 2, the metrics used in the ECOWAS agreement are almost exclusively quantitative. The goals are to ensure that most of women's labour is in the formal sub-regional marketplaces. The priority areas for women include equal access to basic services, peace, stability, and good governance. The role of human rights and cultivating more women-headed firms are key agenda points. Similar to the AfCFTA, the construction of human rights is liberal and explicitly connected to economic participation and engagement. This agreement does specify that access to basic services is a metric that will be measured. The emphasis on economic empowerment is not completely operationalised within the agreement and appears to be another measure of work activism.

Monitoring and institutional accountability are consolidated within member states themselves as outlined in the fifth column of Fig. 2. The capacity building of structures and the organisational capacity of political institutions could be beneficial if the definitions of gender equality, as well as the priorities and metrics, reflect the diverse interests of women's groups. There is no explicit role outlined for civil society and/or women's groups or professional associations. The presence of unions is noticeably absent as well.

Finally, the last section of Fig. 2 indicates that there is no separate gender protocol even though there are two bodies within ECOWAS that are responsible for monitoring the success of gender mainstreaming, that is, the Gender Development Centre and the Special Agency on Gender and Development. Although the bodies exist, they use a liberal approach to addressing gender inequalities, which does not fundamentally place women in decision-making positions. ECOWAS has more administrative bodies tasked with monitoring gender mainstreaming than SADC—such as the centre and special agency mentioned above. The Gender Development Centre was established to collect data on gender equality and potentially establish contact with civil society. Direct networking has not been undertaken systematically with civic society. The ability of groups to contact ECOWAS is reflective of the social capital of their leadership and proximity to regional officials rather their how representative they are of the different needs and priorities of women in member states. The special agency is not institutionally distinct from the centre. Therefore, it is difficult to understand how ECOWAS is distributing the work of gender mainstreaming and providing oversight, contact with women, and a special agency.

Southern African Development Community (SADC)

The SADC components examined include the original articles of formation and in the last section, I evaluate the presence of a gender office or unit. Figure 3 summarises the key findings for SADC and makes some key distinctions from ECOWAS.[INSERT FIG]

FIG. 3: Neoliberal approaches to gender equality in SADC.

Broader Goals of Economic Agreements	Conceptualisation of Gender Equality	Policy Decision Making Authority	Measuring of Successful Gender Equality Mainstreaming	Monitoring & Institutional Accountability	Presence of Unit/Division to Implement Gender Mainstreaming
➤ Regional economic integration ➤ Increase flow goods, services, people ➤ Promote peace and security ➤ Promote self-sustaining development ➤ Harmonise socio-economic policies ➤ Promote the development of human resources ➤ Promote development of technology ➤ Remove barriers to capital, goods and labor flows	➤ Human rights ➤ Economic participation ➤ Declaration on gender & development ➤ Gender equality is a human right ➤ Elimination of gender-based violence ➤ Legal areas, power sharing, decision making, access to and control over productive resources, education, health ➤ Sectoral gender equality integration approach, limitations integration and cohesiveness of framework	➤ Resides among member states ➤ Limited representative civil society participation ➤ Limited professorial or trade association participation	➤ Descriptive inclusion ➤ Full integration into sub-regional economies ➤ Quantitative metrics ➤ Efficiency	➤ To member states ➤ No explicit role for women's groups ➤ No explicit role of civil society ➤ No explicit role for workers associations or unions	➤ Gender Unit, tasked with gender mainstreaming, ➤ Separate protocol gender and development

The first section of Fig. 3 illustrates that blending the economies of the region and making it as easy to move goods, services, and labour across member states as it is within those states is a primary goal of SADC. The promotion of peace and security is listed as an important aim of the agreement. The mutual development and sharing of technology are a part of the provisions. The reference to technology is viewed as inextricably tied to the goal of promoting self-sustained development in the sub-region. Harmonisation of socio-economic policies including the removal of barriers to capital and labour flows are other key components of the treaty.

In column two of Fig. 3, there is a declaration on gender and development and gender equality is defined as a human right. These contentions are important; however, if they are not paired with access to domestic and sub-regional institutions, then it is difficult to address the root causes of inequalities. There is an explicit commitment to addressing significant gender-based violence. The elimination of gender-based violence as a part of gender equality does represent a more expanded understanding of the impacts of the construction of socio-cultural factors on inequalities. The conceptualisation of gender equality includes access to education and health care, control over productive resources, and decision-making power. One other item on the list of necessities is equal protection under the rule of law. It is necessary to include each of these goals to alleviate gender inequities.

Section three of Fig. 3, which describes the stakeholders that have decision-making authority, does not include women's organisations substantively in the process even though they are acknowledged as critical in the preceding section where gender equality is defined. This represents a substantial solvency gap. The SADC members are responsible for the framing of these integration efforts; and if they have undemocratic elements, it prevents the collective agenda of the RECs from representing the interests of all parties.

Figure 3 details the metrics that continue to rely almost exclusively on quantitative measures in section four. They include the same priorities of counting the entry of new women-owned firms into the marketplace. The listing of these key factors does not get fully integrated into a comprehensive set of policies that can be closely monitored and evaluated as depicted in section five. Once again, the domestic governments are responsible for assessing the progress towards attaining gender equality and reporting back to the REC. The limitations in the ability of the state to have feedback mechanisms in place to contact multiple women's groups make it very difficult to rely exclusively on them for monitoring.

The last metric covered in column six of Fig. 3 shows that the gender unit was created to help with the continuous assessment of the gender mainstreaming initiatives. SADC has a specific gender equality protocol that has been designed, unlike ECOWAS which has some specific gender policies for certain sectors like energy. SADC has both a gender protocol and a gender mainstreaming monitoring unit. The Gender Unit has a specific provision to examine gender-based violence unlike the ECOWAS centre and special gender agency. The gender units are significant because their job is to evaluate the progress in securing gender equality in every unit of SADC, which means there is a body independent of member states with this responsibility. Given the limitations of the state, this is important. The limitation of the Gender Unit is that the focus is on policy harmonisation with no direct outreach mechanism for women's groups.

Data Analysis of Gender Mainstreaming Approaches to Integration

There are several ways in which regional trade agreements and RECs' gender equality policies reinscribe neoliberal frameworks. Based on the data, I organised my analysis to highlight the three critical ways in which this occurs. First, by utilising liberal feminist definitions of gender inclusion (overreliance on quantitative data, counting measures, as opposed to other measures of quality of life and the satisfaction of people with their labour conditions and associated income); second, the homogenising of gender mainstreaming needs and experiences of women; third, women do not hold the institutional capacity required to evaluate and monitor integration and hold REC institutions accountable if the provisions are not generating the desired result.

Liberal Feminist Definitions of Gender
Inclusion in Regional Integration

All three agreements define gender equality primarily through the number of women who are counted as beneficiaries in the trade agreements. In this sense, the number of women-owned businesses that are registered as firms is treated as sufficient. These neoliberal features consist of descriptive inclusion, just increasing the number of women involved in economic activities or work that is under the purview and control of the state. This is problematic because it does not augment any of the structural reasons responsible for women's absence or limited participation in the first place. The overreliance on quantitative measures for assessing the attainment of gender equality goals does not include measures of changes in women's power to make decisions around labour and work. My findings align with the viewpoints of other African feminist scholars and the AAPC proceedings which served as the basis for my theoretical framework. The AAPC proceedings explored the limitations of the participation of women in the global economy without protectionist policies. When women who have been exploited by globalisation have little influence over policies that integrate them into markets, they have less economic security overall and the aggregate levels of growth are neither inclusive nor sustainable. The counting of women across economic sectors does little to explain the leadership roles that women have in these sectors. Based on studies of best practices, the most effective way to understand any shifts in women's daily lived economic experiences and potentially connect them back to the adoption of gender mainstreaming frameworks in RECs and the AfCFTA is through interviews, participant observation, and other metrics (Spring, 2009; Tsikata, 2014).

Homogenising the Gender Mainstreaming
Needs and Experiences of Women

Many of the regional and sub-regional integration efforts, which use collective bargaining, do not provide space for different groups of women to shape gender mainstreaming goals or definitions. Examining the quality of women's experiences economically, politically, and socially as a result of the impacts of regional economic groups provides ways to contextualise the statistical data being collected (Kameri-Mbote, 2009;

Kayizzi-Mugerwa et al., 2014). The centring of women's experiences allows a deep dive to identify obstacles and issues preventing them from benefiting from gender equality policies that could be addressed by regional and sub-regional groups. The groups can play a pivotal role in safeguarding women who are participating in multiple markets. The organisations can act as a site of additional resistance to economic exploitation when they have the institutional capacity to make changes to domestic, sub-regional, and regional political structures. When RECs based the objectives of their gender equality policies on small groups of women, the regional bodies: (*a*) fail to fully protect women, (*b*) expose women to neoliberal market forces, and (*c*) mitigate the ability of women to negotiate favourable trade and labour policies on their own terms. Moreover, these agreements remain heavily dependent on the state parties that are often exacerbating gender inequalities in the national contexts. Failing to make these modifications renders gender mainstreaming little more than counting the number of women who are engaged in economic activity ignoring the qualitative components of integration such as increases in revenue, better working conditions, more negotiating power for tariffs, input into safety standards and regulations, and the ability to generate policies that reflect short-, medium-, and long-term needs.

Constraints on Grassroots Women's Institutional Power Within RECs

A re-imagining of the relationships between gender and economic production is essential to move beyond the current growth models. The methods of regional integration that are employed lay more emphasis on access than on transforming existing institutions that are causing the marginalisation in the first place or on establishing new ones. Removing the barriers that place restrictions on the economic activities that women undertake requires identifying the subtle ways in which the policy outcomes focus on descriptive (quantitative) increases rather than substantive (qualitative) increases in women's participation and engagement. Equipping the institutions with the capacity to respond to the needs of different constituencies ensures that women's voices become the impetus for policy and the key to evaluating the efficacy of economic agreements. For example, a rotating schedule could be created for women-headed

NGOs, CBOs, and professional associations to have different groups for each category and serve as observers for each agreement. I would also add a role for two academics and two activists not affiliated with any single civil society group to have observer status as well. These groups and individuals could be embedded within the organisations housing the treaties with two-year term limits. This could help eliminate solvency gaps, such as the one in SADC, where, despite there being some holistic components in the conceptualisation of gender equality, they do not translate into the gender unit as a structural monitoring arm.

Conclusions

The introduction of AfCFTA marked a critical attempt to attain regional economic integration of the continent partly aimed at inclusive and sustainable growth. The reduction in tariffs, increased ease in the mobility of goods, services, and people among member states, integration of information communication technology infrastructure, increased access to domestic, sub-regional, regional, and global markets, and finally changing the position of the continent in global value chains are critical focal points of the AfCFTA and other integration efforts. Women comprise a key demographic that has been identified as an essential stakeholder in these regional integration efforts. Prioritising gender equality has been championed as a mechanism to help ensure that women are incorporated into these processes. While the overarching goals of making sustainable growth including everyone in the society (not just individuals and groups that are already affluent) is critical, the AfCFTA is unlikely to attain these aims if it is based on the same neoliberal logics responsible for the existing global domestic, sub-regional, and regional gender inequalities. This study used a qualitative content analysis of the gender mainstreaming provisions of the AfCFTA, the ECOWAS, and the SADC to assess their relative resistance to and/or accommodation of neoliberal frameworks. My work confirms and empirically illustrates the impacts of the African feminist and Pan-African integration approaches and decolonising development literature critiques.

This article examined how gender equality is defined and operationalised in regional and sub-regional cooperative agreements. It assessed the role of RECs and a continent-wide trade agreement in perpetuating or challenging neoliberal approaches to financialisation. There are four key findings in this study: (*a*) regional integration policies primarily include liberal approaches to regional economic integration and addressing gender equality; (*b*) there is little transformation of underlying state structures and institutions that cause global economic inequalities and gender inequalities at all levels; (*c*) diverse priorities of women are not fully included; and (*d*) women and other most vulnerable and marginalised groups are not formally incorporated into institutions in order to control the monitoring or evaluation mechanisms. This highlights the need for integration policies around gender equality to use the diverse experiences of women within and across national and sub-regional contexts. Providing an empirical study that centres on the experiences of women will uncover institutional barriers to attaining inclusive sustainable growth through regional integration.

The impact that these agreements have on the lives of women highlights the importance of examining and challenging the adoption of neoliberal approaches to gender mainstreaming within and across national, sub-regional, and regional contexts. It is important to understand that if women-owned micro, small, and medium enterprises are gaining access to new markets or having an increase or decrease in revenue streams, the increased participation of women in decision-making and the adoption of alternative cooperative economic strategies can serve to buttress and resist the neoliberal approaches to integration. The local gender dynamics and priorities of women domestically should serve as the central point of theorising regional integration policies and shaping the norms around women's participation. The ability to incorporate multiple definitions of gender equality and the economic priorities of different groups of women into regional economic agreements is required to establish necessary structural changes. This expanded conceptualisation of gender equality that centres local (and national) feminist agendas of activists and scholars as the impetus for economic priorities at the national, sub-regional, and regional levels should be adopted to deconstruct neoliberal integration logics and transform institutions.

References

Abbas, H., & Mama, A. (2014). Pan-Africanism and feminism. *Feminist Africa, 19*, 1–6.

All-African Peoples' Revolutionary Party. (2018). *Statement of issues and recommendations. All African Peoples Conference 2018.* Retrieved from https://ias.ug.edu.gh/sites/ias.ug.edu.gh/files/AAPC%202018-Issues%20%26%20Recommendations_Feb%202019_.pdf

Alter Chen, M. (2005). Rethinking the informal economy: Linkages with the formal economy and the formal regulatory environment. In B. Giha-Khasnobi, R. Kanbur, & E. Ostrom (Eds.), *Linking the informal and formal economies: Concepts and policies* (pp. 75–92). Oxford, UK: Oxford University Press. https://doi.org/10.1093/0199204764.003.0005

Apusigah, A. (2009). The gendered politics of farm household production and the shaping of women's livelihoods in Northern Ghana. *Feminist Africa, 12,* 51–68.

DeMartino, G. (2000). *Global economy, global justice: Theoretical objections and policy alternatives to neoliberalism* (Vol. 4). London, UK: Psychology Press.

Dzisi, S. (2008). Entrepreneurial activities of indigenous African women: A case of Ghana. *Journal of Enterprising Communities: People and Places in the Global Economy, 2*(3), 254–264.

Foucault, M. (1991). Governmentality. In G. Burchell, C. Gordon, & P. Miller (Eds.), *The Foucault effect: Studies in governmentality* (pp. 87–104). Chicago, IL: University of Chicago Press.

Geda, A., & Kebret, H. (2008). Regional economic integration in Africa: A review of problems and prospects with a case study of COMESA. *Journal of African Economies, 17*(3), 357–394. https://doi.org/10.1093/jae/ejm021

Gibb, R. (2009). Regional integration and Africa's development trajectory: Meta-theories, expectations and reality. *Third World Quarterly, 30*(4), 701–721.

Gumede, V. (2019). Revisiting regional integration in Africa – Towards a Pan-African developmental regional integration. *Africa Insight, 49*(1), 97–111.

Hailu, M. B. (2015). Regional economic integration in Africa: Challenges and prospects. *Mizan Law Review, 8*(2), 299–332. https://doi.org/10.4314/mlr.v8i2.2

Harper, S., Zeller, D., Hauzer, M., Pauly, D., & Sumaila, U. R. (2013). Women and fisheries: Contribution to food security and local economies. *Marine Policy, 39,* 56–63. https://doi.org/10.1016/j.marpol.2012.10.018

Hendricks, C. (2015). Creating women's leadership for peace and security in the Greater Horn of Africa. *Feminist Africa, 20,* 43–56.

Jiboku, P. A. (2015). The challenge of regional economic integration in Africa: Theory and reality. *Africa's Public Service Delivery & Performance Review, 3*(4), 5–28. https://doi.org/10.4102/apsdpr.v3i4.96

Kameri-Mbote, P. (2009). What would it take to realise the promises? Protecting women's rights in the Kenya National Land Policy of 2009. *Feminist Africa, 12,* 87–94.

Kayizzi-Mugerwa, S., Anyanwu, J. C., & Conceição, P. (2014). Regional integration in Africa: an introduction. *African Development Review, 26*(S1), 1–6. https://doi.org/10.1111/1467-8268.12102

Korolczuk, E. (2016). Neoliberalism and feminist organizing: from "NGO-ization of resistance" to resistance against neoliberalism. In E. Kovats (Ed.), *Solidarity in struggle: Feminist perspectives on neoliberalism in East-Central Europe* (pp. 32–41). Budapest, Hungary: Friedrich-Ebert-Stiftung.

Mbilinyi, M., & Shechambo, G. (2009). Struggles over land reform in Tanzania: Experiences of Tanzania Gender Networking Programme and feminist activist coalition. *Feminist Africa, 12,* 95–104.

Mkandawire, T. (2014). The spread of economic doctrines and policy-making in postcolonial Africa. *African Studies Review, 57*(1), 171–198.

Naidu, S. C., & Ossome, L. (2018). Work, gender, and immiseration in South Africa and India. *Review of Radical Political Economics, 50*(2), 332–348. https://doi.org/10.1177/0486613416666530

Nkrumah, K. (1963). *Africa must unite.* London, UK: Heinemann.

Niger-Thomas, A. (2003). "Buying futures": The upsurge of female entrepreneurship crossing the formal/informal divide in South West Cameroon. *African Affairs, 102*(407), 365–366. https://doi.org/10.1093/afraf/adg019

Nwogu, N. (2007). Regional integration as an instrument of human rights: Reconceptualizing ECOWAS. *Journal of Human Rights, 6*(3), 345–360. https://doi.org/10.1080/14754830701531112

Nyerere, J. K. (1987). Ujamaa: The basis of African socialism. *The Journal of Pan-African Studies, 1*(1), 4–11.

Nzewi, O. (2009). *The challenges of post-1990 regional integration in Africa: Pan-African parliament* (Policy Brief 57). Centre for Policy Studies. Retrieved from https://africaportal.org/wp-content/uploads/2023/05/polbrief57.pdf

Ofori, P. E., Asongu, S., & Tchamyou, V. S. (2021). *The synergy between governance and economic integration in promoting female economic inclusion in sub-Saharan Africa* (SSRN Research Paper). Retrieved from http://dx.doi.org/10.2139/ssrn.4299366

Ong, A. (2006). *Neoliberalism as exception: Mutations in citizenship and sovereignty*. Durham, NC: Duke University Press.

Ossome, L. (2015). In search of the state? Neoliberalism and the labour question for Pan-African feminism. *Feminist Africa, 20*, 6–25.

Ossome, L., & Naidu, S. (2021). The agrarian question of gendered labour. In P. Jha, W. Chambati, & L Ossome (Eds.), *Labour questions in the global south* (pp. 63–86). Singapore: Springer. https://doi.org/10.1007/978-981-33-4635-2_4

Ryu, Y., & Ortuoste, M. (2014). Democratization, regional integration, and human rights: The case of the ASEAN intergovernmental commission on human rights. *The Pacific Review, 27*(3), 357–382. https://doi.org/10.1080/09512748.2014.909521

Spring, A. (2009). African women in the entrepreneurial landscape: Reconsidering the formal and informal sectors. *Journal of African Business, 10*(1), 11–30. https://doi.org/10.1080/15228910802701296

True, J. (2008). Gender mainstreaming and regional trade governance in Asia-Pacific Economic Cooperation (APEC). In S. M. Rai & G. Waylen (Eds.), *Global governance: Feminist perspectives* (pp. 129–159). London, UK: Palgrave Macmillan. https://doi.org/10.1057/9780230583931_7

Tsikata, D. (2009). Gender, land labour relations and livelihoods in sub-Saharan Africa in the era of economic liberalisation: Towards a research agenda. *Feminist Africa, 12*, 11–30.

Tsikata, D. (2014). Being Pan-Africa: A continental research agenda. *Feminist Africa, 19*, 94–97.

Tsikata, D., & Amanor-Wilks, D.-E. (2009). Editorial: Land and labour in gendered livelihood trajectories. *Feminist Africa, 12*, 1–10.

UNECA. (2010). *Assessing regional integration in Africa IV: enhancing intra-African trade.* Retrieved from https://hdl.handle.net/10855/15956

UNECA. (2023). *Africa's quarterly economic performance and outlook January–March 2023: Expenditure matters for growth and debt sustainability.* Retrieved from https://uneca.org/africa%E2%80%99s-quarterly-economic-performance-and-outlook-january%E2%80%-93march-2023-expenditure-matters-for

UNCTAD. (2022). *Handbook of statistics 2022.* Retrieved from https://hbs.unctad.org/

Wallace, A. (2014). Agency through development: Hausa women's NGOs and CBOs in Kano, Nigeria. *Feminist Economics, 20*(4), 287–288. https://doi.org/10.1080/13545701.2014.963636

Waller, W., & Wrenn, M. V. (2021). Feminist institutionalism and neoliberalism. *Feminist Economics, 27*(3), 51–76. https://doi.org/10.1080/13545701.2021.1883194

A Brief History of Development Initiatives in Africa[*]

Anthony Yaw Baah

Introduction

There have been two types of development initiatives in Africa—initiatives *by* Africans and initiatives *for* Africa. The former refers to country-owned initiatives that were designed and implemented *by* African countries after independence. The latter refers to initiatives that were designed *for* Africa and implemented by or under the supervision of the International Financial Institutions (IFIs).

These initiatives have different features. The Africa-owned initiatives were people-centred, and to some extent, they yielded some fruits, in terms of human development. All other initiatives imposed on Africa, particularly since the 1980s, have been based on the "blind" and ruthless free market ideology, and they have all failed to achieve any significant improvement in human development on the continent.

Unfortunately, the period during which Africans had the opportunity to initiate their own development policies was very short, lasting less than a decade from independence (between 1960 and 1970). Since then, all initiatives have been designed by "aliens" for Africa, and they have all failed. The failure is evidenced by the high incidence of poverty on the African continent, after half a century of independence.

---

[*] This is a revised version of a paper presented at the Africa Labour Research Network forum held in Johannesburg, South Africa, 22-23 May 2003.

I have outlined Africa's development path in the sections that follow, starting with colonial times (the period when Mother Africa was robbed of its natural resources and dignity by the imperialists and empire builders), moving on to the "Golden Decade" of the 1960s (the period of political freedom, self-realisation, self-determination, economic growth, and significant strides in social development), the 1970s (a decade of political instability), the 1980s and 1990s (the decades of decay) and ending with the developments in the present time (a period of uncertainty for Africa).

The Colonial Era: The Period of Robbery and Abuse of Africa

From the outset, let's remind ourselves that the present African countries were created, not by Africans, but by imperialists whose objectives did not include the socio-economic or human development of Africa.

The scramble for Africa at the infamous Berlin Conference in 1884 and the subsequent creation of many small states in Africa was based on pure imperialist greed. We cannot forget this because Africa is still grappling with the "social dissolution" (Stiglitz, 2002, p. 8) that resulted from the indiscriminate division of its peoples without any regard for social cohesion which had kept Africans together for so long. "Colonialism subverted hitherto traditional structures, institutions, and values or made them subservient to the economic and political needs of the imperial powers. It also retarded the development of an entrepreneurial class, as well as a middle class with skills and managerial capacity" (NEPAD, 2001, p. 5).

Therefore, the biggest challenge facing African countries upon their independence was the uphill task of restructuring the economies, which had been set up to generate one or two raw materials for export. The fact that Africa has not yet succeeded in restructuring its economies after more than half a century of independence is an indication of the extent of exploitation of the continent and the ruthlessness of colonialism as well as inappropriate policies imposed on the continent after independence.

Africa in the 1960s: The Period of Economic Growth and Hope

In 1957, Ghana under the leadership of Kwame Nkrumah led the way and mobilised the people to free Africa from imperialist greed. Immediately after independence, the development strategies in Africa had one goal—human development. This was to be achieved within the medium- and long-term development frameworks whose objectives were to eradicate the "colonial structure" that had been imposed on African economies, to speed up economic growth and to improve the living standards of the people.

A key feature of African development initiatives in the 1960s was the pivotal role the new African states played in the social, economic, and human development process—building social and economic infrastructure and providing social services to the impoverished people of the continent. Another important feature of African development initiatives in the 1960s was the adoption of Import Substitution Strategy (ISS) as a key economic development strategy. Among its many other benefits, the ISS ensured adequate protection of local industries and employment. Along with some local free-market capitalist ideologues, the IFIs would come to condemn this with its development strategy with the central role of the state, protection of local industries, and employment. These ideologues saw the state's only role as to protect their economic interests, their lives, and ill-acquired property.

A few other African visionaries, including Kwame Nkrumah, realised that the most effective way to develop Africa and its people was to involve the state directly in economic activities in order to ensure that there was equitable distribution of the benefits from national income and growth. Therefore, the recently established African States made significant investments in social services, especially in the fields of education and health. The construction of economic infrastructure, including roads, ports, communication facilities, and factories, also required significant investments. For example, in the Gold Coast (now Ghana), there were only 208 university students in 1951. By 1961, the number of university students had increased almost six-fold to 1,204. In the health sector, there has been a near tripling of hospital beds from 2,368 in 1951 to 6,155; there has been an increase in rural and urban clinics from 1 to 30; and the number of doctors and dentists has more than tripled from 156 to 500. There were huge investments in transport, communications, and electricity. Tanzania, Zambia, and other African countries followed the same path after they achieved independence.

In order to reduce the dependence of Africa on the colonial powers, i.e. to gain economic independence, ISI became the key element of the development strategies across independent Africa. In Ghana, under Nkrumah's Seven Year Development Plan, 62% of all investments were to go to the social services sector while 38% was earmarked for the "directly productive sector". In trade, African states controlled a substantial proportion of imports of consumer goods and exports. In Ghana, the state-controlled 41% of imports and over 60% of exports (mainly cocoa, gold, and timber). The results were remarkable, in terms of improvement in the standard of living of Africans.

However, by the late 1960s, the momentum of Africa's growth and development had slowed down considerably. The economic slowdown in the late 1960s is usually attributed to "over-investment" in the social sector and corruption. The detrimental and enduring effects of the Cold War on Africa are disregarded, despite the nation serving as one of its frontlines right after independence. The West realised that an increasing number of African countries would probably follow the human-centred path of economic and social development which had proved to be remarkably successful, particularly in Ghana.

The Western powers branded these development policies "socialist policies" because they saw them as a threat to the free-market ideology. They, therefore, sought to interfere in African political affairs through their secret agencies,[1] and in Africa's economic affairs through IFIs— the World Bank and International Monetary Fund (IMF)—in the form of huge investments in infrastructural projects across the continent. A typical example was the West's contribution to the construction of the Akosombo Hydroelectric Dam in Ghana. The World Bank contributed GBP17 million, the USAID GBP9.5 million, the UK GBP5 million, and the Export and Import Bank of the UK GBP3.5 million. The main objective of these investments was for the West to have allies in Africa as part of their Cold War strategy. The long-term objective was to undermine state participation in economic activities in Africa as a strategy to promote the free market ideology. Knowing that indigenous Africans could not immediately take over the major economic activities (because of the

---

1   The secret agencies by nature work secretly so we may never know their *modus operandi*. But the results of their actions are always there for everyone to see. The brutal murder of Patrice Lumumba in 1961 in Congo and the overthrow of Nkrumah in Ghana in 1966 are evidence of the secret actions of secret agents.

lack of credit and requisite management skills), the pull-out of African states from economic activities paved the way for the giant Western multinationals to take over the state enterprises.[2] This strategy worked very well, unfortunately.

The unfortunate part of this conspiracy was that certain African leaders collaborated with their former colonial powers to undermine African unity and its initiatives. This created a division among African leaders, particularly between the French-speaking and the English-speaking countries.[3]

The disunity among African leaders was evident in Addis Ababa when African leaders gathered to form the Organisation of African Unity (OAU) in 1963. African leaders failed to heed Nkrumah's advice that "our essential bulwark against the sinister threats and other multifarious designs of the neo-colonialists is in our political union" and "unless we meet the obvious and very powerful neo-colonialists' threats with a unified African front, based upon a common economic and defence policy, the strategy will be to pick us off and destroy us one by one" (1985, p. xvii). Nkrumah was overthrown in a military coup in 1966 with the active support of well-known secret agents from the West.

Africa in the 1970s: The Period of Political Instability and Economic Decline

Many African states have suffered significant weakening by 1970. There was political instability across Africa. This was the beginning of the economic decline in Africa. The situation was worsened by the oil price shock of 1973 which left African countries crushing under huge foreign debt.

---

2 As a condition for loans from the West to build the Akosombo Dam in Ghana to supply hydroelectric power, a leading US aluminium company Kaiser was to be allowed to invest in Ghana. The tariffs negotiated in 1962 as part of the agreement were still being paid by VALCO until the 2000s. The implication was that poor Ghanaians were subsidising the operation of VALCO for over forty years.

3 A typical example of the colonialists' effort to divide Africa was the signing of the so-called partnership agreement between the European Economic Community (EEC) and the French-speaking countries in Africa in 1963—Yaounde I, followed by Yaoundé II (1969–1975). This partnership was expanded to include African, Caribbean, and Pacific countries in 1975 in Lome, Togo (the so-called Lome Convention).

To create an impression that they cared about Africa and to be able to gain access to the power base as quickly as possible, the World Bank focused on human development issues and provided financial support to health, transport, and rural development. The IFIs set the terms and conditions of loans during this time when African countries were visibly weak. This naturally led to the replacement of human-centred African development priorities with those the IFIs considered appropriate for Africa. The result was a sharp drop in overall investment in social services, and as expected, this led to an equally sharp decline in living standards. Some African economies started recording negative economic growth rates and the incidence of poverty started rising again after some remarkable improvements in the 1960s.

African leaders realised the falling living standards of their people and the marginalisation of the continent. They tried to reverse this trend through regional integration to foster cooperation in various sectors. The formation of the Economic Community of West African States (ECOWAS) and the East African Community (EAC) is an example of such regional cooperation.

The Economic Commission for Africa (ECA) came out with a document—***Revised Framework of Principles for the Implementation of the New International Order in Africa*** which became the intellectual and theoretical foundation of the Monrovia Strategy in 1979 and, a year later, the Lagos Plan of Action and the Final Act of Lagos in 1980. This framework and the subsequent strategies advocated a development strategy for Africa with self-reliance, democratisation of the development process, and fair and just distribution of wealth as the cardinal principles (Adedeji, 2002).

Despite these initiatives, the relatively young African states were unable to overcome the challenges of the 1970s. Therefore, the IFIs were essentially "handed over" to administer the weaker African republics with their weaker economies. From that period until now, the economies of African countries have been in the hands of the IFIs. African states were, thus, stripped of their social and economic policy prerogatives, and since then, every effort by African leaders to "forge their [own] future and to craft their [own] indigenous development strategies and policies has been pooh-poohed by the international financial institutions (IFIs) with the support, or at least the connivance of the donor community [the West]" (Adedeji, 2002, p. 2).

At the beginning of the 1980s, the West forced Africa to follow the World Bank/IMF structural adjustment programmes (SAPs) by tying all their grants and loans to strict adherence to IMF and World Bank conditionalities. The results were disastrous across the continent.

Africa in the 1980s and 1990s: The Period of Structural Adjustment, Poverty, and Misery

By the beginning of the 1980s, all economic and social indicators showed that Africa had been left behind. Mass poverty, starvation, diseases, and ignorance were widespread in Africa. What we witnessed in Africa in the 1980s was well captured in the following statement contained in a paper delivered by the African National Congress (ANC) delegation at a Southern African Development Community (SADCC) conference held in Harare on 28 March 1988:

> "We have seen [in all parts of Africa] the frightened and pleading eyes of both young and old, reduced almost, to animal condition by want and deprivation. We are familiar with the tragic spectacle of children; mothers and fathers rummaging through refuse heaps in search of morsels of food that had been thrown away because they were no longer wanted. Stomachs distended to the point of bursting: eyes protruding sightless from deep sockets; legs so thin you wonder how they manage to support a body that is itself covered in scabs and festering sores; all these the result of man-made conditions that condemn millions to a life of hunger, homelessness, disease, ignorance and absence of protection from cold, heat, rain and the parching winds [of Africa]".

Frantic efforts were made by African leaders with the support of the United Nations, to reverse the trend. Among them were:

- The Lagos Plan of Action for the Economic Development of Africa: 1980–2000 and the Final Act.
- Africa's Priority Programme for Economic Recovery 1986–1990 (APPER) which later became the UN Programme of Action for

Africa's Economic Recovery and Development (UN-PAAERD) (1986).

- The African Alternative Framework to Structural Adjustment Programme for Socio-Economic Recovery and Transformation (AAF-SAP) 1989.
- The African Charter for Popular Participation for Development (1990).
- The UN New Agenda for Development of Africa in the 1990s (UN-NADAF, 1991).

As mentioned in the preceding sections, all these efforts were not supported by the IFIs and the donor community in the West. Instead, Africa became a fertile ground for the experimentation of the Washington Consensus using the so-called official development assistance (ODA) as the main tool.

Based on a World Bank 1981 report (the so-called **Berg Report**), the Bank initiated policy-based lending and tied development assistance to structural adjustment policies with a focus on macroeconomic policies. Another World Bank report in 1989 titled **From Crisis to Sustainable Growth** emphasised "wider issues of state failure" in Africa, stressing governance issues and policy reforms.

In 1994, there was yet another World Bank report with the title **Adjustment in Africa** which emphasised sound macroeconomic and structural management as prerequisites for growth and poverty reduction. As Easterly (2001) put it, it is like these policies did not work so let's try more of them.

With the shift of emphasis from human development to macroeconomic stability (as recommended by numerous IMF and World Bank reports), the ministries in charge of core human development issues such as local government, rural development, education, health, employment, and infrastructural development were downgraded. Instead, the ministries of finance and central banks were promoted since they were dealing directly with the Bank and the Fund. In Ghana, for example, the Ministry of Finance and Economic Planning was stripped of its economic planning functions during the structural adjustment period so that it could focus all its attention on inflation and exchange rate management, among other so-called macroeconomic fundamentals.

Prominent among the policies that were imposed on Africa in the 1980s were privatisation, liberalisation, and fiscal austerity. These policies were dictated by the World Bank and IMF using conditionalities, which were not based on any sound economic reasoning. As Stiglitz (2002, p. 53) rightly pointed out "[t]he problem was that many of these policies became ends in themselves, rather than means to more equitable and sustainable growth. In doing so, these policies were pushed too far, too fast, and to the exclusion of other policies that were needed".

Despite the failure of these policies, the IFIs continued to impose them on Africa throughout the 1980s and 1990s. The two decades of structural adjustment only succeeded in creating many positions and jobs for the so-called "experts" within the Bank and the Fund and increased the number of their missions to Africa. But for the ordinary African people, structural adjustment brought more unemployment, higher cost of living, low wages, poverty, destitution, misery, inequality, higher taxes, poor quality of education, and a huge external debt.

In Ghana, for example, Cleary (1989, p. 50) quotes extensively from Jonah (1987) on the effects of structural adjustment policies on employment as follows:

Retrenchment in the Civil/Public Service has so far gone through three phases. During the first phase 18 April–31 May, 1987, all personnel over 60 years who continued to work without the proper authority as required by existing regulations on re-engagement were retired. Altogether, 3200 persons were affected. During the second phase of retrenchment, 5000 surplus non-teaching staff of the Ghana Education Service were retired. This was completed by the first week of June 1987. The third phase [involved] the retirement of approximately 9000 more people from Civil Service and the Ghana Education Service, not later than the end of October 1987. Altogether, 17,200 employees [have been] retrenched by the end of [1987] ... and the Cocobod (Cocoa Marketing Board) would have sent home about 46,097 workers by the end of December, 1987. And yet this is no more than a beginning of a long exercise.

In the same publication, Cleary recounts the negative human impact of SAPs in Nigeria, Zambia, Central African Republic, and Ghana.

By the end of the 1990s, Africa's situation had, in fact, worsened by all standards. Today, after so many years of adjustment policies, it is estimated that over half of all Africans still live on less than USD1 a day and more than one out of every ten children die before their fifth birthday. In Ghana, real wages in the 1990s were a third of their levels in the 1960s and 1970s. The incidence of poverty increased drastically across the continent during the period of structural adjustment. In some parts of Ghana and many other African countries, the incidence of poverty rose to as high as 80%. Women and children were the most vulnerable.

Income inequality widened in many African countries in the 1980s and 1990s. For example, in 1992, the poorest 10% of the Ghanaian population received a share of 1.2% of total income as compared to the 36% share of the top (richest) 10% of the population. By 1999, the poorest 10% of the population had a share of only 0.3% of total income while the top 10% had increased their share from 36% to 42.5%. The Gini Coefficient in Ghana increased from 0.48 in 1992 to 0.60 in 1999. In Zambia, the bottom 10% of the population received 0.5% while the top 10% received over 50% of total income. In South Africa, the bottom 10% of the population received 1.4% while the top 10% received 42% of total income.

The situation was similar or worse in countries like Niger, Congo, Liberia, Chad, Mali, Malawi, Mozambique, and Sierra Leone.

We cannot deny the relationship between the war and ethnic conflicts we witnessed in Africa (Angola, Mozambique, Sudan, Sierra Leone, Chad, Ethiopia, Liberia, and Cote d'Ivoire) and the extreme poverty on the continent. At the beginning of this century, one out of every five Africans lived in a conflict zone. HIV/AIDS continued to kill thousands of Africans every week. No wonder this period has been rightly described as the "lost decades". But the structural adjustment policies probably killed more Africans than the wars, conflicts, and HIV/AIDS put together. The sad aspect of it is that the IMF and the World Bank never accepted responsibility for the deaths and suffering of these poor Africans. They created a mess in Africa and left it for African governments and their people to clean it.

Africa in the Twenty-First Century: Any Hope?

On the eve of the twenty-first century, the African economic crisis had reached its peak. Most countries had accumulated foreign debt to the tune of over 150% of their GDP over the two previous decades of structural adjustment. Many countries in Africa were forced by the Bretton Woods institutions to spend over a third of their export earnings on foreign debt servicing. As a result of the combination of structural adjustment policies and corruption, living standards plummeted further and the key indicator of well-being—life expectancy—in Sub-Saharan Africa was 30 years less than that in the economically advanced countries—a situation Comrade Fidel Castro of Cuba aptly described as "a true genocide".[4]

Based on a 1996 World Bank report titled *A Continent in Transition* and under intense and sustained pressure from the international civil society organisations to forgive Africa of its huge debt, the bank and the fund came up with the **Heavily Indebted Poor Countries (HIPC)** initiative. This initiative required African and other poor countries in Latin America and Asia to prepare **Poverty Reduction Strategy Papers (PRSPs)** as a condition for debt relief and access to the IMF Poverty Reduction and Growth Facility and the World Bank concessional loans and grants. In the PRSPs, governments were required to demonstrate their commitment to democratic governance, transparency, account-ability, poverty reduction, and the Washington Consensus in return for debt relief and increased assistance. Several African countries prepared the PRSPs. They included Benin, Burkina Faso, Cameroon, Cape Verde, Chad, Congo, Djibouti, Ethiopia, The Gambia, Ghana, Guinea, Kenya, Lesotho, Malawi, Mali, Mauritania, Mozambique, Niger, Rwanda, Senegal, Sierra Leone, Tanzania, Uganda, and Zambia.

In yet another World Bank Report in 2000 titled *"Can Africa Claim the 21st Century?"*, emphasis was placed on the need for reducing con-flict and improving governance, investing in people, increasing compet-itiveness and diversification, improving aid effectiveness, and reducing Africa's dependence on aid.

---

4   Statement by Dr Fidel Castro Ruz, president of Cuba, to the United Nations Financing for Development Conference in Monterrey, Mexico, March 2002. https://www.un.org/webcast/ffd/2002/statements/cubaE.htm

As correctly predicted by civil society organisations and trade unions, the PRSPs and all the World Bank and IMF-sponsored policies failed to alleviate poverty in Africa. The PRSPs probably worsened the plight of poor people in Africa.

Some Recent Development Initiatives

Other initiatives that have been implemented in recent times in Africa include the Millennium Development Goals (MDGs), the Omega Plan, and the Millennium Africa Recovery Programme (MAP) which were combined to form the New Partnership for Africa's Development (NEPAD). The World Bank/IDA developed another initiative known as **Assistance Strategy for Africa (ASAF)** with the purported aim of complementing the efforts of African countries within the framework of NEPAD. The most recent and ongoing development plan is the AU Agenda 2063. These two initiatives are summarised below.

New Partnership for Africa Development (NEPAD)

NEPAD is another strategic framework adopted by African leaders to transform Africa, eradicate poverty, and place the continent on a path of sustainable growth and development, based on a common vision and shared conviction. The NEPAD strategic framework document was adopted by the AU in July 2001 at its thirty-seventh summit in Lusaka, Zambia.

Objectives of NEPAD

The following objectives were to be achieved under NEPAD:

- reduce poverty or eliminate extreme poverty in Africa;
- place African countries, both individually and collectively, on a path of sustainable growth and development;
- halt the marginalisation of Africa in the globalisation process; and
- promote the role of women in all activities (women empowerment).

NEPAD was anchored on the following major themes:

1. **Peace and Security Initiative** (promoting long-term conditions for development and security, building the capacity of African

institutions for early warning, as well as enhancing their capacity to prevent, manage, and resolve conflicts).

2. **Democracy and Political Governance Initiative** (promoting democracy and political pluralism, strengthening the political-administrative framework of participating countries in line with the principles of democracy, transparency, accountability, integrity, respect for human rights, and promotion of the rule of law, and strengthening political governance).

3. **Economic and Corporate Governance Initiative** (promoting a set of concrete and time-bound programmes aimed at enhancing the quality of economic and public financial management, as well as corporate governance).

It was envisaged that Africa would achieve and sustain an average GDP growth rate of over 7% per annum within fifteen years. NEPAD was also designed to ensure that the continent achieves the MDGs.

African Union (AU) Agenda 2063

The AU Agenda 2063 is yet another strategic framework for the socio-economic transformation of the continent within a fifty-year period. This development initiative builds on and seeks to accelerate past and existing continental initiatives for growth and sustainable development including the Lagos Plan of Action and NEPAD, as well as regional and national plans.

After the adoption of the Agenda 2063 framework document by the summit in January 2015 as the basis for Africa's long-term socio-economic development and transformation, the African Union Commission was tasked to prepare the First Ten Year Implementation Plan of Agenda 2063 (2013–2023). This plan, which is the first in a series of five ten-year plans to cover the fifty-year period, was adopted by the summit in June 2015 as a basis for the preparation of medium-term development plans of member states of the Union, the Regional Economic Communities and the AU Organs.

The AU Agenda 2063 was prepared under seven aspirations:

1. a prosperous Africa based on inclusive growth and sustainable development;

2. an integrated continent; politically united and based on the ideals of Pan-Africanism and the vision of Africa's renaissance;
3. an Africa of good governance, democracy, respect for human rights, justice, and the rule of law;
4. a peaceful and secure Africa;
5. an Africa with a strong cultural identity, common heritage, shared values, and ethics;
6. an Africa, whose development is people-driven, relying on the potential of African people, especially its women and youth, and caring for children; and
7. Africa is a strong, united, resilient, and influential global player and partner.

The following are the expected outcomes after the first ten years (2013–2023):

- improvements in living standards across the continent;
- African economies would have been transformed; they would have become more inclusive; and they would have achieved higher and sustainable growth rates;
- African countries would be more integrated economically and politically;
- women, youth, and children would be empowered; and
- Africa would be well-governed and more peaceful.

Conclusion

From the foregoing, it is clear that African leaders and their peoples are struggling to transform the continent, economically, socially, and politically. There have been numerous economic development initiatives in the last six decades or so. But the reality remains that the positive effects of all these initiatives can hardly be felt by the majority of people on the continent.

Africa continues to be at the bottom of the heap in global affairs after more than half a century of independence, despite the various initiatives discussed above. Many African countries continue to rely on the IMF, World Bank, and Western bilateral donors for aid for some important sectors like education, health, sanitation, water, energy, and infrastructural development. Some African countries even rely on grants from these institutions and bilateral aid for food.

But, as Africans, we should always remember what Kwame Nkrumah said many years ago, that it is unreasonable to suppose that foreign powers (and their institutions) affluent enough to give aid to an African State, would not expect some measure of consideration or favour from the state receiving the aid (Nkrumah, 1961).

Western powers and their institutions are not interested in the development of Africa. If they are genuinely committed to supporting Africa in development, what is preventing them from achieving the ODA target of **only 0.7%** of their gross national product?

Economic emancipation remains an unfinished business. Africa should take her destiny into her own hands and develop her own policies, based on the needs of its people. Africa's future lies in her own ability to take bold development initiatives. Africa's future does not lie in neo-colonial partnerships.

References

Adedeji, A. (2002, April 29). "From the Lagos plan of action to the new partnership for African development and from the final act of Lagos to the constitutive act: Wither Africa?" A keynote address at African Forum for Envisioning Africa, Nairobi, Kenya.

African National Congress. (1988, March 28). SADCC's future: Europe's role, Harare, Zimbabwe.

Cleary, S. (1989). Structural adjustment in Africa. Trócaire Development Review, pp. 41–59.

Easterly, E. (2001). The elusive quest of growth: Economists' adventures and misadventures in the tropics. Cambridge, MA: MIT Press.

NEPAD. (2001). A summary of NEPAD action plans.

Nkrumah, K. (1961). I speak of freedom. London, UK: William Heinemann Ltd.

Nkrumah, K. (1968). Dark Days in Ghana. London, UK: Zed Books.

Nkrumah, K. (1985). Africa must unite. London, UK: PANAF.

Stiglitz, J. E. (2002). Globalisation and its discontents. London, UK: Penguin Group.

Pan-African Epistemologies of Knowledge Production: A Deconstruction-Based Critical Reflection[*]

James Dzisah and Michael Kpessa-Whyte

Introduction

Though scholarly interest in Pan-African epistemologies is not new, it has been reinvigorated in recent times due to evidence suggesting that Western-produced knowledge hardly worked in non-Western contexts. To this end, Escobar (1995) documented failures and contradictions in development projects driven by Western knowledge systems in developing countries. Similarly, Chambers (1997) drew attention to errors in Western research-driven development initiatives. As critical opinions in academic circles started to surface, challenging the contextual relevance of knowledge upon which developments in Africa were premised, the World Bank (1998) also published a report acknowledging that knowledge, rather than capital, is the primary factor shaping the trajectory of sustainable economic growth and human well-being. In the context of Africa, these developments generated renewed interest in Pan-African epistemologies and systems of knowledge production, with some arguing

[*] This chapter is a slightly edited version of an article first published in *Contemporary Journal of African Studies*, Vol. 10, No. 2 (2023) and is reproduce here with permission.

that "the basic component of any country's knowledge system is its indigenous knowledge" (Economic and Social Department, 2006, p. 9).

The discourse on Pan-African epistemologies and the broader debate about knowledge production are very often heated due to the roles of colonialism, imperialism, and globalism in subordinating African indigenous ways of knowing (Appiah, 2005; Dei, 2000; Mudimbe, 1988; Ndlovu-Gatsheni, 2018; Ngugi wa Thiong'o, 2012). This is not a settled debate but an evolving one, especially with the emergence of postcolonial scholarship within the broader context of postmodernist approaches. Since knowledge is never produced in a vacuum but within an institutional paradigm that is shaped by historical and contemporary events, Africa and its diaspora, like knowledge itself, is shaped by the evils of enslavement, colonialism, and hegemony (Mamdani, 2016; Mkandawire, 2005; Mudimbe, 1988; Ngugi wa Thiong'o, 1986; Zeleza & Olukoshi, 2004). Compared to Europe's supremacy as the epicentre and model of knowledge creation, the affective nature of the Pan-African epistemological discourse is not a recent development (Adesanmi, 2011; Adomako Ampofo, 2016; Zeleza, 1997; Zeleza & Olukoshi, 2004). This discourse dates to Africa's humiliating encounter with enslavement and colonisation (Mandani, 2016; Mkandawire, 2005; Mudimbe, 1988; Ngugi wa Thiong'o, 1986; Zeleza & Olukoshi, 2004).

Also, the modern realities and experiences of Africa are shaped in the words of Mazrui (1986) by a triple legacy of indigenous heritage arising from time-tested knowledge, Eurocentric capitalism imposed through colonialism, and the jihadist and evangelistic spread of Islam. Similarly, Mudimbe describes the "domination of physical space, the reformulation of natives' minds and the integration of local economic histories with Western perspective as the three complementary projects of colonialism" (1988, p. 15). This historical phase, in the words of Okech, also speaks discernibly to the "inattentiveness to gender" as a visible "category and as a theoretical framework for understanding inclusion, exclusion, and investment in higher education and research" (2020, p. 316). The need for interventions on decolonisation of knowledge and its institutional patriarchal structures featured fervently in the discourse of African feminists who spearheaded the call for dismantling Eurocentric concepts and approaches (Adomako Ampofo & Beoku-Betts, 2021; Amadiume,

1997; Cole, Manuh, & Miescher, 2007; Medie & Kang, 2018; Okech, 2020; Tamale, 2011; Tsikata, 2007).

Rooted in and emanating from these historical events, Pan-African epistemologies and knowledge production in the broader context have re-emerged as a critical discourse, yet still without any proper resolution (Mama, 2003; Nnaemeka, 2005; Oyewumi, 1997). It is appropriate to say that the epistemological position of Europe and its dominant collaborators have permeated the African intellectual landscape. This description applies to both the hegemony of the practice of knowledge production and its consumption (Adomako Ampofo, 2016; Adomako Ampofo & Beoku-Betts, 2021; Mama, 2003; Ngugi wa Thiong'o, 1986; Okech, 2020; Tamale, 2020).

We use the term hegemony not strictly within the confines of Gramscian trappings, which is often status quo legitimising. We situate the hegemonic practices within the perimeters of Foucauldian explications of power and knowledge. This power/knowledge dichotomy stares the African intellectual, whether on the continent or its diaspora, in the face and works both ways in perpetuating what Immanuel Wallerstein (2004) describes as a capitalist-embracing world system. To this end, the African scholar is persistently confronted by a variant of intellectual imperialism that seeks to dismiss, and exclude as irrelevant, knowledge rooted in the African cultural experience unless such experiences are forced to approximate those of the coloniser (Adomako Ampofo & Beoku-Betts, 2021; Mami, 2011; Mandani, 2016; Mkandawire, 2005; Mudimbe, 1988; Ngugi wa Thiong'o, 1986; Shivji, 2018; Zeleza & Olukoshi, 2004). As Chilisa observed, "… it is still the practice in academic debates to invoke Euro-Western belief systems and methodologies to dismiss as irrelevant knowledge from formerly colonised societies" (2011, p. 61). This is why coloniality has become the quality standard of produced knowledge in African educational institutions (Adomako Ampofo, 2016; Adomako Ampofo & Beoku-Betts, 2021; Mama, 2003; Mandani, 2016; Mkandawire, 2005; Mudimbe, 1988; Ngugi wa Thiong'o, 1986; Okech, 2020; Shivji, 2018; Tamale, 2020; Zeleza & Olukoshi, 2004). The common practice in the African academy is that the form and structure of knowledge production and its underpinning narratives must conform to the dictates and structures of the coloniser. This culture of practice accepts the universalising Western epistemologies of knowledge as the "gold standard" and keenly looks forward to its isomorphic mimicry. This hegemonic knowledge production and legitimation is unequivocally captured by Edward Said when he stated that:

> Without significant exception the universalizing discourses of modern Europe and the United States assume the silence, willing or otherwise, of the non-European world...But there is only infrequently an acknowledgement that the colonised people should be heard from, their ideas known (1993, p. 50).

It is clear from the above that to pretend that the knowledge practices within the context of African universities are not part of the problem is just as naïve as indicating that the colonial context and the hegemonic impulses inherent in academic knowledge production from the Global North are figments of our collective imaginations. The question, however, is do our contemporary practices provide the space to pursue what can be recognised as Pan-African epistemologies of production? Is it possible to contemplate its practice purely on Africa's own terms? While these pervasive questions keep reverberating whenever the issue of Pan-African epistemologies of knowledge production is raised, it must be noted that their persistence is not because there is a lack of effort on the part of postcolonial scholars.[1]

However, once we turn on the critical postcolonial gaze to unpack the discourse of epistemologies vis-à-vis global knowledge production, the Western knowledge form becomes the measuring standard. Therefore, in the production and consumption of knowledge through legitimation practices, the Derridean nudges to deconstruct and reconstruct loom large. It must be stated that what we envisaged in this paper is not the application of deconstruction based on logocentrism and mere representations (Derrida, 1973, 1976, 1978). Rather, we deconstruct through the lens of Gayatri Spivak's concept of strategic essentialism.

---

1 For an insight into the debate about the long and detailed history of knowledge production about Africa, see "The Founding of the African Studies Association", by G. Carter, 1983, *African Studies Review*, 26(3/4), pp. 5–9; *African Studies* in the US, by J. Guyer, 1996, Atlanta: ASA Press.

This deconstruction-based postcolonial thought opens the possibility of a viable Pan-African epistemology. Once activated, postcolonial theory's strategic essentialism unleashes African intellectual identity as enmeshed within the cultural norms and values of Africa by providing avenues to reinvigorate indigenous knowledge systems. Thus, within the context of the vexing question of whether there can be fully-fledged Pan-African epistemologies of knowledge, we reopen the debate for a critical self-reflection. This provides ways through which scholars and practitioners reclaim their voices, like the proverbial hunter, with equal control of their tales as well.

The question of reclaiming Pan-African epistemic voices is raised within a discernible ambience that prioritises scholarly accounts of the Global North as the gold standard for assessing postcolonial scholarship. Thus, within the context of African universities, the culture of knowledge production and its practices are so much tinged with residual colonialism. This, in recent times, is anchored through the insistence on such practices as the indexing of scholarly outputs in colonial outlets and the obsession with university ranking scores. These indexing outlets are designed to legitimise and delegitimise knowledge practices emanating from postcolonial sources. For instance, a British scholar who publishes in journals based in the United Kingdom is not confronted with the stigma of publishing only in local journals, by any stretch of the imagination. However, a Ghanaian scholar is scolded, metaphorically speaking, for playing only in the local league.

Despite this, there is a need to interrogate the discourse of knowledge production and its practices in postcolonial society. This deconstruction allows us to redefine the search for Pan-African epistemologies of knowledge production within our collective intent to harness the rich insights of indigenous and postcolonial knowledge. This fits into the original intent and desire of President Nkrumah in establishing the Institute of African Studies as a bastion of a "highly developed code of morals" (Allman, 2013, p. 183). Together, these philosophical and practical instruments of knowledge are to produce authentic Pan-African epistemologies of knowledge that are path-breaking.

The paper is structured around four broad overlapping themes. The next section interrogates the concept of Pan-Africanism. It situates the debate of Pan-African epistemologies of knowledge production within the broader context of what Pan-Africanism meant in the first place and how African knowledge systems have been historically caricatured. The hegemonic practices of knowledge and its legitimation practices are then highlighted. This paves the way for the debate on Pan-African epistemologies of knowledge production within the confines of Gayatri Spivak's deconstruction-laced concept of strategic essentialism. The fourth section details the pathways for Pan-African epistemologies within the immediate African context. The paper concludes that truly Pan-African epistemologies of knowledge production pathways are viable if strategic essentialism is invoked in both theory and practice.

Pan-Africanism and the Debate About the Role of Epistemology

Pan-Africanism, both as a concept and a process, has had very emotional and psychological effects on the people of Africa and its diaspora. As with social science concepts, the term defies a universal definition to the extent that some writers are hesitant to even propose or agree that a definition is discernible (see Ackah, 1999; Geiss, 1974; Langley, 1973; Legum, 1962; Nascimento, 1980; Shepperson, 1962; Thompson, 1973). The vagueness of the term, as suggested by Adi, "reflects the fact that Pan-Africanism has taken different forms at different historical moments and geographical locations" (2018, p. 2).

While the concept of Pan-Africanism still lacks an acceptable definition, its continuing relevance as a process is without doubt. There is an inherent understanding that the process must reflect the totality of Africa and its diaspora (Adi, 2018; Clarke, 1988). The underlying faith in these manifold visions and approaches to exploring Pan-Africanism both as a concept and a process emanates from the shared history and purpose of Africa and its diaspora. The fundamental creed is the notion that there is coherence in Africa's diversity (Adi, 2018). The African Union magazine, *AU Echo*, in January 2013 provided a contemporary definition of Pan-Africanism:

> An ideology and movement that encouraged the solidarity of Africans worldwide. It is based on the belief that unity is vital to

economic, social and political progress and aims to "unify and uplift" people of African descent. The ideology asserts that the fates of all African peoples and countries are intertwined. At its core, Pan-Africanism is a belief that African peoples both on the continent and in the diaspora share not merely a common history, but a common destiny (AU Echo, 2013, p. 1).

If we place our critical gaze on this definition, Pan-Africanism both as a concept and a process has evolved. Emerging at the peak of the slave trade era, Pan-Africanism came to express the practical anticipation that the African continent and its diaspora would be liberated. It must be noted that there are differing accounts relating to Pan-Africanism that are not fully explored in this paper.[2] Justifiably, Pan-Africanism's modern understanding and value emanated from the struggle against colonialism (Adi, 2018). Symbolically, the process was birthed, amplified, and given meaning by the famous statement by President Kwame Nkrumah at the historic declaration of Ghana's independence:

> We have done the battle and we again rededicate ourselves not only in the struggle to emancipate other countries in Africa. Our independence is meaningless unless it is linked up with the total liberation of the African continent (Nkrumah, 1979, pp. 156–171 quoted in Biney, 2011, p. 240).

Political liberation has arrived for many African nations, but the idea of Pan-African epistemologies of knowledge production remains elusive. This situation is not helped by the explicit attempt to deny the geography, intellectual space, and recognition of what can truly be termed Pan-African epistemologies of knowledge. As late as 2007, the disgraced former president of France, Nicholas Sarkozy, arrogantly asserted in a speech that Africa's tragedy is that it has no history and no "idea of

---

2   See Nantambu, K. (1998). Pan-Africanism versus Pan-African Nationalism: An Afrocentric Analysis. *Journal of Black Studies*, 28(5), 561–574 for what he described as an Afrocentric approach to a proper, historical, unifying, and holistic perspective; Clarke, J. H. (1988). Pan-Africanism: A Brief History of an Idea in the African World. *Présence Africaine* 145, 26–56; ʔbádélé Bakari Kambon, Pan-Africanism Defined, at *Definitions of Pan-Afrikanism: Preview to the Ancient Origins*, 2019, https://youtu.be/E8KWImibNyI.

progress" (Adi, 2018, p. 3). But as critical observers have noted, this caricaturing of Africa is not new as outright dismissals of Africa in historical accounts abound (Adi, 2018). Sarkozy's denial was just a return to the Eurocentric path constructed by those before him. For example, in a public lecture at the University of Sussex in October 1963, the historian Trevor-Roper stated:

> Perhaps, in the future, there will be some African history to teach. But at present there is none, or very little: there is only the history of the Europeans in Africa. The rest is largely darkness, like the history of pre-European, pre-Columbian America. And darkness is not a subject for history (Adi, 2018, p. 3).

Unfortunately, Trevor-Roper, just like Sarkozy after him, was only retelling a long-established Eurocentric assertion that sought to deny any intellectual space to talk about Pan-African epistemologies of knowledge production. The well-known German philosopher Friedrich Hegel stated in 1830 that:

> At this point we leave Africa, not to mention it again. For it is no historical part of the World; it has no movement or development to exhibit. Historical movements in it—that is in its northern part—belong to the Asiatic or European World. Carthage displayed there an important transitionary phase of civilization; but, as a Phoenician colony, it belongs to Asia. Egypt will be considered in reference to the passage of the human mind from its Eastern to its Western phase, but it does not belong to the African Spirit. What we properly understand by Africa, is the Unhistorical, Undeveloped Spirit, still involved in the conditions of mere nature, and which had to be presented here only as on the threshold of the World's History (Hegel, 1956, p. 99).

This racist caricaturing of Africa and its knowledge systems is depressing. It is imperative to state that the role of the Institute of African Studies at the University of Ghana was, from the onset, meant to confront these racist caricatures. As indicated by its founding director, Hodgkin:

It was the job of African Studies, not only to expose racist colonial myths ("Africa has no history" for example) but to build up systematically as comprehensive a body of source material as possible to disprove those myths and then to undertake the process of reinterpretation of the evidence and the making available of the results of this interpretation (Allman, 2013, p. 190).

It follows that the University of Ghana's Institute of African Studies was a breeding ground for ideas about what and how Pan-African epistemologies of knowledge production should be developed. Furthermore, several academics have laid out the need for rethinking education and knowledge structures throughout Africa (see Mama, 2003; Mamdani, 2016; Zeleza & Olukoshi, 2004). However, we lost both our bearings and articulation. The attempt to decolonise knowledge as it developed only found expression in the permissive appeal to the oppressors (Prakash, 1995). Our tendency to elevate Western interpretations as universal, interest-free, and value-free while quickly dismissing Pan-African practices led to an endless void from which our cultural norms, scripts, and society were constructed (Prakash, 1995). Interrogating Edward Said's admonition regarding commodities and representations, the reality of our predicament and the task ahead glaringly stare us in the face. As Said aptly articulated,

We live of course in a world not only of commodities but also of representations—their production, circulation, history, and interpretation. In much recent theory the problem of representation is deemed to be central, yet rarely is it put in its full political context, a context that is primarily imperial. Instead, we have on the one hand an isolated cultural sphere, believed to be freely and unconditionally available to weightless theoretical speculation and investigation, and, on the other, a debased political sphere, where the real struggle between interests is supposed to occur. To the professional student of culture—the humanist, the critic, the scholar—only one sphere is relevant, and more to the point, it is accepted that the two spheres are separated, whereas the two are not only connected but ultimately the same (1995, p. 34).

Unfortunately, the African intellectual cannot write in a vacuum. We are situated within an academic world that is saturated with negative statements by non-Africans about ourselves and our continent. This is reasonable given the imperialistic nature of social science (Ake, 1982). As a result, in reconstructing the discourse on Pan-African epistemologies of knowledge production, our very own realities must be front and centre. There is no excuse to steadily hold on to the epistemological ideals that others have constructed for Africa without attempts to produce one that represents our reality.

Regrettably, even in the attempts to deconstruct and reconstruct the very process of knowledge production within the confines of Pan-Africanism, the assemblages of knowledge production are premised on the extent to which the African scholar embraced the Western narrative (Falola, 2004). The West's hegemonic dominance is built on the denigration of indigenous knowledge (Falola, 2005; Oppong, 2013; Yankah, 2004). Paradoxically, indigenous African knowledge systems are not regarded as being on the same level as other knowledge systems when it comes to knowledge generation, even though competition is a fundamental element of creativity and invention. The universalising discourse of the West and the reality of our predicament is that our very own default recognised knowledge mode is enunciated in non-nativized languages and Western-styled educational settings. In the next section, we focus on the global context of knowledge production to highlight how the enterprise of knowledge and its production continues not only to be tinged by the vestiges of colonialism but operates largely within its permeated boundaries.

The Context of Knowledge Production

The pervasiveness of hegemonic discourse on knowledge production and its legitimation is very much a taken-for-granted reality in terms of how non-Western knowledge and its foundational epistemologies are delegitimised. In the classical form of giving a dog a bad name to hang it, knowledge is categorised as science and non-science, with the prototypical non-Western ways of knowing depicted as falling outside the scientific categorisation. So, in the sociology of science literature, the classical Robert Merton provided a romanticised account of science as an epistemic knowledge that is organised around functionalist norms of universalism, disinterestedness, organised scepticism, and communalism (Merton, 1973). These norms that collectively came to be known as the ethos of science provided the institutional context for what was to be accepted or disregarded as knowledge, scientific and non-scientific practice. The "universalism" norm prohibited the scientist's social status and role from being a basis for the validation and acceptance of knowledge claims. The ethos of "disinterestedness" guaranteed neutrality in the assessment of knowledge claims while "organised scepticism" safeguarded the established standards and measures of accepting or rejecting knowledge claims. The ethos of "communalism" detailed knowledge exchanges within the scientific community (Dzisah, 2010). However, we are aware that these scientific ethos as ideal types are farther away from actual practice. However, non-Western knowledge is swiftly discarded due to the theoretical and practical standards established by the scientific mindset.

As broadly defined, one sees an immediate problem in seeking to forge some kind of unity in diversity when it comes to Pan-African epistemologies. In fact, once we turn on the critical gaze, the veiled inherent biases in knowledge production are unmasked. Paul Tiyambe Zeleza was more poignant in stating the obvious:

> ...the terms of global intellectual exchange, like the terms of trade for the so-called developed and developing economies, are decidedly unequal: African studies in the North is a peripheral part of the academy, whereas the Euro-American epistemological order remains central in the African academy. Since the colonial encounter, the construction of scholarly knowledge about Africa has been internationalised both in the sense of it being an activity involving scholars in various parts of the world and the inordinate influence of externally generated models on African scholarship (2007, p. 2).

Zaheer Baber (2003) also revealed elsewhere how practical/technical research is relegated to the periphery while pure/theoretical work is reserved for the core. Admittedly, there is no clear-cut division of intellectual labour, but discerning configurations are visible. As Baber pointedly stated:

> conceptual, theoretical work that sought to universalize its findings from, provincial locations was the preserve of the colonial scholars. Knowledge produced by scholars located in the colonized societies had a particular geographical referent, constituted a case study, and hence had no theoretical contributions to make ... A few notable exceptions notwithstanding, knowledge produced by scholars located in metropolitan societies was deemed to be general and universal in their implication regardless of how local or provincial their terms of reference might be (2003, p. 617).

This development parallels the description of the colonial division of labour in which there is the uncritical affirmation that scholarly outcomes from Africa and its diaspora are inferior and can only serve as raw material that partially solves local issues (Hountondji, 2002). This relegation of African intellectual output to the backyard is not new as has been catalogued by African scholars such as Mbembe (2001) and Mudimbe (1988). However, as Chakrabarty reiterated,

> For generations now, philosophers and thinkers who shape the nature of social science have produced theories that embrace the entirety of humanity ... The everyday paradox of third-world social science is that we find these theories, in spite of their inherent ignorance of "us", eminently useful in understanding our societies (2000, p. 29).

The promptings of these deconstructionist nudges are that we must resituate knowledge production within the idea of open-endedness and reflexivity. This needs to include everything that the legacy of colonialism has caused in our culture and customs. Since production and consumption are intertwined, the deconstruction of how we privileged and reinforced coloniality through routine performativity matrices of journal outlets and citation indexes must be debated. These indexes are nothing but disguised mechanisms that revivify colonial knowledge structures. Ending their privileged status is a starting point for Pan-African epistemologies of knowledge production to re-emerge. We must go beyond these veiled neo-colonial practices by critically reflecting on the production, consumption, and measurement of knowledge.

The reconstruction of what qualifies as Pan-African epistemologies of knowledge rests precisely in going back to the question that Chakrabarty succinctly asked: "What allowed the modern European sages to develop such clairvoyance with regard to societies of which they were empirically ignorant? Why cannot we, once again, return the gaze?" (Chakrabarty, 2000, p. 29). To this end, we need to re-engage those intellectual activities that advance Pan-African epistemologies of knowledge (Falola, 2004; Mamdani, 1999; Mkandawire, 2000, 2002; Quijano, 2007; Zeleza, 1992). There is a need to review what constitutes Pan-African knowledge and the extent to which it must be measured by our very own inherent standards. Also, to what extent must Pan-African knowledge deviate from other knowledge systems? In the next section, we interrogate postcolonial theory as a way of unmasking the hegemonic discourses sustaining the colonial empire and its enduring knowledge base.

Postcolonialism and the Hegemony of Western Knowledge Practices

Postcolonial theory emerged along the lines of revolutionary new frontiers and cultural studies (Gandhi, 1998). These so-called new humanities appeared just as the philosophies of post-structuralism and deconstruction, and became tied to postcolonial theory (Loomba, 1998). The impact of postcolonial theory attracted immediate scrutiny and criticism based largely on its trendiness. It was, therefore, not surprising when Harold Bloom, the famed literary critic, denounced postcolonial studies as being infected with "the disease of resentment" (Hedges, 2000; Go, 2016). Despite attempts by critics to relegate postcolonial theory to non-knowledge, its diversity provided a foundational coordinate (Go, 2016). To this end, the first wave of postcolonial theorists unsettled the Enlightenment notion of objective knowers. This so-called Cartesian subject provided the basis for construing the universe as an objective reality out there. This idealised rendition of the objectivity of knowledge, far removed from the realities of the world, was made untenable. This is because knowledge is relational, whether in its curiosity or neoliberal capitalised format (Dzisah, 2016). More in tune with the postcolonial critique is the fact that knowledge is intrinsically tied to power, especially imperial and colonial power (Go, 2016). This critique went to the core of the idea of Enlightenment. It challenges its universal knowledge claims, teasing that "if the imperial knower cannot pull the 'God trick', then its knowledge is not universal" (Go, 2016, p. 33).

In *Representations of the Intellectual*, Edward Said (1996) provided yet another insight into how universalism claims underlie much of the hegemony of Western knowledge. For instance, a close reading of Marx provided such a universal epistemological proposition in terms of his usage of the categories of "bourgeois" and "pre-bourgeois" or "capital" and "pre-capital". The prefix "pre" signified a notional and sequential relationship (Said, 1996). In the *Grundrisse*, Marx insisted that the emergence of the bourgeoisie and, for that matter, capitalist society produces a historical, philosophical, and universal category—capital. This category depicts the ability to theoretically comprehend the material history of not just Europe but the entirety of humanity. In the process, this universality of history rendered Pan-African knowledge and other non-European history redundant because history must be theoretically based on its differences from the European version. The fact that "cultures are too intermingled, their contents and histories too interdependent and hybrid, for surgical separation into large and mostly ideological oppositions like Orient and Occident" (Said, 1996, p. xii), notwithstanding, the universalism claim continued unabated. As surgically narrated by Dipesh Chakrabarty, in the work of Marx, one just has to substitute the words "Europe" for "capital" and "European" for "bourgeois" (2000, pp. 29–30) to unmask the universal claim of Western hegemony.

In the previous section, we indicated the need to explore what constitutes knowledge within the settings of Pan-African epistemologies of knowledge and the extent to which this knowledge is to be measured. We have already alluded to the fact that scholarship in Africa is responsive rather than proactive due to the epistemological influence of the reality of the West (Falola, 2004, 2005; Yankah, 2004). So, working within this reality, how do we reconstruct Pan-African epistemologies to reflect our cultural and historical practices? In the African systems of thought, the emphasis is on the holistic picture of the larger society. This, as we have already indicated, informed the vision of President Nkrumah in articulating the primary function of the Institute of African Studies (Allman, 2013). The lingering question, though, is why have we abandoned this vision and adopted academic practices that privilege only one form of knowledge, that is, knowledge that is based entirely on the Western performative standards? To put it bluntly, why are contemporary African centres of knowledge production, institutions of research and higher learning insistent that only colonial outlets and their contemporary versions of performance metrics provide the measuring rod of scholarship? Why are African universities taking pride in accepting university rankings performed by Western-based rating agencies, some very dodgy, without any tinge of decolonial intent? (Shivji, 2018).

A major step in the process of deconstructing contemporary knowledge production in the African context is to pay critical attention to the conscious and unconscious perpetuation of the hegemony of Western knowledge systems. This takes the form of the uncritical practice of acclaimed scholarship as based on the geographical location of a journal or its indexed site. The obsession with the hegemonic Western standard must be reconsidered if we are to prioritise Pan-African pedagogical and epistemological approaches (Adomako Ampofo & Beoku-Betts, 2021; Mama, 2003, 2007; Okech, 2020; Oyewumi, 2002; Nnaemeka; 2005). The rallying point for a true constitution of Pan-African epistemologies of knowledge production starts from the rejection of the new indexing colonialism and prioritising, in its place, the uniquely African experiences, where scholarly preparation, appraisal, and the determination of outcomes are rooted within the specific African cultural contexts.

Regarding the question of the extent to which Pan-African knowledge systems must deviate from the Western forms, our ability to deconstruct and simultaneously reconstruct knowledge and the academy will determine the way forward. As we have indicated from the onset, we use the term "deconstruction" in the Derridean fashion only to showcase the possibility of authentic Pan-African epistemologies. This option is only feasible if indigenous knowledges are positioned within the larger framework of institutions, processes, and architecture of knowledge creation that sustain African cultural values. There is a need to recast the discourse and focus on knowledge production practices specifically within the African academy and society, recognising the various ways that we ourselves are perpetuating the hegemony of the West in implied and calculated ways. This is why the deconstructionist perspective allows us to redefine the search for Pan-African epistemologies of knowledge production within our collective intent, which is geared toward harnessing the rich insights of our indigenous knowledges, for a more recognisable paradigm shift.

In fact, until we resituate knowledge production within the idea of reflexivity that takes cognisance of and corrects our overall culture of practices, the search for what constitutes Pan-African knowledge, and its epistemological compass, will remain elusive. The need for reflexivity is critical because our knowledge practices are underpinned by an enduring legacy of colonialism. Indeed, the extent to which we must deviate from the Western hegemonic knowledge as the referent is reflective of how our meanings and interpretations are derived from our uniquely African social organisation and social relations (Mamdani, 2016; Oyewumi, 2002; Quijano, 2007). This way of deconstruction is not new. It has been adopted by postcolonial theorists that are broadly grouped under the lexicon of subaltern studies (Go, 2016) and postcolonial ways (Ngugi wa Thiong'o, 1986, 1993, 2012). However, since Spivak's strategic essentialism is used to frame this paper, we need to delve into the main goal of subaltern studies historiography. As indicated by Go (2016, p. 59), it is intended "to map subaltern agency and excavate the knowledge perspectives, and understandings of colonised groups that have been subjugated by imperial culture".

The subaltern approach that was directed at critiquing "the cultural hegemony of European knowledge" while simultaneously reasserting the "epistemological value and agency of the non-European world" (Gandhi, 1998, p. 44) provides a philosophical perspective and an entry point for the critical reflection on Pan-African epistemologies of knowledge production. For instance, what the subaltern theorist Gayatri Spivak offers as "strategic essentialism" (Go, 2016) provides a path to address the epistemological question relating to the ways of knowing about our reality. The concept of strategic essentialism allows us to simultaneously deconstruct and reconstruct. For instance, it is a fact that, in theory and practice, the category "woman" is not capable of rendering visible the deep-seated heterogeneity of the experiences and practices of "women". However, in a Derridean fashion of deconstruction, we accept the argument that, despite the inherent hegemonic biases toward Western knowledge forms, it is plausible to utilise the concept within the sphere of politics to mobilise and make claims.

As paradoxical as it may sound, this paper, in the light of deconstruction, depends on both postcolonial and Western hegemonic discourses in making the case for critical reflexive Pan-African epistemologies of knowledge production and practice. This paradox stems from the fact that we are deeply ingrained in the various kinds of colonial indoctrination that we were able to map a route for Pan-African epistemologies of knowledge in both theory and practice while remaining within the framework of the Western hegemonic paradigm. In any case, it is the inability of Western epistemology to completely account for African realities that has given rise to recent interest in Pan-African epistemologies. As such, standing on the shoulders of what it considered the shortcomings of the hegemonic Western knowledge systems, the construction of true and meaningful African knowledge systems is possible.

Strategic essentialism in this case enables us to treat social agents as if they are made up of fixed identities just to reclaim their fundamental identity. In other words, our argument, by extension, is that Pan-African epistemologies of knowledge production must simultaneously be fixed and fluid and emerge both from within and outside the academy. The scholarly work of Ayi Kwei Armah and the likes who stood largely outside the academy must be acknowledged in this regard. For instance, his insistence that the university provides the space for effecting desirable social change is very evocative (Armah, 1969, 2006; Mami, 2011).

In blending traditional forms of knowledge practices with the academically normalised ones, the true critical reflective Pan-African epistemologies of knowledge must re-emerge from the throes of the original vision of the Institute of African Studies. However, this time round, it must be much more enduring to enable us to distinctively delineate African indigenous knowledge forms. This approach is not without limitations. It may even be objectively indefensible as Frantz Fanon (1970) indicated

in the book *Toward African Revolution*. Nevertheless, it provided a theoretical route for deconstruction and difference even in the case of Fanon
(1970), where nationalist movements appealed to an indigenous African
past during the heat of the postcolonial struggle if they were wary of the
"paradoxes and pitfalls" of such appeals. However, those appeals, within
the context of decolonisation struggles, provided political values which
anchored the task of defeating colonialism in all its forms.

Furthermore, the concept of strategic essentialism, deployed in
making the case for deconstructing knowledge production and situating
Pan-African epistemologies of knowledge broadly, is also a political and
historiographical device. Its aim is to "recover native agency and voices as
best as the historical archive allows, while nonetheless making visible the
incompleteness of the representation" (Spivak, 1988, p. 205). It implores
us to read the archives of history for the "subaltern subject-effect" and
significantly treat that effect as demonstrating an actual stable identity.
As Spivak put it:

> one writes the subaltern as the subject of history—finding a posi-
> tive subject-position for the subaltern—but only to show that the
> subaltern marks the absolute limit of the place where history is nar-
> rativised into logic, not to establish an inalienable and final truth of
> things (1988, p. 16).

This recasting of the postcolonial archive is for "affirmative deconstruction" (Spivak, 1988, p. 205). Deconstruction for Derrida and its read-
ings for Spivak provide an avenue for a new way of appreciating what is
being deconstructed. Knowledge is indeed power. A critical analysis of
the structure of the production of knowledge and its associated practices,
especially in the African academy, are subservient to the hegemonic dictates of what is Western. As such, in challenging the binaries upon which
knowledge has been constructed, through the prism of deconstruction,
there is the possibility of limiting the destructive impacts of elevating
Western knowledge forms while denigrating non-Western forms. As
such, in our collective resolve, there is the opportunity to provide an
alternative representational strategy that enables us to situate Pan-African

epistemologies of knowledge on a culture of practice that is devoid of neo-colonial simulations.

Pathways for Pan-African Epistemologies of Knowledge Production

In utilising Derridean deconstruction through the lens of postcolonial theory, the different pathways of knowing and conceptualising reality within the context of Pan-African epistemologies of knowledge production look promising. This is because the cumulative nature of knowledge and its implications could shape our practical and subjective experiences and provide cover for deconstructing knowledge that pretends to offer the only mode for decoding knowledge. Framed in this way, the pathway for constructing Pan-African epistemologies of knowledge and, in fact, an indigenous knowledge system differs from the overly positivistic epistemological traditions.

The Pan-African epistemological mode holistically engages the immediate African context. This extensive knowledge base allows us, through the lens of deconstruction-based critical postcolonial theory, to pry open academic discourse, disciplines, and practices. This deconstruction exercise produces a nuanced reconstruction that leaves both the process of knowledge production and practice, substantively decolonised yet adaptive to each emerging situation. This task is not an easy one because the transformative structures of Pan-African epistemologies of knowledge, if not properly anchored, can be disenchanting rather than enchanting. It is important to note, for the purpose of illustration, that we are using the same methodologies as the colonisers. Ochwada (2005) once reminded us about the experiences of African historians caught in the methodological fixes their historical iterations so fervidly critiqued. This admonition is imperative because we need to pay attention to the situatedness of knowledge. Unless we chart a new path and take immediate steps to incorporate in our practices actions that respects the nature of our indigenous knowledge systems, the search for Pan-African epistemologies of knowledge production will remain elusive. This is because the struggle against remnants of colonialism in knowledge production is an endless one. Indeed, a major step forward is in developing and utilising reflective Pan-African epistemologies of knowledge without any apologies (Mkandawire, 2005).

Consequently, the search for enduring Pan-African epistemologies must intensify through a holistic deployment of indigenous African knowledge systems. In addition, within the realm of African universities, the question raised by Mazrui in another context finds a fitting expression here: "Apart from ensuring a climate of academic freedom and the free flourishing of intellectualism, what does society have to do to develop a university before intellectuals and scholars become capable of helping to develop society?" (2005, p. 60). As he explicated, resources are crucial, but we must eschew some of the practices as well. The practices we are referring to in this paper are those that are blinkered and destructive to the original intent of Pan-Africanism, especially its liberatory and transformative versions.

In essence, deconstruction requires the simultaneous reconstruction of knowledge production in a manner that is conscious of the residual effects of existing Western epistemic practices. For instance, the emphasis on the practices such as indexing of scholarly outputs in colonial outlets for most parts only serves as a legacy of colonialism. They provide justifications for delegitimising African indigenous knowledge systems. As Adomako Ampofo has indicated:

> not all voices have the same power—where we speak, and the authority of our voices don't have equal reach, and hence impact our lives differentially. Some voices are marginalized by the way the academy is structured in different places around the globe, exemplified most sharply perhaps by the so-called impact factor syndrome (2016, p. 17).

We are not completely dismissing everything about knowledge production inherited from the colonisers. Rather, we intend to move towards an active Pan-African epistemological gaze that mirrors what Gerald Vizenor (1994) referred to as "survivance". As understood, survivance allows scholars interested in African epistemologies to go beyond resistance, endurance, and survival in a complementary manner, where both the colonised and the colonisers learn from each other (Chilisa, 2011).

Conclusion

We have mapped out the contours of global knowledge production within the prism of Pan-African epistemologies of knowledge production. This is done from the context of the dominant colonial practices that underpin what is recognised and practised as knowledge. This paper, in a way, is contradictory because we make the argument for a critical self-reflection within the African academy in terms of the practices of knowledge and how to revive the discourse of Pan-African epistemologies of knowledge production standing inside those very structures. We depend on both postcolonial and Western hegemonic discourses to make our case. The paradox of our immersion in the colonial reproduction of knowledge is not lost on us, but we contend that it is necessary to stand within the same Western hegemonic paradigm to carve out possibilities, where the Pan-African epistemologies of knowledge are not merely recanted but are re-engaged.

In terms of the dominance and the pervasiveness of the universalising colonial discourses, as Edward Said (1993) has already reminded us, they are very pervasive. We have maintained that the hegemony of power and knowledge that are dominated by the West and quantified inside the African academy in terms of citation index, impact factor, Western-based visibility matrix and university rankings have laid bare the extent to which the discourse of Pan-African epistemological foundations of knowledge remains a weapon of the weak.

The usual practice in the African academy has been the activation of the default mode, that is, the standard practices within which the context of what is considered relevant knowledge is subsumed under the attendant practices of the Western-dominant account. This narrative emanates from the colonial encounter but has been constantly renewed in postcolonial times. For generations now, "philosophers and thinkers who shape the nature of social science have produced theories that embrace the entirety of humanity" (Chakrabarty, 2000, p. 29). Since we live in a commoditised world that is based on the representation of certain cultural elements that are largely Western-based (Said, 1993), the question about how to revive and sustain Pan-African epistemologies of knowledge production are germane and we must indicate that post-colonial scholars have somehow taken the lead (see Adomako Ampofo,

2016; Appiah, 2005; Bodomo, 2013; Dei, 2000; Falola & Jennings, 2002; Mudimbe, 1988; Ndlovu-Gatsheni, 2018; Ngugi wa Thiong'o, 1986; Nnaemeka, 2005; Onyewumi, 1997).

However, within the contours of the African academy, the pressing question has to do with at what material moment will Pan-African epistemologies become the measure of knowledge? At what point will the cultures of practice begin to change to adopt African standards? Despite the pessimism, there is hope, if we start fusing indigenous reality with rationalism (Mazrui, 2005), and encouraging it as the backbone of our academic practices. The task is daunting, but the fact remains that there is the need to continually deconstruct knowledge systems, if we are to eventually reconstruct the paradigms of their production. This is the only way through which we can adequately uproot the pervasive colonial structures reinforcing postcolonial practices.

The process of deconstruction and reconstruction provides a path to correct the psychological damage, distortion, humiliation, and embarrassment visited upon African societies through Western epistemologies. We must embrace Pan-African epistemologies to counter existing theories, correct misinformation, and right intellectual wrongs. The time to act and decolonise these cultures of practices from the African academy is now.

References

Ackah, W. B. (1999). Pan-Africanism: Exploring the contradictions – Politics, identity and development in Africa and the African diaspora. Farnham, UK: Ashgate.

Adesanmi, P. (2011). You're not a country, Africa: A personal history of the African present. Johannesburg, South Africa: Penguin.

Adi, H. (2018). Pan-Africanism: A history. London, UK: Bloomsbury Academic.

Adomako Ampofo, A. (2016). Re-viewing Studies on Africa, #Black Lives Matter, and envisioning the future of African studies. African Studies Review, 59(2), 7–29.

Adomako Ampofo, A., & Beoku-Betts, J. (Ed.). (2021). Producing inclusive feminist knowledge: Positionalities and discourses in the Global South. Bingley, UK: Emerald Publishing Limited.

Ake, C. (1982). Social science as imperialism: The theory of political development (2nd ed.). Ibadan, Nigeria: Ibadan University Press.

Allman, J. (2013). Kwame Nkrumah, African studies, and the politics of knowledge production in the Black Star of Africa. International Journal of African Historical Studies, 46(2), 181–203.

Amadiume, I. (1997). Re-inventing Africa: Matriarchy, religion, and culture. London, UK: Zed Books.

Appiah, K. A. (2005). African studies and the concept of knowledge. Poznan Studies in the Philosophy of the Sciences and Humanities, 88(1), 23–56.

Armah, A. K. (1969). The beautyful ones are not yet born. Portsmouth, NH: Heinemann Educational Books.

Armah, A. K. (2006). The eloquence of the scribes: A memoir on the sources and resources of African literature. Popenguine, Senegal: Per Ankh Publishing Cooperative.

AU Echo. (2013). Issue 5, 1.

Baber, Z. (2003). Provincial universalism: The landscape of knowledge production in an era of globalization. Current Sociology, 51(6), 615–623.

Biney, A. (2011). The political and social thought of Kwame Nkrumah. New York, NY: Palgrave.

Bodomo, A. (2013). African diaspora remittances are better than foreign aid funds: Diaspora driven development in the 21st century. World Economics, 14(4), 21–29.

Chakrabarty, D. (2000). Provincializing Europe: Postcolonial thought and historical difference. Princeton, NJ: Princeton University Press.

Chambers, R. (1997). Whose reality counts? Putting the first last. London, UK: Intermediate Technology Publications.

Chilisa, B. (2011). Indigenous research methodologies. Thousand Oaks, CA: Sage Publications.

Clarke, J. H. (1988). Pan-Africanism: A brief history of an idea in the African world. Présence Africaine, 145, 26–56.

Cole, M. C., Manuh, T., & Miescher, F. S. (Eds.). (2007). Africa after gender? Bloomington, IN: Indiana University Press.

Dei, G. J. S. (2000). Rethinking the role of indigenous knowledges in the academy. International Journal of Inclusive Education, 4(2), 111–132.

Derrida, J. (1973). Speech and phenomena, and other essays on Husserl's theory of signs. Evanston, IL: Northwestern University Press.

Derrida, J. (1976). Of grammatology. Baltimore, MD: Johns Hopkins University Press.

Derrida, J. (1978). Writing and difference. New York, NY: Routledge.

Dzisah, J. (2010). Capitalizing knowledge: The mind-set of academic scientists. Critical Sociology, 36(4), 555–573.

Dzisah, J. (2016). Academic capitalism: Globalization, universities and the paradox of the neoliberal marketplace. Ghana Social Science Journal, 13(1), 1–33.

Economic and Social Department. (2006). Building on gender, agro-biodiversity, and local knowledge: A training manual. Rome, Italy: Food & Agriculture Organization.

Escobar, A. (1995). Encountering development: The making and unmaking of the third world. Princeton, NJ: Princeton University Press.

Falola, T. (2004). Nationalism and African intellectuals. Rochester, NY: University of Rochester Press.

Falola, T. (2005). A mouth sweeter than salt: An African memoir. Ann Arbor, MI: University of Michigan Press.

Falola, T., & Jennings, C. (2002). Africanizing knowledge: African studies across the disciplines. Piscataway, NJ: Transaction Publishers.

Fanon, F. (1970). Toward the African revolution. London, UK: Penguin.

Gandhi, L. (1998). Postcolonial theory: A critical introduction. New York, NY: Columbia University Press.

Geiss, I. (1974). The Pan-African movement: A history of Pan-Africanism in America, Europe, and Africa. New York, NY: Africana Publishing Co.

Go, J. (2016). Postcolonial thought and social theory. Oxford, UK: Oxford University Press.

Hedges, C. (2000). New activists are nurtured by politicized curriculums. New York Times, p. B9. Retrieved from https://www.nytimes.com/2000/05/27/arts/new-activists-are-nurtured-by-politicized-curriculums.html

Hegel, G. W. F. (1956). The philosophy of history. Mineola, NY: Dover Publications.

Hountondji, P. (2002). Knowledge appropriation in a post-colonial context. In C. Odora-Hoopers (Ed.), Indigenous knowledge and the integration of knowledge systems: Towards a philosophy of articulation (pp. 137–142). Cape Town, South Africa: New Africa Books.

Langley, J. A. (1973). Pan-Africanism and nationalism in West Africa, 1900–1945: A study in ideology and social classes. Oxford, UK: Clarendon Press.

Legum, C. (1962). Pan-Africanism: A short political guide. Liverpool, UK: Pall Mall Press.

Loomba, A. (1998). Colonialism/ postcolonialism: The new critical idiom. New York, NY: Routledge.

Mama, A. (2003). Restore, reform but do not transform: The gender politics of higher education in Africa. Journal of Higher Education in Africa, 1(1), 101–125.

Mama, A. (2007). Is it ethical to study Africa? Preliminary thoughts on scholarship and freedom. African Studies Review, 50(1), 1–26.

Mamdani, M. (1999). There can be no African renaissance without an African focused intelligentsia. Southern Africa Political and Economic Monthly, 12(2), 51–54.

Mamdani, M. (2016). Between the public intellectual and the scholar: Decolonisation and some post-independence initiatives in African higher education. Inter-Asia Cultural Studies, 17(1), 68–83.

Mami, F. (2011). Ayi Kwei Armah's intellectuals of the African renaissance. Cadernos de Estudoe Africanos, 21, 163–191.

Mazrui, A. A. (1986). The Africans: A triple heritage. Boston, MA: Little, Brown and Company.

Mazrui, A. A. (2005). Pan-Africanism and the intellectuals rise, decline and revival. In T. Mkandawire (Ed.), African intellectuals: Rethinking politics, language, gender and development (pp. 56–77). London, UK: Zed Books.

Medie, P., & Kang, A. J. (2018). Power, knowledge and the politics of gender in the Global South. European Journal of Politics and Gender, 1(1–2), 37–54.

Mbembe, A. (2001). On the postcolony. Berkeley, CA: University of California Press.

Merton, R. K. (1973). The sociology of science: Theoretical and empirical investigations. Chicago, IL: University of Chicago Press.

Mkandawire, T. (2000). Non-organic intellectuals and "learning" in policy-making Africa. In J. Carlsson & L. Wohlgemuth (Eds.), Learning in development co-operation (pp. 205–212). Expert Group on Development Issues.

Mkandawire, T. (2002). African intellectuals, political culture and development. Austrian Journal of Development Studies, 11(1), 31–47.

Mkandawire, T. (Ed.). (2005). African intellectuals: Rethinking politics, language, gender and development. London, UK: Zed Books.

Mudimbe, V. Y. (1988). The invention of Africa: Gnosis, philosophy and the order of knowledge. Bloomington, IN: Indiana University Press.

Nascimento, E. L. (1980). Pan-Africanism and South America: Emergence of a black rebellion. Buffalo, NY: Afrodiaspora.

Ndlovu-Gatsheni, S. J. (2018). The dynamics of epistemological decolonisation in the 21st century: Towards epistemic freedom. The Strategic Review for Southern Africa, 40(1), 16–45.

Ngugi wa Thiong'o. (1986). Decolonising the mind: The politics of language in African literature. London, UK: James Currey.

Ngugi wa Thiong'o. (1993). Moving the centre: The struggle for cultural freedoms. London, UK: James Currey.

Ngugi wa Thiong'o. (2012). Globalectics: Theory and the politics of knowing. New York, NY: Columbia University Press.

Nkrumah, K. (1979). The autobiography of Kwame Nkrumah. Bedford, UK: PANAF Books.

Nnaemeka, O. (Ed.). (2005). Female circumcision and politics of knowledge: African women in imperialist discourse. Westport, CT: Praeger Publishers.

Ochwada, H. (2005). Historians, nationalism and Pan-Africanism: Myths and realities. In T. Mkandawire (Ed.), African intellectuals: Rethinking politics, language, gender and development (pp. 193–208). London, UK: Zed Books.

Okech, A. (2020). African feminist epistemic communities and decoloniality. Critical African Studies, 12(3), 313–329.

Oyewumi, O. (1997). The invention of women: Making an African sense of Western gender discourses. Minneapolis, MN: University of Minnesota Press.

Oyewumi, O. (2002). Conceptualizing gender: The Eurocentric foundations of feminist concepts and the challenge of African epistemologies. Jenda, 2(1), 1–9.

Oppong, S. (2013). Indigenizing knowledge for development:
Epistemological and pedagogical approaches. Africanus Journal of
Development Studies, 43(2), 34–50.

Prakash, G. (Ed.). (1995). After colonialism: Imperial histories and postcolonial displacements. Princeton, NJ: Princeton University Press.

Quijano, A. (2007). Coloniality and modernity/rationality. Cultural
Studies, 21(2–3), 168–178.

Said, E. (1993). Culture and imperialism. New York, NY: Vintage Books.

Said, E. (1995). Secular interpretation, the geographical element, and the
methodology of imperialism. In G. Prakash (Ed.), After colonialism: Imperial histories and postcolonial displacements (pp. 21–39).
Princeton, NJ: Princeton University Press.

Said, E. (1996). Representations of the intellectual. London, UK: Vintage
Books.

Shepperson, G. (1962). Pan-Africanism and "Pan-Africanism": Some
historical notes. Phylon, 23(4), 346–358.

Shivji, I. (2018). Revolutionary intellectuals. Retrieved from https://
africasacountry.com/2018/05/revolutionary-intellectuals (accessd 6
December 2022).

Spivak, G. C. (1988). Subaltern studies: Deconstructing historiography.
In R. Guha & G.C. Spivak (Eds.), Selected subaltern studies (pp.
3–33). Oxford, UK: Oxford University Press.

Tamale, S. (2011). African sexualities reader. Oxford, UK: Pambazuka
Press.

Tamale, S. (2020). Decolonization and Afro-feminism. Ottawa, Ontario,
Canada: Daraja Press.

Thompson, V. B. (1973). Africa and unity: The evolution of Pan-
Africanism. London, UK: Longmans.

Tsikata, D. (2007). Gender, institutional cultures and the career trajectories of faculty of the university of Ghana. Feminist Africa, 8, 26–41.

Vizenor, G. (1994). Manifest manners: Postindian warriors of survivance. Middletown, CT: Wesleyan University Press.

Wallerstein, I. (2004). World-system analysis: An introduction. Durham, NC: Duke University Press.

World Bank. (1998). World development report, 1998/1999: Knowledge for development. New York, NY: Oxford University Press.

Yankah, K. (2004). Globalisation and the African Scholar. Accra, Ghana: Faculty of Arts, University of Ghana.

Zeleza, P. T. (1992). African social scientists and the struggle for academic freedom. Journal of Eastern African Research and Development, 22, 11–32.

Zeleza, P. T. (1997). Manufacturing African studies and crises (CODESRIA Book Series). Dakar, Senegal: CODESRIA.

Zeleza, P. T. (2007). The study of Africa: Global and transnational engagements (Vol. 2). Dakar, Senegal: CODESRIA.

Zeleza, P. T., & Olukoshi, A. (Eds.). (2004). African universities in the twenty-first century. Vol. I: Liberalisation and internationalisation. Dakar, Senegal: CODESRIA.

Hip-Hop Studies as a Model for Anti-Imperialist Research in Africa[*]

Msia Kibona Clark

Introduction

This paper discusses the intersection of African studies, two interdisciplinary fields that are primarily focused on the study of peoples of African descent: African studies and Hip-Hop studies. African studies has always grappled with imperialist elements and ties to Western agendas, spurring calls to decolonise the field. Hip-Hop studies emerged in the early twenty-first century with a decidedly anti-racist stance with ties to Black feminist, postcolonial, and critical race theories. Hip-Hop studies is not unique in its anti-imperialist approach. We find similar approaches utilised in other interdisciplinary fields, including African studies, and call for similar approaches across major disciplines.

Imperialist methods utilised in the research of communities of colour have led to conversations on the real-life impacts of scholarship on communities of colour. It has also led to considerations of what decolonising the academia may entail. Scholars in social sciences, humanities, natural sciences, and the interdisciplinary fields, such as African studies, have sought to address imperialist research practices in their respective fields.

[*] This chapter is a slightly edited version of an article first published in *Contemporary Journal of African Studies*, Vol. 10, No. 2 (2023) and is reproduced here with permission.

The goal of decolonising work involves an attempt to shift outdated or problematic paradigms. There are examples across disciplines of important scholarship that contributes to the conversation around decolonisation either directly or in practice through the use of anti-imperialist methods.

As a disciplinary field, Hip-Hop studies is relatively young and has absorbed many lessons from the disciplines from which it emerged. The origins of Hip-Hop studies are also tied to the culture of Hip-Hop and its practitioners, with many of the early Hip-Hop scholars coming from their respective Hip-Hop communities. Because Hip-Hop studies scholarship has been influenced by the fact that many of the early researchers in the field were members of the individual Hip-Hop communities. The methodologies employed by Hip-Hop studies scholars have been heavily influenced by Hip-Hop culture itself, since the field has been held, in many respects, accountable to Hip-Hop culture and communities. While the focus of my own research is mostly on African studies, I have discovered that the approaches and methodologies used in Hip-Hop studies are also applicable to other areas of my research.

While Hip-Hop studies has been influenced by Hip-Hop culture, the culture has been heavily influenced by the struggles for independence and civil rights in Africa and the diaspora. Additionally, Hip-Hop culture has often been in a position of having to defend itself against government censorship and public attacks. Hip-Hop studies was in many ways charged with, among other things, accurately representing Hip-Hop culture in academic spaces. Is this degree of accountability attainable in African studies when examining the link between African peoples and African studies?

Hip-Hop studies has not eliminated imperialist methodological approaches to studies of Hip-Hop culture. However, the standardisation of anti-imperialist epistemologies and research practices in Hip-Hop studies has helped to delegitimise research based on imperialist research methodologies. But is this what decolonising African studies would look like? While individual African studies' scholars may use anti-imperialist methods, would the anti-imperialist structure of Hip-Hop studies be a possible transformation for African studies as a discipline? This study will explore the development of Hip-Hop studies epistemologies and anti-imperialist frameworks. The study also imagines a decolonised African studies based on Hip-Hop studies epistemologies. Lastly, the study includes a look at specific Hip-Hop studies approaches, specifically the recognition and involvement of practitioners in knowledge production, and the ways in which the field engages in citational politics.

Hip-Hop Studies

Forman and Neal (2011), Miller et al. (2014), and Harris (2019) trace the emergence of Hip-Hop studies as a field to the early and mid-2000s with an increase in scholarly activity on Hip-Hop from scholars of diverse disciplinary backgrounds, the convening of conferences on Hip-Hop, the development of Hip-Hop archives, the use of Hip-Hop pedagogies in the classroom, and the increase in Hip-Hop courses and academic programmes in institutions of higher education. Hip-Hop studies, Hip-Hop studies scholars, and Hip-Hop studies scholarship are all part of the Hip-Hop culture (Forman & Neal, 2004; Kitwana, 2004; Harris, 2019). In the US, the early Hip-Hop studies' scholars who contributed important text to the canon included Murray Forman, James Spady, Bakari Kitwana, Mark Anthony Neal, Imani Perry, and Tricia Rose. In South Africa, it included Hip-Hop studies scholars Adam Haupt and Quentin Williams. With his 2010 text *Stealing Empire: P2P, intellectual property and Hip-Hop subversion*, Adam Haupt was the first academic to publish a book on Hip-Hop in Africa. All of these scholars were part of Hip-Hop communities that had developed a protectionist stance vis-à-vis social institutions, including academia. This would have a fundamental impact on the development and structure of Hip-Hop studies as a field. Hip-Hop studies sought to legitimise the study of street culture in the academy. There was resistance to the content of Hip-Hop and its social and political relevance (Kitwana, 2004). There has also been resistance to the frameworks and methodologies Hip-Hop studies employs, which may run counter to norms employed in the major disciplines. Prior to the development of Hip-Hop studies as a field, the first generation of scholars to begin writing on Hip-Hop helped establish the field's methodological practices. Harris'(2019) survey of 150 books, book chapters, and academic articles written on Hip-Hop between 1984 and 2000 found common characteristics among this early scholarship. These early scholars primarily conducted "ethnographies that involved interviews, participant observation, living in a particular area for a specified amount of time, taking notes, and building relationships with those in that specific community" (Harris, 2019, p. 11).

In the literature review for this study, an analysis of the seminal text in Hip-Hop studies found several similarities in epistemological approaches. These seminal texts helped establish the recognition of practitioners as scholars. Hip-Hop practitioners would play a central role in informing and shaping the scholarship coming out of the field. Eurie and Spady (1991) include the voices of over 20 Hip-Hop practitioners in their study to help provide historical content. In explaining the value of finding knowledge conveyed orally through Hip-Hop, Eurie and Spady (1991) reference the role of West African oral history and storytellers in providing content to certain historical accounts. Eurie and Spady (1991) call their methodology "hiphopography". We also see this active engagement with Hip-Hop communities in the scholarship of Kitwana (1994, 2002), Rose (1994), Kitwana (2002), Forman and Neal (2004, 2011), Perry (2004), and Chang (2005), who rely on interviews with practitioners and the inclusion of knowledge contributed by Hip-Hop practitioners.

Involving community members in the design and implementation of the research agenda necessitates valuing knowledge that exists outside of the academy. It also requires researchers to see community members as collaborators and not just "key informants". The difference may not seem significant, but the results in the output of research can be. A key informant may not have a say in the research design or output. A collaborator can help to ensure the appropriateness of the research questions and research design and contribute to the accuracy of the interpretations. Redefining the dynamic between the researcher and the communities they seek to research also requires an analysis of the consent form. Acquiring consent is often complicated, and there need to be more effective ways for community members to articulate their consent to participate. Bhattacharya (2021) talks about the impact consent forms can have on the relationship between the researcher and the community. Bhattacharya (2021) calls the consent form "colonial" because of the history of violence tied to similar forms in the very communities within which scholars seek access. Therefore, acquiring consent should be done in a manner that does not require participants to sign a form written in an alienating language, and should be sought in more inclusive ways.

A Hip-Hop Studies Approach in African Studies

Scholars who represent communities of colour have long prioritised decolonising the social sciences. The frameworks and methods used in the major disciplines are rooted in imperialist research methodologies. These methodologies are framed by Global North ideologies and can sometimes be inappropriate in understanding Global South contexts. This kind of research has produced knowledge that has led to warped realities. It is sometimes difficult for scholars of colour, especially those based in the Global South, to challenge the existing narratives. Additionally, academic gatekeepers have maintained these methodologies, which centre knowledge production in Europe and North America, systematically marginalising knowledge produced in the Global South.

It is, therefore, not surprising that calls to decolonise African studies (and other social sciences) have primarily come from scholars representing the Global South and communities of colour. Decolonising African studies includes addressing the discipline's imperialist roots, which have dominated research practices in the field. Scholars in African studies, as well as scholars focusing on other regions in the Global South, have contributed important scholarship identifying problematic theoretical and methodological frameworks employed in research on the Global South. They have also introduced frameworks and approaches that are more appropriate. Interdisciplinary fields such as Hip-Hop studies and African studies are centred on communities that the academy has historically misrepresented, and this misrepresentation has had political and economic impacts. With Hip-Hop studies, the theoretical and methodological approaches may be helpful to research in African studies, which continues to grapple with decolonising. Hip-Hop studies is a newer field that is primarily focused on peoples of African descent, but its history differs from African studies. It is this historical difference that has impacted the current state of each field.

We have mentioned that Hip-Hop studies has early connections to postcolonialism and Black feminism, both of which are also relevant to African studies. Global Hip-Hop studies' scholarship has shown some of the more obvious connections between Hip-Hop and postcolonialism. For example, Rollefson's (2017) text on European Hip-Hop and postcolonialism argues that Hip-Hop has always been a postcolonial culture. Rollefson (2017) asserts that Hip-Hop has always displayed the "postcolonial realities of asymmetry, hybridity, and paradox" (p. 3). Black/African feminism has been widely discussed in Hip-Hop studies. The development of Hip-Hop feminism, and later Ratchet feminism/respectability, is the contribution of female Hip-Hop artists to Black and African feminist thought.

Studies on Hip-Hop have also been focused on Africa. Although there were undoubtedly Hip-Hop scholars that approached the genre from a Pan-African perspective, I hesitate to declare Hip-Hop studies as Pan-African. Hip-Hop has always been unapologetically Black- and African-centred in the sense that it prioritised peoples of African descent. There was also a clear line of descent that was drawn from West African music to Hip-Hop culture. As early as the mid-1990s, scholars like Cheryl Keyes (1996, 2008) and Robert Walser (1995) were writing about Hip-Hop within a broader African cultural context. Hip-Hop studies centres Africa and its diaspora; it has never privileged Euro-American frameworks, and it is rooted in anti-colonial and anti-racist research.

African studies, which has a distinct history, has historically struggled between an African-centred and Eurocentric approach. The former is based on ideas from European studies and the Cold War. (Arowosegbe, 2014; De Ycaza, 2015; Zeleza, 2019). African studies is rooted in Cold War struggles, ideas of European (intellectual) exceptionalism, and racist perceptions of people of African descent (Arowosegbe, 2014; De Ycaza, 2015; Zeleza, 2019). The conversation around decolonising African studies is a reoccurring one. When scholars like Arowosegbe (2014), Ampofo (2016), Zeleza (2019), Kessi et al. (2020), and Mohammed (2021) speak of decolonising African studies, they discuss the decentering of Eurocentric knowledge, Africanising curricula, and understanding connections to racism and neo-imperialism. Hip-Hop studies may offer some lessons in these areas.

It has been important in my work on Hip-Hop as social commentary to approach Hip-Hop as a form of cultural representation. In Africa, we are thus able to use Hip-Hop lyrics to help elucidate important social and political realities. My research utilises the constructivist view of cultural representation, in which cultural representations, whether they be books, music, or films, construct certain realities for us. Cultural representations provide narratives that can be as legitimate a secondary source as a scholarly article. In the research, Hip-Hop music was analysed for its ability to provide information on the impact of neoliberalism, as well as its views concerning gender and sexuality among youth.

It is thus important to work with practitioners as collaborators. African artists presented important challenges to my own ideas around African feminist thought. South African artists Kanyi Mavi and Dope Saint Jude have challenged African feminism and offered alternative ways to think about gender and gender-based violence. In her music, Dope Saint Jude has directly challenged (African) feminism, stating that it has not made enough room for queer voices. In a conversation about her song "Real Talk", in which she states that feminism needs to be more inclusive, Dope Saint Jude states:

> It's easy for us as critical thinkers or people in the academic world to want to have a blanket kind of feminism for one group of people, like Black African feminism. [But] you know it's different, the experience of Black South African women and then within that group, Coloured women. It's different to Black women in a different part of the continent... I am still navigating what it (feminism) means to me and that's what I was trying to explain in the song, this frustration of feminism not accounting for the single mothers or for people who come from different kinds of struggles. For trans women. (Kibona Clark, 2021a, pp. 119-120).

Kanyi Mavi has also challenged (African) feminism for not being in touch with the realities of women's lives in the townships. Through songs like "Umsindo", she offers alternative approaches to what she calls a war against women happening in South Africa and presents ideas that challenge conventional feminist ideas on gender-based violence. When asked to translate the song, which is performed in Xhosa, she says:

That song was literally to stand and speak about that (gender-based violence). And in the song, I say to women, you need to learn and arm up. You need to learn how to protect yourself in a very practical way. And I'm not talking about little groups where you can meet and talk to other women about the fact that you've been hit, or you've been abused. I'm talking about learning how to use a gun, how to use a weapon, protect yourself, learn how to defend yourself. And I know this at this time is not the thing to be preaching. It's a very sensitive time in the world, but it's a very crucial time in South Africa in that it is a war against women. And there is no way to win this war if you cannot protect yourself physically (Kibona Clark, 2021b).

Dope Saint Jude performed "Real Talk" using Gayle, a queer slang popular in Cape Town, and Kanyi Mavi performed "Umsindo" in Xhosa. Both artists were in conversation with women in their communities, and the rest of us were simply listening in. These two Hip-Hop practitioners/activists offer secondary source material that analyses gender dynamics that contribute to other scholarship on the topic. The structure of Hip-Hop studies as a field provides space for the knowledge and contributions from both Dope Saint Jude and Kanyi Mavi to help inform and shape conversations around African feminism and gender in ways that are as significant as texts by any African feminist scholar in the academy.

The irony in proposing that Hip-Hop studies offers epistemological practices that may be used to decolonise African studies is not lost in this study. There has traditionally been scepticism in African studies when it comes to recognising Hip-Hop's intellectual significance. In the USA, much of the early scepticism about Hip-Hop's relevance came from Black scholars themselves. The scholars of US Hip-Hop studies found themselves having to defend Hip-Hop's place in academia and its political impact on their colleagues in the academy (Kitwana, 2004). Kitwana (2004) attributes the struggle for Hip-Hop studies to the early researchers in the field, as well as to the establishment of initiatives like Harvard University's Hip-Hop Archive and the tenacity of undergraduates to pursue Hip-Hop studies. Hip-Hop classes and initiatives were launched in their universities.

Three events were turning points on the status of Hip-Hop in African studies: The Arab Spring in Tunisia in Egypt (2010), Y'en A Marre in Senegal (2011), and Balai Citoyen in Burkina Faso (2013). The participation of Hip-Hoppers in movements that brought important political change in the region resulted in a lot of research resources being directed to the topic. Senegal would become one of the most written-about Hip-Hop scenes in Africa. After Y'en a Marre, several scholars published their research on the relationship between Hip-Hop and the Y'en a Marre movement. Many scholars flew into Senegal to interview Hip-Hop artists and analyse the lyrics of groups like Keur Gui. Between 2012 and 2016, there were over a dozen articles or books and a half-dozen pieces of student research (thesis and dissertations) published on Hip-Hop and the Y'en a Marre movement by scholars in the USA and France.

This recognition of Hip-Hop as a relevant topic in African studies did not necessarily impact the approaches or frameworks to research on Hip-Hop in Africa. Much of the scholarship utilised the same frameworks found in other African studies scholarship on Africa. African studies scholarship on Hip-Hop in Africa has often been disconnected from Hip-Hop studies. Many African studies' scholars who write about Hip-Hop in Africa fail to meaningfully interact with Hip-Hop studies. Important studies on Hip-Hop in Africa have been published by African studies experts; nevertheless, some of these studies have legitimacy issues. As mentioned earlier, standardising anti-imperialist research practices helps to delegitimise research based on imperialist research methodologies, but it does not eliminate it. The scholars of African studies who publish on Hip-Hop in Africa are subject to critique by the Hip-Hop communities they work in. When the legitimacy of their research is challenged, it impacts future access to that community for the scholar, and sometimes for other scholars. African studies scholarship that earns its legitimacy from both the academy and African communities creates an African studies discipline that holds scholars accountable produces more accurate scholarship and benefits communities on the ground.

Communities and Hierarchies

Among the relationships that scholars must navigate in the field are those between themselves and members of the community in which they are conducting their research. There is often a hierarchical structure in which the researcher and community members interact, and in which the researcher often enters with a perceived superiority of knowledge, especially when that knowledge was obtained in Western institutions. Researchers often employ research practices that "reflect the perspective of the powerful and serve to reproduce forms of domination" (Adams, 2014, p. 468). According to Adams (2014), Western researchers tend to form "superficial" relationships with communities they are researching, tending to follow a resource extraction model". Western researchers go through institutional review boards (IRB) to get clearance to conduct their research. Rather than being trained to understand that once they land in country, and prior to beginning their research, securing permissions from local leaders is part of their duty to the community, and they are often taught that seeking permissions is a way to ease their research process. It would be much more effective if scholars were trained to see that securing permissions and support from the local community may also be important for legitimising their scholarly output.

African studies scholarship often imposes Western frameworks and cultural norms on their research of non-Western peoples. Often, Western frameworks or cultural norms are seen as "normal", while non-Western peoples and cultures are "othered" when their cultures and practices differ from Western practices and cultures. Researchers may approach their research with their own biases and preconceived notions of the peoples they are researching. According to Adams (2014), scholars take data and information out of Africa, analyse that data using a Western lens, and produce scholarship that often positions Western culture as normal vis-à-vis non-Western cultures. Adams (2014) criticises the types of interactions Western scholars have in Africa, calling them "superficial interactions" that are only as important as the data scholars are there to "extract". Other than offering the needed permissions, the community has little input in the research being done on them. The role of the community is to provide data. Many scholars have invested in the idea that "it is simply impossible, ridiculous even, to suggest that the object of research can contribute to anything" (L. T. Smith, 2012, p. 123).

On the other hand, in the field of Hip-Hop studies, there is a broader recognition of the need for community involvement. In Hip-Hop studies' approaches, such as hiphopographies, there is an emphasis on ensuring that the research is relevant to the community, and not just academia. According to Alim (2006a), "the researcher does not determine what's relevant; rather, the researcher must rely on the participants of the culture. This ensures that the analysis will be relevant to the community under study" (p. 970). Consciously dismantling "hierarchical divisions between researcher and researched" is a core approach in Hip-Hop studies research (Alim, 2006a).

One way that scholars have recognised the importance of Hip-Hop communities is through the titling of text. Hip-Hop studies has a long history of using Hip-Hop song titles, lyrics, or language in the titles of books, articles, sections, and chapters. *That's the Joint!* (Forman & Neal, 2004, 2011) is both the title of a 1980 song by Funky Four Plus One and a popular Hip-Hop phrase signalling a song's high quality; *Rock the Mic Right* (H. Samy Alim, 2006b) was a line from the 1985 song "La Di Da Di" by Slick Rick and Dougie Fresh; *Native Tongues: An African Hip-Hop Reader* (Saucier, 2011) is the name of the 1980s Hip-Hop collective that was made up of socially conscious artists; the subtitle for *Hip-Hop and Social Change in Africa: Ni Wakati* (Kibona Clark & Mwanzia Koster, 2014) is the name of a song by pioneering Kenyan Hip-Hop group Kalamashaka, and the subtitle for *Hip-Hop in Africa: Prophets of the City and dustyfoot philosophers* (Kibona Clark, 2018) was the name of the pioneering South African Hip-Hop group Prophets of Da City and the 2005 album *Dustyfoot Philosopher* by Somali Hip-Hop artist K'naan.

Community involvement also happens at a more extensive level when practitioners become contributors. Jeff Chang's 2005 book Can't Stop Won't *Stop: A History of the Hip-Hop Generation* features an introduction written by D. J. Kool Herc, who is credited with starting Hip-Hop. My 2014 text *Hip-Hop and Social Change in Africa: Ni Wakati* included chapters by Hip-Hop practitioners who presented their own expert analysis on Hip-Hop and social change in Kenya, Mali, Tanzania, and Uganda. The 2019 text *Neva Again: Hip-Hop Art, Activism and Education in Post-Apartheid South Africa* was edited by three institutionally affiliated academics (Quentin Williams, Adam Haupt, and H. Samy Alim) and one practitioner (Emile Jansen) and included chapters by both academics and practitioners. *Neva Again* is one of the very few academic texts in African studies to include so many chapters by practitioners. Of the book's 30 chapters, twelve are authored entirely by Hip-Hop practitioners, who present histories of Hip-Hop music and breakdance culture in Cape Town, discussions of gender and Hip-Hop, and overviews of Hip-Hop activism in Cape Town. Another important collaboration includes the 2020 article "Sounding Tanzania in the studios of Dar es Salaam" co-authored by Postdoctoral Research Fellow David Kerr and Hip-Hop artist and activist Hashim Rubanza. The collaboration between Kerr and Rubanza is important because, unlike Quentin Williams and Adam Haupt in South Africa, Kerr is a British scholar who did not grow up in Tanzania's Hip-Hop scene. Kerr's collaboration with Rubanza emerged after years of establishing a relationship and collaborations on other projects. The collaborative relationship between Kerr and Rubanza proves that the approach of Hip-Hop studies is not necessarily predicated on the scholar being a member of the same community. It is less about the ethnic or racial backgrounds of the scholars and practitioners, and more about the nature of the collaborative relationships between scholars and practitioners.

The methods used in Hip-Hop research are not brand new or exclusive. There have been discussions about decolonising the social sciences for a long time. In the current #BlackLivesMatter climate, the dialogues are simply getting more attention. Linda Tuhiwai Smith's seminal text *Decolonising Methodologies* (2012) speaks to many of the concerns of scholars in African studies. Smith offers recommendations for approaches to research in Indigenous communities that are familiar with Hip-Hop studies. L. T. Smith (2012) presents the following series of common and unique questions that Indigenous communities may pose to the researcher:

> Whose research is it? Who owns it? Whose interests does it serve? Who will benefit from it? Who has designed its questions and framed its scope? Who will carry it out? Who will write it up? How will its results be disseminated?... Is her spirit clear? Does he have a good heart? What other baggage are they carrying? Are they useful to us? Can they fix up our generator? Can they actually do anything? (pp. 52–53).

We can find similar questions posed to Hip-Hop studies scholars in Africa. In my own research, I have experiences with artists who find interesting ways to test my knowledge of Hip-Hop music and history. Questions frequently concern money and whether I am being paid to carry out the study, or my willingness to pay artists for their time. In some experiences, artists are suspicious of academics based on what has been published about them in the past. Hip-Hop artists read and, more than once, I have found myself on the receiving end of an artist's ire because of their experience with a previous scholar. The relationships a researcher develops with communities and individuals during their research should be taken seriously. Scholars L. T. Smith (2012), Adams (2014), and Bhattacharya (2021) speak about the importance of forming long-term relationships. Often those relationships impact community perceptions of the published research, as well as the experiences of future scholars coming into the community. "… [R]esearch is not an innocent or distant academic exercise but an activity that has something at stake and that occurs in a set of political and social conditions" (L. T. Smith, 2012, p. 46).

Citation Politics

Citational politics involves the practice of centring Western knowledge, and marginalising women and scholars of colour, especially those based outside of the West in academic scholarship. Non-academic voices or sources (such as non-scholarly publications and non-written text) are often omitted from academic scholarship completely, or the work is used without proper attribution, as when a scholar uses an excerpt or quote to introduce or punctuate an argument. In a study, Mott and Cockayne (2017) found that, in geography, there is a tendency towards citing White men or forming what they referred to as "citation cartels", where scholars agree to cite each other's work. Mott and Cockayne (2017), Zeleza (2019), and Kessi et al. (2020) discuss the dominance of White male scholars in academia as gatekeepers. Scholars of colour needing to publish in the so-called top- or mid-tier journals in their field may find difficulty doing so, which impacts their ability to receive tenure or promotion. These structures in academia also effectively silence scholars of colour through citational politics, which centres on White scholars and perpetuates the idea of a (White) Western supremacy of knowledge production. According to Mott and Cockayne (2017), at least in geography, being cited is seen as an indication of relevance and impact. The lack of access to top journals and the lack of presence among reference lists further speaks to the necessity of the decolonisation project.

Citational politics has spurred calls for inclusive citation practices. Mott and Cockayne (2017) call for citation counting, which asks scholars to scrutinise their own references, so they are conscious of who they are citing, and who they are not. Cite Black Women is a movement that emerged in 2017 with a mission to "decolonise the practice of citation by redressing the epistemic erasure of Black women from the literal and figurative bibliographies of the world" (C. A. Smith et al., 2021, p. 3). Cite Black Women resonated with Black women scholars and spread as a movement. In 2018 Cite Black Women released "Cite Black Women Resolutions". The resolutions state:

> 1) Read Black Women's work; 2) Integrate Black women into the CORE of your syllabus; 3) Acknowledge Black women's intellectual production; 4) Make space for Black women to speak; and 5) Give Black women the space and time to breathe (C. A. Smith et al., 2021, pp 4–5).

There are institutions within both African and Hip-Hop studies that actively challenge citational politics. In the beginning, Hip-Hop studies recognised the need to be strategic in how they positioned their scholarship. Hip-Hop studies had to navigate producing scholarship that maintained academic and "scholarly rigor" but did not impose or reinforce elitist or imperialist academic frameworks (Forman & Neal, 2011). Many scholars also recognised that there was a certain amount of accountability to the Hip-Hop community to accurately represent the culture of Hip-Hop. As a result of all of this, Hip-Hop studies' texts are often published with diverse presses, and not always in the traditional university presses. Some of the foundational texts in Hip-Hop studies were not published with university presses. For example, Basic Civitas Books has published several important Hip-Hop studies texts, including Bakari Kitwana's *The Hip-Hop Generation* (2002), Tricia Rose's (2008) *The Hip-Hop Wars*, and Adam Bradley's *Book of Rhymes* (2009). In addition, the *Journal of Hip-Hop Studies*, the *Global Hip Hop Studies Journal*, and *Words Beats & Life: The Global Journal of Hip-Hop Culture*, are the three Hip-Hop studies journals, with the first two being the top two journals in the field. All of the journals accept and publish contributions from scholars and practitioners in each of their issues.

The scholars of Hip-Hop studies often publish with diverse publishers and utilise Hip-Hop artists and their music in their scholarship. In Hip-Hop studies, the artist and their music are used as both primary and secondary sources. The music that artists produce is often used as a primary source that provides data for scholars to interpret. A scholar may perform a textual analysis of song lyrics and music videos in order to explain the significance of an artist's music—for example, Helenon's (2006) study examining the content of French Hip-Hop to reveal the connections to Africa and Blackness found in the lyrics. Helenon's (2006) research sought to understand how these artists "claim their origins, redefine their identity and challenge traditional French conceptions of race and citizenship" (p. 233). Using the music as the primary source, Helenon (2006) used that data to measure and analyze expressions of "Africanness" in the music of French artists of African descent. My 2014 study of gender representations in Tanzanian Hip-Hop used the music and lyrics of female MCs in Tanzania as primary source data to analyse how these artists challenged gender norms and identities through their music. I conducted a textual analysis of the primary source data, the lyrics and music videos of female MCs.

In Alim's (2006b) text *Roc the Mic Right: The Language of Hip-Hop Culture*, he used Hip-Hop lyrics as the primary source in his argument about the existence of a global Hip-Hop Nation Language (HHNL) separate from African American Vernacular English (AAVE). In the text, Alim used the approach in his work by centring the voices of the artists, allowing their music and interviews with artists themselves to provide the narrative. In constructing his argument, he centres the artists, "viewing them as interpreters of their own culture (backflap)".

Also serving as primary sources are participant observation and interviews with Hip-Hop artists. Many Hip-Hop studies scholars include interviews and participant observation as a method for securing primary data. Hiphopographies are commonly used research methods in Hip-Hop studies. They involve researchers working with practitioners in the research design and agenda. There is an emphasis on ensuring that the research is relevant to the community, and not just academia. In their book *Nation Conscious Rap*, Eurie and Spady (1991) help establish important approaches to research in Hip-Hop studies. Interviews are not done at a distance, physical or social, and interviews are seen as more of a shared discourse (Eurie & Spady, 1991). The goal, according to Eurie and Spady, is to represent the community's "cultural realities as accurately as possible" (vii).

Williams' (2017) study on multilingualism in Cape Town Hip-Hop included both interviews and participant observation. Williams' approach did not set up a hierarchy between himself and the artists that were involved in his study. Both Williams and the artists were participants in the study, Williams in the role of participant observer and the artists in the role of practitioner. Each brought their own expertise, and that expertise was equally essential in the final publication. Hip-Hop music and artists are more often primary sources than secondary sources. Secondary sources are sources that are cited because they provide expert analysis or historical background that help support or contextualise the main arguments. One of the common methods of using artists as secondary sources is by including essays authored by practitioners, which as discussed earlier, was done in my 2013 book project as well as the 2019 book project edited by Quentin Williams, Adam Haupt, H. Samy Alim, and Emile Jansen.

The lessons for African studies are significant. The acknowledgement and inclusion of knowledge from outside of the academy is a component of the decolonisation process. It also helps to ensure the research is truly representative and accurate. In my own research, I have relied on knowledge outside of academia, especially from Hip-Hop practitioners, to challenge the appropriateness of my research questions, to improve my arguments, to correct my definitions and uses of terminology, and to help shape my research agenda. Kanyi Mavi, for example, has been a key collaborator in my research, challenging my views on feminism as understood in the academy of African feminist thought. The significance of this cannot be overstated. It not only makes for stronger scholarship, but it also makes the research more relevant and beneficial to the communities themselves.

Conclusion

"… [H]ip hop sits at the confluence of dehumanizing neoliberal globalization and the gritty human realities of postcoloniality" (Rollefson, 2017, p. 3).

The conversations around decolonising African studies have been in motion for several years. The goal of this paper was to contribute the voice of Hip-Hop studies to the conversation in an effort to offer additional approaches to decolonisation. The theoretical and methodological frameworks of Hip-Hop studies have challenged the imperialist research methodologies that are foundational in many disciplines, including those disciplines that service African studies. What Hip-Hop studies offers is an approach in which the relationship between the discipline and the communities it speaks to and for informs the scholarship that is produced. In Hip-Hop studies, there is no separation between Hip-Hop and the study of Hip-Hop (Harris, 2019).

Hip-Hop studies removes hierarchies between researchers and the community, challenging assumptions that the scholar is imbued with superior knowledge. When this happens, it can allow for more productive and relevant research. The involvement of community members and practitioners is not a threat to scholarly research, and Hip-Hop studies shows us that the research often benefits from that involvement. Harris (2019) says that the "methodological approach to studying Hip Hop (studies) and global Hip Hop (studies) entails working with local Hip Hoppas in my community" (p. 22) and that this resulted in a more "thorough portrayal of Hip-Hop" (p. 23).

The benefits of community involvement and investment in a scholar's research are significant and go a long way in serving to decolonise the discipline. The structures in Hip-Hop studies tend to encourage scholars to approach their research in more collaborative ways and to value the knowledge in the community, and of the practitioners. Hip-Hop studies is a young field, and it owes its existence to Hip-Hop communities and cultures. As such, Hip-Hop communities understand the significance of Hip-Hop studies, but also recognise their power within the field. The researcher is not given unquestioned privilege. This dynamic has benefitted scholarship in Hip-Hop studies. African studies may be a long way from having these types of relationships between researchers and the community be a common feature of the field. However, when we look at scholarship on decolonising disciplines, these are the types of relationships that characterise a discipline that has largely created a culture of decolonising practices.

References

Adams, G. (2014). Decolonizing methods: African studies and qualitative research. *Journal of Social and Personal Relationships, 31*(4), 467-474.

Alim, H. S. (2006a) "The Natti ain't no Punk City": Emic views of Hip-Hop cultures. *Callaloo, 29*(3), 969–990.

Alim, H. S. (2006b). *Roc the mic right: The language of Hip-Hop culture.* New York, NY: Routledge.

Ampofo, A. A. (2016). Re-viewing studies on Africa, #Black Lives Matter, and envisioning the future of African studies. *African Studies Review, 59*(2), 7-29.

Arowosegbe, J. O. (2014). African studies and the bias of Eurocentrism. *Social Dynamics, 40*(2), 308-321.

Bhattacharya, K. (2021). *De/colonizing qualitative research: For whom is the work?* (2021 IRDL Scholar's Speaker Series 3). Retrieved from https://digitalcommons.lmu.edu/irdl-speakerseries/3

Bradley, A. (2009). *Book of rhymes: The poetics of Hip-Hop.* New York, NY: Basic Civitas Books.

Chang, J. (2005). *Can't stop won't stop: A history of the Hip-Hop generation.* New York, NY: St. Martin's Press.

De Ycaza, C. (2015). Competing methods for teaching and researching Africa: Interdisciplinarity and the field of African studies. *Ufahamu: A Journal of African Studies, 38*(3), 63-79.

Eurie, J. D., & Spady, J. G. (1991). *Nation conscious rap.* New York, NY: PC International Press.

Forman, M., & Neal, M. A. (Eds.). (2004). *That's the joint!: The Hip-Hop studies reader.* New York, NY: Routledge.

Forman, M., & Neal, M. A. (Eds.). (2011). *That's the joint! The Hip-Hop studies reader* (2nd ed.). New York, NY: Routledge.

Harris, T. T. (2019). Can it be bigger than hip hop? From global hip hop studies to hip hop. *Journal of Hip-Hop Studies, 6*(2), Article 7.

Haupt, A. (2010). *Stealing empire: P2P, intellectual property and Hip-Hop subversion.* Cape Town, South Africa: University of Cape Town.

Haupt, A., Williams, Q., Atim, H. S. A., & Jansen, E. (Eds.). (2019). *Neva again: Hip hop art, activism and education in post-apartheid South Africa.* Cape Town, South Africa: HSRC Press.

Helenon, V. (2006). Africa on their mind: Rap, blackness, and citizenship in France. In D. Basu & S. J. Lemelle (Eds.), *The vinyl ain't final: Hip-Hop and the globalization of Black popular culture* (pp. 151-166). London, UK: Pluto Press.

Kerr, D., & Rubanza, H. (2020) Sounding Tanzania in the studios of Dar es Salaam. *Riffs Journal, 4*(1), 72-85. Retrieved from https://riffs-journal.org/wp-content/ uploads/2020/07/Kerr-and-Rubanza.pdf

Kessi, S., Marks, Z., & Ramugondo, E. (2020). Decolonizing African studies. *Critical African Studies, 12*(3), 271-282.

Keyes, C. L. (1996). At the crossroads: Rap music and its African nexus. *Ethnomusicology, 40*(2), 223-248.

Keyes, C. L. (2008). The roots and stylistic foundations of the rap music tradition. In T. F. Strode & T. Wood (Eds.), *The hip hop reader* (1st ed., pp. 3-16). New York, NY: Pearson.

Kibona Clark, M. (2018). *Hip-Hop in Africa: Prophets of the city and dustyfoot philosophers.* Athens, OH: Ohio University Press.

Kibona Clark, M. (2021a). Matters of representation: An interview with Dope Saint Jude for the Hip Hop African Podcast. *Words Beats & Life: The Global Journal of Hip-Hop Culture (WBLJ), 8*(1), 116-125.

Kibona Clark, M. (Host). (2021b, April 9). Kanyi Mavi, and the cultural & political significance of doing Hip-Hop in Xhosa (No. 66) [Audio podcast episode.] In *Hip-Hop African Podcast.* Howard University. Retrieved from https://hiphopafrican.com/hhap-ep-65-kanyi-mavi-and-the-cultural-political-significance-of-doing-Hip-Hop-in-xhosa/

Kibona Clark, M., & Mwanzia Koster, M. (Eds.). (2014). *Hip-Hop and social change in Africa: Ni Wakati.* Lanham, MD: Lexington Books.

Kitwana, B. (1994). *The rap on gangsta rap: Who run it?: Gangsta rap and visions of Black violence*. Chicago, IL: Third World Press.

Kitwana, B. (2002). *The Hip-Hop generation: young Blacks and the crisis in African American culture*. New York, NY: Basic Civitas Books.

Kitwana, B. (2004). Hip-hop studies and the new culture wars. *Socialism and Democracy, 18*(2), 73-77.

Miller, M., Hodge, D. W., Coleman, J., & Chaney, C. D. (2014). The hip in hip hop: Toward a discipline of hip hop studies. *Journal of Hip Hop Studies, 1*(1), 6-12.

Mohammed, W. F. (2021). Decolonizing African media studies. *Howard Journal of Communications, 32*(2), 123-138.

Mott, C., & Cockayne, D. (2017). Citation matters: Mobilizing the politics of citation toward a practice of 'Conscientious Engagement.' *Gender, Place & Culture, 24*(7), 924-973. https://doi.org/10.1080/09 66369X.2017.1339022

Perry, I. (2004). *Prophets of the hood: Politics and poetics in hip hop*. Durham, NC: Duke University Press.

Rollefson, J. G. (2017). *Flip the script: European hip hop and the politics of postcoloniality*. Chicago, IL: University of Chicago Press.

Rose, T. (1994). *Black noise: Rap music and Black culture in contemporary America*. Middletown, CT: Wesleyan University Press.

Rose, T. (2008). *The hip hop wars: What we talk about when we talk about hip hop—and why it matters*. New York, NY: Basic Civitas Books.

Saucier, P. K. (2011). *Native tongues: An African Hip-Hop reader*. Trenton, NJ: Africa World Press.

Smith, C. A., Williams, E. L., Wadud, I. A., Pirtle, W. N. L., & The Cite Black Women Collective. (2021). Cite Black women: A critical praxis (A statement). *Feminist Anthropology, 2*(1), 10-17.

Smith, L. T. (2012). *Decolonizing methodologies: Research and Indigenous Peoples*. London, UK: Zed Books.

Walser, R. (1995). Rhythm, rhyme, and rhetoric in the music of Public Enemy. *Ethnomusicology, 39*(2), 193-217.

Williams, Q. (2017). *Remix multilingualism: Hip hop, ethnography and performing marginalized voices*. London, UK: Bloomsbury Academic.

Zeleza, P. (2019). *Reckoning with the pasts and reimagining the futures of African studies for the 21st century* (African Peacebuilding Network

(APN) Lecture Series: no 4). Retrieved from https://s3.amazonaws.com/ssrc-cdn1/crmuploads/new_publication_3/reckoning-with-the-pasts-and-reimagining-the-futures-of-african-studies-for-the-21st-century.pdf

Section 2

Opening Ceremony of the AAPC @ 60 at the University of Ghana Cedi Conference Centre on 5th December 2018.

Centring Youth, Women, and Working People in Africa's Struggle for Liberation[*]

Dzodzi Tsikata

In the names of the leaders of the 1958 Conference-Kwame Nkrumah, George Padmore, Tom Mboya, Patrice Lumumba, Franz Fanon, and all the ancestors of the Pan-Africanist and liberation movements too numerous to name, who made immense sacrifices for the upliftment of Africa and its peoples; and on behalf of the indefatigable Conference Planning Committee and Secretariat of AAPC@60, I warmly welcome you to University of Ghana, to the historic city of Accra and to Ghana, on the occasion of this conference to commemorate the sixtieth anniversary of the first All-African People's Conference.

I wish to especially acknowledge the presence of Mr G. A. Balogun, probably the only person in this room who was there in 1958. I also want to acknowledge the presence of Mzee Joseph Butiku, who worked with Julius Nyerere as a young person, and who continues to work to disseminate the ideas of Julius Nyerere and realise his vision through the Nyerere Foundation. I also wish to acknowledge the brilliant and energetic students from Benin, Burkina Faso, Cote d'Ivoire, Ghana, and

[*] Welcome Address at the opening of the sixtieth anniversary commemoration of the All-African People's Conference, 5-8 December 2018.

Nigeria, who were certainly not born at the time of AAPC@1958. This 2018 commemoration is dedicated to them and to their generation of Africans. It is to serve as a reminder of the young people who came together here in 1958 to liberate Africa from the chains of colonialism. We look to you now to take centre stage again and drive the agenda for Africa's future. We want you to ensure that our resolutions speak to your concerns and your vision for Africa. We are looking forward to an intense inter-generational dialogue at this gathering.

I also welcome especially the women who are present at this conference. At the AAPC in 1958, most of the women there served as observers. This did not reflect the true importance of women to the anti-colonial struggles and their many heroic deeds that changed the course of the history of this continent. We can recall, for example, the Aba Women's War of 1929, Nigeria, women's pivotal roles in the Mau-Mau and the Nyabingi struggles against colonial rule in Kenya and Uganda, respectively (Ossome, 2021),[1] and women's struggles against the pass laws in South Africa from the 1950s. As C. L. R. James famously noted, "in the struggle for independence, one market woman ... was worth any dozen Achimota [college] graduates. ... " (James, 1977, p. 56). In July 1960, the Conference of Women of Africa and of African Descent was convened in Accra and hosted by Ghana's women's movements. It was this conference that gave some recognition to women's place in the struggles for African liberation (Manuh, 1993). When the history of our conference, AAPC@60 is written, let it not be said that women were just observers! So, daughters, sisters, and mothers of Africa here gathered a very special welcome to you.

As you know, several significant markers have shaped the fight against colonial rule and the struggles for independence in Africa. For many in Africa, the independence of Ghana in March 1957 was a definitive moment. Similarly, with regard to the elaboration of global Pan-African goals for the liberation and transformation of Africa, 1958 remains a signal moment. Liberation movements, political parties, trade unionists, and progressive groups from across Africa and beyond met in Accra, the capital of the newly independent state of Ghana from 8 to 13 December

---

1 Subsequently published in 2021.

1958 to set an ambitious agenda to change the terms of the relationship between Africa and her colonisers. The '58 conference aimed at the attainment of political independence, consolidating Africa's independence by fostering unity among liberated African states, and instituting measures to reconstruct the economic and social fabric of Africa. What has happened to this agenda of liberation and transformation of Africa? What are our current developmental challenges as a continent? What would it take to achieve total liberation and transform Africa into a united and prosperous continent that serves the needs of all its people, and not only a few?

The Institute of African Studies, the Trades Union Congress (TUC) of Ghana, the Socialist Forum of Ghana (SFG), Third World Network-Africa and Lincoln University, USA, have organized this conference under the theme "Revisiting the 1958 All-African People's Conference—The Unfinished Business of Liberation and Transformation" to find answers to these very pressing questions. The conference aims to bring together groups and individuals working at the forefront of the unfinished business of Africa's liberation and transformation; create a platform for scholars and activists, young and old; to share insights from research and practice and debate and adopt resolutions on Africa's transformation to be presented to the governments and peoples of Africa.

The significance of our conference is underlined by the fact that African communities across the world are marking this anniversary in different ways. We salute them all and wish them wonderful celebrations. The spirit of 1958 is alive and well. And this is as it should be.

For the Institute of African Studies, this conference is in consonance with the mandate given to us by Osagyefo Dr Kwame Nkrumah himself. In his speech, *The African Genius*, which he made at the inauguration of our institute in October 1963, a speech described as "one of the profoundest and most powerful speeches ever delivered by a philosopher-politician", he said:

"One essential function of this Institute must surely be to study the history, culture and institutions, languages and arts of Ghana and of Africa in new African-centred ways—in entire freedom from the propositions and pre-suppositions of the colonial epoch, and from the distortions of those Professors and Lecturers who continue to make European studies of Africa the basis of this new assessment. By the work of this Institute, we must re-assess and assert the glories and achievements of our African past and inspire our generation, and succeeding generations, with a vision of a better future" (Nkrumah, 1963, p. 3).

Nkrumah saw the institute's role in multi-faceted ways, for example, he spoke about the creation of the African library, the decolonisation of education, and the socialisation of a new African—dynamic, forward-looking, and self-confident.

The institute is proud to fulfil the charge enunciated so beautifully in *The African Genius*, a speech which should be required reading for all Africans and friends of Africa. When the University of Ghana asked all its units to determine how they would celebrate the seventieth anniversary of our university, we immediately settled on this as our flagship event. We were guided in this decision by the vision and enthusiasm of Professor Horace Campbell, our most recent Kwame Nkrumah Chair, and by several comrades in Ghana, in Africa and beyond. We thank them all for making this day possible.

Our conference is taking place at a particular conjuncture in Africa. The continent faces grave challenges and immense possibilities. Decolonisation is still a work in progress, with several African territories still under colonialism. The most prominent of these of course is Western Sahara, which is a member of the African Union. Beyond this, true independence and emancipation elude African states and people. The continent is still the primary source of natural resources for the development of other continents, while our people wallow in poverty, disease, and suffer human rights abuses, and our countries remain indebted, under-developed, and under the political and economic control of Western powers and institutions. The Pan-African dream of a united and prosperous Africa is threatened by the forces of globalisation and by global rules of engagement which favour rich over poor nations, and capital over working people. Africans, especially our smallholders, are also experiencing most acutely the fallouts of global warming, created by the economic activities of hyper-capitalism elsewhere.

Against the odds though, we are witnesses to the dynamism and determination of Africa's people, who keep the dream of Pan-Africanism alive in their daily struggles for survival and the construction of innovative cultures of cross-border relations and solidarity.

The crisis of leadership that Africa suffers is at the heart of the unfinished business of liberation and transformation. Many African leaders have been preoccupied with transforming the lives of themselves, families, and friends rather than their people. What must change, as the meeting of the peoples of Africa in 1958 signaled, is that the onus of liberation and transformation of Africa does not lie with only the leaders. Our conference, AAPC@60 is to acknowledge that the transformation of Africa lies in the hands of Africa's people.

And the people, particularly the youth, are making this clear in the current struggles of social movements. The Arab Spring, which many forget started on the African continent is only one such struggle. The Rhodes Must Fall and the Fees Must Fall movements in South Africa have raised questions about the entire purpose of education, the institutional and intellectual cultures of universities, the curriculum, and the racial and gender composition of educational institutions. New social movements of young organic intellectuals such as the "Y'en a Marre" (we have had enough!), movement in Senegal, which is led by musicians, journalists, and students, are advocating a new type of developed thinking and living, and citizenship culture for creating a better Africa. Youth in Togo, Mali, La Cote d'Ivoire, and Burkina Faso have also challenged the rule of kleptocratic dictatorships and have succeeded in exiling leaders who have run African countries without accountability. These young people are the true heirs of the youth who successfully ended formal colonial rule in much of Africa. We hope this conference, reflecting on these youth-led movements across the continent while revisiting the history, ideas, and values of the 1958 conference, will recommit to contributing in our different ways to realise its agenda for Africa's true liberation.

We have laid out an intellectually stimulating and culturally rich programme for the four days. Our seven plenaries are designed to focus both on the current conjuncture as well as the future. Our parallel sessions offer insights on a broad range of issues that concern Africans everywhere under the sub-themes of neo-colonialism and imperialism; Pan-Africanism today; the peoples of Africa (including the diaspora); emancipation of women; global warming; and reparation and restorative justice.

Our cultural programme consists of a film show segment which will run during parallel sessions, a photo exhibition on the 1958 Conference, a palm-wine night of music, dance, and performance; and a music and performance concert to round off the conference on a penultimate day. We hope that you will participate actively in all aspects of the conference, to ensure that the Conference Resolution has your considered input.

We wish to express our profound gratitude to all conference sponsors for their generous support and confidence in this conference. They made it possible to sponsor selected participants from Africa and the diaspora, as well as students from Benin, Burkina Faso, Cote d'Ivoire, and Nigeria.

It is our fervent hope you leave this conference energized and ready to re-engage with vigour in the work to liberate and transform Africa. Let the call of the first All-African People's Conference ring loud and clear, "Peoples of Africa unite! You have nothing to lose but your chains! You have a continent to regain! You have freedom and human dignity to attain!"

I Thank you.

References

James, C. L. R. (1977). *Nkrumah and the Ghana revolution.* London, UK: Allison and Busby.

Manuh, T. (1993). Women and their organizations during the Convention People's Party period. In K. Arhin (Ed.), *The life and work of Kwame Nkrumah* (Papers of a Symposium, pp. 101–127). Accra, Ghana: Sedco; Trenton, NJ: Africa World Press.

Nkrumah, K. (1963, October 25). *The African genius.* Speech at the Opening of the Institute of African Studies, University of Ghana, Accra, Ghana. Accra, Ghana: Ministry of Information and Broadcasting.

Ossome, L. (2021). Pedagogies of feminist resistance: Agrarian movements in Africa. *Agrarian South: Journal of Political Economy, 10*(1), 41–58. https://doi.org/10.1177/22779760211000939

Solidarity Message[*]

Thabo Mbeki

The Vice Chancellor of the University of Ghana, delegates, comrades, and friends, it is a great honour to address this important conference which commemorates the sixtieth anniversary of the All-African People's Conference. That timely and historic conference of 1958 here in Accra under the able leadership of Dr Kwame Nkrumah will always be remembered for its ground-breaking outcomes.

That historic gathering of Africans from all backgrounds with a shared commitment to the African liberation struggle was pivotal in the final onslaught to end colonial rule in Africa.

In the context of South Africa despite travel restrictions imposed by the apartheid regime, South Africa's freedom fighters were not only ably represented at the conference, but those representatives also helped to ensure that a final resolution accepted that armed struggle was in some cases necessary to secure Africa's total liberation in the face of the intransigence of the colonialist and imperialist forces.

The agenda to unite the continent and transform it politically and economically remains a non-finished business to which we must all renew our commitment. I, therefore, commend the Institute of African Studies at the University of Ghana and Ghana's Trade Union and socialist movements for reminding us of the sacrifices of the past, the tasks

---

[*] Delivered at the opening of the sixtieth anniversary commemoration of the All-African People's Conference, 5-8 December 2018.

ahead, and our collective desire to build a free, united, and developed Africa.

This commemoration of the Sixtieth All-African People's Conference is therefore significant for the renewal of the spirit of the African Renaissance, particularly among the young generation of Africans who may be far removed from the events that gave birth to our liberation from colonialism and apartheid. Indeed, the celebration should remind us of the urgent need to close our ranks as Africans and work tirelessly towards the unification of the continent in a manner that truly breaks down colonial barriers and liberates the energies and talents across the continent in our pursuit of African transformation and renewal. Our future fundamentally depends on the Pan-African unity of our continent and its people.

Indeed, this conference can not only be a memorial of our fallen heroes but also an opportunity to produce thoughtful, innovative, and creative blueprints to guide our steps in our forward march to transform and create the African we want. I apologise that I cannot attend the conference due to earlier commitments. However, I am happy to take this opportunity to wish the conference success and thank you very much for your attention.

Solidarity Message*

Kwesi Quartey

I bring you fraternal greetings from the headquarters of the African Union in Addis Ababa, Ethiopia. It is a great honour to be part of the commemoration of the sixtieth anniversary of the All-African Peoples Conference (AAPC) held in Accra in 1958. On behalf of the African Union, I wish to commend the Institute of African Studies of the University of Ghana, and its network of partners for organising this important conference, in part as a remembrance of the journeys, energies, and sacrifices of so many sons and daughters of Africa have had to make in our quest for a free and independent Africa.

The events of 1958, both the meeting of leaders of Independent African States in April and the AAPC in December, did not only signal Africa's potential; they were also the moments that exposed the peoples of Africa to our common challenges and shared aspirations and inspired many to commit to the emancipation of the continent and Africans in the diaspora.

Sixty years ago, between the 8th and 13th of December 1958, the first AAPC was held at the Community Centre of Accra, the capital of Ghana. Under the motto of "Forward to Independence now!" more than 200 delegates from 62 delegations spent a week discussing, moving, and resolving issues relating to Africa's common future. The conference was inspired by several imperatives: the fierce urgency of freedom and

---

* Delivered at the opening ceremony of the sixtieth anniversary commemoration of the All-African People's Conference, 5-8 December 2018.

independence; consolidation of that freedom and independence; the creation of unity and community between the free African states; and the
economic and social reconstruction of Africa. At the end of the week the
conference delegates, who represented a large section of Africa's future
statesmen, unanimously adopted five resolutions relating to Africa and
its future development.

The 1958 AAPC made a major contribution to the defeat of colonial rule. Prior to the 1958 conference, only eight countries—Ethiopia,
Ghana, Guinea, Liberia, Libya, Morocco, Tunisia, and Egypt—were
independent. Two years after the Accra conference, a significant number
of African countries, more than two dozen of them, had successfully liberated themselves and joined the comity of independent African states.
Many of them were led by personalities who had participated in the 1958
AAPC.

It goes without saying that the 1958 AAPC was a watershed moment
in African liberation. Today, we salute the foresight as well as the memories and legacies of Africa's independence leaders and the sacrifices of
Africa's masses—the unsung heroes and heroines of the anti-colonial
struggles—for their relentless efforts and dedication to the struggle. As
we revisit the events of 1958 and attempt to evoke the heroism of the sons
and daughters of Africa, whose sweat, toil, and blood defeated colonialism and liberated many African countries from colonial rule, the most
befitting memorial for their sacrifices is to rededicate ourselves to the
Pan-Africanist dream and commit to vigorously tackling the unfinished
business of liberation and transformation.

Currently, the most comprehensive blueprint for Africa's transformation is the AU's **Agenda 2063: The Africa We Want**, a strategic framework for the socio-economic transformation of the continent over the
next fifty years which builds on past and existing continental initiatives.
Adopted by the Heads of Government at the AU Summit in January
2015, in Addis Ababa, **Agenda 2063** sets out seven key aspirations that
Africans should work towards. These are:

1. a prosperous Africa based on inclusive growth and sustainable
   development;

2. an integrated continent, politically united and based on the ideals of Pan-Africanism and the vision of Africa's Renaissance;

3. an Africa of good governance, democracy, respect for human rights, justice, and the rule of law;

4. a peaceful and secure Africa;

5. an Africa with a strong cultural identity, common heritage, shared values, and ethics;

6. an Africa whose development is people-driven, relying on the potential of African people, especially its women and youth, and caring for children; and

7. Africa as a strong, united, and influential global player and partner.

The achievement of these aspirations to build a united, prosperous, and peaceful Africa is possible if we believe it, truly desire it, and are truly committed to realising it. Sixty years after the first AAPC, we must not be oblivious to the enormity of the unfinished business and the skills, expertise, dexterity, professionalism, activism, sacrifices, and commitment required to finish the task of liberation and transformation. The African Union wishes all the delegates and participants in the sixtieth-anniversary commemoration of the AAPC (AAPC 2018) a productive and rewarding experience. We look forward to the resolutions that will come out of the deliberations.

Our Faith in Our Future is not Without Basis[*]

Akilagpa Sawyerr

Brothers and Sisters from all parts of Africa - continental and global
Representatives of political organisations, and working people's and
women's movements
Students and Youth from all corners of the continent
Distinguished Ladies and Gentlemen

We have come to the end of four days of stimulating and productive engagement with issues that portend far-reaching changes in the way we approach the continuing struggle for African liberation and transformation. It is not my place to attempt even a summary of the significant matters that have emerged from the presentations and extensive discussions we have had these last few days. All I can do is to outline my personal take-aways from the last four days and, perhaps, make one general observation for your further reflection, as we part.

Before doing so, however, I would like, on your behalf and mine, to extend appreciation to the organisers of this conference - The Institute of African Studies, University of Ghana; the Trades Union Congress

---

[*] Concluding Remarks at the closing ceremony of the sixtieth anniversary commemoration of the All-African People's Conference, 5-8 December 2018.

(TUC) of Ghana; the Socialist Forum of Ghana; Lincoln University, the United States of America; and, particularly, the local teams, working parties and support staff who have toiled so hard, for the better part of a year, to plan, organise, and actually deliver this conference so effectively and successfully.

Let me now itemise briefly, the impressions I am taking away from these four days.

First, is the significance of the contacts and connections established, or re-established, during the conference. By bringing together people from all parts of the continent and the diaspora, working in a variety of fields, belonging to different linguistic and age groups, but all committed to the liberation and transformation of Africa, we have opened up new relationships and networking possibilities for the future.

Second, is the bank of brilliant ideas and perspectives that emerged over the course of the conference, especially in relation to cultural/political struggle and economic transformation under contemporary continental and global conditions.

My third takeaway is the palpable air of commitment by all to what could be the new agenda for true liberation and transformation of the continent. Here, I must note what was, for me and, I am certain, for many others, the high point of the conference - the explosion of energy and enthusiasm generated by, not only the presence, but particularly the spectacular contributions of the *youth and student contingents* from 34 countries. Clearly, our faith in the future is not without basis!

Finally, I highlight an issue that, in settings like this, rarely receives the attention it deserves. I refer here to the need to grapple *at the level of theory* with the persistence of *neo-colonialism*, that is, the internal structuring of our economies, both as cause, but also as effect, of the particular conditions under which our economies continue to be integrated into the increasingly globalised system of production and exchange - as sources of raw material and sites for advanced production by others! Given the co-optation of our ruling classes by imperialism, when reference is made to what *we* need to do to liberate ourselves and transform our economies and society, I ask myself: who exactly does the *'we'* refer to? Our current crop of "leaders"? If not, then who? What ideological clarification, what mobilisation and organisation, would it take to identify, motivate and activate the real *we*?

Such questions are particularly pertinent at a time when the reality of neo-colonialism is persistently obscured by the uncritical acceptance of the narrative of "neo-liberalism" - reliance on market forces and foreign investment for development, to put it succinctly - a narrative that makes it possible to speak glibly about African liberation and economic integration, even as measures are implemented that deepen our neo-colonial dependence and fragmentation. How else can one reconcile the establishment of the African Continental Free Trade Area (AfCFTA), reportedly aimed at "accelerating intra-African trade and boosting Africa's trading position in the global market", with the near-simultaneous signing of *Economic Partnership Agreements* (EPAs), under which several African countries have, individually, agreed to liberalize their domestic markets for imports from the European Union?

The question for us is, how do we develop a counter-narrative and effectively integrate it into our struggle for liberation and transformation?

That, I would humbly suggest, is just one of the many outstanding tasks that confront us as we leave this conference.

Let me conclude by thanking each and every one of you for your presence and your contribution to the successful engagements over the past four days. I am sure we will each carry with us the positive atmosphere and the militant message of this conference, and devote ourselves, even more than before, to the prosecution of the unfinished business of the liberation and transformation of Africa.

THANK YOU, AND GO WELL.

Speaking With History: G. A. Balogun with Edem Adotey*

Dr Edem Adotey (EA): Good afternoon, Mr Balogun.

Mr G. A. Balogun (GAB): Good afternoon and you are welcome.

EA: Please tell us something about yourself.

GAB: I was born in Saltpond (Gold Coast/Ghana) on the 2nd of August 1930, which was a Saturday. So even though my name is G. A. Balogun I also have a Fante name which is Ato Kwamena.

EA: What do the initials G. A. in your name stand for?

GAB: My parents were Muslims and so the "G" is Ganiyu which is a servant of God then Akanni in Yoruba means something which you are lucky to have gained or received. For example, if you are walking along some path and you meet something that becomes very dear to you. That is Akanni.

EA: Okay, what does Balogun mean?

GAB: Balogun is Balo and Ogun; Balo is Oba which is chief, and Ogun is war, so it is a chief in war.

EA: Is that Yoruba?

GAB: Yes, my parents were Yoruba.

EA: Do you mean both parents?

GAB: Yes! My mother was born in Saltpond to Nigerian parents. My father came to Saltpond as a young man and that's how my parents got to meet.

---

* G. A. Balogun, national chairman of the Trades Union Congress (TUC) Veterans Association of Ghana is one of the living participants at the 1958 All-African People's Conference.

EA: Oh interesting! So, you are a Saltpond person through and through.

GAB: Yes, after independence or a little before independence, a law was passed that anyone who was born in the Gold Coast, whose parents were also born in the Gold Coast and had stayed here for more than five years, qualified to be Ghanaians.[1] So one, I was born here; two, my mother was born here; and then three, my father had stayed here for more than ten years and so I had the right to choose to become a Ghanaian but I hadn't decided yet.

EA: What made you decide to become a Ghanaian citizen?

GAB: What was going on in the Gold Coast then was very enticing and I was really enjoying it. What enticed me or the petrol that poured into the fire for me was the inauguration of the United Gold Coast Convention (UGCC) in Saltpond in 1947.[2]

EA: Okay, how old were you when that happened?

GAB: Two days after my 17th birthday.

EA: Wow!

GAB: I was born on 2nd August 1930 and so 2nd August 1947 I was 17 years old and then 4th August 1947 was when they inaugurated the UGCC in Saltpond and that was two days after my 17th birthday.

EA: Did you attend the inauguration?

GAB: Yes, I went to the place with my father, and he donated money to them. So, I got there, and I was like wow these guys are talking about politics, about independence, self-government… and that was how the whole thing went into my head and I started exploring, asking questions, doing research into it and all that. That was how the whole thing started. That was really what put the stamp on whether I wanted to be a Ghanaian or Nigerian.

EA: What did you do next?

GAB: From there I started asking where they came from, and I was told they came from Sekondi and so I decided to go to Sekondi and that is how

---

1   The Ghana Nationality and Citizenship Act, 1957 came into effect in May 1957. Under it, one was considered a citizen if one of his/her parents or grandparents was born in Ghana.

2   The UGCC was the first major nationalist party to be formed in the Gold Coast in the post-war era. Its founding members included George Alfred Grant, J. B. Danquah, R. A. Awoonor-Williams, R. S. Blay, E. Akufo-Addo, William Ofori Atta, E. Obetsebi-Lamptey, and Dr E. Ako Adjei. Kwame Nkrumah was invited later in that year to become its General Secretary.

I ended up in Sekondi.[3] When I got there fortunately, the Compagnie Française de l'Afrique Occidentale (CFAO) boss was close to a friend of one of my father's friends and he gave me a job in the company.

EA: Now since you went to Sekondi because of the nationalist movement can you tell us a bit about the UGCC and Kwame Nkrumah?

GAB: CFAO was close to Paa Grant's[4] house, that is when you go around the curve, you will be headed to his house and so when (Kwame) Nkrumah passed by, we would all go out just to wave at him.

On one occasion, we were at Optimism Club in Sekondi near the Police Station, where CFAO employees used to meet and where UGCC used to have their rallies, when Danquah came and introduced Kwame Nkrumah to us as the one who was going to lead the struggle for independence. It was there that he told us. I cannot forget his exact words. He said, "If all of us fail, Kwame Nkrumah will never fail".

EA: In 1949, Nkrumah split from the UGCC and formed his party, the Convention People's Party (CPP). Do you know what led to the split between the UGCC and Nkrumah?

GAB: Those days, all the meetings were for UGCC and then one day something happened. We were hearing some noise from Paa Grant's place, which as I mentioned, is close to our work, that is, just about from here to the Cocoa Clinic Junction [about 100 metres]. We didn't know what was happening and so later we decided to find out. I think it was either Entsa, Kofi Batsa, or one of them because we used to meet regularly together and so it was one of them who told me that the people [leaders of the party] said Nkrumah had brought some veranda boys and girls into UGCC and that was not what they asked him to come and do.[5]

EA: You mean it was Nkrumah's involvement of the masses that led to the split between Nkrumah and the UGCC?

---

3   Sekondi was one of the major towns in the Gold Coast. It is presently regarded as a twin town with Takoradi. Sekondi-Takoradi is the regional capital of the Western Region of Ghana.

4   George Alfred Grant popularly known as Paa Grant was a wealthy timber merchant and the major financier of the UGCC.

5   Verandah boys and girls was a term for the masses or commoners who largely were illiterate or semi-literate and unemployed or employed in the informal sector. They largely slept on people's verandah hence the name.

GAB: That's one of them. On 20th January 1948, Kwame Nkrumah as the General Secretary of the UGCC, had submitted a programme of organisation to the working committee of the Convention. This idea of building upon the masses comes out clearly in the following points contained in Nkrumah's memorandum for reorganisation. So now, what happened? When he gave it to them, they didn't understand mass organisation.

EA: That is the UGCC?

GAB: Yes, the leaders. Basil Davison called them the elder lawyers and chiefs who were the leading protagonists in the struggle for independence for Gold Coast; they were the people who were appointed to the legislative council and who were the spokesmen for the people.

But another important issue was that when Nkrumah came before he wrote this [memorandum for reorganisation], he called the leaders and told them that "… look, you people have been here for 113 years and so if your teacher can teach you for so long and you cannot pass, then he is not a good teacher". That is where the trouble started because they said, "shortest possible time". After 113 years, they are still talking about the "shortest possible time!"; what shortest possible time? If that is the case, then they are not good teachers and so "self-government now! Now! Now!"

EA: What can you tell us about the AAPC in 1958?

GAB: The background to the whole thing was that there were a lot of uprisings in the various countries in Africa. Nkrumah thought that it was important to encourage all these people who were struggling for independence somehow in their own small way. Coming from the background that the independence of Ghana was meaningless unless it led to the total emancipation of Africa, he toured the nine independent states and when he came back, he called the organisations. The idea was to galvanise all of them and let them know that Ghana was ready to assist each and every one of them who was leading the charge both physically and financially. So that was why he called the conference and fortunately, people came.

EA: Were you at the conference?

GAB: Yes.

EA: How did you come to attend the AAPC and in what capacity?

GAB: Initially, they asked all the secretaries of the ministers to come and run the affairs of the conference, but they had not run a conference before and didn't know what to do. So [John] Tettehgah[6] said G. A. [interviewee] please go and help them and so I took over and I did everything.

EA: So, you oversaw the secretariat.

GAB: Yes, I was in charge of the secretariat; myself and T. L. Ogum who was then one of the assistants to Tettehgah.

EA: Which other people were part of the planning committee for the conference?

GAB: The planning committee was mainly Ghanaian. In fact, we were there with some government officers; [Kojo] Botsio was there, George Padmore was there, T. Ras Makonnen (Thomas Griffiths), Dr St. Clair Drake, Eric Hayman was there, [Kofi] Batsa was there, Kojo Addison was there. I think one Habib and some other man, one was from Dahomey and the other from Senegal were also there.

EA: How did you go about organising a conference of such magnitude?

GAB: First, we checked all the credentials of the people and then we formed the standing orders committee and a resolution committee and then there were internal discussions from the committees to discuss political go-ahead, forward march, and solidarity committees that would assist the various organisations.

EA: So how long did it take to plan this conference?

GAB: The actual planning was for about a week.

EA: Where did the resources for the conference come from?

GAB: We did everything! The Ghana government did everything!

EA: Where was the conference held?

GAB: We held it at the Accra Community Centre.

EA: Where is that now?

GAB: It is opposite the Supreme Court, next to the Kwame Nkrumah Mausoleum.

EA: How many trade unions came from across Africa?

---

6 John Tettehgah was the General Secretary of the TUC.

GAB: It wasn't just trade unions because there were about 69 organisations and any organisation that related to politics or advancement was there.

EA: Do you remember the presence of other prominent Africans on the continent?

GAB: I know Patrice Lumumba came, Jomo Kenyatta came, Kaunda came, Joshua Nkomo was there and all these other people ... Sekou Toure! Yes, Sekou Toure, we introduced him to Nkrumah.[7]

EA: What do you mean by "we"?

GAB: I mean Ghana TUC. In 1958, we formed Union Generale Travailleur Afrique Noir (UGTAN) which was an association of Ghana TUC and all French West African countries and Sekou Toure was Secretary General.

EA: What was your official position in the TUC then?

GAB: I was the administrative secretary. In 1960 when he [Nkrumah] opened the Hall of Trades Union, I was the first administrative secretary and at that time we had only a secretary general and an administrative secretary. I was the only person who had headed almost all the departments of TUC from international to economic and social policy.

EA: What really stands out for you regarding the conference?

GAB: Number one, it brought many people who didn't know each other together. The second one is that it was the conference that led us to introduce Sekou Toure to Kwame Nkrumah. Then again, we also got to know other people from other countries as well. For instance, we made [Tom] Mboya chairman of the conference because of the imprisonment of Jomo Kenyatta of Kenya. We wanted him to be released earlier and we wanted attention to be focused there. I mean America and Britain had been involved in various wars and so why were they imprisoning him for fighting for his people?

EA: Thank you very much for sharing these important historical memories of the nationalist and pan-Africanist struggle with us. We are most grateful.

---

7 According to St. Claire Drake, Sekou Toure did not attend the conference, but was in Ghana prior to the conference. He was represented by his wife. See Shepperson, G., & Drake, S. C. (1958). The Fifth Pan-African Conference, 1945 and the All-African Peoples Congress, 1958. *Contributions in Black Studies*, 8(5), 35–66.

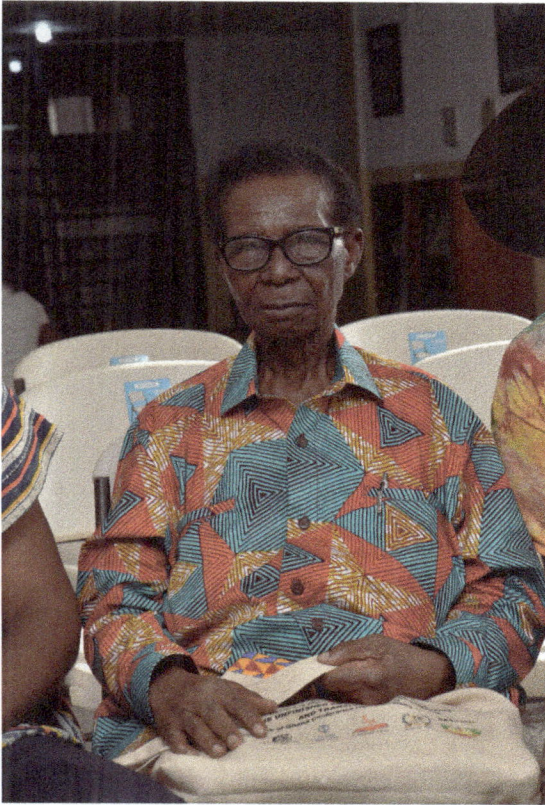

Mr. G.A. Balogun one of the last living participants of the 1958 All-African People's Conference in attendance at the closing ceremony of the AAPC @ 60 on 8th December 2018.

Section 3

Background Paper

Akilagpa Sawyerr, Horace Campbell, Michael Kpessa-Whyte, E. Obodai Torto, Eric Tei-Kumadoe, Kafui Tsekpo, and Peter Bembir

Introduction

The year 2018 marks sixty years since the First All-African People's Conference (AAPC) was held in Accra, Ghana, to galvanise support for independence movements across the continent and nurse the seeds of Pan-Africanism among African peoples at home and abroad. To memorialise the significance of the series of meetings that came to be called the AAPC, the Institute of African Studies (IAS), University of Ghana, in collaboration with other organisations, plans to commemorate this historic event by providing a platform for reflecting on the challenges facing Global Africa in order to revisit the unfinished business of the 1958 Conference. This was the business of the liberation of Africa and a transformation of relations in Africa.

AAPC—Background

Several significant markers shaped the fight against colonial rule and the struggles for independence in Africa. For many in Africa, the independence of Ghana in March 1957 was a definitive moment, but with respect to the elaboration of global Pan-African goals, the year 1958 remains a defining highpoint. The First Conference of Independent African States took place in April of that year in Accra, Ghana, with participation from delegates of the independent African states of Egypt, Ethiopia, Liberia, Libya, Morocco, Sudan, and Tunisia. That was followed in December of the same year by an AAPC, organised by a preparatory committee consisting of members from the independent states listed above, under the chairmanship of Tom Mboya, then General Secretary of the Kenya Federation of Labour. At that time, Kenya was in the midst of a protracted armed rebellion against British colonialism. There was also an armed rebellion in Algeria against French settler colonialism. In all parts of Africa, the people were stirring against colonial rule and apartheid conditions.

The December 1958 AAPC, which was also held in Accra, was attended not only by representatives from the independent states but also by ordinary persons from twenty-eight territories such as Angola, Benin (then Dahomey), Cameroon, Chad, the Congo (then still under colonial rule), Ivory Coast, Kenya, Mozambique, Nigeria, Nyasaland, Rhodesia, Senegal, Sierra Leone, Tanganyika, Togoland, Uganda, and Zanzibar. There was a strong delegation from the Afro-Asian Peoples' Solidarity Council,[1] based in Cairo, Egypt.

Over 300 participants, drawn from political parties and trade union movements and representing over two million Africans, attended this AAPC. The conference also hosted delegations from Canada, China, Denmark, India, the Soviet Union, the United Kingdom, and the United States. One of the major driving forces for the conference was a desire to explore mechanisms through which the countries that had liberated themselves from colonial domination could support the anti-colonial struggle and liberation endeavours in other territories on the continent and in the Caribbean.

The specific objectives of the conference were to: (*a*) encourage the nationalist leaders from the various territories still under colonial rule in their efforts to mobilise the masses or establish political movements for independence and (*b*) develop and agree on an overarching strategy for

---

1   The name of this organisation was changed to the Afro-Asian Peoples' Solidarity Organization in 1960.

executing an African revolution. The conference also tackled the thorny question of the forms of struggle for independence. Regarding this, there were two broad tendencies within the anti-colonial movement. One, represented by George Padmore and Kwame Nkrumah, promoted "positive action" (a variant of the Gandhian nonviolent resistance). The other was represented by Tom Mboya of Kenya and Frantz Fanon of Algeria, who argued in favour of the armed struggles then ongoing in Kenya and Algeria and argued that all forms of struggle against colonialism must be supported. In the final analysis, the conference decided to commend non-violent methods and also to endorse other methods if they were used because the choice was forced on the independence fighters. This led to the formulation "Independence *by any means necessary*", a slogan later popularised in the USA by Malcolm X, who called for black liberation "by any means necessary". Addressing the conference, Tom Mboya indicated that Africans would no longer tolerate any interference in the efforts of Africa to liberate itself from the burden of colonialism. Another notable position taken in the conference was that Pan-Africanism was not confined to a person because of the pigment of their skin. Anyone living in Africa, white or black, could be part of the African liberation struggle, as long as they were committed to the emancipation of Africa and to anti-racist principles.

Dr Kwame Nkrumah, then Prime Minister of Ghana, noted that the priorities of the conference included:

(a) attainment of political independence,
(b) consolidation of independence,
(c) creation of unity among liberated African states, and
(d) economic and social reconstruction of Africa.

The activities of the conference revolved around plenary sessions and five main committees that discussed specific issues relating to the anti-colonial struggle and other objectives of the conference. The major issues for deliberation by the five committees included: (*a*) imperialism and colonialism, (*b*) racialism, (*c*) frontiers and federations, (*d*) ethnicity and traditional institutions, and (*e*) formation of a permanent organisation. Among other things, the conference passed resolutions that condemned imperialism and called for an end to the continuous exploitation of African resources by Western countries. Consequently, the conference declared support for all freedom fighters in Africa and encouraged the independent African countries to pursue foreign policies directed primarily at expediting the liberation of territories still under colonial rule. Specifically, the first AAPC recommended, among other things, the imposition of economic sanctions, including withholding of migrant labour, against apartheid South Africa for its policies of racial discrimination, and urged all African countries to sever diplomatic ties with regimes on the continent that engaged in racial discrimination. Furthermore, the conference called not only for the establishment of a culture of universal adult suffrage and respect for human rights but also for an investigation into complaints of human rights abuses in various parts of the continent, as well as appropriate steps to ensure the enjoyment of human rights by all Africans.

At the end of the conference, it was firmly decided that the idea of an AAPC should be established as a permanent entity with professional staff headquartered in Accra. The purpose of the AAPC would be to foster the desired African unity and to:

(a) promote unity and understanding with all peoples of African descent;
(b) mobilise global public opinion against the abuse of human rights in Africa;
(c) accelerate the liberation of Africa from imperialism and colonialism;
(d) serve as a nucleus for the establishment of a United States of Africa; and
(e) organise similar conferences on an annual basis.

Thus, the First AAPC was not only historic; it remains significant in the struggle for liberation and the quest for African unity, for a number of reasons.

  1. It served as the springboard for the second and third AAPCs held in Tunis (1960) and Cairo (1961), respectively, as well as

similar meetings held in later years to push forward the liberation and continental unity agenda. The Cairo conference called for an immediate end to all forms of colonialism in Africa and urged all freedom fighters to step up their efforts, while the Tunis conference issued a warning against the dangers of neo-colonialism, particularly with regard to the establishment of foreign military bases and economic dependence on the former metropoles.

2. As the first political gathering of ordinary people from various parts of the continent on the continent, the AAPC exposed the delegates to the commonality of the challenges facing Africa and provided an opportunity for networking in the anti-colonial struggle. For instance, in an address during the conference, one of the participants, Patrice Lumumba, later to become Prime Minister of the Congo, said.

This historic conference which puts us in contact with experienced political figures from all over the world, reveals one thing in us: despite our ethnic differences, we have the same awareness, the same anguish, the same anxious desire to make this African continent a free and happy continent that has rid itself of unrest and of fear and of any sort of colonialist domination (Adi, 2018, p. 146).

3. The conference and its follow-up played an instrumental role in generating the needed momentum for independence, as is evidenced by the fact that soon thereafter, particularly in 1960, most African countries were liberated from colonial rule. Particularly noteworthy was the fact that several of the participants, including Patrice Lumumba, left the Accra conference directly to spearhead the struggle and lead their countries to independence.

Following the conferences, Kwame Nkrumah and the forces commit-ted to unity worked hard for the establishment of a permanent organ-isation to support liberation and work for continental unification. This led to the formation of the Organisation of African Unity (OAU) in

May 1963. In 2002, the OAU was transformed into the African Union, with a specific timetable for the full unification of Africa, including plans for a common currency from one common bank of issue, a continental communication system, a common foreign policy, and diplomacy, as well as a common defence system featuring the African High Command. It must be remembered that Kwame Nkrumah had advocated for this strategy at the formation of the OAU in May 1963, and later in his book, *Africa Must Unite* (Nkrumah, 1970).

Contemporary Global Africa

One glaring reality is the fact that there is such limited popular knowledge of the struggle and sacrifices made for independence. For example, many younger Africans would not be aware of the kind of solidarity among the forces fighting for independence that ensured that enormous sacrifices were made in order to win political independence. The massive victory of the Angolan and Cuban forces at Cuito Cuanavale thirty years ago has been erased from the narratives about the decolonisation process. Imperial narratives and disinformation have created the impression, and many in the younger generations believe, that the coming of independence within the continent and the end of apartheid in South Africa were the outcomes of Western beneficence. Thus, the issues that need to be put in context and placed before a new generation of Africans include the current questions of imperial plunder, #Black Lives Matter, the quality of the lives of black working peoples worldwide, education for liberation, the exploitation of women in Global Africa, the future of the youth, peace, environmental repair within Africa, and the questions of reparative justice. It is also important that the Global African family is reminded that there are over twenty-eight colonies in the Pan-African world. The outstanding issues of colonial rule in the Western Sahara, Martinique, Cayenne, Guadeloupe, Puerto Rico, and many other colonial holdouts remind us of the adage that no African country will really be free until all of Africa is free.

It is also urgent that the progressive Pan-African community make special efforts to provide political and material support for our brothers and sisters in Latin America, who are suffering from extreme racist violence. The racism in societies such as Brazil is often kept out of the news by media complicity.

On another front, neo-liberal interventions in all parts of the Pan-African world have oriented the direction of state policies towards the enrichment of a few instead of organising society for the public good. In the wake of the structural adjustment agrarian stagnation, de-industrialisation and the growth of the informal service sectors there is a growing crisis of unemployment and precarious work. Market-based social protection policies have failed to contribute to the creation of healthy, educated, productive, and peaceful societies, but have instead resulted in growing structural inequalities, disaffection, and conflicts arising from the struggle over resources.

Imperial domination and military interventions tended to shift from the optimism of the early postcolonial period to the Afro-pessimism of the 1970s and 1980s. At the end of apartheid, following the defeat of the South African army at Cuito Cuanavale, and the formation of the African Union, there has been a rejuvenation of the ideals of Pan-African Unity. In 2013, at the fiftieth anniversary of the formation of the OAU, there was an amplification of the goals of Unity, with the elaboration of *Agenda 2063*, along with the designation of the global African family overseas as the sixth region of Africa. This rejuvenation of Pan-African ideas has come at a time when there is a recognition of the potential of the demographic dividend of the youthful population of Africa, if only there were appropriate social investments to harness their energy and talent. In Kenya, the triple effect of M-Pesa, the mobile money transfer service; the development of Ushahidi, the leading free online crisis-mapping platform; and iHub, one of the most talked-about innovation lounges on the continent, point to the potentialities of African youth. This demographic asset, combined with the assets of mineral and genetic resources, augur well if the ideas of transformation and reconstruction were to take root in Africa.

This optimistic view is tempered by concerns about the militarisation of politics, youth unemployment, forced migration resulting from a lack of economic opportunities, perennial electoral tensions in some countries, as well as years of political instability and destabilisation in several counties. The NATO intervention in Libya and foreign military forays into Africa point to the fact that African policymakers and activists have to take seriously the warnings of the first AAPC on imperialism and neo-colonialism.

The attractiveness of the resources of Africa has ensured that there are new suitors beyond the former imperial states of Britain, France, Belgium, and the USA. The emergence of new global forces, such as Brazil, Russia, India, and China (BRIC), as well as South Korea and Turkey, all scrambling for Africa's resources, challenge Africans to develop collective approaches to external forces. The nascent regime of agreements, like the Economic Partnership Agreements (EPA) signed between African countries and the European Union, and Defence Cooperation Agreements signed between some African countries and the United States, France, and Britain, raise new concerns about the future of Africa and its preparedness to deal with current manifestations of neo-colonialism and imperialism. The spread of such agreements also raises concerns not only about the extent to which Africa takes the legacy of the freedom fighters seriously but also the possible complicity of African leaders in decisions and actions that obviously undermine the immediate and future prospect of building a united and integrated Africa.

As we commemorate the First AAPC sixty years on, it is apt to restate the call of that first conference:

"Peoples of Africa, Unite! You have nothing to lose but your chains! You have a continent to regain! You have freedom and human dignity to attain!"

And to the colonialists we say: "Hands off Africa! Africa Must be Free!"

The Commemoration—Sub-Thematic Areas

In light of the above, the sixtieth-anniversary commemoration is organised around a number of sub-thematic areas. The sub-themes are selected to take account of the unequal power relations that continue to shape Africa's position in the world, as well as sites of struggle for a new Africa, all reflecting what is considered the unfinished business of the First AAPC.

Peoples of Africa

This sub-theme comprises three significant interrelated areas that reflect the territorial diversity, the youth question, and labour conditions of the peoples of Africa. These organic classifications are global Africa, demographic shifts, and struggles of working people.

Global Africa: The concept of Global Africa is a call for the recognition of unity in diversity of all people of Africa and African descent. The concept contends that Africans at home and dispersed outside of Africa (usually called the *diaspora)* constitute one family. The African Union (AU) has now designated those living outside of Africa as constituting the sixth region of the African Union. The Global Africa idea advocates for the recognition that Africans and peoples of African descent in any part of the world share the common historical and social experiences that shape the consciousness of Pan-Africanism. Historical crimes against humanity such as enslavement, colonialism, and apartheid have served to sharpen the Pan-African consciousness and shaped the formation of organs such as the OAU and, later, the African Union. As Walter Rodney affirmed at the time of the Sixth Pan-African Congress, "One of the cardinal principles of Pan-Africanism is that the people of one part of Africa are responsible for the freedom of their brothers and sisters of Africa, and indeed, black people everywhere should accept the same responsibility".

The question here is to bring back the kind of information-sharing and solidarity that inspired Dr Martin Luther King Jr after he participated in the Independence Day celebrations in Ghana in 1957.

Demographic Shifts: The discussion of demographic shifts focuses on the fact that, for the first time since the trans-Atlantic slave trade, the African population is growing. The projections are that, in the next 30 years, there will be 2.4 billion Africans, a figure estimated to reach 4.1 billion by 2100. Importantly, it is estimated that the population below age 15 will constitute 44%, and that of ages 15–29 will be 30% of the total population of Africa by 2050. The growth of the African population in Latin America will be equally significant. At the same time, in Europe and Japan, unlike in Africa, the indigenous population will decline with the ratio of old persons to working-age persons skewed in favour of the aged. The crucial question is how to optimise the demographic dividend of Africa's youthful population? Related to the optimisation of this youth bulge, is how to create and instil progressive consciousness and competitiveness in the youth.

Struggles of Working People: The working peoples of Africa consist of the mass of poor peasants, the working class, and the cultural workers, who are all caught in the web of precariat labour. Capitalism has intensified the exploitation of black workers. There is a need to grasp the state of workers' and peasant struggles to address the land and labour questions of global Africa and work out how to energise these struggles. The need for independent organisations among these sufferers has been intensified by the ways in which neo-liberal policies have strengthened the military and police forces.

Neo-Colonialism and Imperialism

In the introduction to the book "*Neo-Colonialism: The Last Stage of Imperialism*" (1965), Kwame Nkrumah wrote:

> The neo-colonialism of today represents imperialism in its final and perhaps most dangerous stage. In the past it was possible to convert a country upon which a neo-colonial regime had been imposed into a colonial territory. Today, this process is no longer feasible. Old fashioned colonialism is by no means entirely abolished . . . Once a country has become nominally independent it is no longer possible, as it was in the last century, to reverse the process. Existing colonies may linger on, but no new colonies will be created. In place of colonialism as the main instrument of imperialism, today we have neo-colonialism. The essence of neo-colonialism is that the state which is subject to it is, in theory, independent and has all the outward trappings of international sovereignty. In reality, its economic system and thus its political policy is directed from outside. Today imperialism has taken new forms but with the dominance of finance capital still manifest with the overarching power of the Bretton Woods institutions (Nkrumah, 1965, p. ix).

Clearly, the adverse incorporation of the African economies into the neo-colonial and imperialist global capitalist institutionalised architecture has constrained Africa's trade, production, finance, technological, and investment competitiveness. One of the key effects is the vertiginous debt burden of the continent.

The Debt Burden: The nature of Africa's integration into the current international system ensures that Africa is a price taker. In short, Africans produce and export primary products and generally import industrial products. Prices are generally set by "international market forces", totally dominated by players in the major industrial states; hence, Africa is perennially unable to meet its obligations and continues to borrow to carry out the normal functions of the state and social reproduction. Balance of payments deficits ensure that African governments must finance state expenditure through external borrowing. While the imperial countries, such as members of the European Union, Japan, and the USA, use the expedient of printing money under the banner of quantitative easing, African States are burdened with odious debts. By the end of 2017, the Jubilee Debt Campaign noted that twenty-eight countries in Africa were in debt distress. Intellectual subservience on the part of most African economists prevents them from raising questions about the undemocratic nature of the operations of the Bretton Woods institutions. Alongside this egregious financial vulnerability of the Pan-African world is the ongoing manipulative and exploitative capitalist process of accumulation by dispossession of African lands. Moreover, the development of the illicit global economy ensures that billions are siphoned out of Africa. At a minimum, there is a need for popular awareness on how to curb illicit financial flows.

African Union and Agenda 2063

The African Union has tasked itself with the unification of Africa by 2063. The vision of the AU is to strive for "an integrated, prosperous, and peaceful Africa, driven by its own citizens and representing a dynamic force in the global arena" (African Union, n.d.). *Agenda 2063* provides the strategic framework for the socio-economic transformation of Africa over the next forty-five years. This plan, with its seven clearly defined aspirations, builds on and seeks to accelerate the implementation of existing and past continental initiatives for the full unification of the peoples of

Africa. Western formations are working hard to deflect real understanding of *Agenda 2063* by intense focus on the UN Sustainable Development Goals (SDGs). There is, therefore, a crucial need to foreground the vital importance and urgency of the pursuit of Pan-Africanism and mobilisation of the human capital of the African intelligentsia as a stratagem for continental emancipation. The current leadership must be forced to build the infrastructural basis for a common currency, common military policy or be removed. The timidity that has been exposed in the framing of the African Continental Free Trade Area demonstrates that progressives must continue to promote the free movement of African peoples across Africa. Africans must oppose restrictive immigration practices whether at home or abroad.

Pan-Africanism Today: African descendants outside the continent—in the so-called African diaspora—engage in struggles aimed at transforming the world around them to better serve Africans and humanity at large. Implicit in all Pan-African struggles today is the drive for the full liberation and unification of Africa and an end to racist exploitation.

The African Intelligentsia: This refers to the body of critical literate Africans who produce ideas about the world in which they live and who are not subservient to imperialist Western epistemic orthodoxy. In the case of the progressive African intelligentsia, they seek to ground their concerns in the issues of the full emancipation of the people, and work to decolonise the mind. These intellectuals are engaged in holding the line against brain hacking.

Emancipation of Women

The struggle by women to end all forms of oppression is multifaceted, challenging basic assumptions about contemporary forms of social life. Capitalist exploitation has intensified the oppression of black women, so that the emancipation of the African woman involves struggles against exploitation on four fronts: labour power, patriarchal dominance, racial exploitation, and sexual oppression. Within the Pan-African world, African women face the additional burden of the denial by many Pan-Africanists of the realities of gender oppression. The major question will be to strengthen the linkages among those organising against all forms of patriarchy, sexism, and deformed masculinity.

Reparations and Restorative Justice

For African descendants of the Global African family, the burning question of the crimes of the trans-Atlantic slave trade remains a key issue of international politics. African descendants have been at the forefront of the Third World Conference against Racism (WCAR). In these meetings, held since 2001, the push has been for recognition that the slave trade and slavery constituted crimes against humanity. Reparation, in this instance, is the action of making amends for a wrong done, by providing payment or other assistance to those who have been wronged. Restorative justice calls for the acknowledgement of the past crimes to see how these crimes influence current behaviour, such as the rise of white racism and imperial chauvinism in the current period. One major challenge among Pan-Africanists is to end the silencing of the demands for reparations that are now occurring in official circles in Africa.

Global Warming

There is evidence that Africa is suffering disproportionately from global warming, i.e., the increase in the earth's atmospheric and oceanic temperatures widely predicted to occur due to an increase in the greenhouse effect—with the rise in temperatures of 2°C registering as 3.6°–4° in Africa. Satellite imagery has projected an expansion of the Sahara and Kalahari deserts if there are no drastic measures to reverse global warming. Additionally, Africa is suffering at several domains of the nine planetary boundaries, namely, stratospheric ozone depletion; climate change; change in bio-sphere integrity; ocean acidification; biogeochemical flows (phosphorous and nitrogen cycles), land system change; and freshwater use. The challenge is to promote basic literacy on these questions as a prelude to action.

Conclusion

It is expected that the political, intellectual, and cultural engagement over the course of the Commemoration will provide a platform for drawing, from the spirit and ethos of the First AAPC, inspiration and a drive towards the completion of the mission and tasks of that pivotal event in the history of Africa.

References

Adi, H. (2018). *Pan-Africanism: A history*. London, UK: Bloomsbury Publishing.

African Union. (n.d.). *Vision and mission*. Retrieved from https://au.int/en/about/vision

Nkrumah, K. (1965). *Neo-colonialism: The last stage of imperialism*. London, UK: Thomas Nelson and Sons Ltd.

Nkrumah, K. (1970). *Africa must unite*. London, UK: Panaf Books

The Arts at AAPC @ 60

Eric Tei-Kumadoe and Edem Adotey

Culture has been a site of contestation within the imperialist systems. In this contest, while colonial and neo-colonial institutions have sought to reduce African cultural expressions to the backwater, African thought leaders have challenged these views by asserting an African personality in all its glory. Following in the long tradition of African liberation thought and practice through its numerous actors and institutions that have worked towards the reclamation and affirmation of African culture, the planners of this conference set up a sub-committee to incorporate the celebrations of African culture into the conference. The cultural events organised to celebrate Africa's vibrant cultural heritage included poetry recitals, a photo exhibition, movie shows, and musical performances and concerts including a palm wine music performance under the beautiful African night sky with calabashes of the delicious beverage.

Two types of events were staged during the conference. There were single events like musical performances, concerts, and longer events that ran throughout the conference or even for some months after. The set of events was as follows: poetry performed by Prof Kofi Anyidoho titled "Ancestral Roll Call", and three musical performances spread over three days. They consisted of a welcome performance by Syracuse University's Professor Arthur Flowers, which followed the opening ceremony; a palm wine music performance for day two; and then an African music concert which took place on day three. A photo exhibition that stood for months after the conference and a film screening that ran throughout the conference, except for the last day, was also part of the set of artistic events organised during this momentous gathering. A mini market was also erected for the sale of various items such as beads, fabrics, and bags, among other products. The artistic programmes were intended to offer a complementary platform for learning, participation, and networking. In addition, it sought to lay the foundation for new voyages in search of the incomplete process of liberation.

The renowned Ghanaian academic Prof Kofi Anyidoho kick-started the events with his powerfully evocative poem titled "Ancestral Roll Call" in his baritone voice singing and reciting a poem best suited for a gathering of this nature. It was a solemn yet electrifying account that spanned over 500 years of Global African history condensed in Prof Anyidoho's lines. The poem was an invocation of departed actors in the African liberation struggle against enslavement and imperialism across Global Africa. It celebrated their selfless sacrifices in the effort to lift Africa to where it truly belongs and called upon them to join us and assist us in the unfinished business of African liberation.

The opening ceremony was followed by a photo exhibition aptly named "Re_sisters - Emancipation of Women - Global Africa" which celebrated the role of women in the African liberation struggle, an immense contribution that is usually not given the credit it deserves. It had beautifully curated pictures of these heroines from all walks of life and across Global Africa with succinct information on their contribution to African liberation in addition to photos from the first All-African People's Conference (AAPC) held in Accra in 1958. It was formally opened after the opening ceremony at the conference venue by the Director of the Institute of African Studies, Prof Dzodzi Tsikata. Considering the importance of this exhibition in not only putting faces to these heroines but also stamping these images in people's memories, it was re-mounted at the Institute of African Studies where it stood for several months after the conference.

At the end of the official opening of the photo exhibition, Prof Flowers treated conference participants and guests to a performance that combined folklore, blues, poetry, and spiritualism drawn from African-American experiences. This thrilling performance carried resonances of African philosophies of performance. His array of instruments, including the mbira, was a testament to the unity of African and African–American connections and the enduring cross-Atlantic relations.

The musical performances were interspersed with movies that highlighted Global African experiences. These movies explored themes of the struggle against segregation in the south of the USA; the power of music in the anti-apartheid resistance in South Africa; the place of violence in anti-colonial movements in Algeria; the Haitian Revolution; French colonial massacres of mutinous African soldiers; racism in the Second World War; and the trans-Atlantic enslavement of Africans. In all, seven films were screened. These were *Amandla, Selma, Sankofa, His Majesty's Sergeant, 1804, The Battle of Algiers,* and *Camp de Thiaroye.* Collectively these films conveyed the resilience of Africans in the face of subjugation and exploitation. Each session was followed by engaging conversations with the audience facilitated by graduate students of the Institute of African Studies on the respective themes explored in the films.

Midway through the exhilarating conference, a palm wine music performance dubbed "Palm Wine Night" accompanied by drinks such as palm wine, *pito* and *sobolo* as well as some finger foods, was organised at the forecourt of the Institute of African Studies old building to expose the participants to another aspect of Atlantic crossings. Palm wine music is a popular musical genre in West Africa that has its roots in Caribbean calypso. The combination of the scale of singing, the reliance on the participatory audience, the instruments, costumes, and energy provided by the two bands of the night, the Palm Wine Tappers Band and the Atentenben Band kept many participants on their dancing feet. The participants were also not left out of the musical performances; there was a breathtaking saxophone performance invoking Fela Kuti by scholar and Pan-Africanist, Temitope Maberu-Fangunwa.

There was a musical gala, the "1 Africa Music Concert" on the penultimate night of the conference. It was a blend of different music genres from across Global Africa. The performance included reggae music, hiphop, spoken word, and highlife music. The event which was emceed by one of Ghana's top DJs, Daddy Bosco included some popular artists in Ghana such as Manifest and Knii Lante. The Ghana Police band provided instrumental support for the artists who performed live in the evening. The band also delighted the guests with some popular songs, which were received very well. The audience was very lively and participative, and they stayed on the dancing floor throughout the evening. It is worth mentioning the strong bonds that were formed during these nights of dancing.

The array of artistic programmes put on display over the days did contribute to the overall objectives of the conference. It brought to the fore the importance of the arts in educating people on Africa's history and culture in the "Unfinished Business of Liberation and Transformation" of Africa and its peoples, which was the theme of the conference. It showed participants, for instance, how poetry, music, films, and photos could be powerful mediums for disseminating Africa's rich history and culture. It showed the linkages and continuities of African culture across the Atlantic despite centuries of forcible separation through the trans-Atlantic slave trade. Most importantly, the conference served as a crucial platform for solidifying friendships among individuals of all ages. These new connections have the potential to form the foundation for the unity of the Global African community in realising the Pan-African aspirations in the near future.

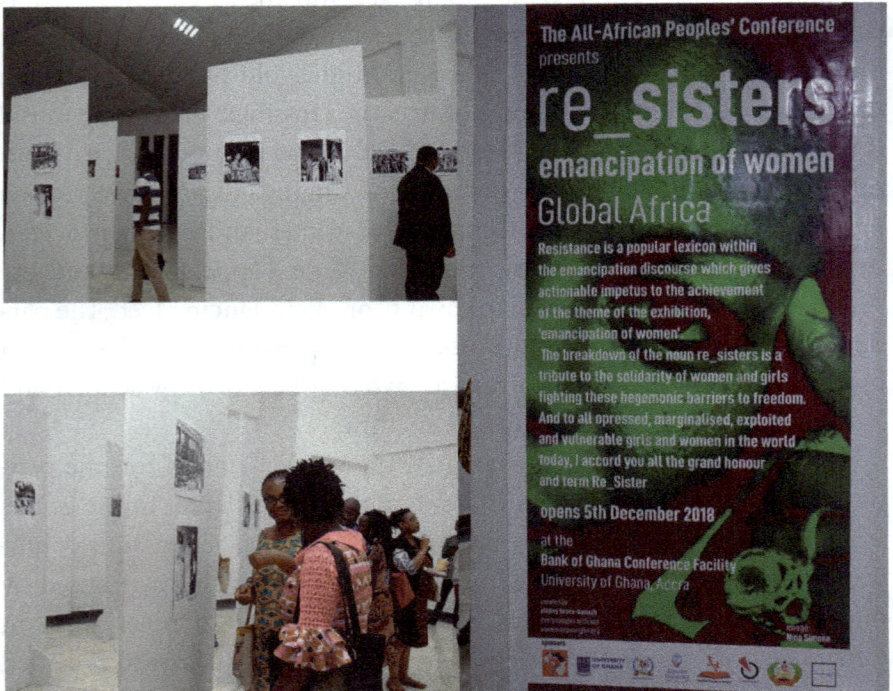

Launch of the AAPC @ 60 photo exhibition titled *Re_sisters - Emancipation of Women - Global Africa* on 5th December 2018.

Active participation at Palm Wine Night a mix of Palm Wine music, Ghanaian drinks, and finger foods held at the forecourt IAS Old Site on 6th December 2018.

1 *Africa musical concert hosted at the Efua Sutherland Drama Studio on 7th December 2018 featuring Dr. Knii Lante supported by the Ghana Police Band (top left), M.Anifest (right), and some participants dancing the night away (bottom left).*

Issues and Recommendations*

Preamble

We, the over 300 Pan-Africanist students, academics, public intellectuals, activists, trade unionists, cultural workers, and working peoples from 34 countries including Algeria, Barbados, Belgium, Benin, Burkina Faso, Cameroon, Canada, Chad, Costa Rica, Côte d'Ivoire, Cuba, Democratic Republic of the Congo, Egypt, France, Gambia, Ghana, Haiti, India, Jamaica, Japan, Lebanon, Namibia, Nigeria, Kenya, Saharawi, Sierra Leone, South Africa, St. Lucia, Tanzania, Togo, Trinidad and Tobago, Uganda, United Kingdom, United States of America, Virgin Islands, and Zimbabwe, on four continents (Africa, the Americas, Asia, and Europe), recently participated in the Sixtieth Anniversary of the All-African Peoples' Conference at the University of Ghana, Accra, from 5 to 8 December 2018.

We deliberated over the four days in plenary and parallel sessions, informal caucuses, and cultural events, and heard two keynote speeches. We also convened six thematic groups to identify issues and recommendations for an official statement on the sixtieth anniversary commemoration. The outcome of these deliberations, which has been the subject of further consultations and revisions, is contained in this statement.

We recognised the quagmire of immiseration plaguing the African masses as a result of neo-colonialism, the contemporary policy of imperialism. We noted the ideological and policy dominance of

---

* Sixtieth anniversary commemoration of the All-African People's Conference, 5-8 December 2018.

neo-liberal capitalism and the oppressive economic and social policies that have impoverished African populations and engendered perennial warfare. We recognised the sham independence, balkanisation, and debilitating borders inherited from the colonial era that have been counter-productive to the forces of African liberation, unity, and social transformation. We noted our keen awareness of the environmental deterioration that has accompanied capitalist operations and exacerbated global warming to the detriment of humanity. We expressed dismay that the problems that bedevilled Africa at the time of the first All-African People's Conference of 1958 still afflict Africans throughout the planet.

Our conference prioritised the voices and concerns of the youth, the working peoples, and the oppressed women of Africa, recognising that these social forces are at the forefront of struggles to deal with the unfinished business of the All-African People's Conference of 1958. Our collective vision to end the oppression of African women, the working people, and youth goes hand in hand with the need to organise these sectors of Africa's population and thereby improve their self-conscious agency and the quality of their lives.

We also noted that the decolonization of minds, the political remobilization, and the restoration of all African people's lives depend on instilling in them a Pan-African historical consciousness. We also recognised the need to illuminate the historic debt owed to African people by imperialist usurpers and capitalist exploiters. We vowed to use the arts and new tools of political mobilisation and education for the emancipation of Africans and the transformation of Africa.

We are also critical of the lethargic performance of the current leadership of the African Union (AU) with respect to addressing the challenges facing Global Africa. This has allowed our states to welcome foreign military bases and intrusions of former colonial powers in the affairs of independent African states. We contend that electing progressive leaders in Africa will strengthen the AU in the long run, just as a core group of leaders within the Organisation of African Unity (OAU) was able to forge ahead with the OAU Liberation Committee that spearheaded the fight against apartheid.

Our resolve to rectify all the challenges facing Global Africa today is reflected in this statement, which we have issued to guide further deliberation and action on the issues we have prioritised.

1. **On Pan-Africanism Today and Tomorrow and Building a New Politics of Substantive Democracy and Security**

We note the following as matters of concern:

- the process of decolonisation is incomplete as there are African territories still under colonial rule;
- the dominant political systems in Africa today are based on a Euro-American hegemonic construct, largely imposed through colonial rule and post-colonial control, incompatible with some key African beliefs, cosmologies, and values, and unable to deliver substantive democracy to the peoples of Africa;
- elite capture and control of processes and institutions of governance have resulted in politics and practice in many African countries that are exclusive, non-representative, and undemocratic;
- the following persist:

  - weak economic institutions that are unable to ensure equality and equity or effectively enforce regulatory mechanisms designed to protect African economies from exploitation and natural resource pillage;
  - weak and unrepresentative political parties that lack Pan-Africanist orientation;
  - ossified, colonially created national borders that inhibit mobility and freedom of movement within Africa;
  - official Pan-African organisations that are not sufficiently reflective of Pan-Africanism or aspirations of the majority of African peoples at home and abroad;
  - ongoing cleavages and very minimal interactions amongst the peoples of Global Africa (i.e. continental and diasporic Africa);
  - the underutilisation of the mobilising potential of the arts and newly emerging communications technologies and social media.

<u>We commit to addressing these issues and make the following key</u>
<u>recommendations:</u>

- Global Africans must immediately end any and all existing forms of formal colonial rule of African peoples. Specifically, we call for the end of the colonial control of the Western Sahara by the government of Morocco;
- Global Africa should create systems of inclusive democracy that address issues of representation, equity, and fairness for all groups in Global Africa and reflect the spirit and ideals of Pan-African emancipation;
- the dominant elite political class must be replaced by formations that represent and empower diverse social groups (such as farmers, peasants, youth, precariat, labour, traders, and cultural workers) in all branches of government in Africa;
- Global Africans should support the formation of political parties undergirded by Pan-African ideals, goals, and objectives;
- serious and concrete steps must be taken to dismantle colonial borders created during and after the Berlin Conference of 1884/85;
- the decision to institute an AU Passport should be expedited and implemented fully in the shortest possible time. The eligibility criteria for passports should include the entire Global African family, to facilitate visits to and movement within Africa at minimal cost;
- development, control, ownership, and use of facilitative technology and media, including newly emerging technologies and social media, should be encouraged;
- there is an urgent need to consolidate the use of local languages on social media to deepen and widen the space of interaction within Global Africa;
- policies and practices must be put in place to regulate the control and ownership of information and communications media to promote smooth interaction amongst Africans;
- African organisations must intensify support for the Black Lives Matter Movement and other continental and global struggles.

2. On Pan-African Epistemologies for Knowledge Production

<u>We note the following as matters of concern:</u>

- Africa-centred epistemologies (how we know what we know), that is, the frameworks and methodologies for how we know, discover, and theorise, are necessary for the production and validation of knowledge that empowers;
- knowledge is power and knowledge is ideological; thus, institutions that transmit knowledge should be recognised as instruments of power and locations of political struggles;
- no "knowledge products" are truthful in an absolute sense. Africans have been wilfully miseducated by the imperialists to denigrate indigenous knowledge. Their collective intellectual capabilities have been undermined to facilitate subjugation and marginalisation;
- knowledge production in African universities is characterised by exclusionary class, race, and gender politics and elitism. This is because many African universities are based on the Western European model which is different from earlier models used in Africa;
- in African universities today, the complex disciplinary organisation of knowledge has proved unconducive to addressing Africa's pressing development challenges;
- the African intelligentsia have been perpetuating colonial knowledge and privileging Western perspectives on the world;
- only with the end of colonial rule did it become possible to establish new schools of history that better reflected the perspective and interests of African peoples such as the Dakar School, the Dar es Salaam School, and the Ibadan School. Kwame Nkrumah was instrumental in the establishment of the Institute of African Studies at the University of Ghana to spearhead an intellectual revolution to accompany Africa's social revolution. All these initiatives are struggling against an ever-stronger tide of Western hegemonic scholarship on Africa.

<u>We commit to addressing these issues, and make the following key recommendations:</u>

- Global Africans should be able to access the knowledge and self-knowledge that empowers generations. Such knowledge should be taught at the earliest grade levels possible in Africa;
- there is a great need to democratise and decolonise knowledge production in Africa beyond the walls of Western-style universities;
- Global Africans need to create independent learning institutions that are Pan-African in content and context;
- Global Africans ought to develop (an) African language(s) that can be used across Africa, and include non-verbal languages such as dance to communicate;
- academic scholarship should be joined with civic activism. This means that our institutions and struggles will include Pan-Africanist scholars and activists working together;
- Global Africans should create curricula that enhance our collective Pan-African personality, and work with these curricula in a diversity of spaces, both within and outside the formal education systems;
- Pan-African knowledge products should utilise multimedia productions;
- Pan-African knowledge producers should study and understand policy processes and identify and engage with the perspectives and fears of policymakers to ensure the influence of African-centred scholarship on policy processes, policies, and outcomes;
- that the All-African Peoples' Conference be organised at shorter intervals of time (perhaps every two years).

3. On Ending Imperialist Domination and Transforming Africa's Economies

<u>We note the following as matters of concern:</u>

- Africa's economies are structurally dependent on the production and export of raw material commodities which feed industrial production, job creation, and incomes in other economies. Africa retains the negative environmental and social burdens of this type of production;

- internally, the most important sectors of Africa's economies are dominated by Western transnational capital. Despite current anxieties across Africa, China does not yet control any economic sector in Africa even as its influence is increasing rapidly;
- African states act as protectors and promoters of the rights of foreign investors. Currently, bilateral investment treaties (BITs) and international investment agreements (IIAs) offer foreign companies excessive rights with little, if any obligations;
- Africa's ruling elites are largely comfortable overseeing realities within which there is widespread unemployment, a crisis of livelihoods in rural areas, and urbanisation amidst deindustrialisation. As a result, there are growing inequalities—class, gender, generational, and regional—across Africa;
- increasingly precarious working conditions are undermining the livelihoods of workers in the "informal" economy. This, together with increasing unemployment and a rise in the number of youth who have never been in formal employment, has resulted in deteriorating living conditions in many African countries.

We commit to addressing these issues, and make the following key recommendations:

- there must be the stemming, and return, of illicit outflows of capital from Africa;
- the economic systems of African countries must be redesigned and directed towards facilitating the self-reliance and self-sufficiency of African states and their peoples;
- the peoples of Africa must reclaim the African state to ensure the domestication of local capital and to direct local capital and resources to domestic industrialisation to serve the interests of the working people of Africa;
- the process of domestic industrialisation must be directed towards serving local needs for goods and services and the

development of local markets so as to ensure food sovereignty, sustainable production, and the dignity of livelihoods;

- domestic industrialisation aimed towards stimulating local production must be directed towards education, health, housing, transportation, and infrastructure, as well as industries that are beneficial to the people at large;
- Global Africans must develop and disseminate analysis that promotes the understanding that neoliberalism and the neoliberal economic system are anti-people, anti-solidarity, anti-collective, and are bolstered by the expansion of debt and numerous debt cycles which perpetuate crisis and undermine the sovereignty and autonomy of African states as well as their control of their political economy;
- African economies must have effective trade barriers and protections;
- African states must promote genuine custodianship of natural resources, foster democratic decentralisation, and ensure that any economic activity is ecologically sustainable;
- African states must develop mechanisms which account for the economic "value-added" of migrants and develop strategic backwards linkages with both the historic and contemporary diaspora communities;
- Global Africans must rein in and dismantle the power over African economies of foreign states, financial capital, transnational corporations (TNCs), and other corporate forms and place restraints on the self-aggrandisement, state capture, and corruption of local elite;
- African states redesign banking systems to create a peoples-centred banking system based on financial cooperatives such as credit unions as an important model to direct people's resources and generate projects that are paid, designed, and controlled by peoples' currency and agency;
- African states reimagine an economic system based on a partnership between state and cooperative enterprises across all sectors;

- Global Africans recognise and actualise the centrality of the state with regard to transforming Africa's economies;
- promoting development strategies rooted in Pan-Africanism and regional integration based on the recognition that most African economies are too small and weak to carry out the sustainable transformation, is imperative.

4. On Climate Change and Environmental Repair

We note the following as matters of concern:

- a global capitalist order, in which Africa is inundated with capitalist production that is profit-motivated, has contributed significantly to deforestation and forest degradation;
- new, destructive visions of nature have infiltrated and destroyed the indigenous African relationship with nature;
- indigenous institutions and values considered nature to be sacred. The current conception of nature as dualistic and separate from humans, which has led to environmentally unsustainable production practices, has been imposed on Africans;
- unsustainable mineral exploitation, dominated by foreign firms, rips Africa of its natural resources, while industrial waste destroys rivers and streams;
- Africans themselves play a role in environmental destruction that contributes to global warming. Practices such as littering of plastics and other waste material is a major challenge for most of Africa's natural environments;
- there is a lack of sensitisation on the destructive effects of illegal mining on the natural environment in Africa.

We commit to addressing these issues, and make the following key recommendations:

- Global Africans must be committed to planting and caring for trees. In this regard, it is especially important that indigenous trees be preserved;

- Africans must return to indigenous relationships with nature, where nature is not a commodity to be exploited for human benefit but integral to humanity in a sustainable manner. A Pan-African vision is needed in this respect;
- the full involvement of communities in the management of nature is imperative, and communities must be primary beneficiaries of resources from nature;
- information on climate change and global warming must be made available to communities to guide the actions of people;
- African governments should place more land in the hands of local farmers and encourage sustainable farming practices to encourage food sovereignty and ecological conservation;
- increased sensitisation of the harmful effects of certain local practices on lands and forests is vital to efforts at reducing global warming;
- African regional bodies, governments, and communities should hold the private sector responsible and task it through stringent regulations to repair and restore the environments destroyed through the activities of individual corporate entities;
- universities in Africa need to increase research on desalination of seawater to increase the provision of water for agriculture and domestic consumption, especially in drier regions of the continent, to reduce pressure on and degradation of inland water bodies;
- African countries and governments must invest in the recycling of by-products to reduce waste ought to be increased, and reduction in wasteful consumption encouraged;
- climate change should be recognised as an important economic issue by the AU.

5. On Restorative and Reparative Justice

We note the following as matters of concern:

- the current discourses on reparations and restorative justice are limited to what others can do for Global Africa, but this should extend to what we can do for ourselves as Africans on the continent and Africans in the diaspora. We cannot wait for external reparations before we repair ourselves and our environment;

- there is a need for a new paradigm to understand the changed economic situation after 1492 and for the interpretation of African history for the cause of reparative justice;
- the use of a positivist legal framework in explaining justice in Africa is inimical to the cause of reparative and restorative justice;
- the UN Conference Against Racism of 2011 has recognised slavery as a crime against humanity. Most African states have not incorporated this reality into their current international relations policies. In this respect, institutional failure in Africa is the cause of current forms of slavery and human trafficking in Africa. We condemn all forms of modern slavery including the trafficking of human bodies arising out of the institutional failure on the African continent;
- debates about the issue of reparations are critical to the effort to clarify and implement the outcomes of the WCAR Programme of Action;
- it is important to recognise that reparations are not necessarily about money, but mainly about the dignity of the Africans.

We commit to addressing these issues, and make the following key recommendations:

- there should be a push for the establishment of a global education programme on reparative and restorative justice in the context of WCAR outcomes to assist in the clarification and identification of perpetrators in both the trans-Atlantic slave trade and the trans-Sahara slave trade;
- Pan-Africanists must organise to secure recognition of the historic ecological debt and reparations owed to Africa's people for slavery and colonial plunder;
- that an All-African dialogue on reparations be established. This dialogue should be modelled on the South African Truth and Reconciliation Commission and should allow all states and

civil society groups in Global Africa the opportunity to share experiences and feelings and to seek healing for our collective roles in the African slave trade, both as victims and perpetrators;

- there must be clarity on the recipients of reparations for Africa—survivors of the enslaved outside Africa and Africans on the continent;
- there must be mandatory inclusion, in the curricula in Global African secondary and tertiary education systems, of compulsory courses on the history of Africa and the African diaspora. This curriculum change is urgent to reverse the currently dominant view that Africans were enslaved to be Christianised and modernised;
- African, Caribbean, and other-African majority states in other parts of Global Africa should engage in self-reparation, particularly in the following areas: resource and land reclamation and restoration, correction of education systems, return of lost populations, removal of the legacies of the colonial system including images, nationalisation of African assets in the name of the working people, and correction of legal frameworks in Africa;
- there must be a systematic effort to ensure the return of cultural artefacts taken from Africa during the colonial period and afterward;
- African states must show support and solidarity with the Caribbean Community (CARICOM), ten-point plan, and Global Africa Congress' twelve-point.
- the AU Commission on Reparations should advance the cause of reparations and restorative justice in Global Africa.
- that Global Africans support the Boycott, Divestment, and Sanctions (BDS) campaign against the State of Israel until this state recognises the social and political rights of the Palestinian people;
- universal African citizenship and free movement of African labour across Global Africa must be realised to curtail and stop modern forms of enslavement and trafficking of Africans;
- awareness, analysis, and action are required for social change. Our patience in going through the process will lead to a more likely successful outcome in the struggle for reparation and restoration.

6. On Youth, Workers, Progressive Women, and Africa's Transformation

We note the following as matters of concern:

- Africa is blessed with a youthful population. However, there is much-sustained work to be done to ensure that the potential of Africa's youth is fully realised for the benefit of all the peoples of Africa;
- unemployment and underemployment are currently complicating the full inclusion of the youth in their efforts to achieve the realisation of their potential;
- African women and girls continue to suffer physical and psychological violence, marginalisation, and discrimination, which threaten the full realisation of their personhood and citizenship; LGBQI persons—men and women—are at particular risk in this connection;
- the persistence of certain cultural practices and patriarchal institutions in state and civil society normalise, endorse, encourage, and perpetuate gender inequalities across Global Africa. Institutions and processes of socialisation often teach rigid gender roles that emphasise the inferiority and subordination of girls and women to males, thus perpetuating blatant inequity and inequality between men and women in all realms—economic, cultural, social, and political;
- violence and discrimination against women are often carried out with impunity, facilitated by patriarchal and increasingly militarised states, and compounded by the absence or collapse of critical social services and the privatisation of public goods;
- African workers have lost many of the victories of an earlier era such as the rights to collective bargaining and the rights to decent wages and a decent quality of life;
- only the strengthening of the organisations of working peoples, women, and the youth across borders, economic sectors, and industries can strengthen the peoples of Africa.

<u>We commit to addressing these issues, and make the following key</u>
<u>recommendations:</u>

- Global Africans should value and harness the creativity and innovations of the youth, recognising them as an integral part of bringing our collective vision to fruition;
- those privileged with positions of leadership must fully appreciate and actively fulfil their responsibilities in preparing, including, and providing for youth in every aspect of work;
- Global Africans must recognise, in particular, the need for holistic African-centred education systems and spaces, which embrace the rich diversity of our past and present realities and experiences as African people, and prepare our children and youth to be the agents of Africa's transformation into the future that we envision for ourselves;
- Global Africans should nurture trans-border and trans-sector youth movements, including those working with particular constituencies, e.g. students, professional associations, trade unions, and other organisations of working people;
- different movements working towards Africa's transformation must be linked up, catalysing, and facilitating the organising across borders of all kinds, including across the continent and diaspora to make these separate initiatives one emancipative movement that recognises and embraces diversity and inclusivity within the collective vision for a united, strong, Africa;
- children and youth must be at the heart of these movements, and be provided with appropriate spaces and processes for their full inclusion, regardless of their abilities, location, or place in society;
- women and girls must be welcomed as active, integral, and full members in the Pan-Africanist emancipatory movements, and efforts made to bring in and create support structures as appropriate for all those who have been historically excluded or marginalised in our movements, such as rural women and LGBTIQ persons;
- Global Africans must realise, respect and enforce women's full political, social, cultural, and economic rights under appropriate legal and policy frameworks;

- African states must create comprehensive social services systems that provide appropriate and holistic systems of support for all girls and women, and pay attention to the unique needs of non-traditional family units, such as those headed by single women, as well as those particularly at risk in contexts where their safety and security are compromised;
- all individuals, institutions, and governments committing violence against African peoples, and particularly against all girls and women, must be held accountable;
- Global Africans must find, document, celebrate, and amplify our feminist ancestors and recuperate women's histories of struggle and enduring economic, social, and political contributions to the African experience.

Issued this 15th Day of February 2019, at Accra, by the Organising Committee of the Sixtieth Anniversary Commemoration of the All-African Peoples' Conference (AAPC).

UNIVERSITY OF GHANA

IAS

TWNAfrica

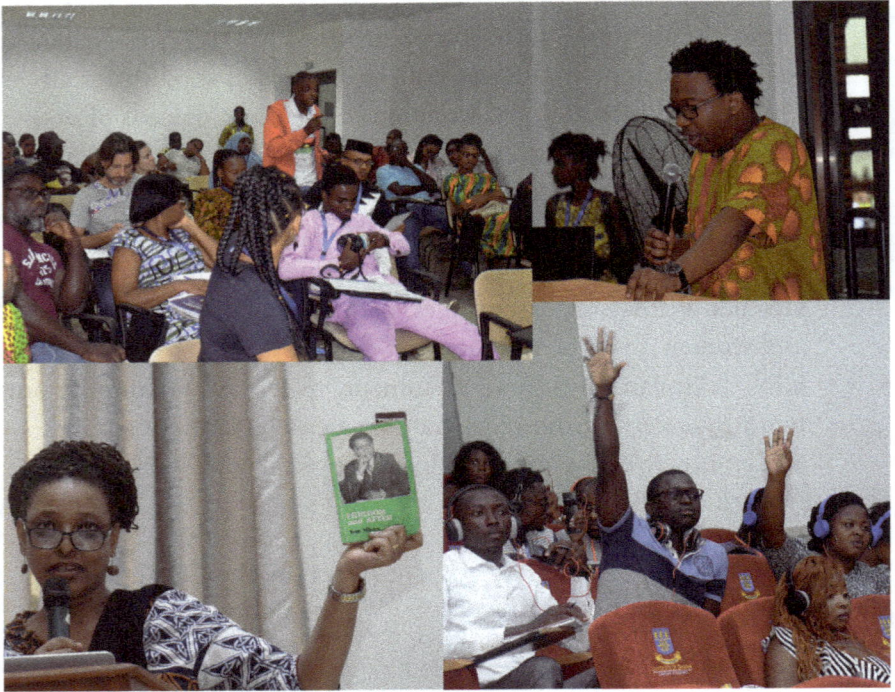

Vibrant interaction with panelists and participants and plenary sessions and panels throughout the conference.

EXHORTATION

De Geas of Rickydoc: An Exhortation

Arthur Rickydoc Flowers

I am Flowers of the Delta Clan Flowers and the Line of O. Killens.
I am hoodoo, I am griot, I am a man of power, my words true
words, my story true story, my lies true lies, I am Mythmaker . . .

Weaver of conjure, worker of storm, castor of bones and tomorrow's truth, I make myth tomorrow, as I define so shall it be, for you see, my friend, I am a conjuror, a dread delta hoodoo come to call thru seared mouthharp lungs to me, o mighty race, for I've had Visions. I've seen the Promised Land. It is in me like Fire.

It is I, Rickydoc Rootdocta, come to call you 1stborn,. You who walked first on two feet, you should not be the last, listen firstborn, eh, to de Geas of Rickydoc, and I will give you a Mission greater than your Adversity, I will give you a Destiny, I will give you Power. When my people gather together like this, in Peace and Love and Harmony, that place, that gathering place, this space, you and me, eh, Holyground.

cast your vision, young hoodoo, as far as you
can see, determine the challenges the tribe
will face, prepare the tribal soul to meet them.

This What I See:
I see a Culture respected throughout the Galaxy. Guide and Guardian of Humanity's Quest to Evolve. To be. Guardian of Human Destiny. Greater Nubia is what I see.

I propose an African Way, so evolved, so illuminated, everybody in the world wants to partake. A Way that will encompass all those who come against us. The Cross, the Crescent, East and West, they must all understand they are guests in Africa and not conquerors. I submit that cultural survival in the twenty-first century will be determined by which cultures that contribute to the globalised future and which wither away.

Look at the condition of the Pan-African World today, and it is difficult not to despair. We are yet and still the bottomfeeders of the earth. Everywhere in the world that you got Black People they on the bottom of their respective society. *Everywhere.* Can't blame everywhere on nobody else. Somehow someway we must transform into strength the weaknesses that have crippled us in global competition. *Listen to me.* O ancient race in deep decline. Yet so clearly perched on the cusp of Greatness. Standing at the crossroads, which way will we go.

Got to Work the tribal soul/culture.
Transform Blackfolk Souldeep.
Everywhere.

The Longgame is always spiritual. Struggles against our enemies must always be subject to the struggle within. When Mandela was released from 27 years of captivity, he could easily have called for vengeance but he called instead for a society better than the one they replaced. It is easy to call out the transgressions of others but it is among our own that we must be heard. If we would reclaim our legacy as God's Holy Instrument, we must stand on Higher Ground.

I ask that you take responsibility not only for your own Destiny but the destiny of all creature great and small. When moving a culture or peoples you must think in generations or strategies are ineffective, frustration and burnout certain. You must be comfortable with the glacial pace of social change and human destiny. Phases of struggle come and go, you win some, you lose some, you keep struggling.

What my mentor, Babajohn Killens, the Great Griot Master of Brooklyn, called being a "long-distance runner." What I call the Longgame. Shaping our generations into the people we want most to be.

To win this race will require planning, pacing,
discipline and stamina, and a belief in our ability to
win the long, protracted struggle, we must construct
one hundred year plans, two hundred year plans, we
must construct institutions for generations unborn.

Babajohn Killens

All traditions must periodically reform themselves. If the African Way is to survive the inroads of those hunting African souls as they once hunted bodies, it will have to be a Better Way. An enlightened and empowered Way. A true advance in spiritual understanding and evolution wrapped in an appealing mythology of universal value—*one closer to the truth of things*—finessing them all with strategic grace and dem hoodoo blessings, a globalised culture so strong/illuminated/powerful/beautiful that everybody in the world wants to claim African.

My understanding is the true test of a good, healthy spiritual tradition is that its adherents lead good, healthy lives, brimming with strength and meaning, beauty and grace. That they build strong, healthy communities. Open gates, O Traveller, cosmic doors to the Divine, the Great Mojo in its many names and infinite manifestations.

I believe we must give the African Peoples of the World a vision of themselves as a People of Power and Purpose, a vision they can believe in, one that calls them to their very best, generation after generation, and one they feel compelled to live up to. Forever.

Once upon a time a poser heaped scorn and
abuse upon the Babajohn to which the Babajohn
replied—Demoja, my friend, Hoodoo Peace.
Disarmed, the stranger walked off confused. How,
asked a trainee, did you handle that so well.
Hoodoo Blessings, the Babajohn reply, I gave
him what I had to give. I hoodooed him . . .

Gon Re-myth my people as survivors that will thrive under any adversity, finesse any challenge, foreseen or unforeseen, that Destiny throws on us. We've climbed some difficult mountains, you and I, our struggle has always been epic and we have always overcome.

What we cannot afford to do is get caught up in yesteryear. Again. The winning hand is not the strongest force but the one fighting tomorrow's battles today. Too often Pan-African Playas an ideological generation or two behind. The fundamentalists I guess gon always be fundamentalists, but the cutting edge got to move on. We got Work to do.

It's like you standing there and you mack mack macking
and its an epic mack and you got to keep macking, keep
weaving that magic mack macking until everything around
you is transformed and a new world is born and when you
falter the world thins until you catch it again, and suddenly
they see it, see it like you see it fullgrown, the Long March
of the Firstborn, a star faring folk leaping at the sun . . .

I say we consider the security and prosperity of our generations the Prime Directive, I say we calm, cool, and collected, forever vigilant, deploying a multifaceted strategic/tactical posture in constant calibration, some moves bold and strong, some hidden in shadows, others waiting silently in the wings. The protracted mobilisation of an entire culture, *Conch War*, every possible sector of African society, every member of it—each unto self an Army.

Grandmasters of the Longgame. Trickeration. Strategy.
The Key That Opens All Locks. I say we got this.

There are times, fleeting moments, when you being strong, disciplined, and productive, or you've written the perfect passage, participated in an historical moment, helped a loved one/stranger, that you are acutely aware of yourself as historical, epochal, mythical, history in the flesh. There are moments when you have placed yourself so precisely in the historical continuum's centre of balance that you are aware of being Godforce. *A Focal Point of Reality and Illusion. A Nexus of Generational Possibility.* Conjuring Reality into Being through the sheer force of your Will, your Work, your Craft, your Game.

If you pull it off, you and your works will be studied and modelled in the hearts and aspirations of generations to come. To the extent that your works are relevant and significant to those generations, to that extent are you Immortal. *Immortal.* Every move, every word act deed positioning you as Ancestral Force. Tell me. What would you have future generations think when they think of you. What would you have them feel.

I believe that we are here to craft of the raw material we are given a good if not Great Soul. Just what will your contribution to the Struggle be. What contribution will you make to the Amelioration of the Human Condition, the Social Contract, without which we are but beasts in the field. I hope you leave here, this moment here, this here Crossroads moment here, you and me, here me, renewed and refreshed in the Struggle of Life, confident in the Victory of all that is good. Ready to roll.

Folk think Prophecy is foretelling the future. Au contrary. Prophecy is correlating current behaviour with destinic consequence: *Continue to conduct yourselves in this manner and your generations will suffer. Listen to me and they will thrive. God told me this.*

Awaken the sleeper, Protect the weak, Guide the strong.

And when you come to the Crossroads always take the Highroad, always strive to be Greater than you are.

The Illuminated Children of the Sun.
Humanity's Living Ancestors.
God's True Chosen.

May your days be full of Passion, may your lives be full of Grace
May your Works serve many Generations, may gods Blessings be
on us all—demoja demoja demoja—gods Blessings on us all.

I am. Rickydoc Trickmaster.
De High Hoodoo of Memphis.

You need me you call
me, I will come.

List of Contributors

Edem Adotey is a historian and a Senior Research Fellow at the Institute of African Studies, University of Ghana. He is a Pan-African scholar-activist with research interest in African borderlands. His works explore the intersection between borders and ethnic identities, citizenship, nationalism, and Pan-Africanism. These have been published in journals such as *African Affairs, Africa, History in Africa, Third World Quarterly, Nations and Nationalism, Journal of Borderlands Studies* and *Contemporary Journal of African Studies* His current book project examines chieftaincy and rituals in the (un)making of Ewe identities on the Ghana-Togo borderlands, c. 19th to present times. He is a Fulbright scholar and an American Council of Learned Societies (ACLS) fellow.

Kofi Anyidoho is a poet, literary scholar, educator, and cultural activist. He is a retired Professor of Literature at the English Department, University of Ghana, Legon. Anyidoho has won many prizes for his poetry, including the Valco Fund Literary Award, the Fania Kruger Fellowship for Poetry of Social Vision, the Langston Hughes Prize, the Davidson Nichol Prize, and the BBC Arts and Africa Poetry Award. His published creative works include five collections of poetry: *Elegy for the Revolution* (1978), *A Harvest of Our Dreams* (1984, 1993), *Earth Child* (1985), *Ancestral Logic & Caribbean Blues* (1993), and *Praise Song for The Land* (2002). He has also published *Akpokplo* (a play in Ewe and English: 1977, 1997) and *GhanaNya* and *Agbenoxevi,* CD & Cassette recordings of his poetry in Ewe. Anyidoho was the first occupant of the Kwame Nkrumah Chair in African Studies at the University of Ghana-Legon, a member of the Executive Committee of Council for the Development of Social Science Research in Africa (CODESRIA) (2008-2011) and the Director of its African Humanities Institute Programme.

Anthony Yaw Baah is the Secretary General of the Trades Union Congress (Ghana). He holds PhD in Economics from the University of Sussex in the United Kingdom, MSc in Financial Economics from the Norwegian School of Management and B.A (Hons) in Economics with French from the University of Ghana. He has received other academic awards including certificates from Harvard Business School Executive Education Programme, International Institute for Labour and Cooperative Studies from Israel, the World Bank Institute in Washington D.C, and a diploma from the International Labour Organisation Training Centre in Turin, Italy. He is currently a member of the Governing Body of the International Labour Organisation in Geneva, Switzerland and a member of the National Development Planning Commission (NDPC) of Ghana. He has previously served on the Management Committee of the Institute for Statistical, Social, and Economic Research of the University of Ghana, Advisory Board of the International Centre for Development and Decent Work (ICDD) of the University of Kassel, Germany, governing board of National Pensions Regulatory Authority (NPRA) of Ghana, and Ghana Statistical Service (GSS) board.

Peter Bembir is a PhD Candidate at the Institute of African Studies (IAS), University of Ghana. He researched peacekeeping's professional and medical influences on the structures and behaviour of the Ghana Armed Forces and its personnel. Before the doctoral work, Peter was a senior research assistant to the Kwame Nkrumah Chair in African Studies. He has undergraduate and postgraduate training in Political Studies, and Development Studies respectively from the Kwame Nkrumah University of Science and Technology, Ghana, and the University of Cambridge, UK. Among several research and training experiences, Bembir was an assistant investigator in research to remedy the impact of climate change on security and livelihoods in the Lake Chad Basin and a field manager for an impact evaluation of healthcare intervention in the Volta Region.

Horace G. Campbell is an internationally known peace and justice activist. He holds a joint Professorship in the Department of African American Studies and the Department of Political Science at Syracuse University. Professor Campbell has published widely. His most recent book is *Global NATO and the Catastrophic Failure in Libya: Lessons for Africa in the Forging of African Unity* (Monthly Review Press, USA, 2013). http://monthlyreview.org/product/global_nato_and_the_catastrophic_failure_in_libya/His most well-known book, *Rasta and Resistance: from Marcus Garvey to Walter Rodney* (Africa World Press, Trenton, 1985) is going through its eighth printing, and has been translated into French, Spanish, Turkish and Italian. He has also authored *Barack Obama and 21st Century Politics: A Revolutionary Moment in the USA* (Pluto Press, London 2010). He is also the author of *Reclaiming Zimbabwe: The Exhaustion of the Patriarchal Model of Liberation.* He has published more than 100 journal articles and a dozen monographs as well as chapters in edited books. In the period 2016-2018 he served as the Distinguished Kwame Nkrumah Chair, Institute of African Studies, University of Ghana. His interventions on current politics and international affairs appear on the Counterpunch site and Democracy Now. He was one of the four rapporteurs for the International Commission of Inquiry on Systemic Racist Police Violence against People of African Descent in the United States. https://inquirycommission.org/. He is the Chairperson of the Global Pan African Movement (North American delegation).

Msia Kibona Clark is an associate professor in the African Studies Department, Howard University, Washington, DC, USA. Her research explores themes such as Hip-Hop in Africa, African feminism, and the influence of social movements on cultural production. Msia has published several articles, book chapters, and reviews in academic journals and popular media outlets. Her work not only sheds light on rich and diverse African Hip-Hop communities but also addresses critical social issues. Her recent book *African Women in Digital Spaces* explores the use of social media for advocacy by women across Africa and the diaspora. In addition to her publications, she has curated exhibitions on African culture and photography and is the host of The Hip-Hop African Podcast.

James Dzisah teaches sociological theory, globalization, and Development at the Department of Sociology, University of Ghana. He holds a PhD in sociology from the University of Saskatchewan,

Saskatoon, Canada, and has lectured at the Department of Sociology, University of Saskatchewan, and Nipissing University both in Canada. He was a postdoctoral research associate of innovation at the Newcastle University Business School, Newcastle upon Tyne, UK. His research work revolves around sociology of science, globalization and development. He currently serves as a consulting editor for the Triple Helix Journal and is an editorial board member for the International Journal of Innovation Science. He has published two edited books, several journal articles, and book chapters.

Arthur Rickydoc Flowers, native of Memphis, is the author of novels, creative nonfictions, and graphic texts. He has been Exec. Dir. of The Harlem Writers Guild and various nonprofits. He is professor emeritus, Syracuse University, a practitioner of Literary Hoodoo, the High Hoodoo of Memphis (bonified) and a performance artist in the griotic school of African American literature – *Welcome to Rickydocs Traveling Medicine Show. Whatever ails you I will cure it for sure. If I can't cure you, I will ease your troubled mind.*

Mjiba Frehiwot is a Senior Research Fellow at the Institute of African Studies at the University of Ghana. Dr. Frehiwot researches, debates and thinks deeply about Pan-African consciousness and how to decolonize and re-Africanize knowledge production in Global Africa. Her primary research focuses on Pan-Africanism, African political thought, and social movements in Global Africa. Mjiba served as the head of the Conference secretariat for the 60th anniversary of the All-African Peoples Conference. She is an Associate Editor with *Feminist Africa* and is the Treasurer of the African Studies Association of Africa.

Michael Kpessa-Whyte is an associate professor with the History and Politics Section of the Institute of African Studies (IAS), University of Ghana, Legon, Ghana. He holds a PhD in comparative public policy from McMaster University, Hamilton, Canada. He was the Social Sciences and Humanities Research Council of Canada (SSHRC) Post-Doctoral Fellow at the Johnson-Shoyama Graduate School of Public

Policy, University of Saskatchewan, Saskatoon, Canada. Between 2013 and 2016, he was a policy advisor in the Office of the President of the Republic of Ghana and the executive director of the Ghana National Service Scheme. Prof Kpessa-Whyte has co-edited the *Public Policy in Ghana: Conceptual and Practical Insights* (Palgrave-Macmillan, 2024) and several peer-reviewed journal articles and book chapters.

Thabo Mbeki is a former president of South Africa (1999 – 2008) and Chairperson of the African Union (2002 - 2003). He was also twice chairperson of the Southern African Development Community (SADC). A noted pan-Africanist, he has championed the African Renaissance project. He is the recipient of numerous awards for his work. In 2012, he was awarded the African of the Year by the Daily Trust newspaper of Abuja, Nigeria for his efforts in mediating peace talks between North Sudan and South Sudan. The Rand Afrikaans University conferred an Honorary Doctorate on him in 1999 and in 2000 he received the Honorary Doctor of Laws from the Glasgow Caledonian University. The Thabo Mbeki Foundation was launched in 2010 to continue his vision of African integration and development.

Georges Nzongola-Ntalaja is professor emeritus of African studies at the University of North Carolina in Chapel Hill and Howard University in Washington, DC. He served as President of the African Studies Association (ASA) of the United States and of the African Association of Political Science (AAPS). His book, *The Congo from Leopold to Kabila: A People's History* (Zed Books, 2002), won the 2004 Best Book Award from African Politics Conference Group (APCG), a coordinate organization of the ASA. He has held three positions in the United Nations Development Programme (UNDP) as a Senior Governance Adviser to the Federal Government of Nigeria, Director of the Oslo Governance Centre (OGC) and as Director in charge of setting up the Africa Governance Institute (AGI), a think tank for African states. He has also held positions in the public sector as Diplomatic Advisor to DRC Prime Minister Etienne Tshisekedi (1992-93) and as the Ambassador of the DRC to the United Nations from January 2022 to August 2023.

D. Zizwe Poe is a professor of Pan-Africana Studies at Lincoln University in Pennsylvania. He is a life-long Nkrumahist scholar/activist and organizer of Pan-African activity. Professor Poe is best known for his work on *Kwame Nkrumah's Contribution to Pan-Africanism: An Afrocentric Analysis*. He served as an active member of Nkrumah's second political party, the All-African People's Revolutionary Party, for a quarter of a century. He has worked in academic institutions from 1984 until the present continuously focusing on the works of Pan-African liberation organizations. Professor Poe has participated in numerous international endeavours and presented discussions on Pan-Africanism in the United Nations, African Union, Senegal, Nigeria, Ghana, Libya, and Egypt consistently connecting the importance of "historical consciousness" and mass empowerment.

Kwesi Quartey is a retired diplomat with extensive service in Ghana's diplomatic missions abroad. These include Ghana's Embassies and High Commissions in Cotonou, Cairo, Brussels, and Havana. He served as Deputy Head of Mission in London and as a Permanent Representative of the Ghana Mission to the United Nations in New York. He was former Secretary to the cabinet and Deputy Minister of Foreign Affairs and Regional Integration under President John Mahama. Between 2017 and 2021 he served as the Deputy Chairperson of the African Union Commission. In this position he was responsible for ensuring that the operational systems were fully functional and aligned, to enhance the institutional capacities of the Commission, organs, liaison offices and specialized agencies.

Akilagpa Sawyerr, former Secretary-General, Association of African Universities, and President, Ghana Academy of Arts and Sciences, has been engaged in radical Pan-African scholarship and civil society activism since starting his law teaching career at the University of Dar es Salaam, Tanzania. With the degree of Doctor of the Science of Jurisprudence from the University of California, Berkeley, Akilagpa Sawyerr has held teaching, visiting, research and other positions at universities in all parts of Africa, Papua New Guinea, the UK, the US, Canada, and Germany. A Companion of The Order of the Volta, and former Vice-Chancellor of the University of Ghana, he has led several national, Pan-African and international non-governmental organizations, including STAR-Ghana; Institute for Democratic Governance; Third World Network-Africa; Council for the Development of Social Research in Africa (CODESRIA); the Global Development Network; and served on several others, including Commonwealth of Learning; UNDP Human Development Report; and Committee on Freedom and Responsibility in the Conduct of Science (CFRS), International Council for Science (ICSU). Professor Sawyerr's research and publications cover international trade and investment law, international negotiations, mining and energy law, and higher education.

Issa Shivji is Professor Emeritus in Public Law at the University of Dar es Salaam. He was professor of law at the University of Dar es Salaam until his retirement in 2006 after 36 years of service. He was the first incumbent of the Mwalimu Julius Nyerere Professorial Chair in Pan-African Studies at the same University, 2008-2013. Shivji has published some 15 books and monographs and numerous articles and book chapters in national and international journals. His latest book co-authored with two other colleagues is a three-volume biography of Julius Nyerere titled Development as Rebellion (Mkuki na Nyota 2020). Professor Shivji chaired the Presidential Commission of Enquiry into Land Matters (Tanzania) in 1991-92. He is a recipient of several awards including two honorary doctorates in law from the University of East London, UK (1997) and University of Rhodes, South Africa (2009).

Eric Tei-Kumadoe is a doctoral candidate at the Institute of African Studies, University of Ghana, Legon. His research interests revolve around the multifaceted dimensions of anticolonial resistance by historical figures, ordinary people and workers. His dissertation project is a historical examination of resistance to forced labour policies in the mines of colonial Ghana. Tei-Kumadoe has a multidisciplinary background in philosophy, psychology, African literature, history, oral traditions and urban studies. He has been involved in teaching at his university and research collaborations on agrarian economies, labour, peacekeeping, mining history and decolonisation.

Obodai Torto is a development sociologist and works as a Research Fellow in the Institute of African Studies, University of Ghana. Also, at the University of Ghana, he serves as an affiliate lecturer at the Centre for Migration Studies and Centre for Social Policy Studies. His research focuses on political economy of development, peacebuilding, security, and humanitarian aid, globalization, energy transition, natural resources management and development, sustainability, rural & agricultural development, and forced migration/displacement. He received his PhD in Sociology (Development Studies option) at the University of Waterloo, Canada.

Kafui Tsekpo's research interest straddle leadership, security, and society; public (social) policy design; migration, security and development; development nexus and decolonial knowledge systems. Over the past 10 years part of his working and research engagement has centred around issues of inclusivity, peacebuilding, nation-building and transformative development in Africa. Kafui has held teaching positions at the Institute of African Studies, University of Ghana. He is presently a Fellow of the South African Research Chair in Social Policy at UNISA, Pretoria, and an affiliate of the African Leadership Centre, King's College London/Nairobi. He is a member of the Ghana Inclusive Development Research Network, International Public Policy Association, Development Studies Association, South African Sociological Association, the Ghana Studies Association and the Conflict Research Network-West Africa. Kafui has several peer reviewed journal and book publications to his credit.

Dzodzi Tsikata, a Pan-Africanist feminist scholar activist is a Distinguished Research Professor of Development Studies at SOAS, University of London and Adjunct Professor at the Institute of African Studies, University of Ghana. She was Director of the Institute of African Studies (2016-2022) and served as the Chair of the Organising Committee of the 60th Anniversary Commemoration of the All-African Peoples Conference of 1958. Her research in the last thirty years has been on the gender of land and labour relations of agrarian and urban informal economies in Africa and their social policy underpinnings. Dzodzi is the Managing Editor of Feminist Africa and a member of the editorial collective of *Agrarian South: Journal of Political Economy*.

www.ingramcontent.com/pod-product-compliance
Lightning Source LLC
Chambersburg PA
CBHW050330270326
41926CB00016B/3397